Political Parties, Interest Groups, and Political Campaigns

Political Parties, Interest Groups, and Political Campaigns

Ronald J. Hrebenar
University of Utah

Matthew J. Burbank
University of Utah

and

Robert C. Benedict
University of Utah

Westview Press
A Member of the Perseus Books Group

Copyright © 1999 by Westview Press, A Member of the Perseus Books Group

Published in 1999 in the United States of America by Westview Press, 5500 Central Avenue, Boulder, Colorado 80301-2877, and in the United Kingdom by Westview Press, 12 Hid's Copse Road, Cumnor Hill, Oxford OX2 9JJ

Find us on the World Wide Web at www.westviewpress.com

Library of Congress Cataloging-in-Publication Data
Political parties, interest groups, and political campaigns /
Ronald J. Hrebenar, Matthew J. Burbank, and Robert C. Benedict.
    p.   cm.
Includes bibliographical references and index.
ISBN 0-8133-8007-3 (hc).— ISBN 0-8133-8008-1 (pbk.)
    1. Political parties—United States.   2. Pressure groups—United
States.   3. Electioneering—United States.   I. Hrebenar, Ronald J.,
1945–   .   II. Burbank, Matthew J.   III. Benedict, Robert C.
JK2261.P643   1999
324.7'0973'09049—dc21   99-20304
                                                                                                      CIP

The paper used in this publication meets the requirements of the American National Standard for Permanence of Paper for Printed Library Materials Z39.48-1984.

10   9   8   7   6   5   4   3   2   1

To Michiko, Mary, and Judy

Contents

Tables and Illustrations

Tables

Figures

Boxes

Preface

This book is about political parties, interest groups, and political campaigns. Until recently, these three subjects were often taught in three separate courses, but we had noted a movement to combine all three in one course, which happened at our university when it switched from quarters to semesters in the summer of 1998.

Two Westview editors encouraged us to write this book. Jennifer Knerr, then political science editor, initiated the project and her successor, Leo Wiegman, encouraged us to finish it. We wish to thank both of them for their support and assistance. We also thank Kristin Milavec, our project editor, and Nora Wood for her assistance with the index.

We have tried to incorporate the most recent information and data into this manuscript. The reader will find the various themes supported with data from the 1998 general elections. Our central theme is the greater interaction of interest groups and political parties in political campaigns of all types. The 1998 elections provided more evidence in support of this pattern. We tried to synthesize materials about the role that parties and interest groups play in American political campaigns. Then we placed our analysis into a historical framework and tried to explain how the once dominant parties have now joined with interest groups to use modern political campaigning techniques in both candidate- and issue-centered campaigns. The link in this analysis is our broad definition of "campaign," which includes the traditional party-led, candidate-centered campaign, the lobby-led policy campaign in governmental and public opinion arenas, and other types of political campaigns in many other arenas.

This book tries to avoid much of the debate that has dominated the discipline of political science for so long about the decline of political parties as essential actors in our contemporary political system. We believe that parties continue to be essential actors but are now sharing their role in political campaigns with interest groups. This debate has largely run its course and contributes little to the current appreciation and understanding of modern political organizations. The new reality of such organizations is that they have moved much closer together and have joined to dominate our politics through their common focus on political campaigns. The following is that story.

This book was jointly edited by all three of us. However, each of us had primary responsibility for the following chapters: Ron Hrebenar, Chapters 8, 9, and 10; Matthew Burbank, Chapters 2, 3, and 4; Robert Benedict, Chapters 5, 6, and 7. Chapters 1 and 11 were jointly written by Ron Hrebenar and Matthew Burbank.

Ronald J. Hrebenar
Matthew J. Burbank
Robert C. Benedict
Salt Lake City

1

Parties, Interest Groups, and Campaigns

An Introduction

Parties, interest groups, and campaigns are the essence of contemporary American politics. Political parties were invented in the United States in the late 1790s and have dominated American politics ever since. In the early decades of the republic, interest groups were subordinated to the much more powerful parties. But as the range of government activities gradually expanded, powerful interest groups paid more attention to politics. By the late 1800s, Washington, D.C., had become a major arena for lobbying. However, the real power of "pressure group" politics was on the state level as various lobbies came to dominate state capitals. As one commentator noted, "Standard Oil did everything to the Pennsylvania legislature except refine it" (Thayer 1973, 37). In 1908 a political scientist named Arthur F. Bentley called interest groups the core unit for understanding politics, and that observation seems even more true as the century ends.

Interest groups have so extended their range of activities that they are now challenging political parties in the latter's traditional campaign lair. Campaigns now provide a common arena for both political parties and interest groups. Of course, there have been interest groups in campaigns throughout our political history. The rapid growth of the new Republican party in the 1850s, for example, was largely driven by various abolitionist groups that used the party as a vehicle to pursue their policy goal of ending slavery. Similarly, the great increase in Democratic party power in the 1930s was in part a reflection of the increased political power of labor unions and their support of Democratic party campaigns. Although interest groups and political parties have long been key players, the role they have played in the drama of American politics has changed considerably over the past few decades.

Our theme in this book, then, is that as the role of political parties and interest groups in American politics has changed, elections have become the modern battleground. Candidates, parties, and interest groups all seek to dominate the media and influence skeptical voters in order to gain a hold on what has become an increasingly volatile issue agenda. We define the concept of campaigns broadly to include both candidate and issue campaigns that occur in electoral, governmental, or public opinion arenas. The changes that have produced a new style of American political campaigns have in some ways changed the nature of our democratic process. Parties began to lose control over electoral campaigns with the rise of candidate-centered campaigns in the 1950s. In recent years, they have lost even more of their once nearly total control to rising numbers of interest groups with seemingly limitless amounts of money and all the consultants, modern political tools, and media they can buy. Clearly, contemporary American political campaigns, whether designed to elect a candidate to public office or sell a policy preference to the public, have changed along with the relationship between political parties and interest groups. This book explains how political organizations and political processes have come to this point.

The Changing Nature of American Political Campaigns

Returning to the "good old days" of past political eras, when the parties ruled the political scene, or even to the days of candidate-dominated elections, is not a realistic option. We have entered a new political era in which parties and interest groups are both deeply involved in political campaigns. As James Reichley (1996, 12) has concluded:

> We are not going back to the times in the late nineteenth and early twentieth centuries when the major parties were like great popular armies, almost churches, which fought in well-drilled and enthusiastic ranks in each campaign. Other forces—the media, interest groups, citizen watchdog organizations, professional campaign consultants—will continue to rival the parties for influence in our politics.

1896 and 1996: A Comparison of Two Campaigns

Political parties and interest groups have long been (and still are) fundamental to American politics; thus it is fair to ask if their involvement in campaigns has really changed. We illustrate our general argument with a brief comparison of two presidential campaigns, the elections of 1896 and 1996. Although a hundred years separate the campaigns, it is fair to compare them because in many ways the election of 1896 signaled the beginning of a new style of campaigning in American national elections and can even be called the first modern media campaign in our history. Millions of posters, billboards, pamphlets, and buttons were distributed, including more than 300 million pieces of campaign literature in over a dozen languages. More than 1,400 surrogate speakers crisscrossed the nation in support of the Republican candidate, William McKinley, alone.

Similarities between the election campaigns of 1896 and 1996 include the two major parties, the Republicans and Democrats. Indeed, each party represented essentially the same core constituencies in 1896 and 1996—Republicans drawing most of their support from business and Democrats claiming to use the power of government to help ordinary citizens.

Money was important in both elections as well. Although the national election of 1996 has been widely identified as the most expensive ever, the money spent in the election of 1896 was also remarkable for its day. The Republican campaign alone was estimated to have cost $6–7 million, a far cry from the estimated $100,000 Lincoln's campaign spent in 1860.

A key difference, however, between the election of 1896 and the election of 1996 is the role played by parties, candidates, and interest groups. In 1896, Republican William McKinley ran against Democrat William Jennings Bryan. McKinley was a little-known member of the House of Representatives from Ohio; his being selected over the better-known Speaker of the House from Maine, Thomas B. Reed, was largely the result of the urging of a wealthy Ohio businessman, Mark Hanna. Hanna, perhaps the first of the modern corps of professional campaign managers, went to various important industries and asked them to give a certain percentage of their wealth to the campaign in order to ensure a probusiness federal administration. The banking industry, for example, was asked to give one-fourth of 1 percent of its capitalization, and Standard Oil contributed the then huge sum of $250,000. Democratic party activists, badly divided over the issue of silver currency, met at the party's national convention in Chicago and chose another little-known candidate, Nebraska congressman William Jennings Bryan. Bryan won the Democratic presidential nomination largely because of his thundering "Cross of Gold" speech delivered at the convention.

During the campaign, Bryan traveled across the nation giving thousands of speeches, whereas McKinley gave almost none. McKinley preferred to stay home while his media and surrogate speakers carried his campaign to the nation for him. The result is well known. McKinley won a sizable victory and the Republican party dominated American politics for the following three decades until the Great Depression brought Democrat Franklin Roosevelt to power in 1932.

One hundred years later, in 1996, a new era of party-group relationships had clearly emerged in the presidential campaign. In a series of primary elections, Republicans chose a well-known and long-serving member of the Senate, Robert Dole, over a host of contenders, despite concerns about his age, his status as a Washington insider, and, more importantly, his lack of skill in the use of modern media. At a carefully choreographed national convention, Republicans were treated to speeches by an array of prominent people and elaborately produced videotapes "introducing" their candidate and the campaign themes. At their carefully staged convention in Chicago, Democrats renominated the incumbent president, William Clinton. Clinton, as the nation subsequently discovered in 1998, had some personal flaws but once again proved to be adept at campaigning and using media.

Both major candidates were financed by $60 million from the federal government. The real action, however, was in party fund-raising. The national parties sought to raise "soft money"—large donations that could not legally be given to the campaigns but could be given to the parties for "party building" activities. Interest groups gave money to the parties but, even more importantly, also spent money independently of parties or candidates to support their own issue positions. The AFL-CIO used its money-raising power to accumulate a campaign war chest of more than $30 million, which it used to facilitate the Clinton reelection campaign and target dozens of Republican members of Congress who had been elected in the 1994 GOP victory. Small businesses and some larger corporations viewed the AFL-CIO campaign efforts with concern and organized a countereffort, spending nearly the same amount in support of Republican and conservative candidates for Congress.

Money raised from interest group supporters was an important element both in 1896 and 1996. As Jessie Unruh, the late Republican boss of California politics once said, "Money is the mother's milk of politics." For at least a hundred years (and probably longer) this has been true. What has changed is the way interest groups provide money for campaigns. In 1896 parties organized the gathering and spending of money. Today interest groups still help fund parties with so-called soft money contributions, but they also give directly to individual candidates through political action committees (PACs), and even run their own independent issue campaigns.

Thus, even though political parties, candidates, and interest groups were involved in both elections, they played different roles. In 1896 party bosses and party activists selected candidates at their national conventions who were largely unknown prior to running for president. In 1996 there were no party bosses and the nominees of the parties were known long before the party conventions were actually held. In 1896 the campaigns were conducted by party supporters largely at the behest of powerful state or local party leaders. Indeed, Bryan was something of an anomaly for being directly involved in his own campaign. In 1996 each of the two major candidates had an extensive campaign organization that was entirely independent of his political party. Both candidates, but especially President Clinton, used their appeal as candidates to raise funds for their party organizations. Moreover, the 1996 election actually began shortly after the 1994 midterm elections, when both the Republican challengers and the Democratic incumbent began to position themselves on issues, raise money using leadership PACs, and begin spending on media ads well in advance of the summer conventions or even the primaries.

In both 1896 and 1996 the parties and the candidates were supported by particular interests and opposed by others. In 1896 these interests—Bryan's silver miners and McKinley's Wall Street financiers—worked through the party to support the candidate because only the parties were capable of mobilizing voters and winning the election for their candidates. In 1996 groups with strong views gave money to candidates and parties, but they also spent money independently in an effort to sway voters. The differences between these two elections are quite significant. The 1896 election was contested entirely within the framework of the Republican and Democratic parties; the 1996 elections were fought among many more organizations: the two major parties plus dozens of powerful interest groups. The political parties have lost their monopoly on elections. Today there are many actors in our electoral dramas.

Parties, Campaigns, and Interest Groups: Themes

The relationship among parties, interest groups, and campaigns is a dynamic one. The overlapping of parties and interest groups in the 1996 and 1998 campaigns was especially noticeable; in some congressional districts interest groups seemed to be more active than the parties. In previous eras, the parties were certainly the dominant organizations in the electoral arena, although interest groups may have been present.

Political scientist Paul Herrnson (1998) has suggested that the relationship between parties and interest groups, in congressional campaigns at least, has changed considerably over the years. From the time strong party organizations emerged in the 1840s and into the 1940s, the political parties dominated the relationship. The parties had few rivals in terms of organizing political campaigns during this period. But beginning in the early 1950s with the rise of professional campaign managers and political consultants, the candidates themselves began to dominate the modern, media-oriented style of campaigns. They could buy anything the parties once provided (and a great deal more) without incurring the costs associated with having the party be responsible for electing the candidate. Parties eventually became service agents and contracted out a variety of campaign services to their candidates after they realized that they had lost their campaign monopoly to the private sector of "hired guns." This period lasted until the late 1970s, when post-Watergate reforms changed the rules of political finance in a way that reemphasized the contributions that parties could make in a campaign. These reforms collapsed in the early 1990s, however, and by the 1996 elections it was apparent to all that lawyers and strategists had discovered huge loopholes in federal restrictions on interest group money and activities in federal campaigns. The current "postreform" period is one of largely unregulated political campaigns in which interest groups can and often do play a major role in electing members of Congress as well as candidates for other offices (Herrnson 1998).

As political parties lost control of campaigns, the essential nature of modern campaigns changed. Once, campaigns were relatively short-lived events, designed to mobilize core groups of party supporters to vote in general elections. Two months of active campaigning, from Labor Day to the first week of November, was sufficient to awaken voters and herd them to the polls in most election years. Campaigning longer was viewed as counterproductive, since it would waste time and money. But when candidate-centered elections became the norm, campaigns had to focus on selling the candidate to a wide group of potential supporters. Many potential supporters were not loyal members of the party or were independents who lacked a significant attachment to any party. Candidate image management has become the centerpiece of campaigns. Candidates have their images created, maintained, or shifted via the mass media—particularly television. The first successful use of television in a national political campaign occurred fifty years ago in Eisenhower's 1952 presidential campaign. Candidate campaigns are now the episodic organizations of professionals and experts that political parties once were. These professional campaigners now wander the country, moving from one campaign to another like the "hired guns" of the Old West.

This new style of media campaigning is very expensive and requires candidates to raise enormous amounts of money. The 1998 California governor's race cost nearly $100 million. Major senatorial races in the late 1990s often cost between $10 million and $25 million; spending $1–2 million in a congressional campaign is no longer unusual. Even state legislative races have become increasingly costly. In major states they have begun to look just like congressional races in their use of media and political consultants. As a consequence, candidates spend more of their time on fund-raising activities. It has been estimated that a senatorial candidate facing a tough race in a major state would have to raise about $10,000 a day for each of the 2,190 days of that six-year term. The need for such huge amounts of campaign money raises serious questions about the relationships between candidates and the political action committees that provide a growing proportion of those funds.

Advocacy advertising campaigns also represent an important change in the role of interest groups, which have long had a "public" or educational front as well as a "private" or lobbying front. Today, however, interest groups have come to play a significant role in elections and in shaping public opinion. Interest groups as well as politicians use political action committees as vehicles to promote candidates and issues, raise money, and sway voters.

The Study of Parties, Interest Groups, and Campaigns

This book organizes the study of political organizations and modern campaigns into three main parts. The first four chapters focus on the study of political parties and their role in American politics. Chapter 2 introduces political parties and describes their development in the first two hundred years of American political history. Chapter 3 presents the organization of contemporary political parties. Chapters 4–5 locate parties within the context of the American electoral system and the living body of the American political system, the electorate.

The second part of the book focuses on the relationship between political parties and contemporary political finance (Chapter 6) with consideration of the growing importance of fund-raising and all the problems associated with "political money." Chapter 7 relates how American campaigns have changed and how political parties have tried to adjust to their loss of dominance in modern campaigning.

The third part brings interest groups into the discussion. Chapter 8 links political campaigns and interest groups, and Chapter 9 discusses various types of interest group campaigns in the issue advocacy sectors. Finally, the book concludes with an analysis of the internal aspects of interest groups and describes how they relate to groups' participation in political campaigns of all types.

As Figure 1.1 suggests, campaigns are the linkage between political parties and interest groups, and the nature of that linkage has changed. More and more, the activities of parties and interest groups overlap in the various arenas of American politics. Those arenas include the various legislatures from Congress to the councils and commissions in the nation's cities and counties; executives and bureaucracies from the federal government down to the local library special districts; and judicial chambers from the Supreme Court to city or district courts in the fifty states. Increasingly, the thousands of elections that are periodically contested witness the activities of both parties and interest groups. Previously, interest groups were more interested in issue campaigns conducted in initiatives and referenda,

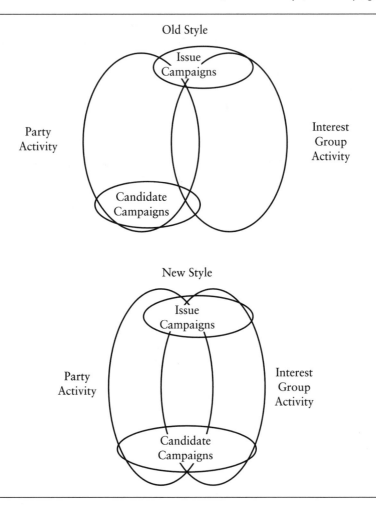

FIGURE 1.1   The Old Style and the New Style of Election Campaign Activities

but now they are often important participants in party and candidate campaigns.

Parties at one time dominated American political campaigns and government. That is not the case in today's politics and government. In many places, interest groups are as important, if not more important, than their party rivals. This is the new style of American politics: parties, interest groups, and campaigns.

2

The Development of Political Parties in America

The history of political parties in the United States is colorful and complex. Over the course of more than two hundred years of American elections, numerous political parties have competed for votes. Some parties, such as the contemporary Democratic and Republican parties, have existed as continuous organizations for extended periods of time. Other parties, such as the Prohibition party or the Socialist party, fielded presidential candidates for years but with little success. Still other parties existed for only an election or two, or competed in only a few states.

In this chapter we focus on changes that have occurred in the major political parties over the course of electoral competition in the United States. As Table 2.1 shows, we identify four distinct periods of party organization. American parties have changed over time in response to new political and social conditions. The first parties to emerge in this nation were composed almost entirely of elite national politicians. In organizational terms, political parties were elite caucuses that helped unite politicians and allowed them to advance their common policies. These early parties also became a means for politicians to seek support among the small number of voters in various states. As the electorate grew in the 1820s and 1830s, parties became more organizationally sophisticated in order to mobilize large numbers of voters. The period of mass party organizations saw the development of elaborate national conventions, party platforms, mass rallies with partisan speakers, and highly effective techniques for mobilizing voters. By the dawn of the twentieth century, however, strong party organizations were under attack. Changing social conditions and Progressive legislation led to a decline in party organization. The existing parties did not disappear, but these newly "reformed" parties had to adapt to the new political rules laid down by state governments. Beginning in the 1950s and 1960s, however, conditions again changed, particularly with the advent of television and political polling. In the present era of "candidate-centered" elections, parties have become organizations dedicated to providing the technology and services that candidates need to get elected. In short, the political parties of the 1990s differ from the organizations that existed in the 1940s or the 1890s, their structure and activities having changed to adapt to new political circumstances.

The history of political parties has often been described in terms of "realignment theory" (see Box 2.1). Although realignment theory has many strengths, it also has an important weakness: It implicitly assumes that parties have remained essentially the same over the course of American history. Consequently, realignment theory does not provide a clear understanding of the role of political parties in contemporary electoral politics. As historian Joel H. Silbey (1991b, 3) states, realignment theory "has not been able to account for what has happened over the past generation of American politics, despite the often frustrating search by scholars to locate the electoral realignment that was due in 1964, 1968, or thereabout." Indeed, Silbey (1991a, 1991b) argues that realignment theory is a viable explanation for electoral change only for the period of American history, roughly 1830 to 1930, in which political parties had the ability to mobilize large numbers of voters. Since our purpose in this book is to explain the role of political parties, interest groups, and campaigns in contemporary American politics, we have chosen to emphasize how American political parties have changed over time. We believe that an examination of the partisan and organizational changes that have occurred in the United States will help to provide a more complete understanding of contemporary political parties in American politics.

TABLE 2.1   Organizational Change and the Major American Parties

Years	Organization	Major Parties	Key Elections
1796–1828	Elite caucuses	Federalists Jeffersonian Republicans	1800, 1824
1840–1900	Mass organizations	Democrats Whigs Republicans	1840, 1860, 1896
1900–1960	Reformed parties	Democrats Republicans	1912, 1932, 1952
1960–present	Service parties	Democrats Republicans	1960, 1968, 1980

SOURCE: Created by the authors.

BOX 2.1 Realignment Theory

Beginning in 1896, the Republican party won seven of the nine presidential elections leading up to 1932. Starting in 1932, the Democrats went on to win the next five presidential elections in a row. Clearly, something changed in 1932. The purpose of realignment theory is to offer an explanation for the periods of stability and change in national electoral competition.

There are two fundamental concepts associated with realignment theory. The first is the concept of a "party system." A party system is a period of time in which there is stable competition between two major political parties. A party system may be a period of relative equality between the major parties, so that election contests are highly competitive. More commonly, however, a party system is characterized as a period in which one party is dominant. Under normal circumstances, the dominant party is expected to win presidential elections and control Congress as well.

The second fundamental concept is "realignment." Realignment is the process by which party systems change. Political scientist V. O. Key (1955, 1959) described two types of realignment: critical elections and secular realignment. A critical election is a single election that marks the end of an existing party system and the beginning of a new party system. The election of 1932, which ended Republican dominance and ushered in a new period of Democratic dominance, is often identified as a critical election. A true critical election, according to Key (1955), should exhibit a sharp break from past election results and should be durable. In contrast to a critical election, realignment may occur over a series of elections. Change that occurs over a series of elections is called a "secular realignment." Although secular realignments do not show a sharp break with past voting patterns, they result in durable new alignments. The elections between 1856 and 1860, which led to the demise of the Whig party, the split of the Democratic party, and the emergence of the Republican party, are often cited as an example of a secular realignment. A period in which the previously stable alignment of a party system begins to break down but has not been replaced by a new alignment is referred to as "dealignment." Thus, an existing party system may change as a result of a critical election or a process of secular realignment; it may also experience dealignment.

Scholars generally agree that realignment theory identifies five distinct party systems with the following approximate dates and major parties:

1. 1796–1816, First Party System: Jeffersonian Republicans and Federalists
2. 1840–1856, Second Party System: Democrats and Whigs
3. 1860–1896, Third Party System: Republicans and Democrats
4. 1896–1932, Fourth Party System: Republicans and Democrats
5. 1932–, Fifth Party System: Democrats and Republicans

(continues)

BOX 2.1   (continued)

There is a good deal of debate among scholars as to why and how realignment occurs. The conventional view, however, is that a party system reflects the enduring appeal of the dominant political party to a coalition of social groups in the electorate. A realignment, then, comes about when changing political circumstances, such as economic hardship or the emergence of a new political issue, alter the appeal of a party to members of the electorate (Sundquist 1983).

Although realignment theory maintains its appeal in historical terms, a number of scholars have questioned its ability to explain contemporary American electoral politics (e.g., Ladd 1991; Silbey 1991b). The debate is far from over, but important questions have been raised about whether we are likely to see another realignment given the nature of contemporary American electoral politics.

The First Parties

Ratification of the Constitution and establishment of a new national government created the conditions for the emergence of national political parties in the United States. For the first time, there was a national government that could exercise power apart from the state governments. These new federal institutions transcended the local political groups and notable families, which provided cohesion for politics in the states. Still, there was no rush to organize national political parties after the Constitution was ratified in 1788.

National Politics in an Antiparty Era

Political parties were not formed in the earliest days of the republic because they were regarded as, at worst, an outright threat to the operation of republican government or, at best, a necessary evil (Hofstadter 1969, 16–28). Nearly all the leading figures of the constitutional period regarded political parties as detrimental to the "public good." As practical politicians, these leaders recognized that people have differing interests and opinions. But they believed that political competition based on organized groups, what James Madison called "factions," would lead to disorder and disharmony. Indeed, one of the strongest justifications for the Constitution was that it created a new government with enough power to solve practical problems but made the exercise of power diffuse enough to discourage dominance by any one group. As Madison wrote in *The Federalist Papers,* no. 10, "among the numerous advantages promised by a well constructed Union, none deserves to be more accurately developed than its tendency to break and control the violence of faction." Years later, as he prepared to leave the presidency, George Washington warned that the formation of parties "agitates the Community with ill-founded jealousies and false alarms, kindles the animosity of one part against another, foments occasional riot and insurrection." The ideas expressed by Madison and Washington reflected widespread antiparty sentiment based on the view that parties would make it more difficult to reach agreement on actions to promote the public good.

Early on, political parties were simply not necessary. The conduct of politics at both the state and national levels was largely an elite affair with participation in public office dominated by a few people from powerful families. The number of people eligible to vote was small, as most states limited eligibility to property-owning men. Opportunities for public debate were limited by the difficulty of communication in a predominantly agrarian society. As a result, there was little need for organizations designed to mobilize citizens to vote or to provide a vehicle for politicians to communicate their views to the electorate.

Thus, when the Constitution was established, there was little practical need for organized political parties and a widespread view among leading members of the new government that organized factions would be harmful. With President Washington in office, it was possible for a short time to operate the new national government without political parties. Yet, ironically, it was a series of disputes over political issues during Washington's administration that led to the formation of the first American political parties.

The Emergence of American Political Parties

The Federalist and Jeffersonian Republican parties came into existence in the late 1790s as a result of policy differences between two members of Washington's administration, Thomas Jefferson and Alexander Hamilton. The debate centered on what role the federal government should play in economic activity (Beeman 1994). Treasury secretary Alexander Hamilton pressed for the national government to assume responsibility for paying the debt that individual states had incurred during the Revolutionary War. Later, Hamilton pushed for the creation of a national bank to carry out the economic policies of the central government. Hamilton's plans were opposed by many who had been against the creation of a federal government in the first place, the Anti-Federalists, and even by some political leaders who had supported ratification of the Constitution.

Hamilton's economic policies were opposed from within the Washington administration by Thomas Jefferson. The differences between the two men were exacerbated by their sharply different views over matters of foreign policy. In 1793, as a result of the French Revolution, the new government in France declared war on Great Britain and called upon the United States for assistance. Jefferson, though anxious to keep America out of war, sided with the French. Hamilton, concerned that American merchants would lose valuable trade with Britain, argued that the change in government resulting from the French Revolution made French claims to American assistance invalid. The debate was resolved by President Washington's declaration of American neutrality in the war between France and Britain.

Maintaining a neutral position was not easy, however. Disagreements about American policy arose between supporters of France and supporters of Britain in the United States. Further, a series of disputes arose between the United States and Britain over shipping. These disputes were resolved by a treaty with Britain negotiated by John Jay. The Jay Treaty was ratified by the Senate in the summer of 1795 by a close vote. When the provisions of the Jay Treaty became public, opponents raised highly charged objections to provisions that they regarded as favoring merchants and others with interests in trade with Britain.

Although the Jay Treaty was ratified by the Senate, opponents tried to block its implementation by voting down funds in the House of Representatives. This effort, led by none other than James Madison, was a key development in the organization of the first American political party. Treaty opponents were narrowly defeated, but the House debate "marked one of the first organized attempts by an opposition group to defeat an important administration proposal" (Hoadley 1986, 137).

The debate over the Jay Treaty was a turning point for several reasons. First, the series of votes in the House related to the question of funding the Jay Treaty showed solid evidence of consistent partisan voting by members of the House (Hoadley 1986, 135–139). Though the divisions were not sufficiently strong to argue that party organization had been established in Congress, they do provide clear evidence of an emerging opposition to the policies of the president's administration. A second significant development was that after losing in Congress, treaty opponents attempted to make their case among the electorate. Opponents of the Jay Treaty organized a series of mass protest meetings held in towns from Georgia to New Hampshire (Charles 1956, 83). Here, for the first time, was evidence of popularly supported political parties on a national level.

Supporters of the Washington administration's policy were alarmed by the actions of its opponents. Though each group believed that its members were the true supporters of "republican principles," it was increasingly clear that there were marked differences in the domestic and foreign policies of each side. With these policy differences in mind, supporters of the administration promoted the candidacy of John Adams for president and Thomas Pinckney for vice president in the upcoming election in 1796. Through private correspondence, those opposed to the administration's policies supported Thomas Jefferson for president and Aaron Burr for vice president.

Debate over the Jay Treaty and the direction of relations with France and Britain were important matters dividing the two sides. Despite the policy differences, there is little evidence of party organization or party labels being used in the presidential or congressional elections of 1796. Indeed, because the election was conducted according to the original Constitutional provisions, John Adams was elected president by the electoral college and Thomas Jefferson was elected vice president, since he had the second highest number of electoral votes, even though Jefferson was Adams's opponent in the election.

Actions taken during President Adams's time in office, including passage of the Alien and Sedition Acts, spurred the creation of party organization. Supporters of Adams, commonly identified by this point as Federalists, won a strong majority in the congressional elections of 1798. By the time of the presidential election of 1800, however, the superior organizational efforts of the Jeffersonian Republicans and divisions among the Federalists resulted in a victory for Thomas Jefferson.

The election of 1800 marked an important milestone in the organizational development of political parties—the selection of candidates by congressional caucus. In 1800 members of Congress organized themselves into competing Republican and Federalist party caucuses to nominate candidates for the presidency. The Federalist members of Congress chose John Adams for president and Charles Cotesworth Pinckney for vice president, whereas the Republican caucus nominated Thomas Jefferson and Aaron Burr. Though none of the candidates actively campaigned for office, preferring to leave such unseemly conduct to their supporters, there was abundant evidence of strong partisan sentiment. "Electioneering was done by newspaper, pamphlet, and occasional public meetings. . . . Jefferson was accused of being a Jacobin, an atheist, and a French agent; Adams was asserted to be an autocrat and a slavish admirer of the British monarchy" (Morison 1965, 80).

The Republican candidates had a clear majority in the electoral college vote, but the election had to be decided in the House of Representatives because a tie had occurred between Jefferson and Burr. Federalists attempted to take advantage of the circumstance and maneuvered to get Burr elected president instead of Jefferson. After a great deal of political wrangling, Jefferson was elected president with Burr as vice president.

With the election of 1800, evidence of party competition had become clear. The Federalist party, associated with leaders such as John Adams and Alexander Hamilton, advocated the broad exercise of federal power to promote commerce and a policy of strong ties with Great Britain, the most important commercial and military nation of the day. The Republican party, led by James Madison and Thomas Jefferson, was wary of Britain and favored maintaining the American alliance with France and did not favor the use of federal power to promote commerce.

Several important points should be emphasized about the creation of political parties. First, the political parties that developed in the 1790s can best be characterized as elite caucuses. The parties did not develop as organizational entities that existed outside of Congress; rather, the parties were predominantly groups of like-minded members of Congress who met to express their views and plan strategy. The true birthplace of the first political parties was Congress (Hoadley 1986). The newly created Jeffersonian Republican party, for example, first endorsed candidates for the presidency and Congress and only later became involved in state elections (Ladd 1970, 81). Indeed, winning national elections was so significant to the early political parties that the Constitution was changed to accommodate this new reality. As the election of 1800 demonstrated, the Constitution's original method of selection, which gave two votes to each elector to cast for two different candidates, was not well suited to the practice of having political parties select candidates for both positions. This difficulty resulted in the Twelfth Amendment, ratified in 1804, which required electors to cast one ballot for president and a second for vice president.

Second, political parties emerged in the United States for essentially pragmatic reasons. The politicians who founded the parties were not consciously seeking to do so. What these politicians wanted was support for their policies. To gain support, they sought to influence voters, win elections, and satisfy diverse group interests; consequently, parties were invented (Chambers 1967, 10). The pragmatic origin of political parties is significant because, as we noted above, the prevailing political views of the day were very much antiparty. Despite the antiparty culture, political parties came into being to promote the policies advocated by contending groups of elites. Ultimately, political parties came to be recognized not just as sources of divisiveness but as vehicles for the expression of contending political views. Accepting the legitimacy of political opposition within the constitutional framework was a significant step in the development of a truly democratic form of government.

Finally, from their origins in Congress, parties became a tool for engaging a broader range of citizens in the debates of national politicians. Leaders such as Madison, Jefferson, and Hamilton sought to organize support for their side by contacting local officials or influential citizens in the various states. One organizational technique of the day was the use of "committees of correspondence." These committees were composed of well-known state leaders who would write to like-minded citizens throughout the state and urge them to hold local meetings (Ladd 1970, 81). Of course, the extent of party organization varied widely from state to state. In Pennsylvania and New York, party organizations flourished, whereas other states did not experience the development of persistent party organizations and had only short-lived periods of party competition.

The Demise of the Federalists

Competition between the first parties lasted for only a short time. If we date the inception of organized parties from the election of 1800, it is clear that the competition was all but over by 1816. Deprived of national office by Jefferson's victory in 1800, the Federalists never regained their pre-1800 electoral strength and soon disappeared from the national political scene (Ladd 1970, 83). A crucial blow to the party's hopes for a comeback occurred when leaders called the Hartford Convention during the War of 1812 to discuss the future of New England. The convention discussed proposals for New England states to secede from the United States. As a result, "a stigma of unpatriotism, from which it never recovered, was attached to the Federalist party" (Morison 1965, 128). The last Federalist to run for the presidency was Rufus King of New York in 1816. King won only three states, and his weak showing further diminished the party's competitiveness.

Why did the Federalists disappear? One explanation is that when the War of 1812 ended, foreign policy ceased to be a strong basis of contention between the parties or in American society generally. Also, because party loyalties and party organization were quite uncertain at the time, it was relatively easy for aspiring politicians to shift to Republican ranks as that party came to dominate the national government. Finally, the various party leaders had no intention of creating parties as independent organizations. Political leaders of the time viewed politics as a duty rather than a profession; thus, there was little commitment to building long-lasting political organizations.

After Jefferson served two terms as president, his close ally James Madison was elected president in 1808 and reelected in 1812. During Madison's term in office, the Jeffersonian Republican party came to dominate national politics. By the time that James Monroe was elected president in 1816, the Republicans encountered no effective opposition. Without an opposing political party, whoever secured the Republican party's nomination in the congressional caucus was assured of winning the presidency. In the congressional caucus, James Monroe of Virginia narrowly defeated William Crawford of Georgia. The period after Monroe's election as president has since been known as the "era of good feelings" in recognition of the decline of partisanship. Still, this period from 1816 to 1824 was marked by the maneuvering of ambitious politicians within the dominant Republican party.

Transition to a New Party System

James Monroe was reelected in 1820 without opposition. The party of Jefferson had truly come to dominate national politics, yet change was occurring. In particular, a generational shift was under way as leaders from the constitutional period such as Washington, Jefferson, Madison, and Monroe moved from the political scene. A new generation of political leaders, including Henry Clay, John Calhoun, and Andrew Jackson, were becoming prominent. New political issues also emerged. The Missouri Compromise of 1820 had temporarily removed slavery as a divisive issue, but issues such as protective tariffs, the establishment of a national bank, and the need for internal improvements were hotly debated.

The election of 1824 marked an important transition. The election signaled the end of the "era of good feelings" as rivalry for the presidency intensified. The presidential election of 1824 was contested by four candidates, all Republicans. Competition to become the party's nominee revealed the organizational weakness of the Republican party and, in particular, the weakness of the congressional caucus as a method for selecting the party's presidential nominee. William H. Crawford from Georgia, Treasury secretary in Monroe's administration, was selected by the congressional caucus as the party's nominee. Unfortunately for Crawford, the caucus was poorly attended. Only 66 of 212 Republican members participated. As a result, other candidates emerged to contest the nomination. Henry Clay, the Speaker of the House, was nominated by his home state legislature in Kentucky. Senator Andrew Jackson from Tennessee was also nominated by his home state legislature. Finally, several state legislatures chose to nominate John Quincy Adams of Massachusetts. John C. Calhoun of South Carolina, Monroe's secretary of war, was unable to garner sufficient support for his presidential aspirations and so consented to be nominated as the party's candidate for vice president.

After the campaign ended and the electoral votes were counted, however, no candidate had the necessary majority of 132 electoral votes. Andrew Jackson was the leading candidate with ninety-nine electoral votes, but John Quincy Adams had eighty-four, William Crawford had forty-one, and Henry Clay had thirty-seven. Because there was no majority in the electoral college, the House of Representatives decided the election. In the House, each state got one vote as stipulated in the Constitution. After striking a deal with Clay for the votes of his supporters, John Quincy Adams was elected president by the House on the first ballot, receiving the votes of thirteen out of the twenty-four states. Once sworn in as president, Adams named Clay to be his secretary of state.

Supporters of Andrew Jackson were outraged at having been outmaneuvered and denounced the deal between Adams and Clay as a "corrupt bargain." Jackson's supporters immediately began planning for the next election. The coalition of Jackson's supporters had little in common except their hope for a Jackson victory. Martin Van Buren led the remnants of the Crawford forces into Jackson's camp, joining Vice President Calhoun and other politicians. Thus, as the election of 1828 approached, there was still only one dominant party, the Republicans, but two very clear factions: the Jackson-Calhoun coalition, strongest in the western and southern states, and the Adams-Clay supporters, who were strongest in New England.

The Mass Party Era

Though Andrew Jackson was defeated in his bid to be president in 1824, it was hardly the end of his political career. Indeed, the three presidential elections of 1824, 1828, and 1832 were largely defined in terms of support for (or opposition to) Andrew Jackson (Shade 1994, 48). Political parties as independent organizations with strong support in the popular electorate did not become fully evident until 1840. Still, the roots of these new political organizations were set in the Jacksonian period. In partisan terms, the key events of this period were the transformation of the party of Jefferson into the party of Jackson and the emergence of a new opposition party. In organizational terms, the key events were the demise of caucus-based parties and the growth of a mass electorate.

The Expanding Electorate and the Arrival of New Parties

The election of 1828 was the first since 1800 in which the leading candidate was not nominated by congressional caucus. Jackson was nominated by state legislatures, local mass meetings, and state conventions. In the election of 1828, Andrew Jackson won 56 percent of the popular vote and 178 electoral votes to defeat the incumbent, President John Quincy Adams.

The campaign between Adams and Jackson was not a high-minded debate featuring opposing philosophies of government. Rather, it was highly personal and negative, with supporters of Jackson charging President Adams with corruption and, in return, Adams's supporters raising questions about Jackson's personal conduct. More importantly, however, the 1828 campaign was perhaps the first truly popular presidential campaign. The campaign featured parades, speeches at mass meetings, and other public demonstrations of support to involve citizens in the process. As Table 2.2 shows, between 1824 and 1828 there was a substantial increase in both the number of citizens casting ballots and the turnout rate; the number of voters participating in 1828 was more than triple the size of the active electorate in 1824.

TABLE 2.2   Growth of the National Electorate: Votes and Turnout in Presidential Elections, 1824–1860

Election	Number of States	Total Votes Cast	Turnout %
1824	18	365,833	26.7
1828	22	1,148,018	57.3
1832	23	1,293,973	56.7
1836	25	1,503,534	56.5
1840	25	2,411,808	80.3
1844	25	2,703,659	79.0
1848	29	2,879,184	72.8
1852	30	3,161,830	69.5
1856	30	4,054,647	79.4
1860	32	4,685,561	81.8

SOURCES: Total votes are from *Congressional Quarterly's Guide to U.S. Elections,* 2d ed. (Washington, D.C.: Congressional Quarterly, 1985). Estimates of turnout are from Walter Dean Burnham, "The Turnout Problem," in A. James Reichley, ed., *Elections American Style* (Washington, D.C.: Brookings Institution, 1987), 113.

As president, Jackson rewarded his supporters through patronage politics—the "spoils system." Rewarding supporters with material benefits such as government jobs or government business was hardly new in American politics. Still, as historian Samuel Eliot Morison (1965, 165) explains:

> It is a fair statement that Jackson introduced the spoils system into the federal government, and that he never regretted it. His theory, stated in his first annual message, was that "the duties of all public offices" were so "plain and simple" that any man of average intelligence was qualified; and that more would be lost by continuing men in office than could be gained by experience.

During Jackson's first term in office, however, a key element of his coalition was altered when Jackson had a falling out with Vice President John Calhoun over personal and political differences. Martin Van Buren of New York, a supporter of Jackson's since the election of 1824, became the president's heir apparent. The election of 1832 thus featured Jackson running for reelection with Martin Van Buren as his vice presidential candidate. The remnants of the old Adams-Clay faction, using the name National Republicans, nominated Henry Clay and John Sargeant. The election also included a prominent third party, the Anti-Masons, who ran William Wirt and Amos Ellmaker.

The election of 1832 marked two important milestones in party organization. The first was the use of party conventions to nominate presidential candidates. The National Republicans used a convention to nominate Clay and

Sargeant, as did the supporters of Jackson, who met in Baltimore to endorse Jackson and nominate Van Buren for vice president. But the first national party convention, held in 1831, was organized by the Anti-Masonic party. The Anti-Masonic party itself was the second milestone. Not only was it the first significant third party in a presidential election, it was also the first "extralegislative" party to nominate a presidential candidate. That is, the Anti-Masons were not organized around a congressional or an administrative faction but represented the views of ordinary citizens, in this case, citizens who were opposed to secret societies, such as the Masons. Although the Anti-Masonic party did not last long as a political force, the party is notable for its origins and its ability to nominate and run a presidential candidate.

Andrew Jackson was reelected in 1832 by a sizable margin. His second term, however, was filled with difficulties. Jackson's activities as president had created a diverse group of political opponents, who by 1834 were referring to themselves as "Whigs." The name was chosen because the Whigs had been the party of opposition to royal government during the American Revolution. It was intended to remind people of the high-handed ways of "King Andrew," as opponents called Jackson.

Though united in their opposition to Jackson's administration, the Whigs could not unite behind a single presidential candidate, in part because of the rudimentary nature of their party organization. In 1836 the Whigs ran three regional candidates: William Henry Harrison, who competed in fifteen states; Hugh Lawson White, who was the Whig candidate in many southern states; and Daniel Webster, who ran in his home state of Massachusetts. Martin Van Buren, Jackson's chosen successor, ran against these various regional candidates using "Democratic Republican" as his party label.

Van Buren won the election, but the Whigs had reason to be encouraged. The three Whig candidates combined got roughly 738,000 votes (49 percent), compared to 764,000 for Van Buren (51 percent). The Whigs also demonstrated an ability to compete in the southern states, which Andrew Jackson had previously dominated completely. Though the Whigs proved to be capable of attracting votes, the election of 1836 was not a simple contest between two political parties. No fewer than five presidential candidates and eight different tickets received votes in the electoral college balloting (Shade 1994, 45). And, for the only time in American history, the Senate was required to select the vice president in accordance with the Twelfth Amendment because no candidate had a majority of electoral votes. The Senate elected the Democratic Republican candidate, Richard Mentor Johnson.

Whigs Versus Democrats

The four presidential elections between 1840 and 1852 featured competition between two clearly defined and well-organized parties, the Whigs and the Democrats. Prior to 1840, candidates had competed under a variety of labels, and party organization was often rudimentary. After 1840, the parties consistently held national conventions to nominate candidates and began to write platforms, a mark of the increasing organizational sophistication of the political parties.

The election of 1840 was marked by an intense campaign that attracted enormous popular attention. As Table 2.2 shows, nearly 2.5 million citizens voted in 1840, and the turnout rate was 80 percent. President Van Buren was nominated for reelection by his party, now calling itself the Democratic party. The Democrats drew up a detailed platform but could not agree on a vice presidential candidate and so left that choice to the electors from each state. The Whig party held a convention in 1839 and nominated William Henry Harrison of Ohio, a folk hero from his military exploits at the Battle of Tippecanoe in 1811, and John Tyler of Virginia. The campaign of 1840 was long on symbolism and short on substance, exemplified by the Whig campaign slogan, Tippecanoe and Tyler too! The Whigs attempted to capitalize on Harrison's status as a war hero and contrasted Harrison's image as a plainspoken farmer with the allegedly aristocratic manners of Martin Van Buren. Historian Samuel Eliot Morison (1965, 200) summed up the election as follows:

> The reason why the 1840 campaign became the jolliest and most idiotic presidential contest in our history is that the Whigs beat the Democrats by their own methods. They adopted no platform, nominated a military hero, ignored real issues, and appealed to the emotions rather than the brains of voters. Expectations of profit and patronage were employed to "get out the vote," and the people were given a big show.

Harrison defeated Van Buren but died after only a month in office and was replaced by the vice president, John Tyler. The Whig party also won control of Congress in 1840. Henry Clay, who had been passed over by the Whigs for the party's presidential nomination, served as leader of the Whigs in Congress. Tyler and Clay, both seeking to lead the Whig party, were soon at odds over the issue of reestablishing the Bank of the United States, and the first Whig administration ended in disarray.

Disputes within the Whig party helped the Democrats regain the presidency in 1844. The Democrats nominated James Polk, while the Whigs chose Henry Clay to carry their presidential standard. The election of 1844 featured a third-party challenge from the Liberty party, an antislavery party that had grown out of the abolitionist movement. Though it won about 2 percent of the vote nationally, the Liberty party split the Whig vote in New York and helped Polk and the Democratic party carry New York's thirty-six electoral votes (Rosenstone, Behr, and Lazarus 1996, 50).

In 1848 the Whigs recaptured the White House by again nominating a military hero, Zachary Taylor. The Democrats chose Senator Lewis Cass from Michigan as their presidential candidate. Unfortunately for the Democrats, Cass's moderate position on the question of extending slavery into new territories satisfied neither the southern branch of the party nor the more antislavery elements of the northern party. In fact, some northern Democrats, especially a group of New Yorkers known as "Barnburners," backed the candidate of a new third party, the Free Soil party. The Free Soil party opposed the extension of slavery into the territory recently acquired from Mexico and chose as its candidate Martin Van Buren, the former president. Ultimately Taylor won the election but died after a brief time in office and was replaced by Vice President Millard Fillmore. Democrats regained the presidency in 1852, when Franklin Pierce defeated Whig candidate Winfield Scott. The remnants of the Free Soil party again contested the presidency in 1852, but the party was not as important as it had been in 1848.

The election of 1852 was the last to feature a contest between Whigs and Democrats. The collapse of the Whig party was due, in large part, to the nature of its electoral coalition. The Whigs were a truly national party that relied on the joint appeal of economic progressivism and social conservatism (Reichley 1992, 97–102). The political issues surrounding the question of slavery caused enormous disruption throughout American politics during the 1840s and 1850s. The reemergence of slavery as a political issue led to the demise of the Whigs as an organized party. The slavery issue also split the Democratic party into northern and southern wings, and it ultimately created the conditions for a new political party, the Republicans.

Both Whig and Democratic parties foundered on the issue of slavery. Yet, in terms of party organization, the changes that occurred during the 1840s were remarkable. By 1850 party organizations had greatly surpassed the rudimentary parties of the 1820s and had indeed become mass party organizations. Unlike the parties of the 1820s, the parties of the 1850s were truly national in scope. After 1840 "the nature of the presidential contest changed from one rooted in cohesive state interests to one structured by national parties that penetrated into the states" (Shade 1994, 49). The pursuit of national appeal led the major parties to "balance" their presidential and vice presidential candidates in an effort to maximize their appeal to different parts of the nation. More importantly, party organizations of the 1850s were much more institutionalized than earlier parties. Party conventions, those national meetings of party supporters to nominate a presidential ticket, had become established and the parties regularly issued platforms spelling out their positions. Finally, by the middle of the nineteenth century American political parties had become the primary connection between average citizens and government. As Table 2.2 shows, the size of the eligible electorate had grown substantially, at least for white males, and parties were the vehicles for getting out the vote as well as rewarding supporters with the tangible benefits of office.

The Civil War and the Rise of the Republicans

The collapse of the Whig party and the split of the Democratic party in 1860 created an opportunity for a new political party. The Republican party, however, did not simply replace the Whigs (Gienapp 1987). In the early 1850s the political party that seemed poised to take over from the Whigs was the American party. The American party grew out of an anti-immigrant and anti-Catholic movement organized into secret societies called the "Know-Nothings" because of members' pledges to say that they knew nothing of such organizations (Reichley 1992, 108–110). After Democrat Franklin Pierce was elected in 1852, the Know-Nothings began to organize politically and nominated candidates to run under the American party label. In 1854 the American party swept state elections in Massachusetts, winning the governorship and dominating the state legislature. The next year, the party won control of state legislatures in three New England states as well as in Maryland and Kentucky.

By the mid-1850s, the American party appeared poised to become the next major political party. But then it too foundered on the slavery issue. In 1856 the American party's national convention ended in disarray due to differences between northern and southern delegates over the Kansas-Nebraska Act. The Kansas-Nebraska Act was legislation passed in May 1854 by Democrats in Congress that effectively repealed the Compromise of 1820, which had banned slavery in northern territories. The American party adopted a platform supporting the Kansas-Nebraska Act and thus supporting slavery in the eyes of northern delegates, who promptly left the convention. The convention nominated former president Millard Fillmore as its candidate for president. While accepting the nomination, Fillmore disavowed the anti-Catholic views of the party. Thus, with Fillmore as the American party candidate and with an apparent proslavery plank in the party's platform, northern voters who were either anti-Catholic or antislavery had little reason to support the party.

Passage of the Kansas-Nebraska Act was also instrumental in the creation of the Republican party. Meetings were held in many cities and towns throughout the north in 1854 to oppose any action by Congress that allowed the expansion of slavery. At one such meeting held in Ripon, Wisconsin, participants called for the fusion of former Whigs, antislavery Democrats, supporters of the old Free Soil party, and dissatisfied Know-Nothings into a new Republican party. This new party struggled initially to compete against the American party for support in northern states (Gienapp 1987).

American party candidates stressed the issues of temperance, anti-immigration, and anti-Catholicism, whereas the Republican party increasingly became defined by its opposition to the extension of slavery.

In 1856 the Republican party nominated celebrated western explorer John C. Frémont for president. The election of 1856 featured a three-way race between Frémont, Democrat James Buchanan, and American party candidate Millard Fillmore. Though Buchanan won the election narrowly, the Republican candidate did remarkably well, winning 33 percent of the national vote despite having no support in southern states. Perhaps most importantly, Frémont finished ahead of both Buchanan and Fillmore in most northern states, thus establishing the Republican party rather than the American party as the Democrats' chief rival. "Defeating the Know-Nothings to become the dominant opposition party was the most important victory that the Republican party would ever win in its long and storied history" (Gienapp 1994, 72).

The election of 1860 confirmed the Republicans as the dominant party in the North and led to the splintering of the Democrats. The election was contested by four candidates: Abraham Lincoln of Illinois, the Republican candidate; Senator Steven A. Douglas of Illinois, Lincoln's old nemesis and the candidate of northern Democrats; Vice President John Breckinridge of Kentucky, the candidate of southern Democrats; and Senator John Bell of Tennessee, the nominee of the Constitutional Union party. Yet in most states, the contest boiled down to a two-party fight: Lincoln versus Douglas in the north, Bell versus Breckinridge in the South. The election attracted considerable popular attention and voter turnout rose to 82 percent.

While remaining an antislavery party, the Republicans added several economic issues to their campaign platform, such as support for western homesteading and a protective tariff, to attract a broader base of votes. Republican efforts paid off. Lincoln carried all of the free states of the North and West except New Jersey, whose electors were split between Lincoln and Douglas. Bell won Kentucky, Virginia, and Tennessee, while Douglas carried only Missouri and part of New Jersey. Breckinridge won nine states in the Deep South plus the border states of Maryland and Delaware. In electoral votes, Lincoln had 180, Breckinridge, 72, Bell, 39, and Douglas, 12. After 1860 the Republicans clearly replaced the Whigs and the American party in the northern states and became the dominant national party, since the Democratic party was divided into northern and southern wings.

Shortly after the election, several southern states left the Union and the Civil War began. In the North, many Democrats supported the war and took the name "War Democrats." Other Democrats, "Copperheads," opposed the war and provided opposition to the Lincoln administration. Some scholars have argued that the beneficial effects of a functioning two-party system were a factor in the Union victory (McKitrick 1967). Strong political opposition forced the Lincoln administration to maintain party unity and seek support from others when possible. The Confederate government, on the other hand, was without a party system and thus had no outlet for organized opposition. The greatest source of opposition to Lincoln's war effort, however, came from within his own party. "Radical Republicans" in Congress wanted greater congressional guidance of the war effort, emancipation of the slaves, and political reconstruction of the South after the war.

In an attempt to reduce the influence of the Radical Republicans, Lincoln resorted to coalition politics and broadened the Republican party to include War Democrats. First in Ohio and later in other states, the new Republican party became the Union party. Although some Radical Republicans would have preferred another candidate in 1864, the Union party nominated Lincoln for reelection. Lincoln defeated George B. McClellan, the War Democrats' nominee and a former general in the Union Army.

Following the end of the war and the assassination of Lincoln, Vice President Andrew Johnson, a War Democrat, took over as president. As efforts to reintegrate the southern states into the Union progressed, Johnson and congressional Republicans crossed swords. In 1868 congressional Republicans had Johnson impeached by the House of Representatives and very nearly convicted in the Senate.

As the southern states reentered the Union, Democrats resumed the role of the main opposition party. In the summer of 1868, the Democratic party attempted to restore some of its political vitality by nominating Horatio Seymour, a moderately conservative governor of New York, as its candidate for president. The Republican party sought to overcome its own internal fissures by nominating a war hero, Ulysses S. Grant, as its presidential candidate. Grant swept the election, winning most of the northern states and seven reconstructed southern states for a total of 214 electoral votes to 80 for Seymour. Grant's first administration was beset by difficulties, including opposition to his renomination from within his own party. Still, Grant was popular with voters and he won reelection easily in 1872.

Despite the disruptions of the Civil War, the parties remained robust organizations. In large part, the need for strong organization was spurred by close competition between Republicans and Democrats from the mid-1870s to the 1890s. Republicans had a strong base of support in the North and Midwest and strong ties to business. Democrats moved to regain control of the southern states, with the easing of federal intervention, and continued to do well in many northern cities. The partisan balance of the period extended to both Congress and the presidency. In the five presidential elections between 1876 and 1892, Republicans won three. One of those Republican victories was the controversial election of 1876, when Republican Rutherford Hayes defeated Democrat Samuel Tilden in the Electoral

College even though Tilden had more popular votes. Democrats managed to win the presidency in 1884 and 1892 with Grover Cleveland, former governor of New York and a strong supporter of business, as their candidate.

Party Machines

In the years following the Civil War, party organization reached its zenith in the political "machines" that dominated many American cities in the late nineteenth and early twentieth centuries. Party loyalty and concern with organization helped boost voter turnout to around 80 percent. As millions of people immigrated to the cities, mostly from European nations, they were quickly enrolled in the voting "armies" of the two parties.

Party machines existed primarily, though not exclusively, in urban locations with large populations of working people. As political scientist William Crotty (1994, 134–135) notes, party machines operated in a straightforward fashion:

> The machine and its leaders wanted political power. Political power led to personal wealth. To gain power, the machine needed to control public office by determining who the candidates were and by assuring them a loyal and predictable vote in elections. In return, the quid pro quo was that the machine provided services and tangible, material rewards on a personal basis for those who supported it.

Both Republican and Democratic party machines existed, although the Democratic party often had more appeal among urban immigrants because Republican leaders often supported political positions regarded as anti-immigrant, such as prohibition or English language laws (Reichley 1992, 141–143). Party machines were not, however, ideological in nature. They were fundamentally pragmatic organizations; their chief concern was to gain control of local government as a source of patronage and money.

One of the first and most enduring machines was Tammany Hall, established in New York City in 1787 (Mushkat 1971; Allen 1993). At the outset, Tammany was a nonpartisan benevolent society that entered politics to promote the presidential candidacy of Thomas Jefferson. Later, Tammany was run by William Marcy Tweed and the Tweed Ring. "Boss" Tweed used the Tammany organization to make money. "Under Tweed, Tammany changed from an organization primarily dedicated to winning elections to one brazenly employed for wholesale thievery" (Allen 1993, 81). After Tweed was jailed for corruption, "Honest John" Kelly took over the leadership of Tammany and turned it into an efficient vote mobilizer. "Kelly, it was said, 'found Tammany a horde and left it a political army'" (Reichley 1992, 143).

The financial (and at times political) corruption associated with machine politics undermined democracy in some cities to the point that elections became meaningless. If supporters of the party machine felt it was necessary to maintain control, they would have party workers stuff ballot boxes, hire "repeaters" to travel from poll to poll voting for the machine's candidates, or simply terrorize their opponents. Yet party machines also provided benefits by helping to acculturate immigrants and, in the days before the welfare state, by providing working people with jobs and other tangible goods. As a result, party machines "fostered support for the governing system among the poor and the recently arrived by presenting a benign and supportive face to government bureaucracy" (Crotty 1994, 137).

Given their preoccupation with control of local government, the urban political machines were important to national parties primarily because they could supply votes for national candidates. Party machines existed in many cities across the United States from Boston, New York, and Philadelphia in the East to Cincinnati and Chicago in the Midwest to San Francisco in the West. Each organization was rooted in local politics and adapted to local conditions. Although some organizations, such as the Daley machine in Chicago, prospered in the 1950s and 1960s, for the most part the heyday of urban party machines occurred in the decades following the Civil War, years of unprecedented growth for American cities.

The Reform of Political Parties

The rise of party machines was tied to economic, social, and political conditions in a rapidly urbanizing nation. Conditions that helped create strong urban parties influenced national politics as well. America changed in the decades following the Civil War as it was transformed from an agricultural nation into an industrialized one.

A negative consequence of these changes was the feeling some Americans had that they and their communities no longer controlled their own fate. Farmers depended on commodities prices set in the world market; the speculations of financiers and wealthy industrialists affected economic conditions throughout the nation. Increasingly, the leaders of both major parties represented the views of leaders of business and industry and not of laborers or debtors. This situation bred frustration and tension, and when the first major industrial depression hit, the party system could no longer function as it had in preindustrial days.

Populism and the Decline of the Democrats

As America became more industrial and urban, farmers in the Midwest, South, and West lost much of the political influence they had traditionally enjoyed in a predominantly agricultural nation. Many farmers, believing that their interests were being ignored by both Democrats and Republicans, formed organizations dedicated to representing the interests of farmers. Between 1870 and 1896, a number of organizations emerged and experienced varying degrees of political success. For example, in 1873 the Granger movement had thousands of local Granges but by 1876 had come to an end politically. One political party, the Greenbacks, advocated printing paper money not backed by metal currency as a response to the economic problems of the day. The Greenbacks had close ties to the Granger movement and ran presidential candidates in 1876, 1880, and 1884. It was, however, the People's party, generally known as the Populists, that most directly threatened the continued dominance of the two major parties. In 1892, Populist candidate James Weaver received over 8 percent of the national vote, won twenty-two electoral votes, and carried the farming states of Kansas, Colorado, Idaho, North Dakota, and Nevada.

By the early 1890s, Democrats had restored themselves to prosperity in national politics. The Democrats won control of Congress and captured the White House with Grover Cleveland in 1892. Cleveland was a probusiness Democrat who was as conservative on economic questions as any Republican. Unfortunately for Democrats, even as President Cleveland was taking office in 1893, the economy was slipping into a financial "panic." Banks failed, businesses went bankrupt, industrial production slowed, and thousands of workers became unemployed.

Rather than adopt policy proposals favored by Populists and some Democrats—issuing currency backed by silver—President Cleveland worked hard to ensure the stability of the gold standard. Cleveland exercised his power over federal patronage as a way to encourage Congress to repeal laws promoting paper or silver-backed money. Cleveland also attempted, with less success, to reduce the rates of the Republican-supported tariff. The nation's economic difficulties were compounded by a wave of industrial strikes that stemmed in part from workers reacting to layoffs or wage cuts. Though pleasing to large businesses and the financial sector, Cleveland's policies did little to help farmers, small businesses, organized labor, or people looking for work, thus "fixing indelibly in the minds of many voters an association between the Democratic party and economic hard times that was to last for more than 30 years" (Reichley 1992, 167).

In the midterm elections of 1894, Republicans regained control of both houses of Congress. Democrats' poor showing in the midterm elections put them in a difficult position for the upcoming presidential election of 1896. Clearly, no Democratic candidate associated with President Cleveland would be in a strong position.

Blaming their political troubles on the "hard money" policies adopted by the Cleveland administration, many Democrats supported a "free silver" plank in the party's platform. At the Democratic convention in the summer of 1896, the party selected William Jennings Bryan, a former member of the House of Representatives from Nebraska, as their presidential candidate. Bryan was a gifted speaker and evangelical Christian who won the nomination largely on the strength of his speech to the convention. Bryan closed his speech, favoring the "free silver" position, by evoking a brilliant rhetorical image: "We shall answer their demands for a gold standard by saying to them, you shall not press down upon the brow of labor this crown of thorns. You shall not crucify mankind upon a cross of gold."

Bryan's "Cross of Gold" speech secured the Democratic nomination and placed the Democratic party on the side of farmers and advocates of silver currency and against big business, the banks, and other supporters of the gold standard. The Populist party convention, meeting shortly after the Democrats, also chose Bryan as their presidential candidate. Bryan's presidential campaign was an attempt to bring together a coalition of evangelical Protestants and people from the predominantly rural western and southern states. Although Bryan made some efforts to attract urban working-class voters, he attacked not only big business and "big money" but big cities as well.

Republicans chose William McKinley, a former congressman and governor of Ohio, as their presidential candidate. Under the direction of businessman Marcus Hanna, the Republicans ran an efficient campaign financed by the very businesses that Bryan attacked. The keys to the election, however, were that Republicans were successful in getting urban workers to identify their interests with the Republican party and that Bryan was largely unsuccessful in his appeal to Protestant voters of the North and Midwest (Kleppner 1987, 59–89). As James Sundquist (1983, 164) has noted:

> Bryan's campaign polarized sentiment on what, for his purposes, was the wrong basis. He did not set class against class; he set rural against urban. When in his Cross of Gold speech he spoke of "*your* cities" and "*our* farms," he cast out of his circle not just urban capital but urban labor too.

Republicans appealed to urban workers by supporting an industrial tariff as a way to save jobs. Republicans also opposed silver currency and pointed out to urban workers that it would mean less money in their pockets if they were paid in inflated dollars.

McKinley won the election with 51 percent of the national vote, carrying all the large industrial states of the Northeast and Midwest plus California and Oregon. Bryan swept the southern states and won most of the sparsely populated western states but received only 176 electoral votes to McKinley's 271. The electoral coalition of business and northern urban workers that the Republicans established in 1896 proved to be quite durable. Republicans went on to win every presidential election from 1896 through

1928 with the exception of two, the 1912 and 1916 elections. Bryan ran twice more as a Democrat in 1900 and 1908, but he was defeated soundly by McKinley in 1900 and by William Howard Taft in 1908.

The election of 1896 was the end of the Populists as an electoral force. As the economy gradually recovered during McKinley's administration, the appeal of the Populist message diminished. Although a Populist candidate for president ran in the next three elections, the party got less than 1 percent of the national vote in each.

The Influence of the Progressives

During the first decade of the twentieth century a new wave of reform demands swept the nation. The Progressive movement, as it was known, did not result from a single cause or seek a united goal; rather, it grew from a diverse set of roots (Reichley 1992, 186–193). Common among Progressives was a desire to improve the process of government. Progressives espoused many reforms that would eventually have an impact on the party system, including voter registration and ballot reform, referendum and citizen initiative, direct primaries, recall elections, nonpartisan elections, stronger civil service regulations to limit patronage, and expansion of the electorate particularly for women. In general, Progressive reformers were hostile to political bosses and the party machines that had come to dominate many city and state governments. Many of the reforms initiated during the Progressive era were intended to weaken party organizations.

Despite the antiparty tone, Republican leaders were able to adapt to many Progressive demands, and Theodore Roosevelt became identified as one of the Progressive leaders. Roosevelt was McKinley's vice president in 1900 and became president after McKinley was assassinated in 1901. Roosevelt went on to a sweeping victory in 1904, winning every state except the eleven states of the old Confederacy and the Border South states of Kentucky and Maryland.

The conservatism of William Howard Taft, Theodore Roosevelt's successor, left many Progressives feeling betrayed. After being denied the 1912 Republican nomination, Roosevelt formed a third party, the Progressive or "Bull Moose" party. Split into two camps, regular Republicans and Progressives, the Republican majority lost the presidency to Democrat Woodrow Wilson in 1912. Wilson won again in 1916 over Republican Charles Evans Hughes in an extremely close contest. The Bull Moose ticket polled enough votes in 1912 to put the regular Republican party into third place, but most of Roosevelt's supporters rejoined the Republican ranks after 1912. The Progressive party also ran a popular candidate, Robert LaFollette, in 1924. Although LaFollette got only 16.5 percent of the national vote, he carried his home state of Wisconsin and finished a strong second to Republican Calvin Coolidge in a number of northern and western states.

Whether as a separate party or a faction within existing parties, Progressives constituted an important political force. They were successful in large part because they were able to get many of their reforms adopted by politicians in the major parties even though they often worked against the interests of the party organizations. In short, Progressives were able to use the popular appeal of their proposals to implement change.

The Creation of the New Deal Coalition

Republican domination of the White House was restored in 1920. Though Republicans had a dominant coalition, party support was highly sectionalized: The South was solidly Democratic, whereas the Northeast and the Midwest were solidly Republican. Urban voters and rural Republicans continued to provide Republican majorities for Harding, Coolidge, and Hoover in 1920, 1924, and 1928. Indeed, in 1928, Republican Herbert Hoover won 58 percent of the popular vote and 444 electoral votes to Democrat Alfred Smith's 40 percent and 87 electoral votes.

When city voters shifted to the Republican side in 1896, it helped ensure almost solid Republican victories through 1928. But the shifting loyalties of urban voters in the North once again proved decisive in 1932. Actually, the loyalties of urban voters were in flux throughout the 1920s and began to shift toward the Democratic party during the 1928 candidacy of Alfred Smith (Key 1955). As governor of New York, Smith had become a spokesman for urban immigrants and their families and attracted a new class of voters to the Democratic party. Republicans began to lose their urban base early in the 1920s and reached rock bottom in 1936 with Roosevelt's second-term landslide.

The presidential election of 1932 marked a monumental shift in the political fortunes of the two major parties. In 1928, Republican Herbert Hoover carried all but eight states, six of which were in the South. By 1932, Hoover carried only six states; Democrat Franklin Roosevelt won all the other states and amassed 472 out of 531 electoral votes. The shift to the Democrats in 1932 followed an economic crisis of unprecedented magnitude—the collapse of the stock market in 1929 followed by the depression—resulting in high levels of unemployment and economic dislocation. The Hoover administration's response, in keeping with orthodox economic views of the day, was to keep the federal government's budget in balance and to let the business cycle run its course. Much as the panic of 1893 had earned the Democrats the label of "the party of hard times," the economic collapse of the early 1930s had the same effect for Republicans.

Research on the voting patterns of the 1930s suggests that some of the Democratic gains came as a result of Republicans who converted to the Democratic party (Erikson and Tedin 1981; Sundquist 1983, 229–239). Other scholars, however, point out that millions of young people, many from immigrant families, reached voting age between 1924 and 1932 and argue that it was these new voters who flocked to the Democratic party in the early 1930s and helped to establish a new period of Democratic dominance (Anderson 1979). Whether through the conversion of previously Republican voters or through the mobilization of a new generation of voters, the political response to the trauma of the depression created a preference for the Democratic party that was to last for many years.

Having campaigned on the rather vague promise of a "new deal," once in office Roosevelt moved quickly to use the powers of the federal government to tackle the country's economic problems. Although parts of Roosevelt's New Deal program would be declared unconstitutional by the Supreme Court and its effectiveness was uncertain, Roosevelt's actions were clearly endorsed by the electorate. Democrats won a huge majority of seats in both the House and the Senate in 1932 and increased those majorities in 1934. Following Roosevelt's win in 1932, the New Deal coalition was composed primarily of the solidly Democratic states of the Deep and Border South, the Rocky Mountain states of the West, and working-class voters of the large northern cities. Roosevelt went on to win elections in 1936, 1940, and 1944; in each election Roosevelt got a clear majority of the popular vote and won over four hundred electoral votes.

Although retaining its minority status, the Republican party improved its prospects in the latter years of the New Deal period. Democratic strength in Congress declined in 1938 and 1940. In 1942, Republicans won half of the nation's governorships, including New York and California. Republican performance in the 1940 and 1944 presidential elections showed some improvement over 1936, when Republican Alfred Landon of Kansas lost in a landslide. Landon carried only two states, Maine and Vermont. But in 1940, Wendell Wilkie carried ten states, and by 1944 Thomas Dewey carried twelve states. The improvement in Republican electoral fortunes stemmed from increasing dissatisfaction with the Democrats, but Republicans had also taken steps in the "out" years to improve their party's organization. For example, in 1936 the Republicans named their party's general counsel, John Hamilton, full-time party chairman, the first time either party had a paid party chairman (Goldman 1990, 401).

Republicans were thus looking forward to campaigning against President Harry Truman in the 1948 election after four straight defeats at the hands of Franklin Roosevelt. Truman, the former senator from Missouri who was added to the Democratic ticket in 1944, became president in 1945 after

Roosevelt's death. By 1948, Truman faced considerable opposition within the Democratic party as well as from Republicans. After a convention fight over a civil rights plank in the party's platform, anti-Truman southerners walked out of the convention. Southern "States' Rights" Democrats, commonly called "Dixiecrats," backed South Carolina governor Strom Thurmond as their presidential candidate. The goal of the Dixiecrats was to stop Truman's civil rights agenda by throwing the presidential contest into the House of Representatives, where the southern states hoped to exert greater leverage to strike a political deal. In addition to the Dixiecrat split, some liberal Democrats tried to push Henry Wallace to run as a "Progressive" candidate. Wallace had been vice president during Roosevelt's third term and a member of Truman's administration until his resignation. Wallace disagreed with Truman chiefly on the issue of relations with the Soviet Union in the postwar period.

With the Democratic coalition in disarray, it appeared that the Republican nominee, New York governor Thomas Dewey, would be the inevitable victor. Truman's campaign was underfinanced, poorly staffed, and not well supported by the party organization. Truman, however, proved himself to be a remarkable campaigner and conducted a 30,000-mile railroad tour to take his message to the people. Given the disunity among the Democratic factions, Truman's campaign featured attacks on the "big money" Republicans represented by Thomas Dewey and the Republican Congress. Truman's attacks rallied a sufficient number of New Deal Democrats for him to pull off a surprise victory. Dewey got 45 percent of the national vote and won sixteen states, primarily in the Northeast and the plains states. Dixiecrat candidate Strom Thurmond won four Deep South states. Truman won the remaining twenty-eight states and received 303 electoral votes, despite winning only 49 percent of the national vote.

Decline of the Democrats

In hindsight, Truman's 1948 victory can be seen as the last election featuring a dominant New Deal coalition. The volatile nature of the Democratic coalition had become clear when Truman's reelection was challenged within his own party from both the left, over foreign policy, and the right, over civil rights. Although elements of the New Deal coalition continued to influence Democratic electoral strategy into the 1960s and 1970s, the tensions apparent within the party in 1948 would ultimately lead to the dissolution of the New Deal coalition.

In 1952, Republicans selected a World War II military hero, Dwight D. Eisenhower, as their presidential nominee. Eisenhower was selected at the Republican convention over Senator Robert Taft of Ohio. His long service in office and his deep dedication to the party led to Taft's being known as

"Mr. Republican." The selection of Eisenhower, a popular outsider, over Taft, a party stalwart, has led some commentators to argue that this choice was the first indication of a new era of candidate-centered politics (Broder 1972). Indeed, for both Democrats and Republicans, the 1950s were a low point for party organizational strength.

Eisenhower proved his appeal to voters by winning two national elections over Democratic candidate Adlai E. Stevenson. Eisenhower won over 55 percent of the national vote in 1952, carrying all but nine states; in 1956 he won 57 percent of the popular vote, carrying all but seven states. Even the solidly Democratic South showed some signs of weakening as Eisenhower won Florida, Tennessee, and Virginia in 1952 and carried all three of those states plus Louisiana and Kentucky in 1956. In 1952, Republicans also obtained a narrow majority in both the House and Senate. Democrats regained the House in the 1954 midterm elections and would not relinquish control to the Republicans until 1994.

Party Organizations in the Modern Era

The postwar period witnessed several significant developments leading to changes in parties and campaigns. One was the rise of television. Television advertising for candidates was introduced during the Eisenhower-Stevenson presidential contests of the 1950s. As television ownership became widespread, this new technology transformed the conduct of campaigns. Newspapers had long been a staple of partisan communication, and politicians had used radio broadcasts since the 1930s. But television enabled candidates to communicate with potential voters in a far more direct fashion. Perhaps most significantly, television allowed candidates to bypass party organizations and party workers. In short, it contributed to a new era of candidate-centered rather than party-centered elections. Of course, television was not the only factor, but combined with other developments the spread of television changed the nature of modern campaigning.

Long-term organizational change was also under way. Party machines, so essential as vote mobilizers in the late nineteenth and early twentieth centuries, were gradually dying. Changes in federal, state, and local laws extended civil service protection to government employees and weakened the ability of party politicians to dispense patronage. Without patronage, party organizers could not raise money or command the votes of supporters. Other factors also contributed to the decline of party machines, such as the changing demographics of cities as the flow of immigrants slowed and city residents moved from urban neighborhoods to suburban areas. These changes weakened local party organizations, and the focus of party activities shifted from local to national parties. During the 1960s, the national committees of both major parties, the Republican National Committee

(RNC) and the Democratic National Committee (DNC), began to play a more active role in efforts to promote the administration's policies when the party controlled the White House and shape policy positions for the parties. The national parties, especially the Republicans, increased the number of professional staff and improved fund-raising at the national level.

Party Competition and Candidate-Centered Elections

Democrats returned to the White House in 1960, when John F. Kennedy defeated Republican Richard Nixon in one of the closest contests in U.S. political history. Kennedy got 49.7 percent of the popular vote while Nixon received 49.6 percent; Kennedy won the election by 114,673 votes out of the 68 million votes cast. Despite his charismatic image, Kennedy's lack of a clear policy agenda made him vulnerable as the 1964 election approached. In an attempt to strengthen his support in the South and to patch up a quarrel between Texas Democrats, President Kennedy made a trip to Dallas in November 1963. It was on that trip that he was assassinated. Vice President Lyndon Johnson assumed office and went on to lead the Democrats in the 1964 elections.

The contest for the 1964 Republican nomination pitted the conservative wing of the party, with its base of support in the West and the South, against the more liberal eastern wing of the party. The spirited nomination battle involved a number of candidates but came down to conservative favorite Senator Barry Goldwater of Arizona and New York's Nelson Rockefeller. In June, Goldwater edged out Rockefeller in a close contest in the California Republican primary. Goldwater's nomination marked a shift in the balance of power within the Republican party away from the Wall Street establishment toward conservative activists from the western states.

In the general election, Johnson won a landslide over Goldwater, in part by playing on voters' fears that Goldwater was too conservative. Johnson won 61 percent of the popular vote and carried all but six states. Democrats increased their majority in the House and the Senate. The only good news for the Republicans was that Goldwater won the electoral votes of five Deep South states plus his home state of Arizona. Johnson's strong showing allowed him to pursue aggressively his "Great Society" legislative agenda, which included federal support for education, the Voting Rights Act, and the Medicare program.

The Democratic triumph was short-lived. By 1968 the Democratic party was badly split over Johnson's Vietnam War policy. Southern Democrats were unhappy with Johnson and northern Democrats over civil rights. Johnson's attempt to seek renomination faltered early in the process. Johnson won the preference vote in the Democratic party primary in New

Hampshire in March 1968. But an antiwar candidate, Senator Eugene Mc-Carthy of Minnesota, polled 42 percent of the vote. Johnson's weak showing encouraged not only the McCarthy campaign but other Democratic hopefuls as well. Robert Kennedy entered the race shortly after the New Hampshire primary. Although he may have been able to retain his party's nomination, President Johnson decided against seeking a second full term and withdrew from the nomination contest.

After Johnson withdrew, Vice President Hubert Humphrey joined the race. Although McCarthy and Kennedy were the leading candidates through the Democratic primary elections, Robert Kennedy was assassinated after the California primary, and only McCarthy and Humphrey were left as the Democratic convention approached. The regular Democratic organization backed Humphrey, who was nominated despite the fact that McCarthy went into the convention with the most pledged delegates.

The 1968 Democratic convention in Chicago was a disaster for the party. Antiwar protestors and police clashed during the convention, leading Senator Abraham Ribicoff of Connecticut to denounce the "gestapo tactics" of the Chicago police during televised coverage. Ribicoff's speech drew a vehement protest from Chicago mayor Richard Daley, who was on the convention floor at the time. In the general election, Democrats faced another challenge, this time from dissatisfied southern Democrats supporting the candidacy of George Wallace, segregationist governor from Alabama running on the American Independent party label.

On the Republican side, Richard Nixon was again selected as the party's nominee and chose Spiro Agnew of Maryland as his running mate. Nixon won a close victory over Humphrey in the general election with 43.4 percent of the popular vote, compared to 42.7 percent for Humphrey and 13.5 percent for Wallace. By 1972, however, Nixon used the advantages of incumbency skillfully and defeated Democratic nominee George McGovern in a landslide. Nixon won 61 percent of the popular vote and swept every state except Massachusetts (McGovern also won the three electoral votes of the District of Columbia). Nixon's victory in 1972, however, did not result in Republican dominance. Democrats maintained control of Congress and Nixon's reputation was soon undermined by the Watergate scandal. Any hope of a new Republican majority based on Nixon's wins in 1968 and 1972 eroded with the resignations of first Agnew and then Nixon. The backlash against Republicans became evident in the 1974 midterm elections as a new crop of Democrats was elected to the House of Representatives.

After its 1968 convention debacle, the Democratic party embarked on a series of reform efforts that resulted in greater national party control over the presidential nomination process. In response to vocal complaints from party activists and others that Humphrey's selection at the 1968 convention was essentially undemocratic, the party convened a commission headed by George McGovern, senator from South Dakota, and Donald Fraser, congressman from Minnesota. The McGovern-Fraser commission made a series of far-reaching recommendations about delegate selection that were adopted by the DNC and put into place during the 1972 presidential nominating process. These reforms helped to increase participation within the party, but they further weakened the ability of state and local party organizations to control their delegates.

One of the first beneficiaries of the new rules was none other than George McGovern. McGovern was able to use the new rules, which opened up participation in the party to his advantage, as he campaigned for the party's nomination against Senator Edmund Muskie of Maine. Although McGovern's nomination ended disastrously for the Democrats in 1972, the Democratic party continued to "reform" party rules over the course of the next four general elections. One of the most important consequences of the reforms enacted by the Democratic party was the increased prominence of primary elections in the presidential nomination process (a topic covered in more detail in Chapter 4). The increased use of primary elections to select delegates for national party conventions affected Republicans as well as Democrats because states changed their laws in response to Democratic party reforms. The shift to primary elections in turn affected how candidates would compete for their party's nomination.

Shifting Party Fortunes in the Contemporary Era

Changes in the presidential nominating process became evident in 1976, when a dark horse candidate, Jimmy Carter, won the Democratic nomination. Carter, the former governor of Georgia, was virtually unknown on the national political stage at the beginning of 1976. But Carter was able to use a relatively strong showing in early primaries to establish himself as a credible candidate and defeat his better-known rivals for the Democratic nomination. In the primaries and in the general election, Carter ran as a political "outsider" who was not a part of the Washington establishment.

Carter's opponent in the 1976 general election was Republican Gerald Ford, the incumbent president. Ford had been minority leader of the House but was appointed vice president by Richard Nixon after Spiro Agnew resigned. Ford became president in 1974 after Nixon resigned. Ford faced stiff competition for the Republican nomination from Ronald Reagan, whose candidacy was strongly supported by conservative activists. Ford managed to prevail in a close contest.

In the general election, Carter won a slim majority of the popular vote, 50.1 percent. Carter's victory, particularly his showing in southern states, led some Democrats to see the revival of the New Deal coalition. But political events during the Carter administration crushed any hope for a return of Democratic dominance. Although President Carter had some successes, economic problems at home and a foreign policy crisis put Democrats in a difficult situation leading into the 1980 elections. At home, the economy was suffering from both high inflation and stagnant growth, a condition termed "stagflation." Abroad, the Soviets had invaded and occupied Afghanistan, reigniting Cold War worries about Soviet expansionism. Perhaps even more telling in the media age was the prolonged crisis of Americans held hostage in Iran. In short, Carter's campaign for a second term had significant obstacles to overcome. Among the first of these was a challenge within his own party during the Democratic primaries from Senator Edward Kennedy.

Republicans nominated Ronald Reagan as their candidate in 1980. One of Reagan's competitors for the nomination, John Anderson, was highly critical of his economic policy in the primaries and ultimately decided to run as an independent candidate in the general election. Reagan's nomination was partly a consequence of efforts to mobilize conservative activists within the party begun by Goldwater's supporters in 1964. Though Reagan was most strongly supported by Republican conservatives, his personal appeal as a candidate and his ability to communicate his message effectively cemented his support among Republicans and attracted other voters as well. Reagan, with running mate George Bush, won the 1980 election with a slight majority of the popular vote, 50.7 percent, but a commanding 489 electoral votes. Carter finished with 41 percent of the popular vote, and independent candidate John Anderson got 7 percent. Perhaps even more heartening for Republicans was that they picked up twelve seats in the Senate, giving them control, and thirty-five seats in the House. Although Democrats continued to maintain control of the House of Representatives, Republican fortunes had clearly improved since the Watergate scandal.

In 1984, President Reagan was easily reelected, with nearly 59 percent of the popular vote, over Democrat Walter Mondale. Reagan did well in all areas of the country and with virtually all social groups, with the exception of African American voters, Hispanic voters, and urban voters. Indicative of the era of candidate-centered elections, the coalition of supporters was more a "Reagan coalition" than a "Republican coalition." Despite the scope of Reagan's victory at the presidential level, Republican gains in Congress were modest. They gained fourteen seats in the House, though Democrats still held a substantial majority, and Republicans lost two seats in the Senate.

The results of the 1988 presidential election supported the view that 1984 was more of a Reagan coalition than a Republican one. In 1988, George Bush, who had served as Reagan's vice president for two terms, easily defeated Democrat Michael Dukakis. After a lackluster campaign, Bush won 54 percent of the popular vote to Dukakis's 46 percent. In comparison to Reagan's showing in 1984, however, Bush's support was several percentage points lower than Reagan's among nearly all social groups (Pomper 1989). Further, Democrats managed to maintain control over both houses of Congress (Democrats had regained control of the Senate in the 1986 midterm elections). Thus, despite three convincing wins at the presidential level, the Republican party could not demonstrate a dominant coalition because of its inability to control Congress. Instead, divided party government continued, with Republicans controlling the executive branch and Democrats, the legislative branch.

In 1992 it appeared that Democrats might have found a way out of the stalemate of divided party government. The 1992 election matched incumbent President George Bush against a little-known Democrat, Governor Bill Clinton of Arkansas. Bush had the advantage of his leadership in the Gulf crisis, which had pushed his presidential approval ratings to nearly 90 percent in March 1991, but the disadvantage of sluggish economic performance in the year preceding the election. Bush had faced a challenge from Patrick Buchanan in the Republican primaries. Although Buchanan's campaign was potentially divisive because of his appeal to social conservatives, President Bush was easily renominated. Among Democrats, Clinton emerged as the nominee only after a hard-fought battle with several other contenders.

Another factor in the 1992 election was a major independent candidate, H. Ross Perot, a billionaire Texas businessman. Perot got into the race, dropped out, and then reentered the race in September. Perot's candidacy made the outcome more unpredictable than usual. On election day, Bill Clinton was elected president with only 43 percent of the popular vote to George Bush's 37 percent and Ross Perot's 19 percent. Despite his small plurality in the popular vote, Clinton carried thirty-two states and the District of Columbia for a total of 370 electoral votes to Bush's 168. Perot failed to win any electoral votes but did make a strong showing in a number of states, particularly western states.

Coming out of the 1992 elections, the Democrats controlled the executive branch and both houses of Congress. Unfortunately for the Democratic party, President Clinton's first years in office were not highly successful and Republicans were able to take advantage. In the 1994 midterm elections, Republicans scored an important breakthrough, gaining fifty-two seats in the House and eight seats in the Senate to take control of both the House and Senate for the first time since 1952.

Going into the 1996 presidential election year, the scope of the Republican victory in 1994 should have put Republicans in a strong position. President Clinton, however, was able to use the circumstance to his political credit. With no challenge from within his party to his renomination, and with a strong economy, Clinton was able to position himself as a "new"

Democrat. The Republican challenger, Senator Robert Dole from Kansas, had to survive a difficult primary challenge to win the nomination. The 1996 campaign included another challenge from Ross Perot, who had worked to create a new third party, the Reform party.

With the aid of a strong economy, Clinton and running mate Albert Gore were able to win reelection handily. Clinton finished with 49 percent of the popular vote to Dole's 41 percent and Perot's 8 percent. Clinton won most of the states of the far West, the Midwest, and the Northeast, whereas Dole won most of the plains states, including Texas, and the southern states. Although Clinton's victory was good news for Democrats, Republicans suffered only minor losses in the House and managed to retain control. Republicans actually gained seats in the Senate in 1996 to increase their majority. After the 1996 election, the era of divided party government continued, but with Republicans controlling the House and Senate and Democrats, the White House.

The pattern of national election results since World War II shows that neither party has established a clear-cut advantage. At the presidential level, and increasingly in congressional elections as well, election outcomes hinge far more on the candidate and the campaign than on firmly established partisan coalitions.

The Changing Nature
of American Political Parties

An examination of the history of American political parties from the ratification of the Constitution to the late twentieth century reveals complexity and at times confusion. Still, some broad patterns are clearly discernible.

The central theme of this chapter is that American political parties have changed enormously in adapting to changing political circumstances. Perhaps the most important point to recognize is that successful political parties in the United States are highly pragmatic organizations. Although the political environment may change, political parties have maintained their goal of getting, or keeping, their supporters in power through the election process. Even as political parties have changed, this aspect of political parties has remained constant.

When political parties first emerged in the 1790s, they functioned as little more than meeting places for elected officials who either opposed or supported the president's administration. The first parties provided a way of collecting elected national leaders into more or less cohesive groups that shared views on some of the important issues of the day. These parties existed primarily as caucuses—organized meetings of political leaders. The first parties fulfilled the real need for an organized means for politicians to rally support for their policy positions.

As the United States grew, political parties became a means for organizing the expanding electorate. By the 1840s, political parties had developed into mass organizations that incorporated political supporters into the process of choosing presidential nominees and developing the party's platform. Political parties existed as organizations outside of, and in addition to, the organizations that served members of Congress and the executive. Political parties became the chief means for political leaders to communicate with supporters across the country. Indeed, some party leaders, both Democrats and Republicans, honed their organizations to become effective mobilizers of votes as they sought to control patronage jobs and government services. Although these party machines existed in states and counties across the nation, the most notorious were the ones that ran large cities such as New York, Boston, Chicago, Philadelphia, Kansas City, and San Francisco.

From the 1890s to the 1920s, a series of reforms were enacted that substantially reduced the power of political parties. These Progressive-era reforms directly undermined the control that parties could exert over their supporters. For instance, the introduction of the direct primary, in which voters, not party leaders, choose a party's nominee, reduced the power of political bosses. As these and other reforms were introduced, political corruption eased somewhat. There were, however, unintended consequences as well. For example, fewer people participated in elections when the link between parties and the tangible rewards of being a party supporter were broken.

The parties did not wither away but increasingly became creatures of state government. New laws defining how candidates could get on the state's ballot or when primary elections would be held have enshrined the major political parties in the legal code. Political parties continued to provide a means for organizing legislative and executive business and, outside of government, continued to recruit candidates for office. But the heyday of strong party organizations that could mobilize large masses of voters was over.

One consequence of the decline of strong party organizations was the system of candidate-centered elections we see today in the United States. New technologies, such as television, telephone polls, and direct mail, have shifted the central focus of elections onto the candidates and their personal campaign organizations (Wattenberg 1991). The parties adapted to these circumstances by becoming "service organizations" (Aldrich 1995). In response to the new style of campaigning, which emerged most forcefully in the 1960s and 1970s, contemporary parties have responded by providing the services that candidates seek. Parties organize workshops for potential candidates covering topics such as how to organize a campaign and how to dress for television. Parties also provide services such as polling, legal advice concerning campaign finance laws, policy papers on important issues, and telephone banks for voter registration or mobilization. Although service organizations are a far cry from the old party machines, this organizational shift appears to be a successful adaption of contemporary political parties to the realities of electoral competition.

3

The Organization of Contemporary American Parties

In some ways, the contemporary Republican and Democratic parties resemble midsized corporations. They maintain permanent headquarters in Washington, providing space for key executives who worry continually about the competition, a sizable number of employees who range from technical experts to receptionists, and many other trappings of corporate life. But concluding that the major political parties operate like most corporations would be a serious misreading of the nature of American parties.

The two major American political parties are not organized along strict hierarchical lines but are made up of several loosely connected organizations. The various organizations that compose a modern party may be on the same team but are not necessarily part of a single command structure. At the center of each major party is its national committee, the Republican National Committee (RNC) or the Democratic National Committee (DNC), headed by a national chairperson. Yet the national chairperson is not the party's sole authority. Unlike a corporate chief executive officer, the party chair must work in conjunction with members of Congress and, if the party controls the White House, members of the president's administration. Not only must the party chairperson coordinate actions with elected officials in Washington, but he or she is not in a position to issue orders that will be carried out in Kansas or Idaho because each state has its own party organization subject to state law and is not a creature of the national party.

The important point is that the political parties are not the same as most modern, hierarchical organizations such as General Electric or Microsoft. Rather, each major party is a complex network of organizations with overlapping responsibilities and decentralized power. Why do the party organizations retain these loosely connected structures? In large part because

45

American parties are a product of a complex political environment, a result of federalism and the separation of powers, and these structural features allow for maximum flexibility. Indeed, this flexibility has allowed the parties to adapt to the changing circumstances of American politics.

The adaptability of the parties to new political circumstances is well illustrated by changes that have occurred in the United States since World War II. The 1950s were in many ways the low point for American party organizations. The full force of Progressive reforms designed to weaken party machines and end political corruption had hit the state and local parties. The weakening of local parties hurt the national parties as well because the national parties had always relied on state and local organizations for resources. Even worse, just as the party organizations were in the doldrums, candidates were discovering that they could use new technologies, principally television, to appeal directly to voters. With this new technology and the resources to use it, candidates more than ever became the stars of the political show. The 1960s marked a transition to an era of "candidate-centered" elections (Wattenberg 1991).

Over the course of many years the parties adapted to these new circumstances by becoming "service" organizations. At the presidential level, campaign organizations have become self-contained entities complete with media consultants, pollsters, speech writers, state organizers, and the rest. Presidential candidates, in short, can largely conduct their operations without relying on a party organization. Most candidates, however, do not have that luxury. Thus, rather than try to revive the glory days of past political machines, modern political parties have moved to provide the services that candidates need. Both the national and state parties provide candidate training, help with direct mail appeals, advise on media advertising, and deliver a variety of other services.

Our purpose in this chapter is to examine the complex structures of contemporary American parties in the era of parties as service organizations. We begin at the grass roots with the people who are the lifeblood of the party organizations, the party activists. Next, we examine the state and local parties and conclude with the national party organizations.

Party Activists

Comparing party organizations in different democratic nations allows us to identify two types of organizations: mass parties and cadre parties (Duverger 1963, 63–71). Mass political parties have a large number of dues-paying members, who compose the bulk of the party organization. Mass parties are typically organized hierarchically with members participating, through local organizations, in the selection of party candidates and the party's positions on issues. An example of a mass political party is the British Labour party. Though its membership is down from its peak in the late 1970s, the Labour party still has roughly 4 million members, most of whom are affiliated to the party through membership in trade unions (Pelling and Reid 1996, 197–199).

Cadre parties, on the other hand, do not have many members. Instead, cadre parties are composed of small groups of activists who come together for a short period to get candidates elected to office. During an election, a cadre party may have a large number of activists working to promote the party's candidates; after the election, the party organization typically dwindles to a few officials. Because there is no base of members to organize, in practice the structure of a cadre party is rarely hierarchical, more often resembling a loose network of connections among candidates, officials, and a few dedicated activists (Schwartz 1990).

American parties are cadre parties. American political parties do not have large numbers of dues-paying members or strong hierarchical structures. Rather, American party organizations tend to be composed of a few party officials who maintain the party organization between elections. At election time, however, party activity increases and citizen activists pitch in to work for the party or its candidates.

The Social Basis of Party Activism

Who are these party activists? In general, we know that people who take an active role in the life of parties, whether as convention delegates, local party officials, or campaign volunteers, are not typical of other citizens. According to estimates from the American National Election surveys, only about 3 percent of the adult population reports having worked for a party or a candidate in recent election years. Party activists, as a group, are better educated, have higher incomes, and are more likely to have professional occupations than most citizens. As is true with other forms of political participation in the United States, there is a social distinction with regard to involvement in parties and campaigns: People with higher socioeconomic status are more likely to participate than people with lower socioeconomic status (Verba and Nie 1972, 129–133; Verba et al. 1993).

The socioeconomic distinctiveness of party activists is true of both Democrats and Republicans. As Table 3.1 shows, among delegates to the 1992 national party conventions, 72 percent of Democrats and 67 percent of Republicans had a college or a postgraduate degree, whereas only 24 percent of all citizens had attained that level of education. Similarly, 39 percent of Republican delegates and 28 percent of Democratic delegates had household incomes of more than $100,000, compared to only 6 percent of citizens.

TABLE 3.1   Characteristics of Party Convention Delegates

| | Convention Delegates | | |
	Republican %	Democrat %	All Citizens %
Education			
High school or less	10	8	52
Some college	23	20	23
College graduate	22	18	16
Postgraduate	45	54	8
Family Income			
Under $30,000	4	9	45
$30,000–59,999	26	31	35
$60,000–99,999	31	32	14
More than $100,000	39	28	6
Race			
White	91	77	84
Non-white	9	23	16
Labor Union Member			
Yes	4	29	10
No	96	71	90
Ideological Identification			
Extremely liberal	0	12	3
Liberal	2	56	25
Moderate	15	25	31
Conservative	70	7	37
Extremely conservative	13	0	4

SOURCES: Compiled by the authors. The raw data for convention delegates are from: Richard Herrera and Warren E. Miller, *Convention Delegate Study, 1992* [computer file] (Ann Arbor, Mich.: Interuniversity Consortium for Political and Social Research, 1995). The raw data for the sample of American citizens are from: Warren E. Miller, Donald R. Kinder, and Steven J. Rosenstone, *American National Election Study, 1992* [computer file] (Ann Arbor, Mich.: Interuniversity Consortium for Political and Social Research, 1993).

The survey results in Table 3.1 show the similarity of Democratic and Republican delegates in socioeconomic terms, but there are differences among party delegates as well. Democratic delegates are more likely to be racial minorities and are more likely to belong to a labor union than Republican delegates. Republican delegates are much more likely to identify themselves as "conservative" or "extremely conservative," whereas Democratic delegates are more likely to call themselves "liberal" or "extremely liberal." The characteristics of national convention delegates are broadly similar to descriptions of state and county party leaders (see Huckshorn 1976; Gibson et al. 1986).

In socioeconomic and ideological terms, party activists clearly differ from most citizens. What leads people to become party activists? As with political participation generally, one factor associated with party activism is an exposure to partisan activity at a young age. People whose parents were involved in partisan activities are more likely to become activists as adults than people from politically inactive families (Jennings and Niemi 1981; Beck and Jennings 1982). A comparison between lifelong Democratic activists and activists who converted to the Republican party revealed that activists whose parents had been involved in politics were less likely to switch parties (Clark et al. 1991).

Thus, involvement in political parties appears to be a function of both resources and learning. People with higher socioeconomic standing are more likely to take an active role in a party organization because they are more likely to have the necessary personal resources. Of course, not all party activists are people with high socioeconomic status and certainly not all people of high socioeconomic status participate. Clearly, learning the value of participating in partisan activity from parents who engage in such actions can be a crucial motivation for individuals to become involved.

Incentives for Activism

Of course, there are distinctions among party activists, one of which is their incentive for getting involved. Three types of incentives for involvement in political organizations have been identified: (1) material, (2) purposive, and (3) solidary (Clark and Wilson 1961; Wilson 1995, 30–55).

Material incentives are tangible payoffs to the individual activist in return for participation. The tradition of party bosses providing government jobs to people who helped to get the party's candidates elected is an example of a material incentive for party activism. Purposive incentives, on the other hand, are less tangible rewards. A purposive incentive is a motivation based upon a sense of purpose. In other words, individuals become active in party activities in order to promote some larger cause such as the appeal of a particular candidate or a strongly held issue position. Individuals who get involved in party activities primarily because they believe in a particular issue or candidate are said to be motivated by purposive incentives. Finally, a solidary incentive is a motivation to become involved in party activity for social reasons such as friendship or group affiliation (see Crotty 1986). Campaign and party volunteers are often recruited to serve in the party by people they know.

The distinction between material and purposive incentives for party activists is a key difference between "professional" and "amateur" party activists. Professional activists (or "pragmatists" as they are some times called) are motivated primarily by material incentives. Although the days of vast numbers of patronage jobs are gone, involvement in a political party or campaign is often a stepping-stone to a job as a staff person, an appointment to an advisory board, or some other tangible reward. Professional activists are primarily concerned with winning elections because it is by winning that material rewards become available. In contrast, amateur activists (or "purists") are drawn to parties or campaigns by a desire to promote a particular issue position or a particular candidate. Thus, for amateurs, winning elections may not matter as much as supporting the "right" candidate or advocating the "correct" position on an issue, even if the candidate or position is not popular.

Both Democrats and Republicans have experienced tensions between amateur and professional activists within their ranks. In a now classic study, political scientist James Q. Wilson (1962) studied amateur Democratic activists in three cities, Los Angeles, Chicago, and New York. These amateur activists were chiefly concerned with promoting various liberal policies within the Democratic party and attempting to make the party itself more open to citizen participation. These activists formed "Democratic clubs," organizations that existed separately from the party. For activists in these Democratic clubs, the opposition was less the Republican party than it was the local "regular" party organization controlled by party professionals.

The differences between amateurs and professionals were starkly displayed in the Democratic party's presidential nomination process in 1968 (for an excellent summary, see Blum 1991, 287–310). In late 1967 and early 1968, a variety of amateur activists, especially college students, were drawn to the presidential campaign of Senator Eugene McCarthy because he opposed President Lyndon Johnson's Vietnam policy. Despite the passion of McCarthy's amateurs, professional activists led by Mayor Richard Daley of Chicago easily outmaneuvered McCarthy's supporters at the party's national convention in Chicago. Support from Daley and other party professionals was essential to Vice President Hubert Humphrey's nomination. Most professional activists considered Humphrey more electable than Senator McCarthy.

Although the professionals were able to control the nomination in 1968, dissatisfaction with the nomination process led many amateur activists to demand changes in the party's nomination procedures. Ultimately, these changes helped to weaken the control of professionals such as Mayor Daley and, in 1972, helped the candidate of the party's liberal wing, Senator George McGovern, win the party's nomination for president. More recently, amateur activists have been important to candidates such as Jesse Jackson in his bid for the presidential nomination in 1984 and 1988.

Republicans too have witnessed the struggle between professionals and amateurs. For example, many supporters of Arizona senator Barry Goldwater's bid for the presidency in 1964 were amateur activists drawn to Goldwater more for his conservative views than his broad electoral appeal.

As one Goldwater delegate at the 1964 Republican convention put it, "I'd rather stick by real principles this country was built on than win. Popularity isn't important; prestige isn't important; it's principles that matter" (quoted in Wildavsky 1965, 397). Though Goldwater was soundly defeated by Lyndon Johnson, conservative activists energized by his candidacy had a lasting impact on the Republican party. One of Goldwater's supporters was none other than Ronald Reagan, who, at the urging of other Goldwater supporters, went on to run for governor of California (Reichley 1992, 333). More recently, amateur activists within the Republican party have been prominent supporters of candidates Patrick Buchanan and Pat Robertson (see Hertzke 1993, 157–171).

The contrast between amateur and professional activists captures an important element of party politics—the ongoing tension between principles and pragmatism. But we should not exaggerate this distinction, for several reasons. First, many people are involved in party politics for mixed reasons, including policy and issue concerns, commitment to the party, and personal concerns (Miller and Jennings 1986, 91–96). Second, there is a clear value in having relatively porous party structures that allow activists to flow in and out depending on their concerns. The influx of amateur activists into party politics during the 1960s raised concerns about possible negative consequences for party competition, but those negative effects never fully materialized (Miller and Jennings 1986; Herrera 1995). Amateur activists who are initially unsuccessful may become disenchanted and drop out of party politics or may stay and accept the value of pragmatism (Dodson 1990). On the other side of the coin, even the most hard-boiled professional activists have issues and principles they care about.

Although differences in motivation may allow us to classify party activists as professionals or amateurs, it is clear that both pragmatism and principle matter for individuals experienced in party politics. The authors of a study of state party activists concluded that "despite a strong tendency among our respondents to opt for ideological purity over electability in the abstract . . . Democratic and Republican activists were actually more concerned with electability than with ideology in choosing a party nominee" (Stone and Abramowitz 1983, 946).

State and Local Parties

Party activists are the lifeblood of the parties, but it is the state parties that have traditionally provided the organizational skeleton of American political parties. Although the nominating conventions provided a national focus, real power often rested with the state and local party officials who could deliver the votes. For most of American history, the national parties have served as umbrella organizations for a confederation of state parties.

The national parties depended on state and local organizations for resources and votes. State and local parties are no longer dominant, however, because the national parties have become more structurally sound and professional in the post–World War II period. Still, state and local parties have not fallen by the wayside. State and local parties too have adapted to the changing circumstances of the American political scene.

State Parties and State Laws

Political parties are not discussed in the Constitution nor, for most of our history, have they been the subject of federal law. Instead, to the extent that political parties are provided for in the law, it is state law. The regulation of political parties differs markedly among states. Five states (Alaska, Delaware, Hawaii, Kentucky, and North Carolina) traditionally have had very limited regulations, whereas states such as Ohio, Illinois, Texas, and New Jersey have developed elaborate legal regulation of state parties (ACIR 1986, 128–143).

The regulation of political parties had its roots in the late 1880s and early 1890s, when states began to adopt the Australian ballot. Prior to this time ballots were printed by the parties themselves and distributed to voters by party workers. When governments began to print official state ballots, all candidates were listed with their party affiliation. As party scholar Leon Epstein (1986, 165) has pointed out:

> The official ballot recognition of parties in 1888–90 provided the legal arguments for the most important regulation that followed. From its inception, official ballot recognition required that a party's nominations be certified by party officers to government officials, and that only officers of certain parties—usually those polling a certain percentage of votes at the previous election—could thus certify.

Prior to the issuance of official state ballots, political parties were regarded as essentially private associations. After the adoption of the Australian ballot, which automatically provided positions on the ballot for state-recognized political parties, state governments had a greater interest in regulating the operation of political parties. It occurred over the course of several decades, but the switch to state printed ballots was the beginning of the transition from political parties as strictly private associations to parties as "public utilities" (Epstein 1986). As public utilities, political parties gained legal recognition and, more importantly, their nominees gained routine access to the state's ballot. In return, the parties had to accept regulation by state government of their organizational structure and conduct of public business.

All states have laws governing election procedures and ballot access. As part of the regulation of the electoral process, states may have laws that define what constitutes a political party. State laws differ, however, on the extent to which they regulate the composition and internal working of political parties. In some states, the law may provide general guidelines as to how political parties are to be structured. For example, the law in Georgia (1998, 21–2–11), a state with a tradition of limited regulation, specifies that

> each political party shall establish and maintain a state executive committee exercising state-wide jurisdiction and control over party affairs and a county executive committee in each county in which it holds a primary, exercising county-wide jurisdiction and control over party affairs. . . . The state executive committee of each political party shall formulate, adopt, and promulgate rules and regulations, consistent with law, governing the conduct of conventions and other party affairs.

Although Georgia's law does specify the existence of a state executive committee and county executive committees, it leaves the conduct of party affairs largely up to these party bodies. In contrast, states with a tradition of heavy regulation provide more extensive requirements about the structure of parties and the procedures they are to follow. Ohio law, for example, distinguishes among major, intermediate, and minor parties, based on the percentage of votes received in gubernatorial or presidential elections. For major parties it specifies the time when a state convention may be held, the composition of delegates to the state convention, and the membership and election procedures for the party's controlling committees. In sum, to a greater or lesser degree, states have come to regulate the structure and composition of parties as well as the rules and procedures by which parties are to operate.

Because regulation was intended to eliminate corrupt election practices, the power of state governments to regulate parties went unchallenged for many years. Two decisions by the Supreme Court in the 1980s, however, have given party organizations greater freedom from state regulation. In *Tashjian v. Republican Party of Connecticut* (1986), the Supreme Court ruled that the state of Connecticut could not prevent the state Republican party from allowing registered independents to vote in its primary elections. Shortly afterward, the Court ruled in *Eu v. San Francisco County Democratic Central Committee* (1989) that certain California regulations were an unconstitutional burden on the First Amendment liberties of political parties. California had passed legislation that prevented party endorsements in primary elections, limited the length of time a person could serve as state party chair, and required the state party chair to rotate between residents of southern and northern California. The Court declared that California's regulations were unconstitutional because "a State cannot justify regulating a party's internal affairs without showing that such regulation is necessary to ensure an election that is orderly and fair" (*Eu v. San Francisco County Democratic Central Committee* 1989, 1025).

These rulings raise questions about how extensively states can regulate party organizations and suggest that parties might be able to exercise more discretion in the conduct of their business. It is, however, unlikely that state laws regulating parties will undergo extensive challenge any time soon. Many state regulations are not particularly burdensome, and most party activities are already in accordance with state law. If parties regard state regulation as intrusive, though, there is now legal precedent for limiting state regulation unless the law is clearly necessary to promote the governmental interest in conducting free and fair elections.

State Party Organization

State parties are typically governed by a state central committee headed by a state party chairperson. The composition and duties of the state party central committees are determined by state law as well as the party's own rules. Most states have laws that specify how the party's central committee is to be composed, whereas other states simply leave it up to the parties themselves. In states that specify, there are generally two methods for selecting members. One method requires that members be elected in primary elections. Few states use this system and it is not favored by party officials because it limits their ability to influence the composition of their own central committee. More commonly, state laws require that central committee members be selected by state or county conventions. The convention method allows state party leaders more ability to influence the composition of the state central committee.

The duties of state central committees depend on state laws, party rules, or past practices. In some states, the party central committee is directly responsible for selecting delegates to the national party convention or is charged with writing the state party's platform. For the most part, however, state central party committees are a mechanism for broadening the representation of the party and a means for shaping party policy. For example, if the state party chair wants to launch a new fund-raising campaign or organize a voter mobilization program in the state, working with central committee members would be a good way to gather support (whether or not it required formal approval by the central committee).

A state central committee is the formal policymaking body, but day-to-day operations are usually handled by the state party chair. In most states, the state party chair is selected by the central committee, although other states require that the chair be elected by the delegates to the state party convention. State party chairs are generally chosen for a two-year term. State party chairs may remain for extended periods, but the more usual pattern is for the state chairperson to serve only for a short time. Two or three years is a common length of service for a state party chairperson (Huckshorn 1976, 46; Reichley 1992, 389). The job of a state party chair can be a demanding one. Formal duties differ from state to state, but the primary responsibility of a contemporary chairperson is to represent the state party organization both within the state and within the national party organization.

Within the state, the party chair must work to coordinate the efforts of various party constituencies. Political scientist Robert Huckshorn (1991, 1060) has identified four internal party responsibilities of a state chairperson: (1) to maintain a good working relationship with local party leaders and activists; (2) to maintain an effective relationship with the elected members of the state central committee; (3) to provide elected state officials, such as the governor or state legislators, with political help as necessary; and (4) to administer party headquarters and employ staff to carry out the goals of the party organization. Huckshorn's list provides a good sense of the various relationships within the state party that a chairperson has to cultivate. Of course, the job also involves developing relationships outside the party as well. For example, state party chairs should have good relations with a broad array of people outside the party organization such as potential campaign contributors, local businesspeople, union officials, and members of the media.

How well the state chairperson is able to carry out these duties depends on many factors in addition to personal ability, including the party's partisan performance and the status of the party organization. The party's partisan performance refers to how well the party has done in recent elections, in particular, whether the party controls the governorship or not. In a study of state party leaders, Huckshorn (1976, 69–95) identified three roles for state party chairs, depending on whether their party controls the governorship: (1) the political agent, (2) the in-party independent, and (3) the out-party independent. Political agents are state chairs selected by the incumbent governor and expected to serve as a partisan agent for the governor. In contrast, an in-party independent chairperson is usually selected without the support of the incumbent governor and so is regarded as being able to act on behalf of the party independently from the governor. Finally, when the chairperson's party does not control the governorship, the state party chair is classified as an out-party independent, since selection as chair depends on the individual's standing within the party.

Another factor that affects the chairperson's job is the current strength of the state party organization. Research by Cotter et al. (1984) has shown that there are substantial differences in the organizational strength of state parties. An important component of organizational strength is the extent of "bureaucratization" of the party, that is, the presence of professional leadership, paid staff, and regular sources of funds. Nearly all state parties now have a paid executive director, and some state parties have well-established sources of income and paid staffers to run party operations on a routine basis. Other state parties, however, have less money and fewer professional staff members. Thus, it stands to reason that a state party chair who takes over an organization with a reliable source of funds and knowledgeable professional staff will be able to concentrate time and effort on recruiting candidates or developing strategy for an upcoming campaign. State chairs who inherit less proficient organizations will have to spend more time raising money, trying to fill party positions, and engaging in other routine activities.

State political parties differ in terms of their electoral success, the extent of regulation by state law, and their organizational strength. Yet all state parties share the goal of winning elections. The bottom line for political parties is to get their candidates into office, and much of what state parties actually do can be summarized in terms of this goal. In their study of state parties, Cotter et al. (1984, 19–26) identify state party activities as falling into two categories: institutional-support and candidate-directed activities. Institutional-support activities "enhance the capacity of the party organization to perform as a service bureau for a broad clientele and thus to generate broad support" (Cotter et al. 1984, 19). Party fund-raising, voter registration drives, analysis of issues, staffing party positions, and publishing a party newsletter are examples of activities that maintain or enhance a party's institutional ability. Candidate-directed activities focus on getting candidates elected to office. Recruiting people to run for office, conducting campaign seminars, and providing assistance with campaign finance laws are examples of the candidate-directed services that state parties perform.

Local Parties

The most basic operational unit of party organization in the United States is the county level (or the equivalent unit in states such as Alaska and Louisiana). County party organizations may be composed of wards or precincts, but these units seldom have their own organizational structure. Most county parties have formal rules for their operation and are usually headed by a county chairperson. Unlike state organizations, however, county organizations are not very bureaucratic. A few county party organizations are highly organized, such as the Cook County Democratic party in Illinois or the Nassau County Republican party in New York, but most county organizations are run by volunteers with few resources. In sum, local party organizations are more personalized and less professional in their organizational structures than state parties. The more personalized leadership found at the county level has one notable benefit—less turnover in leadership. In contrast to state party chairs, county party chairs tend to remain in the same office for a longer period of time (Cotter et al. 1984, 44). Although county parties do not have the resources of state parties, that should not be taken to mean they are inactive. In fact, research on local parties has demonstrated that they are far more organized and active than scholars had suspected (Cotter et al. 1984; Gibson et al. 1986). Table 3.2 lists a number of activities reported by local party leaders in a survey (Gibson, Frendreis, and Vertz 1989).

The list of activities undertaken by local parties during an election year suggests several things about the nature of local parties. First, the activities undertaken by local parties are similar for both Republicans and Democrats. Although Republican local parties report slightly higher levels of activities, the differences between the parties are surprisingly small. It appears that party organizations operate in a similar fashion at the local level regardless of partisanship. This conclusion fits with the finding that, in organizational terms, local parties tend to be quite similar. This does not hold true at the state level, however. State Republican parties are generally more sophisticated organizationally than state Democratic parties (Cotter et al. 1984). At the local level, however, there are less notable differences between parties. "Generally, it is the larger, industrialized, and somewhat

TABLE 3.2   Activities of Local Party Organizations

Activity	Republican %	Democrat %
Distribute campaign literature	91	89
Organize campaign events	87	85
Distribute posters and signs	81	83
Arrange fund-raising events	83	80
Hold registration drives	78	79
Organize telephone campaigns	78	76
Prepare press releases	75	72
Contribute money to candidates	76	68
Send mail to voters	75	66
Conduct door-to-door canvassing	69	67
Buy newspaper advertisements	66	61
Buy radio/TV advertisements	36	38
Use public opinion surveys	26	22
Buy billboard space	10	10

NOTE: Figures are the percentages of local party organizations that reported engaging in the activity in the 1984 election.

SOURCE: Adapted from James L. Gibson, John P. Frendreis, and Laura L. Vertz, "Party Dynamics in the 1980s: Change in County Party Organizational Strength, 1980–1984," *American Journal of Political Science* 33, no. 1 (1989): 73–74. Reprinted with permission of the University of Wisconsin Press.

wealthier states which have the strongest local party organizations," both Democratic and Republican (Cotter et al. 1984, 51).

The activities in Table 3.2, listed from most common to least common, suggest something else about the nature of local parties. The more common activities conducted by local parties tend to be those that involve mobilizing volunteers; the least common are those that require sizable amounts of money. Nearly all the local parties during the 1984 elections reported distributing literature, organizing campaign rallies, or distributing yard signs. Considerably fewer local parties reported conducting activities that required money, for example, buying advertisements on radio or television or renting billboards. The differences in these activities emphasize that local parties tend to thrive on people, whereas state and national parties thrive on money.

Changes in State and Local Parties

Over the last several decades state parties have undergone a revitalization due, in large part, to their adaptation to the service party role. Research on state and local parties has demonstrated that now, in comparison with the 1950s and 1960s, they have more money, are better organized and more professional, and engage in a broad range of activities designed to help candidates and build party organization (Cotter et al. 1984; Gibson, Frendreis, and Vertz 1989; Reichley 1992).

Of course, this change did not occur quickly, nor has it occurred uniformly across states. In general, the strengthening of party organization and greater activism of state and local parties have come about as a result of policies initiated by the national Republican party (Bibby 1994; Reichley 1992). The Republican party's persistent minority status nationally in the 1960s led the party to concentrate on improving its organizational capacity to assist candidates. As a result, Republicans began to provide cash and political expertise to help state Republican parties and established a decided structural advantage over many state Democratic parties. Only later, in the mid-1980s, did the national Democratic party respond with similar programs; it has been able to narrow the gap in recent years.

Another significant development has been the growth of legislative campaign committees in many states (Gierzynski 1992; Shea 1995). Legislative campaign committees (LCCs) are organizations that collect contributions from donors, usually interest groups, and distribute campaign contributions to candidates running for the state legislature. Much like their counterparts in Congress discussed later in this chapter, these organizations are structured by party (Democratic or Republican) and chamber (House or Senate). In New York, for example, four LCCs operate in the state: House Republicans, House Democrats, Senate Republicans, and Senate Democrats. Active LCCs are estimated to exist in a majority of states (between thirty and forty) in the 1990s. In New York, Wisconsin, Ohio, Indiana, Washington, and Illinois, LCCs are highly advanced entities that can provide a range of services to legislative candidates in addition to making direct contributions. In general, LCCs are most fully developed in states with professional legislatures, highly competitive state elections, and, to a lesser extent, a tradition of weak state parties (Rosenthal 1994).

The development of LCCs suggests several important points. First, the emergence of LCCs has been fueled by the growing importance of money in state and local campaigns. It can be difficult for candidates in low-profile state elections to raise money, yet the cost of running for such offices has risen across the country. Thus, LCCs provide a mechanism for established state legislators to raise money from individuals and groups and use it to assist candidates from their party. In an important sense, then, the creation of LCCs is an extension of what has happened at the national level and reflects the efforts of political leaders to adapt to contemporary circumstances.

Second, the spread of LCCs underscores the ambivalent nature of state party organizations. On the one hand, LCCs may strengthen party loyalties by funneling interest group money to legislators through a party-related organization. Newly elected legislators may feel an obligation to other members of their legislative party rather than to specific interest groups or wealthy donors. On the other hand, although organized along party lines, LCCs are organizationally separate from state parties. At times, an LCC may even compete with a state or local party organization. Daniel Shea (1995) describes a special legislative election in New York in which squabbling over campaign strategy between the local Democratic party and the Democratic Assembly Campaign Committee ended up hurting the Democratic candidate.

Finally, LCCs are not always oriented toward party goals. In addition to the "caucus" type of LCC created by Democrats or Republicans in the legislature, we are also seeing the development of "leadership" LCCs (Gierzynski 1992, 39–43). A leadership campaign committee differs from a caucus LCC because it is controlled by a legislative leader. An extraordinary example of the use of a leadership LCC occurred when the Speaker of the California Assembly, Willie Brown, used his personal LCC to dole out $2.9 million in 1982 and $2.4 million in 1984 to state legislative campaigns. Brown used his leadership committee rather than the Democratic party's LCC in order to maximize his personal control over the distribution of campaign contributions. Although the California example is an extreme case, some scholars point out that the use of leadership LCCs may encourage state legislators to be loyal to particular legislative leaders rather than political parties (Reichley 1992, 392; Rosenthal 1994).

Over the past thirty years, state parties have adapted to their role as service parties. State parties today are stronger and more professional organizations than they were in the 1960s. Local parties are not the dominant party machines of the late nineteenth and early twentieth centuries, but they remain organized and active. The increased organizational strength of state and local parties raises a question: Do the services supplied to candidates and the campaign activities conducted by the parties actually help candidates win elections? The answer to this question appears to be a qualified yes. There is evidence indicating that a state party that is organizationally stronger than its competitor has greater success in gubernatorial elections (Cotter et al. 1984, 101). The evidence for local parties is less clear-cut. Overall, there appears to be little relationship between local party strength and votes for the party's candidates. Local party strength does, however, appear to be positively associated with recruiting candidates to run for the state legislature and even for Congress (Frendreis, Gibson, and Vertz 1990).

State and local parties have, for the most part, adapted well to the new realities of candidate-centered elections. In most states, the political scene today is more complicated than it was forty years ago. In addition to political parties, states have seen a proliferation of political consultants, an increase in the number of interest groups and political action committees, and the emergence of new organizations such as the legislative campaign committees. The state parties, in particular, have responded by becoming more professional and active. But the demand for greater professionalism may be coming at the cost of reduced autonomy. In the 1980s and 1990s, state parties have come to rely increasingly on resources provided by their national parties. It is too soon to say whether the traditionally decentralized American party structure is becoming more centralized. The phenomenon of national parties transferring resources to the states is a relatively recent development. Still, these changes point to the need to understand what is occurring within the national parties.

National Parties

Change in the national parties has followed different paths for Democrats and Republicans. Both parties maintain the same essential structures, but Democrats have pursued change through internal reform, whereas Republicans have focused more on changing the performance of their party.

After the tumultuous convention of 1968, Democrats undertook a series of reforms designed to make the party's nomination process more open to and more representative of party constituents. Beginning with the McGovern-Fraser commission, Democrats changed the party's rules for selecting delegates and established procedures ensuring that state parties would comply with national party rules. Efforts to reform the nomination procedures were not settled easily, however. The Democrats set up additional reform commissions after the 1972, 1976, 1980, and 1984 general elections that were designed to remedy defects perceived in the previous election nomination.

Although Democrats focused on the nomination process, leaders in the Republican party chose to improve the performance of their central party organization. The linchpin of this strategy has been to raise more money for the national party and to use the cash to provide services for candidates and state parties. Under the leadership of party chair Ray Bliss (1965–1969), the Republicans essentially invented the service party organization.

Although the two parties pursued different paths in the 1970s and 1980s, developments in one party led to changes in the other as well. Because changes in the Democratic party led states to modify their nomination procedures, the Republican nomination process also changed to meet new state requirements. More dramatically, Democratic party leaders realized by the mid-1980s that they were seriously behind the Republicans in the ability to raise money and provide services to candidates. Somewhat belatedly, the Democratic party has made a concerted effort to catch up with Republican innovations in party organization. Thus, as the twentieth century draws to a close, the national parties retain their traditional structures, adapted to the realities of contemporary politics.

Party Conventions

Formal authority for both major political parties is vested in national conventions that meet every four years. The delegates selected to attend the Republican and Democratic conventions are responsible for choosing the party's nominee for president, approving the party's platform, and approving any changes to party rules or organization. Though formally the supreme authority in party matters, the national conventions are clearly less important today than they were prior to World War II.

One reason for the diminishing importance of conventions is the growing number of state primaries (a point discussed in more detail in the next chapter). Since the 1970s, the process of selecting each party's nominee for the presidency has been determined by the selection of pledged delegates in state primaries rather than at the convention itself. Another change concerns control over the party's platform. Although delegates can still influence the party platform, the process of writing the platform is usually carefully monitored by supporters of the presidential nominee. Since the nominee is usually known prior to the convention, supporters of the nominee try to prevent the party from adopting potentially damaging platform planks on the eve of the general election campaign. Finally, even though the national conventions decide the organizational structure and rules of the party, the responsibilities of running the party's increasingly complex affairs are handled by the national committee and the chairperson of the national committee.

Although the national conventions have become less important as decisionmaking bodies, they are still important as symbols of the parties. They bring together representatives from across the United States to perform the party's most significant functions—selecting the presidential ticket and writing the platform.

In practice, modern conventions have stopped being a mechanism for selecting the party's nominee and become a showcase for the party's presidential candidate. Because national television coverage of the conventions allows candidates to present themselves and their major campaign themes to viewers virtually unchallenged, the nominee's supporters script the party convention to control the party's image with the attentive electorate. Debates regarded by party insiders as divisive or overly technical are relegated to nontelevised times; speakers who appear in prime time are carefully selected and coached to emphasize particular themes. At the 1996 Republican convention, for example, the Dole campaign selected Representative Susan Molinari from New York to give the convention's keynote speech, scheduled Colin Powell to speak during prime-time coverage on the first night of the convention, and featured Elizabeth Dole, the candidate's wife and a former secretary of transportation in the Reagan cabinet. Choosing these individuals to represent the Republican party was clearly an effort to select speakers who would provide a positive image for the Republican ticket (Just 1997, 86–87). In sum, party leaders see the convention as a way to present a carefully crafted view of the party and its candidates to the voters.

Do efforts to control the convention help the party's nominee? There is little evidence to suggest that voters are attracted to a party by its convention, but there is some anecdotal evidence to suggest that a poor convention may hurt. For instance, in contrast to the carefully scripted 1984 and 1988 conventions, the 1992 Republican convention that nominated President George Bush for reelection was marked by considerable controversy, mostly over a speech given by Patrick Buchanan. Although controversy over the Buchanan speech probably did not contribute to Bush's defeat, it certainly did not help the Bush-Quayle ticket focus attention on the themes they wanted to communicate to voters.

Another way to assess the effect of a party convention is to examine the "convention bounce," the difference in a candidate's intended vote before and after the party's nominating convention. Prior to the 1996 Republican convention in San Diego, for example, about 30 percent of registered voters in a Gallup poll indicated they would vote for Robert Dole. In weekend polling after the convention that formally nominated Dole and running mate Jack Kemp, 41 percent of registered voters said they intended to vote

BOX 3.1 How Would a New Party Organize a Convention? The 1996 Reform Party

The convention practices of the Republican and Democratic parties—speeches by party notables, adoption of the platform, dramatic roll call of the states, and noisy acceptance speech by the nominees—have developed over many years. These practices exist because of party rules or simply by tradition and have been adapted to the media age only in recent years. Of course, none of these traditions would be binding on a new party holding its first convention.

How would a new party arrange a convention? In 1996 we had the opportunity to find out. Former independent candidate Ross Perot helped organize a new political party, the Reform party, and created a new format for its nominating convention. First, the party mailed out nominating ballots in July to about 1.3 million citizens who either were registered members of the party or had signed one of its ballot-access petitions. Any candidate who received more than 10 percent of the nominating vote was included on the final nominating ballot sent out in the first week of August. Party supporters could vote by mail, telephone, or e-mail.

The Reform party held a two-stage convention process. The first convention meeting, held in Long Beach, California, on August 11, featured speeches by the candidates on the final ballot. Two candidates spoke to a gathering of an estimated 2,500 Reform party supporters: Richard Lamm, former governor of Colorado, and Ross Perot, billionaire businessman. After the Long Beach convention, party supporters had one week to vote (although mail ballots could have been sent earlier), and votes were tallied by an independent accounting firm. The results were announced on August 18 at a second party meeting, held in Valley Forge, Pennsylvania. The second meeting was billed as the "campaign kick-off" for the Reform party and featured a speech by the nominee, Ross Perot, who received roughly two-thirds of the final votes.

The contest between Lamm and Perot for the Reform party's nomination was a mismatch given Perot's independent candidacy in 1992 and his crucial role in starting the party, but it did serve to increase media attention for the fledgling party. Balloting by party supporters was an effort to make the process more directly democratic, in contrast with the system of elected delegates used by the Democrats and Republicans. The direct balloting was not without its problems, however. Over 1 million final ballots were mailed out, but only about 49,000 were returned. The use of telephone balloting proved to be even more problematic. According to media reports, of the 68,000 telephone ballots cast, roughly 64,000 were invalid. Despite the technical troubles, the Reform party process may provide a glimpse into the future of nominating conventions.

SOURCES: Rhodes Cook, "Third Parties Push to Present a Respectable Alternative," *Congressional Quarterly Weekly Report* 54 (1996): 1986–1988; Deborah Kalb, "Perot Gets Reform Party Nod, Will Take Matching Funds," *Congressional Quarterly Weekly Report* 54 (1996): 2396–2397; Bill Stall, "Same Notes, Different Style for Perot, Lamm," *Los Angeles Times*, August 12, 1996, A1; Bill Stall, "Reform Party's Nominating Process Runs into Snags," *Los Angeles Times*, August 16, 1996, A31; and Robin Toner, "Lamm Far Behind," *New York Times*, August 18, 1996, 1.

for the Dole-Kemp ticket. Thus, Dole got an eleven-point "convention bounce" (see Table 3.3). Because candidate and party receive several days of nearly exclusive attention from the national media, including hours of prime-time coverage, the candidate's approval rating usually jumps immediately after the party's nominating convention.

TABLE 3.3   Convention Bounce for Major Party Presidential Candidates, 1964–1996

Year	Candidate	Party	Bounce
1996	Dole	Republican	11
	Clinton (I)	Democrat	5
1992	Clinton	Democrat	16
	Bush (I)	Republican	5
1988	Dukakis	Democrat	7
	Bush	Republican	6
1984	Mondale	Democrat	1
	Reagan (I)	Republican	4
1980	Reagan	Republican	8
	Carter (I)	Democrat	10
1976	Carter	Democrat	9
	Ford (I)	Republican	4
1972	McGovern	Democrat	0
	Nixon (I)	Republican	7
1968	Nixon	Republican	5
	Humphrey	Democrat	2
1964	Goldwater	Republican	5
	Johnson (I)	Democrat	0

Average Bounce, 1964–1996
    All candidates   = 5.8
    Republican candidates   = 6.1
    Democratic candidates   = 5.6
    Out-party candidates   = 6.9
    In-party candidates   = 4.8
    Incumbent presidents   = 5.0

NOTE: (I) denotes an incumbent president. For each election year the out party traditionally holds the first convention and so is listed first.

SOURCES: Compiled by the authors from Gallup poll data. Data for convention bounce for 1964–1992 are from Lydia Saad, "Average Convention 'Bounce' Since 1964 Is Five Points," *Gallup Poll Monthly* 371 (August 1996): 8–9. Convention bounces for Dole and Clinton are calculated from the Gallup polls prior to and after the two conventions reported in David W. Moore, "Perot Candidacy Hurt by Major Party Conventions," *Gallup Poll Monthly* 371 (September 1996): 4–5. To calculate Dole's convention bounce, the August 5–7 Gallup poll was the preconvention poll and the August 16–18 Gallup poll was the postconvention poll. For Clinton, August 23–25 was the preconvention poll and August 30–September 1 was the postconvention poll.

As Table 3.3 shows, since 1964, when Gallup first asked the intended vote questions just before and just after the conventions, the average convention bounce has been about 6 percent. Republican candidates have fared slightly better on average, at 6.1 percent, than Democratic candidates, at 5.6 percent. Between 1964 and 1996, the "out party" (the party not holding the presidency) generally received a higher bounce because it traditionally holds its convention first. On average the out party has a convention bounce of 6.9 percent, whereas the party in power has an average bounce of 4.8 percent (with the seven incumbent presidents averaging a 5 percent convention bounce).

Of course, the size of the bounce depends on how the candidate was perceived before the convention as well as what happened at the convention. In 1964, for example, Republican Barry Goldwater got a respectable 5 percent bounce after the Republican convention, whereas President Johnson got no discernible bounce. But President Johnson's lack of bounce was due, no doubt, to the fact that he had a 69 percent approval rating prior to the convention. In recent years, candidates representing the party out of power have done particularly well. Prior to 1992, the Gallup poll recorded only one double-digit increase—Jimmy Carter's 10 percent bounce in 1980. In 1992, Bill Clinton recorded the largest convention bounce measured by Gallup, 16 percent, attributable in part to the dramatic exit of Ross Perot from the presidential race just prior to the Democratic convention (Saad 1996). In 1996, Republican Robert Dole got a two-step bounce. His intended vote numbers went up about 9 percent with the announcement that Jack Kemp would be his running mate just prior to the start of the Republican convention. The Dole-Kemp ticket went up an additional 2 percent by the end of the convention (though different polls produced very different estimates of the size of Dole's increase; see Morin 1996).

The summer nominating conventions have been an important ritual for American parties since the nineteenth century and have been broadcast on television since 1952. Yet in recent years there has been growing dissatisfaction with the conventions and a decline in the number of hours shown on television. With the growth of state primaries and pledged delegates, the party's nominee is generally known well in advance of the convention. As a result, instead of being the climax of the nomination process conventions have become the opening of the general election campaign. Party leaders may regard a strong show of party unity as a valuable opportunity, but the increasingly choreographed convention proceedings shown on television have resulted in fewer viewers and dissatisfaction among journalists with the lack of "real" news stories. As veteran ABC news anchor Ted Koppel put it during the 1996 Republican convention in San Diego (Laurence 1996, 4),"this convention is more of an 'infomercial' than a news event. Nothing surprising has happened. Nothing surprising is anticipated.

Frankly we expect the Democratic convention in Chicago to be much the same."

Because of the significance of conventions to the major parties, it is unlikely that there will be major changes in this system any time soon. Yet, after 1996, it is clear that the heyday of saturation television coverage is over.

The National Party Committees

Both major parties rely on a national party committee to conduct party business between conventions. The two national committees are similar in function, but they differ markedly in membership. The Republican National Committee (RNC) uses a traditional method of representation based on states. Three members are selected from each of the fifty states and five additional areas (the District of Columbia, Virgin Islands, Guam, American Samoa, and Puerto Rico). The three representatives are the party chair and one national committeewoman and one national committeeman selected from each state. The RNC thus has a total membership of 165, representing all the states and additional areas equally, regardless of state population or party performance. In contrast, the Democratic National Committee (DNC) is far larger than the RNC and membership criteria are more complex. Prior to 1972, DNC structure was similar to the current RNC structure. In 1972, however, as part of the reforms recommended by the McGovern-Fraser commission, the party convention approved a change in representation on the DNC to increase participation in the party and enhance the representation of groups that had previously been underrepresented. Members of the DNC are selected from four constituencies: (1) the states and territories, (2) elected officials, (3) special constituency organizations, and (4) at-large members. The most numerous group of representatives is the one selected from states.

Membership in the DNC is not apportioned equally to all states but is based on population and past support for Democratic candidates. Each state sends at least two delegates to the DNC, but larger states and states that have elected Democrats to office are apportioned additional seats (using the formula for apportioning national convention delegates discussed in the next chapter). In addition, the DNC consists of the state party chair and the next highest Democratic party official of the opposite sex from each state and six additional areas (District of Columbia, Virgin Islands, Guam, American Samoa, Puerto Rico, and "Democrats abroad"). Currently, there are 212 elected state representatives and 112 state party officials, thus accounting for 324 DNC members. The DNC also includes twenty-five members who are elected officials at the national, state, or local level. The DNC reserves places for Democratic leaders in the House and Senate, as well as members of the Democratic Governors Association, the

Democratic Mayors Conference, and local officeholders. There are also a small number of places on the DNC for Democratic party officials and representatives of three affiliated groups: Young Democrats, College Democrats, and the National Federation of Democratic Women. Finally, the DNC includes places for up to sixty-five additional members to increase the representation of women, young people, and minority group members. Its total size varies, but the DNC usually has in excess of four hundred members.

Both Democrats and Republicans leave the selection of national committee members from the states to the state parties and state laws. In some states, national members are selected by the state party central committee or at a state party convention, whereas other states use primary elections to select members for the national committees.

The full national committee for both parties is far too large and meets too infrequently, usually twice a year, to govern the party effectively. Management tasks for the national committees, such as approving budgets, are handled by an executive committee. In keeping with differences between the parties, the RNC has a relatively small executive committee whereas the DNC has a larger executive committee. The RNC executive committee consists of eleven members of the full RNC, three members appointed by the chair and eight members elected from four regional caucuses of states, as well as the RNC chair and cochair and other RNC officials. The Democrats' executive committee includes members of the DNC from the state regional caucuses as well as DNC officials and the chairs of various affiliated organizations.

In practice, the chairperson of the national party committee is primarily responsible for running the party between elections. The chair of each major party's national committee is formally elected by the full national committee, although in practice the selection of the party chair is heavily influenced by the incumbent president or presidential nominee. Typically, only when the party not holding the presidency replaces its chairperson after the presidential election is there a competitive election for party chair. After Republicans lost the 1996 presidential election, for instance, members of the RNC elected Jim Nicholson, a national committeeman from Colorado, as the new chairman in a closely contested election in January 1997. In contrast, when the party wins the White House, the president usually chooses the chairperson. After winning in 1992, President Clinton appointed the sitting DNC chair, Ronald Brown, to his cabinet and picked his 1992 campaign manager, David Wilhelm, to replace Brown. Wilhelm was duly elected chair by members of the DNC.

President Clinton's recent choices to head the Democratic party have been rather innovative. In 1995, Clinton named two people to chair the party. Donald Fowler, a state party leader from South Carolina, was named national party chair and Christopher Dodd, a senator from Connecticut, was named "general chair" of the party. In effect, Senator Dodd served as a high-profile spokesman for the party, and Fowler handled the day-to-day responsibilities. President Clinton was apparently satisfied with this unorthodox arrangement because he again named two people to head the party. Steven Grossman, a former state party chair in Massachusetts and former president of AIPAC (American Israel Public Affairs Committee), was named national party chairman, and Governor Roy Romer of Colorado was selected as general party chair. Whether the Democrats continue this arrangement in the future will depend on whether other Democratic officials see it as an effective means of promoting the party's message.

The position of national party chair can be a demanding one. The goals for the chair of the DNC or RNC depend to a large extent on whether the party currently holds the White House. For the party in power, the party chairperson is selected by the president and is expected to be a public advocate for the administration while having precious little influence over policy decisions. The chair of the party out of power has more freedom to target the administration for political criticism while preparing for future elections. Generally, it is the job of the party chair to raise money to pay off debts or build up funds for future campaigns, get a team in place for upcoming congressional or presidential elections, assist state parties in recruiting candidates, and develop issue positions and campaign themes for the party as a whole.

If the party does well, the chairperson may be rewarded. Ronald Brown's selection to head the Commerce Department was widely regarded as a reward for the Democrats' success in the 1992 elections. If the party does poorly, the chairperson may take the blame. After the Democrats' disastrous showing in the 1994 midterm elections, David Wilhelm resigned as chairman and was replaced by the party's executive director, Debra DeLee, who served as chair until President Clinton named a new party chair in January 1995. Similarly, after the 1996 election in which the Republicans failed to capture the presidency, Haley Barbour stepped down as head of the RNC. Though the people who serve as chair of the national committee of either party rarely serve for extended periods of time, most former party chairs remain active in politics after their service as party chair ends.

The Congressional Campaign Committees

Although not part of the formal party structure, congressional campaign committees (CCCs) are an important element of both major political parties. Each party in both houses of Congress maintains a campaign fund. The House committees are the National Republican Congressional Committee (NRCC) and the Democratic Congressional Campaign Committee (DCCC). The Senate committees are the National Republican Senatorial

Committee (NRSC) and the Democratic Senatorial Campaign Committee (DSCC).

The CCCs have been in existence for some time. The first congressional campaign committee was formed by House Republicans shortly after the Civil War, whereas the Senate committees were created after the ratification of the Seventeenth Amendment in 1913, which provided for direct election of senators (Kolodny 1998). Although they have existed for a number of years, these committees have become more prominent in recent years because of the increasing importance of money in congressional campaigns. The CCCs are organized and led by members of the House or the Senate and, since the 1980s, have employed a large number of staff in election years. Paul Herrnson (1995, 79) reports that in 1992 the Republicans, who tend to be better organized and financed, had 130 staff members working for the NRSC and eighty-nine staffers for the NRCC, whereas the DCCC had sixty-four and the DSCC thirty-five full-time staffers.

The primary function of the CCCs is to use the advantage of incumbency to raise money to assist the party's candidates in House or Senate elections. Especially in recent years the parties have been highly effective at raising money, and the congressional committees have been an important part of the fund-raising effort for both parties. Table 3.4 shows the amounts that various components of the parties have collected since 1975, when the Federal Election Commission was created to monitor campaign finance. The data in Table 3.4 show that both parties have improved their fund-raising prowess over this time period, consistent with the development of the service party orientation. Table 3.4 also shows the sizable advantage that Republicans have maintained over the Democrats in fund-raising, although the Democrats have narrowed the gap in recent years.

The Republican congressional campaign committees have been more consistent fund-raisers, accounting for roughly 30 percent of the Republican total over the years. Despite Democratic dominance in Congress over most of this period, the DCCC and DSCC have not been as consistent in contributing to the total of Democratic party funds. The Democratic congressional committees have, however, improved over this period. In 1975–1976 the Democratic committees contributed about 13 percent of the party's total, but that rose to over 22 percent in 1995–1996.

The congressional campaign committees raise money mostly from PACs, although they collect from individual contributors as well. Once the funds are raised, the committees provide direct contributions to congressional candidates, both incumbents and challengers, and may spend money independently in key states or districts to help their candidates. The leadership and staff of the congressional committees try to target money as strategically as possible, though studies indicate that Republicans have been more successful in targeting funds than Democrats (Dwyre 1994a; Hernnson 1995,

TABLE 3.4   Major Party Fund-Raising: Receipts of Party Committees,
1975–1996 (in millions of dollars)

	Republican Organizations			
	RNC	*NRCC*	*NRSC*	*State*
1975–1976	29.1	12.2	1.8	–
1977–1978	34.2	14.1	10.9	20.9
1979–1980	77.8	20.2	22.3	33.8
1981–1982	84.1	58.0	48.9	24.0
1983–1984	105.9	58.3	81.6	45.4
1985–1986	83.8	39.8	86.1	42.6
1987–1988	91.0	34.7	65.9	66.0
1989–1990	68.7	33.2	65.1	39.3
1991–1992	85.4	35.3	73.8	72.8
1993–1994	87.4	26.7	65.3	75.0
1995–1996	193.0	74.2	64.5	128.4
	Democratic Organizations			
	DNC	*DCCC*	*DSCC*	*State*
1975–1976	13.1	0.9	1.0	–
1977–1978	11.3	2.8	0.3	8.7
1979–1980	15.4	2.9	1.7	9.1
1981–1982	16.5	6.5	5.6	7.6
1983–1984	46.6	10.4	8.9	16.8
1985–1986	17.2	12.3	13.4	11.2
1987–1988	52.3	12.5	16.3	44.7
1989–1990	14.5	9.1	17.5	44.7
1991–1992	65.8	12.8	25.5	73.7
1993–1994	41.8	19.4	26.4	55.6
1995–1996	108.4	26.6	30.8	93.2

NOTE: These data are from the Federal Election Commission and so include only amounts subject to federal reporting requirements. The "state" category includes money raised by various state and local political party committees.
SOURCES: Figures for 1975–1976 to 1985–1986 are from Paul S. Herrnson, *Party Campaigning in the 1980s* (Cambridge: Harvard University Press, 1984), 32–34. Post-1986 figures were compiled by the authors from Federal Election Commission data.

85–87). As a general rule, established incumbents in safe seats should be less likely to receive help from their campaign committee than incumbents who face tough reelection fights or challengers in competitive contests.

In addition to providing contributions directly to candidates' campaigns, congressional campaign committees may use "coordinated expenditures" by which the party spends money on behalf of its candidates. Coordinated expenditures often involve spending for campaign consultants, media time, production of campaign commercials, opinion polling, or candidate training. These services can often be used to help several candidates simultaneously, for instance, by conducting a statewide opinion poll or by holding a campaign seminar for congressional candidates. In addition to providing resources, the senators or representatives who are chosen to head their respective campaign committees are often active in recruiting congressional candidates well before the campaign season starts. A call from a well-known member of Congress with a promise of assistance from the congressional campaign committee can be a positive incentive for individuals contemplating running for the House or Senate.

The recent prominence of the congressional campaign committees reflects an important lesson about the contemporary national parties: Formal structure is often less important than control of resources. The idea of incumbent politicians collecting funds to assist all candidates from their party may appear to be the very essence of party commitment. Although organized by party, congressional campaign committees are not part of the formal structure of the major parties. That is, the campaign strategies and fund-raising undertaken by the CCCs are controlled by members of Congress, not the party chair or the national committee. There is, of course, a very practical reason for members of Congress to assist their party's other candidates: Congress is organized by party, and being the majority party is tremendously advantageous (Kolodny 1998). Ambitious members of the same party may cooperate to promote their own good, which is not to imply that they are part of a strong hierarchical organization. Members of Congress and party officials seek the same goal and may coordinate their efforts, but neither group controls the actions of the other.

Contemporary Parties and the Service Party Role

The formal structure of American political parties is much the same today as it was at the turn of the century. Both major parties are composed of a loosely organized collection of state and local parties united through the mechanisms of a national party committee and a nominating convention. But comparing the outward similarity of the party structures misses the enormous changes that the parties have experienced.

The major political parties have changed because they had to adapt to new social and political circumstances. Quite apart from partisan concerns, American society has changed dramatically in ways that have affected the parties. In the nineteenth century, when there were high levels of immigration as well as internal migration from farms to cities, it was possible for strong local parties to organize masses of voters in an effort to control city governments. With immigration in decline and population movement going from the cities to the suburbs, urban political machines lost dominance of the political landscape. The development and spread of electronic broadcast media, first radio and later television, meant that citizens were no longer reliant on local newspapers or word-of-mouth communication for political information. Prior to the development of the mass electronic media, it made sense to campaign through organized rallies and candidate speeches. Using radio and television, candidates can communicate directly to voters and have no need for party organization as an intermediary. In sum, political parties, like other organizations, had to adapt to broader social changes.

There were also important changes in the political environment in which parties operate. Legislation passed during the Progressive era substantially changed party organization and operation. State adoption of the Australian ballot and subsequent passage of direct primary laws limited the control that party organizations had exercised over who appeared on the ballot under the party's label. Voter registration, limits on the ability of elected officials to hire and fire government employees, nonpartisan elections, and other laws took their toll on party organizations. By the 1950s, state and local parties were no longer the dominant political organizations they had been in some areas, even though a few party machines managed to keep going in the 1960s (Mayhew 1986).

The combination of social and political change meant that party organization had reached its nadir just as new technology, especially television, was allowing candidates to speak directly to voters, bypassing the party organization altogether. The presidential election of 1952 was the first to feature televised advertisements for a presidential candidate; from that point on the medium became more accessible to candidates for a range of offices. An important consequence of the development of televised campaigning was that a candidate's personal campaign organization became more central and the party organization became less important to the candidate. The 1950s and 1960s thus marked a transition period. Party organizations were in the process of long-term atrophy, and candidates were beginning to take advantage of new technology to market themselves to voters.

The parties responded to these circumstances by adopting a "service party role." As service parties, the political parties have the primary function of providing services to candidates. Parties do not attempt to control or compete with the candidate's separate campaign organization; rather, the parties seek to recruit and assist candidates who can run under the party's label and win. In a sense, this has always been central to the role of political parties in the United States. What has changed, however, is the prominence of election contests. No longer do parties simply seek to mobilize "their" voters; now both parties and individual candidates must use sophisticated strategies to try to motivate party supporters and appeal to independent or swing voters at the same time. In the next chapter, we look at the rules that govern these electoral contests.

4

The American
Electoral System

American political parties are something of a paradox. American political parties are among the oldest continuously established party organizations in the world and play a vital part in the conduct of American politics. Yet, by comparison with nearly any other democratic nation, American political parties are weak organizations that cannot control even such essential functions as determining which candidates run under the party's label.

Though seemingly contradictory, these two characterizations of American political parties are, in fact, quite compatible. American party organizations continue to exist and play an important part in American government because they have been able to adapt to the unique political environment of the United States. The American electoral environment itself is largely responsible for the type of political party system that exists in the United States today. In this chapter, we examine three important features of American election rules: the plurality system, the nomination process, and the electoral college.

Electoral Systems

One of the most fundamental features of any democratic system of government is the set of rules used to decide elections. The electoral rules help to determine the number of political parties, the competitiveness of elections, the stability of government, and even how well citizens' policy preferences are translated into public policy. Before explaining the effects of the American electoral system, we need to discuss electoral systems in general.

The political consequences of various electoral arrangements have been carefully studied by political scientists (see, e.g., Lijphart 1990, 1994; Rae 1967; Taagepera and Shugart 1989). Most scholars agree that the two most important features of any country's electoral system are the electoral formula and the district magnitude (Lijphart 1994, 10). Electoral formulas are the rules for deciding who gets elected. Most democracies in the world today use one of the following types of electoral formulas: (1) proportional representation systems, (2) plurality systems, and (3) semiproportional or mixed systems (Lijphart 1994, 10). Of these three types, the semiproportional system is the least common and will not be the focus of our attention. More important for our purposes is the distinction between proportional representation systems and plurality systems.

Most democratic nations use proportional representation (PR). Proportional representation systems award seats in the legislature based on a party's proportion of the total vote. For example, a party that gets 40 percent of the popular vote should get about 40 percent of the seats in the legislature. There are a number of methods that may be used for determining how candidates are selected, but various PR systems share the idea that representation in legislative assemblies ought to be roughly proportional to overall support within the electorate. Some methods of PR are more favorable to parties that win relatively larger percentages of the vote; others treat parties relatively equitably.

The magnitude of electoral districts is the most significant determinant of how proportional a PR system is. Countries that use proportional representation have "multimember districts," meaning that two or more representatives are elected from the same geographic area. District magnitude, then, refers to how many representatives are elected from a particular district. Some PR countries, such as Ireland, have relatively small district magnitudes; the number of representatives per district is typically between three and five. Other nations have relatively large district magnitudes. In Israel, for example, the entire nation serves as one electoral district for the 120 members of the legislature. The relationship between district magnitude and the degree of proportionality in the electoral system is easy to identify: The larger the district magnitude the more proportional the system can be (Rae 1967; Lijphart 1990; Taagepera and Shugart 1989, 112–125).

In contrast to PR, plurality systems are nearly always used in conjunction with single-member districts. A single-member district means that only one representative is elected from a geographic district. There is no logical necessity for using single-member districts with a plurality system. Two or three candidates with the most votes could just as easily be chosen from a given district; but in practice nations with plurality methods tend to use single-member districts.

With a plurality formula, the decision rule is quite simple: The candidate with the most votes wins. The plurality formula, also known as "first past the post," is used in the United States, the United Kingdom, Canada, India, and, until quite recently, New Zealand.

A related but slightly different electoral formula is the "majority-plurality" method that has been used at various times in France. The majority-plurality system requires the use of two ballots. On the first ballot, a candidate who receives a true majority of votes wins. If no candidate wins a majority in the first ballot, a second ballot is held and the winner is determined by a plurality of the votes. Although more than two candidates may participate in the second ballot, in practice the second ballot is a contest between the two strongest candidates, as weaker candidates withdraw and attempt to form an alliance with one of the remaining parties. In the United States, a similar type of electoral arrangement has been used in Louisiana (see the discussion on primary elections later in this chapter).

Since state governments in the United States are largely free to determine their own election laws, in theory a whole variety of electoral systems could be used. In practice, however, nearly all elections use a plurality electoral system, although some states and localities have experimented with different systems at times.

Plurality elections are used most often in the United States for several reasons. First, the plurality system is an efficient way to determine election outcomes. Because the candidate must simply win more votes than any other candidate, not a majority of the votes cast, the winner of the election is easily determined, whether two candidates or twenty candidates are competing for office. Of course, in a two-candidate election the results from a plurality system and a majority system would be the same. With three or more candidates, however, the plurality system still produces a clear winner, whereas a majority system may or may not produce a candidate with a majority of the votes. Another reason for the widespread use of the plurality system is tradition. The plurality system was used in England and has been commonly adopted by nations with a British colonial heritage.

Although plurality systems have advantages, they have limitations as well. One potential difficulty, particularly with multicandidate elections, is that a plurality electoral formula tends to exaggerate the power of a plurality of voters. Consider the following hypothetical circumstance. Suppose that candidates from three parties (Party A, Party B, and Party C) were competing in ten single-member districts under a plurality electoral system. Further, suppose that the results in each district were the same: Party A's candidate got 35 percent of the vote, Party B's candidate got 33 percent of the vote, and Party C's candidate got 32 percent of the vote. Under a plurality system, Party A's candidates, who won the most votes in each district, would win *all* the seats in the legislature. That is, even though only 35 percent of voters supported it, Party A would get 100 percent of the seats. Thus, a plurality electoral system may translate a small plurality of support, 35 percent in our example, into a legislative majority.

Contrast the results just described with a PR system. If the ten seats had been part of one multimember district and the three parties had each earned the same percentages of the vote, Party A would likely get four seats and Parties B and C would each win three seats. Party A would still be advantaged by an electoral formula that translated 35 percent electoral support into 40 percent (four of ten) of the legislative seats, but the bias under the PR system would be much less than under a plurality method. Although PR would produce legislative representation more nearly matching the level of support within the electorate, it would not provide one party a clear majority in the legislature. In order to control a majority of the ten votes within the legislature, two of the parties would have to form a coalition.

The effects of a plurality electoral formula are readily apparent in real election results as well. Table 4.1 shows the outcomes from two recent British elections to illustrate these effects. Notice that in 1992 the two major parties in Britain, the Conservative party and the Labour party, were both advantaged by the plurality electoral system. In 1992 the Conservatives got 42 percent of the national vote but won 52 percent of the seats, sufficient for a slim majority in the House of Commons. Labour, in turn, received 34 percent of the vote but managed to win nearly 42 percent of the seats. In the 1997 election, the Labour party was able to turn a plurality of the popular vote, 44 percent, into a firm majority by winning 64 percent of the seats in Parliament. The Conservatives, on the other hand, did not even

TABLE 4.1   Effect of the Plurality Electoral Method: Election Results from
             Britain, 1992, 1997

	Percentage of Vote	Number of Seats	Percentage of Seats
British Election 1992			
Conservative	41.9	336	51.6
Labour	34.4	271	41.6
Liberal Democrats	17.9	20	3.1
Other	5.8	24	3.7
Total	100	651	100
British Election 1997			
Conservative	31.4	165	25.0
Labour	44.4	419	63.6
Liberal Democrats	17.2	46	7.0
Other	7.0	29	4.4
Total	100	659	100

NOTE: The "other" category includes the Scottish National Party, Plaid Cymru (Welsh nationalist party), and the parties of Northern Ireland.
SOURCE: Compiled by the authors.

get the usual benefit of being a large party, as they came away with only 25 percent of the seats in the House of Commons after getting over 31 percent of the popular vote.

The party that has fared least well under the plurality electoral laws in Britain has been the Liberal Democratic party. The party's base of voters is spread across large parts of the country and is not concentrated in a few constituencies. The Liberal Democrats have the curse of finishing second in many constituencies. In contrast, the parties that make up the "other" category tend to be small parties whose support is concentrated in a few constituencies. These parties include Scottish and Welsh national parties as well as the parties of Northern Ireland. Because their appeal is limited to certain constituencies, none of these parties gets a large share of the national vote, but they stand a better chance of getting a plurality of votes in those areas in which their support is concentrated. For a third party in a plurality system, it is better to have concentrated support than support thinly spread across a wide area. Election outcomes in which seemingly more popular parties get less representation in Parliament than highly localized parties have led some political observers in Britain to call for changes in the electoral laws.

These examples show an important feature of electoral systems: The way that votes are translated into seats has substantial political consequences. One of the best-known statements of this relationship is "Duverger's Law," so named because it was proposed by French political scientist Maurice Duverger. Duverger (1963, 217) stated, in effect, that plurality electoral methods were associated with two-party political systems and PR electoral methods with multiparty systems. Duverger (1963, 403–412) also noted that plurality systems tend to result in more durable governments than PR systems because of the political difficulties associated with maintaining government coalitions. Of course, Duverger's Law does not hold in all cases. Canada serves as a contemporary example of a nation with a plurality electoral system but more than two major political parties.

Nonetheless, the logic of Duverger's analysis is still helpful in explaining an important feature of American politics. Despite the existence of a number of third parties at times in American history, the United States is correctly described as having a two-party system. One of the chief reasons for the dominance of two large parties is that the plurality electoral system in effect punishes minor parties. In a PR system, small parties that can attract 10–15 percent of the total vote stand a good chance of gaining representation in the legislature. With a plurality system, a party that cannot get the most votes in at least some districts will not be represented. Many third parties have discovered that in a plurality system it may be better to ally themselves with one of the major parties in order to have some influence, rather than go it alone and get nothing. In part as a result of our plurality system, American parties tend to be broad-based electoral coalitions designed to enhance the candidates' chances of winning.

Nominations

The plurality electoral system that predominates in American elections is not the most widely used, but it is employed in other democratic nations. When it comes to nominating candidates for office, however, the process that the United States uses is unique: a state-run direct primary. It was not always that way however. As discussed in Chapter 2, when parties began to organize in this country, candidates for office were chosen by means of a caucus of party supporters within the legislative branch. As parties began to develop "extraparliamentary" organizations, however, the legislative caucus was replaced by a party convention in which supporters from across the state or the nation gathered to elect the party's nominee. Although the legislative caucus system and the convention system have flaws, they both have the advantage that the party's candidates are selected by people closely affiliated with the party itself. That is, the party controls its own nominations.

In most democratic nations, candidates are selected by the parties (Ware 1996, 257–288). Most political parties have developed their own internal rules for selecting candidates. In Britain, for instance, the selection of candidates to run for Parliament is left entirely to the parties to determine. The Conservative party provides a list of candidates who have met certain party criteria, but otherwise the selection of the party's candidate is made by members of the local constituency party. The Labour party has a more complex set of rules set by the central party, but candidates are nevertheless selected by the local parties. Other nations, such as Germany, have certain rules established by the government regarding the process parties must use to select candidates. Yet, even in Germany, the selection of candidates for office is primarily a decision left to the parties.

In the United States, however, candidate selection is determined more by state government than by the parties themselves. The method for selecting party nominees used most widely in the United States is the direct primary. In a direct primary, it is the voters who decide the party's candidate for the general election rather than party officials or party activists. It is not the primary itself that is unique; political parties in other nations have used primary elections to select candidates. What is unusual about the American system is that it is mandated by the states. As one scholar put it, "The distinctiveness of the American experience lies not so much in the use of primaries *per se,* nor in state regulation of the nomination process, but in the sheer extent of state involvement in this aspect of party activity" (Ware 1996, 260).

Extensive state government involvement in the nomination process in the United States stems from the Progressive era. The direct primary was championed by Progressive reformers as a way to make the selection of candidates more democratic and to limit the power of "party bosses." Wisconsin was the first state to adopt a statewide direct primary system, in 1903. Wisconsin was a stronghold of the Progressive movement, but other states adopted the innovation and by 1920 a majority of states were using the direct primary. Today, some form of the direct primary is in place in every state, although there is considerable variation among states.

State Primaries

States have a variety of rules governing the nomination process. Further, the system used by a particular state at any point in time is subject to change as state officials and state parties attempt to improve the system or, in some cases, simply seek partisan advantage by altering the electoral rules. Despite the complexity of keeping up with current state law and party rules concerning the nomination process, several broad patterns can be discerned.

As with general elections, primary elections allow any legally registered citizen to participate. The criteria for determining who is eligible to vote in a primary represent a fundamental distinction in the primary election process. In general, four types of primary elections are currently in use:

1. closed primaries
2. open primaries
3. blanket primaries
4. nonpartisan primaries

In states with closed primaries, only voters who are registered as Republicans or Democrats can vote in that party's primary. For example, if you were a resident of New York and wanted to vote in the Republican primary, you would have to be a registered voter and also a registered Republican to obtain a ballot for the Republican primary.

Most states hold closed primaries, but there are differences among states as to when voters must register. The bulk of states that hold closed primaries, including the large states of Pennsylvania, New York, and Florida, require voters to register their party affiliation well in advance of the primary election. In some closed primary states, notably Ohio and Iowa, registered voters may change their party registration at the polls on the day of the primary election. Some states, such as Massachusetts, allow voters who are registered but have not declared a party affiliation to declare at the polls and vote in one of the party's primaries. In addition, some state parties allow unaffiliated voters to vote in the party's primary election. Although Connecticut's closed primary law prohibited the practice, the Supreme Court ruled in the case of *Tashjian v. Republican Party of Connecticut* (1986) that the state could not prevent the Connecticut Republican party from allowing unaffiliated voters to participate in its primary. Despite variations in state laws, closed primaries allow only a party's registered supporters to vote in the party's primary. A majority of states use some form of closed primary.

In contrast, states with open primaries do not require voters to register their party affiliation prior to the primary. Currently, about twenty states use one of two major types of open primary. In about half of the open primary states, including Texas, Illinois, and Indiana, voters are required to ask for the ballot of one party or the other when they appear at the polls. Although all registered voters may participate in either the Democratic or Republican primary regardless of their own partisan affiliation, they must at least publicly request a party's primary ballot (some states allow these public declarations to be challenged by a party's poll watchers). In an even less restrictive form of the open primary, registered voters are given the primary ballots of both parties and are allowed to choose, in the privacy of the polling booth, which primary they will vote in. States such as Wisconsin, Michigan, Minnesota, Utah, Hawaii, and Montana use this least-restrictive form of an open primary.

Two states, Alaska and Washington, have a tradition of using what is called a "blanket primary." In 1998 these two states were joined by California, which used the blanket primary for the first time in its June primaries. California's switch from a closed primary to a blanket primary came about as a result of a citizens' initiative, Proposition 198, passed in 1996.

The blanket primary is a variant of the open primary in which the primary contests of both parties are included on a single ballot. Unlike an open primary in which the voter must choose one party's ballot or the other, in a blanket primary voters may shift between party primaries for different offices. The ballot for a blanket primary looks much like a general election ballot with voters free to vote for, say, a Republican candidate among all the candidates for governor and then vote for a Democratic candidate among the candidates for a House seat.

In the 1996 primary in the state of Washington, for example, a voter could choose any one of fifteen candidates for governor: six Democrats, eight Republicans, and one Socialist Worker. The nominee for each party is the candidate from that party with the most votes. In the 1996 Washington gubernatorial primary, the four candidates with the highest vote totals were: Gary Locke, a Democrat with 24 percent of the total vote; Norman Rice, a Democrat with 18 percent; Ellen Craswell, a Republican who won

15 percent; and Dale Foreman, a Republican who got 13.5 percent of the vote. Thus, Locke won the Democratic nomination and Craswell, the Republican with the most votes, won the Republican nomination. The blanket primary allows voters maximum freedom to participate in interesting or hotly contested primary elections, but it does so at the expense of party control.

The final type of primary is unique to the state of Louisiana. Since 1978, Louisiana has used a "nonpartisan" or "all-party" primary in which all the candidates for a particular office are listed on the same ballot regardless of party. If one candidate wins a majority of the votes cast in the primary, usually held in October, there is no general election for that office. The winner of the primary is declared the winner based on obtaining a majority of votes in the primary. If no candidate wins a majority, then the general election features the two candidates who got the most votes in the primary regardless of party. Thus, a Louisiana general election may feature one Republican and one Democrat or even two Republicans or two Democratic candidates to determine the winner.

The future of Louisiana's nonpartisan primary, however, is uncertain. The Supreme Court, in the case of *Foster v. Love* (1997), has ruled that because Louisiana's primary in effect elected federal officials before November it violated the federal law mandating a uniform election day throughout the nation. As a result of a divisive debate among politicians over how to modify Louisiana's system, the issue has yet to be conclusively resolved.* Although Louisiana may continue to use some form of an open primary, the Supreme Court has ruled that the primary system may not, in effect, evade federal law in regard to when federal officials are elected.

From the perspective of the party organizations, closed primaries are preferable to other types of primary election arrangements. Closed primaries are preferred because they effectively minimize the threat of "crossover" voting or, even worse, "raiding." Crossover voting occurs

---

*After the Supreme Court's ruling, a special session of the Louisiana state legislature was unable to reach a decision about how to change the state's primary elections to conform with federal law. The legislature's inaction ultimately led to a ruling by a federal district judge that moved the date of Louisiana's 1998 federal primary elections from October to the first Tuesday in November to coincide with all other national elections. The judge ruled that any required runoff elections for House or Senate seats would have to take place in December (neither the Supreme Court ruling or the federal district court ruling applied to elections for state offices). Thus, while voters in every other state were voting in general elections for their members of Congress on November 3, 1998, voters in Louisiana were technically casting their ballots in a primary election. In practice, however, it did not make any difference because the winners in the congressional races, all incumbents, won a majority of the votes in the November primary and thus avoided the need for runoff elections.

when voters who are not regular supporters of a party participate in the party's primary election. For example, if the Republican party in an open primary state were having a closely contested primary and the Democratic candidate faced no opposition, some independent or even Democratic party identifiers might be inclined to vote in the Republican primary. "Raiding" would occur if Democrats chose to participate in the Republican primary with the intention of purposefully voting for the Republican they believe to be the weaker general election opponent.

Proponents of strong parties argue that closed primaries are preferable because they prevent the threat of nonsupporters influencing a nomination. Despite this concern, studies of crossover voting in open primary states have found little evidence to suggest that the practice is widespread or that voters act strategically to try to weaken their opponents (Abramowitz, Mc-Glennon, and Rapoport 1981; Hedlun and Watts 1986; Wekkin 1991).

All states have provisions for primary elections to select candidates for the general election, and most states use only a primary election system. A number of states, however, provide for a system of party conventions in place of, or in addition to, primaries (Council of State Governments 1996, 157–158). The most commonly used format is the "convention-first" method, which allows parties in Colorado, Connecticut, New Mexico, New York, North Dakota, and Utah to hold state party conventions prior to the primary. The chief advantage of a convention, from the perspective of the party organization, is that party activists are able to exercise greater control over their nominees than they would in a pure primary system.

The type of nomination system can influence the outcome of the election. In Utah, for example, state party rules allow candidates who can demonstrate strong support among convention delegates—at least 60 percent for Democrats and 70 percent for Republicans in 1996—to become the party's nominee and avoid a primary altogether. In the state Republican convention held in May 1996, several candidates were competing for the nomination of the second congressional district. By the final ballot at the state convention, 67 percent of Republican delegates voted for candidate Todd Neilson, whereas 33 percent supported Merrill Cook, a Republican who had run as an independent and then returned to the Republican party. Although Neilson clearly had more support than Cook among Republican activists, he did not have the 70 percent support necessary to become the party's nominee without a primary. Subsequently, in the state's open primary election, Cook defeated Neilson, in part due to Cook's greater name recognition among primary voters. Although a majority of Republican party activists would have preferred that Cook not be the party's nominee, primary voters chose the better-known candidate to represent the party. Cook went on to win the House seat in the November 1996 election.

Other states use their party caucus-convention systems in different ways. One state, Iowa, requires a party to hold a convention after the primaries to select the party's nominee if no candidate in the primary receives more than 35 percent of the vote. Indiana, Michigan, and South Dakota use primaries for top state offices such as governor but let the parties select nominees for other offices at party conventions. Currently, two states, Alabama and Virginia, allow state parties to choose whether to hold a party convention or use the state primary to select nominees.

Virginia's system has attracted attention recently. In 1994 the Virginia Republican party chose to hold a convention to select their nominee for the U.S. Senate race. The Virginia Republican convention selected Oliver North, a former Reagan administration national security staff member who gained national prominence because of the Iran-Contra affair, over James Miller, a former Reagan administration budget official. Although opinion polls indicated that Miller might fare better in the general election against incumbent Democratic senator Charles Robb, a strong contingent of North supporters was able to secure the nomination for their candidate in the Republican convention. Though his ardent supporters helped him get the nomination, Oliver North lost to Charles Robb after a hard-fought general election campaign. In summary, the mixed convention-primary systems used in some states allow state party organizations and party activists a greater role in the selection of their party's nominees than does a straight primary election method.

Presidential Primaries

In addition to selecting nominees for state office, primary elections have also come to play a prominent role in the selection of presidential candidates. In primary elections for state offices such as governor, voters choose their preferred candidate to be the party's nominee. The presidential nomination, however, is formally determined at the party's national nominating convention. Thus, what is actually being determined during a presidential primary is who the delegates to a party's national convention will be. The process for selecting delegates is complex because it involves the national parties, the state parties, and state laws.

The rules of the national parties determine the allocation of delegates to the states. Both the number of delegates and the allocation rules differ between the major parties. Republicans have fewer delegates attending their national convention than Democrats. In 1996 the Republicans had 1,984 delegates and the Democrats had 4,295 delegates. Republicans allocate the number of delegates for a state or territory based on population and award additional or "bonus" delegates to states with a strong record of the Republican presidential candidate carrying the state or of electing Republicans to state offices. In contrast, Democrats use a formula based on population and the average vote for the Democratic presidential candidate in previous elections (Pika and Watson 1996, 8–9). Democrats, but not Republicans, also provide for "automatic" delegates, or "superdelegates" as they are sometimes called. Automatic delegates are elected officials, such as governors and members of the House or Senate, and elected party officials who become convention delegates by virtue of their offices.

The national parties can, if they choose, influence the selection rules that states use to award delegates to winning candidates. For the most part, Republicans have left the question of delegate selection to the states, whereas Democrats have tried hard to influence the selection process. Because the process is about selecting delegates to each party's national convention, the national parties have the leverage to influence the states by refusing to recognize delegates who are selected in ways that do not conform to party rules.

The traditional method used by states was "winner take all," in which the candidate who gets the most votes gets all the state's delegates. The winner-take-all system is based on the same logic that guides the plurality electoral formula discussed earlier in this chapter. Since the mid-1970s, however, the Democratic party has had a rule against using winner take all and has required states to use some form of proportional representation in awarding delegates. In 1992, Democrats again changed their rules to improve the application of proportional representation to ensure that any candidate who wins at least 15 percent of the vote receives some share of the state's convention delegates.

Within constraints imposed by the national parties, the states choose the method of delegate selection. The exact procedure by which convention delegates are selected differs from state to state. Currently most states use a primary election to determine delegate selection, with a small number of states using caucus-convention systems. Presidential primaries involve voters casting their ballots either for delegates directly or for their preferred candidate, who is then awarded delegates based on the vote. In a caucus-convention system, in contrast, the state parties hold a series of local meetings at which citizens who attend the meetings indicate their preference for the party's candidates and select delegates to attend the next level of meetings up to the state convention. National convention delegates are then elected at a state or congressional district convention.

Participation is considerably higher in primary elections than in caucus-convention meetings. In presidential primaries, much like general elections, candidates must emphasize a broad appeal to many different voters. As a result, candidates with name recognition and the resources to mount a media campaign usually do better than candidates without these advantages in states with primary elections. In caucus-convention states, on the other hand, campaign organization is an important factor. Candidates with strong campaign organizations that can get their supporters to attend local meetings are much better off than candidates who lack strong organizations. Thus, the states of New Hampshire, which holds the first primary, and Iowa, which holds the first caucus, provide a demanding test for presidential campaigns. Though neither Iowa nor New Hampshire is particularly representative of people in other states, together they do provide an early test of both a candidate's voter appeal and campaign organization.

States also choose when to hold their elections, again in conformity with national party rules. Traditionally, the presidential primary season ran from late February to early June. Over the course of the last several elections, however, a number of states have moved up their primary or convention dates in order to ensure having their election before the selection process is over. The shift to earlier primary dates is called "front-loading."

In 1996, Senator Dole had the Republican nomination largely wrapped up by the end of March. As a result of dissatisfaction with front-loading, the Republicans adopted new rules at their 1996 convention to encourage states to hold their 2000 primaries or conventions in April, May, or June. The new Republican rules attempt to entice states to hold their primaries later in the season by awarding progressively larger numbers of bonus delegates to states with later elections (Stanley 1997, 35). Despite this incentive, in 1998 California continued the trend toward front-loading by moving its primary date for presidential elections, which had already been moved from early June to late March in 1996, to early March.

Since 1968 there has been a marked increased in the number of states holding primary elections. As a result, a greater proportion of delegates to the national conventions are now selected in primaries rather than by caucus-convention. In 1968 seventeen states held Democratic primaries and sixteen states held Republican primaries, accounting for about 35 percent of the convention delegates for each party. Other states selected their delegates through some variation of the caucus-convention system. By 1996, in contrast, thirty-six states held Democratic primaries, accounting for 63 percent of the delegates, and 43 states held Republican primaries, selecting 88 percent of the Republican delegates.

The chief reason for the shift to primaries was the internal reforms undertaken in the Democratic party after the 1968 Democratic national convention. Although the McGovern-Fraser commission did not intend to compel states to use primary elections, in practice the new rules that the Democrats adopted led states to drop caucus-conventions as a method for selecting delegates and institute primaries. Moreover, even though these changes were initiated by the Democratic party, they also affected the Republicans. When states changed their laws to comply with Democratic party rules, the new procedures usually applied to both parties. Thus, primary elections have come to dominate the presidential selection process since the 1970s.

The Impact of Primary Elections

Progressive reformers urged the use of primary elections to open up elections to greater citizen participation and simultaneously weaken the power of party leaders over their organizations. Has the widespread adoption of primary elections brought about these intended consequences? For the most part, the answer is yes. Certainly, primary elections do increase the number of citizens participating in the selection of party nominees. It is abundantly clear that more citizens vote in primary elections than participate in caucus meetings. Yet in most states the turnout for primary elections is considerably below that of general elections. Thus, although citizens can involve themselves in the selection of party nominees, most voters choose not to do so. In a sense, then, the intent of the Progressive reformers has been achieved only partially; more citizens participate in primaries than in caucuses, but those voters who participate in primary elections are still a minority of those eligible to participate.

The effect of primaries on party structures, however, is more clear-cut. The widespread adoption of primary elections for state offices did weaken the control of party leaders and ultimately the power of state and local party organizations. By the 1950s, state and local political parties were clearly weaker organizations in most states than they had been at the turn of the century prior to the adoption of the direct primary. Other factors such as changing demographics and laws limiting patronage appointments also played a role, but the impact of direct primaries on the weakening of party organizations should not be overlooked. Although some states allow the parties greater latitude to use a caucus-convention system, the candidate selection process is still very much guided by state regulation.

The move to primary elections in the presidential nomination process, on the other hand, can be seen as more of a consequence of the weakening of party organization than a cause. The growth of presidential primaries was largely an unintended consequence of efforts by the Democrats to modify their internal party operations. Indeed, the ability of the national parties, both Democrats and Republicans, to influence state laws with regard to delegate selection can be interpreted as a sign of vigorous party organizations.

Of course, even after the parties make their nominations, the states continue to play an important role. How the electoral college shapes the conduct of the general election for the presidency will be examined next.

The Electoral College

When citizens cast their ballots for governor, senator, or state legislator, the winner is the one candidate who receives a plurality of the votes cast. The only exception is the office of the president. The president, of course, is chosen by the vote of the electoral college rather than the popular vote. Perhaps because it is a unique institutional arrangement, the electoral college has attracted a good deal of attention. Since the impact of the electoral college on presidential elections is often not well understood, it is worth discussing in some detail.

The origins of the electoral college are rooted in the Constitutional Convention of 1787. During the debate over the new Constitution, Charles Pinckney and others spoke in favor of the president's being selected by members of Congress so that states would be represented in the process. James Madison and others argued in favor of a president elected directly by popular vote. The idea of having a group of prominent individuals from the states, later known as electors, be responsible for selecting the one nationally elected official was a compromise (Mead 1987, 73; Glennon 1992, 7–10). To meet Pinckney's concerns, the electoral college provided a way for states to be central to the election of the national executive, since the selection of electors would be left to the states. To meet Madison's concern with keeping the president distinct from Congress, the electors were to convene in the states, and members of the House and Senate were prohibited from serving as electors.

Equally important, the electoral college provided a way to avoid the obvious practical difficulties of holding a national election in a predominantly rural nation in which citizens had limited access to information about political events in their own state, let alone information about what was happening in distant states. Thus, the local notables who were expected to serve as electors would meet in their states to cast their votes for president, and those votes would be sent to Congress to be counted. Recalling the antiparty sentiment common to political elites of the day, the electoral college was designed as a practical way for state elites to select a national leader.

Problems with the workings of the electoral college were exposed by the election of 1800. As specified in Article 2, section 1 of the Constitution, electors were to cast two ballots. The candidate with a majority of electoral votes would become president and the person with the next highest number would become vice president. By the election of 1800, however, political parties had appeared. The Jeffersonian Republican party had organized a ticket of Thomas Jefferson for president and Aaron Burr for vice president. Republicans had a clear majority in the electoral college, but when Republican electors in the states dutifully cast one vote for Jefferson and one for Burr, it left the two candidates tied. Because of the tie vote, the election had to be decided in the House of Representatives. Although Jefferson prevailed, it was not without a good deal of political maneuvering by both Federalist and Republican supporters.

The election of 1800 led to the ratification of the Twelfth Amendment in 1804. It specifies that electors "shall name in their ballots the person voted for as President, and in distinct ballots the person voted for as Vice-President." The Twelfth Amendment sought to avoid the problem that arose in 1800 by requiring distinct votes for president and vice president. The amendment also limited the number of candidates the House could consider to the top three in the event that no candidate had a majority (originally the top five were considered by the House).

The Twelfth Amendment did solve the problems of 1800, but three subsequent elections have raised questions about the functioning of the electoral college. In 1824 four presidential contenders won electoral votes but none had the required majority: Andrew Jackson had ninety-nine, John Quincy Adams had eighty-four, William Crawford had forty-one, and Henry Clay had thirty-seven. Because only the top three candidates would be considered by the House, Clay agreed to ask his supporters to back Adams. When the decision was made in the House, John Quincy Adams was elected president despite Jackson's greater popular support.

In two other elections, the candidate with fewer popular votes won because of the electoral college. In 1876, Democrat Samuel J. Tilden appeared to have defeated Republican Rutherford B. Hayes by winning 260,000 more popular votes. Disputes over electoral votes cast in Louisiana, South Carolina, and Florida, however, prevented either candidate from obtaining a majority of electors. Because the votes from the three southern states were disputed, the election was not decided in the House. A special electoral commission was set up to resolve only the contested ballots. The actions of the electoral commission were shot through with partisan politics, and ultimately Rutherford B. Hayes was elected president in one of the most questionable presidential elections in American history. Finally, in 1888, Democrat Grover Cleveland was defeated by Republican Benjamin Harrison in the electoral college, even though Cleveland had won about 100,000 more popular votes. Cleveland's revenge came in 1892 when he was re-elected to the White House with a Democratic majority in Congress.

In spite of the controversy surrounding a few elections, the workings of the contemporary electoral college are fairly straightforward. Each state has a number of votes to cast in the electoral college that is equal to its combined number of representatives in the House and Senate. For example, Colorado has eight electoral votes because it has six members in the House of Representatives and two Senators. Because the number of House members from a state can change after a census, the number of a state's electoral votes can also change. No state, however, has fewer than three electoral votes because that is the constitutional minimum of representatives in the House and Senate. Representation in the electoral college for residents of Washington, D.C., was set by the Twenty-third Amendment, ratified in 1961. The District of Columbia currently has three electoral votes, so there are 538 electoral college votes (435 members of the House plus 100 Senators plus 3 for the District of Columbia). Thus, 270 electoral votes constitute the majority required to be elected president.

Article 2, section 1 of the Constitution specifies that each state legislature determines the selection of electors, except that members of the House or Senate may not be appointed electors. Prior to the development of political parties, members of the state legislatures themselves chose the electors. After 1832, however, all the states adopted a system for allowing electors to be chosen by popular vote (with the partial exception of South Carolina, which continued to select electors by the state legislature until 1860).

Today, states rely on state parties to provide lists of nominees to be electors should that party's candidate win a plurality of the popular vote in the state. Most states require that the party's elector nominees be chosen at the state party convention, whereas a few states require the nominees to come from the state party central committee. Twelve states, including Alabama, Kansas, Texas, and Washington, allow the parties to use whatever method they wish to provide nominees (Berns 1992, 11).

Who are the electors? Because potential electors are selected by the state parties and cannot be members of the House or Senate, they are most often prominent state or party officials. Governors, members of the state legislature, state party chair and vice chair, or retired officeholders are often nominated to serve as electors should the party's candidate carry the state. Because electors are chosen by the parties and are usually individuals with a history of service to the state and party, the problem of "faithless" electors is rarely encountered. A faithless elector is one who votes for a candidate other than the candidate who carried the state. Some states have laws that require electors to vote for the candidate who carries the state, though only a few states specify a penalty for not doing so. "Because only eight of the more than 16,000 electors chosen since the first election have not honored their pledges, the faithless elector phenomenon is an occasional curiosity rather than a perennial problem" (Berns 1992, 13).

Electoral college votes are awarded using the winner-take-all method, meaning that the candidate for president who wins a plurality of the popular vote in a state gets all of that state's electoral votes. The only exceptions currently are Maine and Nebraska, in which some of electoral college votes are based on the popular vote in the congressional districts (thus it is possible to split the electoral votes of Maine and Nebraska). It is this process of awarding electoral votes on a winner-take-all basis that exaggerates the majority of the winning candidate. For example, in 1996 President Clinton was reelected with just shy of 50 percent of the popular vote, but he won 379 electoral votes—a full 70 percent of the electoral college votes. Clinton's plurality of the popular vote was thus translated into a convincing majority by the electoral rules. It is also the winner-take-all system that allows the potential for an "undemocratic" result in which a candidate wins fewer total popular votes but carries enough states to win an electoral college majority.

Since disputed presidential elections are so rare, does it matter whether or not the United States uses an electoral college? One common complaint about the electoral college is that the winner-take-all system tends to encourage presidential candidates to concentrate their attention on the largest states. A candidate could secure an electoral majority by campaigning in, and winning, only eleven states. A candidate who carried the ten largest states and either Virginia or Georgia could secure the 270 electoral votes needed to win.

Is the electoral college system to blame for attention that presidential campaigns lavish on a handful of states such as California, New York, and Texas? Oddly enough, the electoral college tends to slightly overrepresent less populated states such as Wyoming, Delaware, Alaska, and North Dakota because each state gets two votes for its senators regardless of its population. Thus, states with small populations actually get more weight in the electoral college than they would get based purely on popular votes. In other words, if there were no electoral college and the presidential elections were decided by the national popular vote, campaigns would still concentrate on the largest states because that is where most of the voters are.

Still, the existence of the electoral college does influence the conduct of presidential campaigns. Although it is possible for a candidate to secure an electoral college majority by concentrating on only eleven states, in practice no candidate would be sufficiently sure of winning the largest states to campaign in such a fashion. The structure of the electoral college affects how candidates allocate their campaign resources, since winning the presidency is ultimately a matter of getting a majority of electoral college votes (Bartels 1985).

To illustrate the effect of the electoral college on campaign strategy, consider the circumstances of the Dole campaign in September 1996. Following the nominating conventions, the Dole-Kemp ticket trailed Clinton-Gore in most national opinion polls. Although examining national polls can help some aspects of campaign strategy, by September the campaign is a battle for the states. Table 4.2 shows how, according to our calculations, Dole's strategists might have evaluated the likelihood of their candidate's winning various states. The states are arranged in five categories from "sure win" to "sure loss," with the "toss-up" states in the middle. Note that if Dole were to carry all the "sure win," "likely win," and "toss-up" states, he would have nineteen more electoral votes than needed to reach the 270 mark (64 + 65 + 160 = 289). Given these calculations, Dole could afford to lose Kentucky (8) and Tennessee (11) but could not afford to lose Ohio (21), Illinois (22), or Florida (25).

TABLE 4.2   How the Electoral College Affects Campaign Strategy: Hypothetical Dole Campaign State List for 1996

Sure Win		Likely Win		Toss-up		Likely Loss		Sure Loss	
AL	9	AZ	8	CO	8	CA	54	AR	6
AK	3	IN	12	FL	25	CT	8	DC	3
ID	4	TX	32	GA	13	DE	3	HI	4
KS	6	VI	13	IL	22	IA	7	MA	12
MS	7			KY	8	LA	8	VT	3
NE	5			MT	3	ME	4	WV	5
ND	3			NV	5	MD	10		
OK	8			NH	4	MI	18		
SC	8			NJ	15	MN	10		
SD	3			NC	14	MO	11		
UT	5			OH	21	NM	5		
WY	3			TN	11	NY	33		
				WI	11	OR	7		
						PA	23		
						RI	4		
						WA	11		
64		65		160		216		33	

SOURCE: Constructed by the authors.

Arranging the states in this fashion might have helped the Dole campaign make difficult decisions about allocating campaign resources. For example, should the campaign buy time in the Los Angeles media market or divert resources from California into key "toss-up" states such as Florida or Illinois? Table 4.2 shows that California is not part of Dole's winning coalition of states and suggests that campaign resources would be better used to pursue the electoral votes of other states. This type of calculation also suggests why states such as Idaho or Kansas would receive fewer resources from the Dole campaign: Dole strategists would expect their candidate to carry those states. If the candidate were to be in danger of losing Kansas or other staunch Republican states, no amount of campaign resources could prevent an electoral college defeat. Knowing what states are crucial to getting the necessary majority within the electoral college can help campaign strategists use resources effectively.

All presidential campaigns engage in such electoral college calculations and have a strategy to win enough states to gain an electoral college majority. Of course, in some elections, such as Reagan's landslide victory in 1984, the calculations are a mere formality. Yet in competitive presidential elections, careful use of limited resources may help win a crucial state and secure a winning majority. In deciding how to classify their chances of winning a state, campaigns typically take many factors into account: past voting patterns, current polls, the strength of the state party, the strength of state candidates such as a governor or senator, key issues, and, of course, the home states of the presidential and vice presidential candidates. In the excitement of the campaign, it is not always possible to conduct all activities according to the overall strategy. Nevertheless, the electoral college does influence how candidates conduct their campaigns and may affect the outcome of elections as well.

The Impact of Electoral Rules

Stated bluntly, the theme of this chapter is that the rules of the electoral game matter. Elections in the United States are dominated by two big political parties in large part because of the plurality electoral system. If states were to adopt proportional representation, competitive smaller parties might well grow. With the widespread use of the plurality rule, however, it makes sense that the two dominant parties are broad-based electoral coalitions. By allowing state parties and state politicians the freedom to pursue election based on local issues, the national parties do not present a clear and coherent ideological message. They do, however, maximize their chances of winning control of both state and national governments by letting Arizona Republicans and Massachusetts Republicans, or Wisconsin Democrats and Mississippi Democrats, seek election according to what will win in their state.

American political parties are organizationally weak in comparison to parties in other democratic nations, in part due to state control of nominations. Direct primary laws make it impossible for state parties to control even the seemingly essential function of selecting party candidates. The adoption of the Australian ballot and the direct primary by the states was largely responsible for transforming political parties from essentially private organizations into "public utilities" closely regulated by state law (Epstein 1986). In sum, state election laws passed in the late nineteenth and early twentieth centuries have profoundly altered the political environment in which the parties operate.

Of course, it is not just state laws that matter. Two features of the Constitution, federalism and the electoral college, have had a decided impact on the nature of political parties and electoral competition in this nation. The American federal system leaves control over the matter of elections largely to the states. In recent years federal legislation, such as the Voting Rights Act of 1965 and the Federal Election Campaign Act of 1971, has introduced some federal control over the conduct of elections. Still, the bulk of election rules are left to the states to determine. As our discussion of the electoral college has shown, even in presidential elections the states are still central to the American electoral process.

5

The Changing
American Electorate

A key task of political parties is to mobilize the public to support party candidates at the ballot box. However, a changing electorate and its increasingly tense relationship with the parties makes mobilization difficult. The public does not overtly attack the parties and the candidates they choose but maintains a lengthy "open season" of criticism about them. For example, nearly half (49 percent) of the respondents in a recent poll stated that neither party was better able to control the top problem facing their community; 40 percent expressed a similar view about the top problem facing the country (Times Mirror Center 1994, 29). When asked what it means to be a Republican, over half of those questioned in another poll said that Republicans are for "rich, powerful, moneyed interests." Democrats fared little better, as only one in five said being a Democrat means being "for working people" (Broder 1990).

Citizens who do go to the polls continuously express anger or frustration about their choices, although an increasing number decide not to engage in such traditional activities as voting. Polling conducted in 1996 found that only 51 percent of voters were satisfied with the choice of presidential candidates; among nominal Dole supporters the dissatisfaction was even higher: Only 31 percent were satisfied with the choices available.

The electorate also shows its disdain for parties and candidates by either staying at home during primary and general elections or crossing party lines. The purpose of presidential primaries is to take the choice out of the party's "smoke-filled rooms" and give the electorate an important role in decisionmaking. Although primaries proliferated after 1968, participation by the voting-age population gradually decreased, reaching its lowest figure of 19.6 percent in 1992 ("A Correction" 1992). Most of the decline occurred in Democratic presidential primaries, with participation falling to slightly less than 12 percent. Republican participation remained steady at slightly more than 8 percent of eligible voters ("Democratic Primaries Show Drop in Turnout" 1992). Empirical evidence also indicates a general shift away from the established parties, particularly the Democratic party. Throughout the 1980s voter identification with the Democratic party dipped, and a sizable number of voters defected from the Democratic party label.

In this chapter we develop four themes. First, participation in conventional forms of political activity other than voting has remained steady over the past thirty years, but this trend has been accompanied by a dramatic decline in voter turnout. As a result, parties must operate in a world of declining voter allegiance. Second, Democratic party identifiers have decreased, but the increase in the number of self-proclaimed "independent" voters is accompanied by questions about their degree of independence. Third, party identification remains a key predictor of how the electorate will vote, and fourth, with the exception of race, membership in social and economic groups is less predictive of identification with parties or candidates than in the past. Parties must therefore build coalitions around other factors, such as the values of voters, as well as voter allegiance to specific issues to win at the ballot box. In this chapter we also profile the changing American electorate—the "new" independents, the ticket splitters, the nonvoters, and the growing number of older voters.

Parties and Limited Political Participation

Parties depend on their external environment. The general electorate is a major determinant of party activities and services. By providing (or not providing) the parties with skills, resources, and personnel, and by articulating demands (or not doing so), the electorate shapes the parties' political performance. Thus, in evaluating the criticism of party services and activities, we should keep in mind the resources that the two major parties have available to them. The charge that parties concentrate on winning elections and not on formulating policies must be evaluated in terms of low voter turnout and even lower participation in other types of political activity.

Many people hold that it is important to participate in the political process that selects our decisionmakers. In a national sample, 85 percent of those interviewed felt it was their duty as a citizen to always vote (Ornstein, Kohut, and McCarthy 1988). Academicians also extol the virtues of citizen participation. In building a case for citizen involvement, political scientists suggest a wide range of social and personal benefits. They argue that citizen involvement is important because participation makes the individual a "better" person and participation results in "better" decisions.

Although most Americans agree that everyone ought to participate in the political decisionmaking process, only a limited number do so. Extensive

TABLE 5.1   Types of Political Participation, 1952–1996 (in percentages)

Year	Voting Reported	Persuade Others How to Vote	Campaign Button or Political Sticker	Contributed Money to the Campaign	Attended Rallies or Meetings	Worked for a Party or Candidate
1952	73	27	n.a.	4	7	3
1956	73	28	16	10	7	3
1960	79	33	21	12	8	6
1964	78	31	16	11	9	5
1968	76	33	15	9	9	6
1972	73	32	13	10	9	5
1976	72	37	8	16	6	4
1980	71	36	7	8	8	4
1984	74	32	9	8	8	4
1988	70	29	9	9	7	3
1992	75	37	11	7	8	3
1996	77	29	10	6	6	3

SOURCE: National Elections Studies. Available at: <www.umich.edu/~nes>.

surveys undertaken by Henry Brady, Sidney Verba, and associates link participation to four resources—political interest, time, money, and civic skills (communications and organizational ability). In general, political interest is linked to turnout, and civic skills are important to acts requiring time (e.g., working for a campaign or writing a letter to a public offical). The monetary resoues necessary for contributions are the least equally distributed resource (Brady, Verba, and Schlozman 1995). Table 5.1, profiling citizen activities over several election years, underscores the lack of participation. For activities requiring little time, such as attempting to persuade others how to vote, about a third of those polled engaged in them. The figure does vary by election year; with third-party candidate Ross Perot on the ballot in 1992 the percentage jumped to 37 percent, a level not attained since the 1976 election. As to activities that demand some additional sacrifice, such as contributing time or money to the parties, 15 percent or less of the electorate gave a favorable reply. Activities that demand the most time, such as working for a party or a candidate, attracted only 3 to 4 percent of respondents in the National Election Studies.

Trends in Turnout and the Puzzle of Participation

To theorists of democratic politics, U.S. voter turnout levels, anemic when compared with other countries of the world, suggest a lack of interest in politics at best or raise questions of legitimacy about the U.S. system at worst. When Bill Clinton's 1992 electoral victory represented less than 25 percent of the voting-age population, did his policies come anywhere close to the preferences of the remaining three-quarters of the voting-age population? For political parties the key issue is mobilization: How can a party cajole, exhort, or even beg potential voters to go to the polls in sufficient numbers to give it victory? Thus the success or failure of parties in mobilization has a major impact on voter turnout. To address the concerns of both the parties and the theorists, it is necessary to (1) consider historical trends in turnout, (2) note which groups in society are turning out in greater or lesser numbers, and (3) identify the factors that have the greatest impact on turnout.

In the United States turnout is usually defined as the proportion of the voting-age population, including both citizens and noncitizens, who do go to the polls. Table 2.2 traced turnout in the 1800s and noted that during the turbulent years from 1840 to 1860 turnout ranged from 70 percent to 80 percent. Table 5.2, which displays trends during the period after women

TABLE 5.2   Trends in Voter Participation, 1920–1996 (in percentages)

Year	Estimated Population of Voting Age (in millions)	Number of Votes Cast (in millions)	Percentage of Votes Cast
1920	61.5	26.8	43.6
1924	66.2	29.1	43.9
1928	71.0	36.8	51.9
1932	75.6	39.8	52.5
1936	80.1	45.6	57.0
1940	84.3	49.8	59.1
1944	90.6	47.9	53.0
1948	95.6	48.8	51.1
1952	99.9	61.6	61.6
1956	104.5	62.0	59.3
1960	109.7	68.8	62.8
1964	114.1	70.6	61.9
1968	120.3	73.2	60.9
1972	140.8	77.7	55.2
1976	152.3	81.6	53.5
1980	164.6	86.6	52.6
1984	174.4	92.6	53.3
1988	182.6	91.6	50.1
1992	189.5	104.4	55.1
1996	196.5	96.5	49.1

SOURCES: *Current Population Reports*, series P-20, nos. 100, 453 (Washington D.C.: U.S. Bureau of the Census, 1991). Figures for 1992 and 1996 are from the Federal Election Commission, "National Voter Turnout in Federal Elections: 1960–1996." Available at: <www.fec.gov>.

gained the vote, reveals three different patterns. In the period from 1920 to 1948 a turnout rate greater than 55 percent was very unusual, occurring only in 1936 and 1940. The high point for turnout occurred between 1952 and 1968, when participation rates ranged between 59 and 62 percent. Since that time the figures have edged down to levels closer to 50 percent. Attracting the electorate's attention is even more difficult in nonpresidential elections, as turnout rates of 40 percent are the norm.

The lower turnout rates led Richard Brody (1978) to pose the "puzzle of participation", since measures taken in recent years should result in equaling or surpassing the participation levels of the 1960s. States eased requirements for voter registration by enacting several reforms, and shifts within the electorate in terms of education, income, occupation, and turnout by women should increase participation. Instead, with the exception of 1992, turnout has been seven to ten percentage points below that of the 1960s. Data from the National Election Studies (NES), as well as the profile contained in "No Show '96: Americans Who Don't Vote," a survey of those who indicated they would "definitely not vote" or "probably not vote" in November, will be used to explore this puzzle (Northwestern University 1996).

Gender, Race, and Region

Table 5.3 utilizes National Election Studies data about self-reported turnout in presidential elections. This survey has several strengths; however, because self-reported turnout is not checked against the voting rolls, substantial overreporting of turnout occurs. If the 77 percent who reported voting in in 1996 (Table 5.1) actually did go to the polls, 112.5 million votes would have been cast, compared with the 96.5 million who actually voted (Table 5.2).

Women reported increased turnout in the 1960s, compared with the 1950s (Table 5.3), which helped narrow the gap between men and women. With the exception of 1984, however, men reported greater turnout than women. The self-reported voting rates are at odds with other data. Exit polling indicates that since 1980 more women have voted than men. Similar results are found in census surveys. In 1992, 62.3 percent of women reported they voted, compared to only 60.2 percent of men. These data do not solve the issue of declining participation, but they do hold important implications for political parties, which must determine whether a specific set of "women's issues" exists (including abortion, child care, health insurance, gun control) and whether sufficient group solidarity exists on these issues to tip the balance in a close election.

Turnout levels by race and region are inextricably linked. The impact of the civil rights movement is shown in Table 5.3. Black self-reported turnout increased from 35 percent in 1956 to 68 percent by 1968. This trend had

TABLE 5.3 Self-Reported Turnout, 1952–1996 (in percentages)

	1952	1956	1960	1964	1968	1972	1976	1980	1984	1988	1992	1996
Gender												
Male	80	80	84	80	78	76	77	73	74	72	77	78
Female	69	68	75	76	74	70	68	70	74	68	74	75
Race												
White	78	76	82	80	77	74	73	72	75	72	77	78
Black	33	35	53	65	68	65	65	67	66	60	67	68
Region												
South	48	53	66	62	68	61	64	69	66	57	65	71
Nonsouth	81	79	83	82	79	77	74	72	77	76	80	80
Education												
Grade sch./some high sch.	66	63	69	69	64	59	59	57	57	50	51	57
High school	85	79	87	82	84	75	70	70	70	62	71	69
Some college	87	90	88	89	79	84	83	76	81	78	83	81
College degree	93	89	93	88	89	90	87	91	91	92	93	90
Family Income Percentile												
0–16	53	53	65	64	60	60	54	56	53	47	52	62
17–33	69	65	71	73	66	63	65	68	69	59	68	65
34–67	76	76	81	79	79	70	71	72	74	71	77	77
68–95	85	83	85	86	87	86	80	81	84	82	88	85
96–100	95	90	94	88	93	90	91	87	91	96	90	96
Year of Birth												
1975 or later	**	**	**	**	**	**	**	**	**	**	77	52
1959–1974	**	**	**	**	**	**	**	57	53	49	65	68
1943–1958	**	**	**	48	61	66	62	63	74	73	78	80
1927–1942	58	58	70	71	75	77	79	78	80	77	83	82
1911–1926	73	74	83	83	84	79	79	82	83	81	81	85
Party ID												
Democrat	72	73	79	76	75	73	73	72	74	69	78	76
Independent	49	55	57	55	58	51	55	49	54	45	56	50
Republican	83	78	87	87	82	81	79	80	80	77	79	84

** Not avaliable within the category. SOURCE: National Election Studies.

the expected impact on the South as a region, raising the reported turnout by 15 percent between 1956 and 1968. Since that time period, the gap between white and black voters has narrowed to ten percentage points, which is about the same gap that was reported between southern and nonsouthern states. Indeed, for the time period covered by Table 5.3, 1996 marked the first time more than 70 percent reported voting in southern states.

Education and Voter Registration

Although gender, race, and region provide some reasons for increased voter turnout in the 1960s, they do not shed much light on recent declines in participation. Education is an indicator that holds more promise, as numerous studies of voting behavior indicate that level of education is the socioeconomic variable most closely associated with levels of turnout (Wolfinger and Rosenstone 1980, 35; Teixeira 1987, 30–31). Additional education raises confidence and cognitive skills, which makes it easier to cope with the "smoke and mirrors" often surrounding politics.

Education levels have been rising during the past several decades. According to the National Election Studies, between 1960 and 1996 the percentage of the white electorate not graduating from high school fell from 47 to 13 percent, whereas the percentage of college graduates rose from 11 percent to 28 percent. As expected, in any one election college graduates reported turnouts thirty to forty percentage points higher than those with some high school or less. But how are education levels linked to declining participation over time? The greatest reported participation rates for the "some college" and "high school" groups in Table 5.3 occurred from 1952 to 1968. If average reported turnout for this period is compared with the average for 1972–1996, in the "some college" category, the decline is 6 percent, whereas for high school graduates a 13 percent drop is found, as well as an 8 percent decrease for those with grade school or some high school education. In contrast, among college graduates, a very slight increase of 0.5 percent is found when the averages for the two periods are compared.

The other factor that should stimulate increased participation is changes in voter registration procedures. People are more likely to participate if they can register easily and quickly. In the South after World War II, three legal requirements were used to disenfranchise black voters—literacy tests, poll taxes, and periodic registration. Literacy tests, in which voters had to prove their ability to read and write, were abolished by the Voting Rights Act of 1965. Poll taxes, which assessed a fee to register to vote, were outlawed for federal elections by the Twenty-fourth Amendment to the Constitution, adopted in 1964 and later extended to all elections by the Supreme Court. Periodic registration, which required citizens to reregister to vote, was gradually eliminated by the states.

Yet another problem that needed to be addressed was voter mobility. In the 1980s about one-third of Americans changed their address every two years. States responded to greater voter mobility by enacting registration by mail, along with such other measures as shorter state residency requirements (thirty days) and bilingual registration material (Teixeira 1992, 29). These steps lowered the costs of voting. The major remaining barrier is the closing date—the last day by which people can register. Over 90 percent of Americans must register between two weeks to a month before the election, whereas Arizona and Georgia require a fifty-day period. At such times, interest in elections is far from its peak.

Political scientists have argued that if a timely means of reregistering mobile voters were found, voter turnout would rise, although little agreement exists on the level of increase (Wolfinger 1991; Squire, Wolfinger, and Glass 1987; Teixeira 1992, 111–112; Nagler 1991).

For many years legislation in Congress to permit postcard registration of voters in all states was blocked by Republicans, who feared increases in both election fraud and the registration of potential Democratic voters. Congress did enact legislation in 1993 to make it easier for mobile voters to register. State and local governments must offer voter registration by mail, and at disability offices, military recruitment centers, and motor vehicle registration offices. The National Voter Registration Act (NVRA) went into effect in January 1995. In its first two years it processed 41.4 million applications or transactions, of which 27.5 million were newly registered voters. About 14 million changed their registration address, 8.7 million were deleted from voter lists, and 7.1 million were put in an "inactive" category and would be removed if they did not vote in 1998 (Federal Election Commission 1997b). Of those who registered for the first time, or updated their registration, about half did so through driver licensing agencies and a third used mail registration. Another 12 percent relied on public assistance agencies (Piven and Cloward 1996, 39–40). Elected officials' major concerns were whether or not those newly registered voters would actually turn up at the polls and, if so, which party they would favor. The preliminary indications are that the newly enfranchised did not show up in sufficient numbers to offset an overall 6 percent decline in 1996 compared with 1992. Indeed, in the data contained in the profile of nonvoters in Box 5.1 about those who *chose* not to vote indicates that removing barriers such as registration laws would make no difference in whether they take part in the democratic process.

If education levels have risen and more lenient registration laws have been enacted, why has turnout not increased over the last twenty years? Education and voting laws did lead to small increases in participation, but both were swamped by such other factors as a marked decline in mobilization efforts by the parties. In Table 5.4, Steven Rosenstone and John

---

BOX 5.1   Profile of Nonvoters

The Doers (29 percent of total)
Less than 45 years old
Earn more than $30,000 a year
College educated
Volunteer; write or call politicians
Follow what's going on in government some or most of the time
Say they will vote but often are not registered

The Unplugged (27 percent of total)
Less than 30 years old
Earn less than $30,000 a year
Don't discuss politics; don't volunteer
Move often; do not feel connected to their communities
Do not like government institutions

The Irritables (18 percent of total)
Middle-aged
Earn more than $30,000 a year
Believe their vote does not matter
View political environment with skepticism
Choose not to vote

The Don't Knows (14 percent of total)
Over 45 years old
Earn less than $30,000 a year
High school education
Have few political opinions
Largely ignore politics
Often not registered to vote

The Alienated (12 percent of total)
Over 45 years old
Earn less than $30,000 a year
Have a negative view of government
Do not often read newspaper or watch news shows
Do not plan to vote in November

SOURCE: Northwestern University Medill School of Journalism, "No Show '96: Americans Who Don't Vote," 1996 (survey of 1,001 likely nonvoters).

Hansen (1993) took the characteristics of 1960 voters and statistically "transformed" citizens of the 1960s into citizens of the 1980s by giving them the profile of 1980 voters, including more education, lower political efficacy, and less attachment to political parties and candidates. The results

TABLE 5.4   Decomposition of the Decline in Voter Turnout in Presidential
Election Years Between the 1960s and 1980s

Change	Effect on Percentage Change in Turnout Between 1960s and 1980s	Percentage of Decline in Turnout Explained
Increased formal education	+2.8	
An easing of voter registration laws	+1.8	
A younger electorate	–2.7	17
Weakened social involvement	–1.4	9
Declining feelings of efficacy	–1.4	9
Weakened attachment to and evaluations of political parties and their candidates	–1.7	11
A decline in mobilization	–8.7	54
Net change in voter turnout	–11.3	100

SOURCE: Steven J. Rosenstone and John Mark Hansen, *Mobilization, Participation and Democracy in America* (New York: Macmillan, 1993), 215.

of the table reflect how much more or less likely the 1960s electorate would be to participate in elections if their attributes paralleled those of the 1980s electorate.

The table allows us to fit together the first pieces of the puzzle of participation: In the 1980s, advances in educational level did raise turnout, which was about 2.8 percent higher than it would have been, and the liberalization of registration laws accounted for another 1.8 percent increase. Yet these factors were swept aside when compared with other factors, which will be examined briefly.

A Younger Electorate

Table 5.4 identifies one very important reason for the decline in turnout (17 percent): a younger electorate. One impact of the baby boom generation is that in 1960 only 27 percent of the 1960 electorate was under thirty-five, whereas by the mid-1980s the figure jumped to 40 percent. The Twenty-sixth Amendment, which lowered the voting age to eighteen in 1972, immediately enlarged the size of the voter group least likely to participate. That year 48 percent of the newly enfranchised eighteen to twenty-one-year-old citizens reported voting. Estimates of actual participation by this group are much lower, with about one in three participating by the end of the 1980s (Teixeira 1992, 37–38). Yet another indicator of disinterest is a 1989 survey among 1,000 youths, in which only 12 percent rated voting as a basic tenet of good citizenship (Simpson 1992, 66).

Lower participation by younger voters is not totally due to a lack of interest in politics. In the survey of likely nonvoters in Box 5.1, those labeled "Doers" are involved with their community and interested in politics. This group is disproportionately young, well educated, and affluent. Nearly half (48 percent) are between the ages of eighteen and twenty-nine; 55 percent have attended college, and 55 percent make over $30,000 a year. This group has positive feelings about national government institutions, but many have not registered to vote. Whether this is due to giving almost total priority to their careers is not clear, but this group provides one example of lower turnout rates among the younger electorate.

As to what might be done to attract younger people to the polls, several innovative attempts show how difficult the task is. In the early 1990s, music industry representatives began a Rock the Vote series of public service announcements to encourage young music fans to register and vote. Cynics suggested a less civic minded purpose: Record industry executives wanted youthful registered voters to derail any congressional regulation of music lyrics. Although she was unregistered at the time, one public service spot featured Madonna, skimpily dressed and draped in the flag, singing, "If you don't vote, you're going to get a spanky." Not even this threat (or enticement) had much of an impact on participation levels among younger voters. MTV repeated the Rock the Vote spots in subsequent elections and in 1996 presented a series titled "Choose or Lose," which featured interviews with the candidates and profiles of the campaign issues. Although some criticized such attempts as nonsubstantive "pop participation," an interview with Bill Clinton did include discussion of relevant issues such as parental notification for teens who seek abortions. Moreover, MTV profiles of the issues were four minutes in length, permitting more substance than the average network news report.

Social Involvement and Political Efficacy

Table 5.4 shows that 9 percent of the decline in turnout is explained by weakened social involvement. People who engage in casual conversation with family, friends, and coworkers learn more about the candidates and issues, thus lowering the costs of voting. They are more aware of the problems and issues facing the community and have a greater stake in seeing these issues resolved. On the other hand, new residents in a community face the more immediate demands of relocation, including housing, schooling, and finding local merchants for services. Interest in the local community takes time to develop, as does encouragement to participate in voting by friends or acquaintances (Squire, Wolfinger, and Glass 1987; Popkin 1991, chap. 10). Thus, under what Gerald Pomper and Loretta Sernekos call the "bake sale" theory, an increasing number of mobile citizens are not fully integrated into the community; they do not feel at home at the neighborhood bake sale or the ballot box (Pomper and Sernekos 1991). Several indicators that reflect social connectedness are home ownership, years in the home, marital status (spouses have interpersonal ties with their partner), years in the community, and church attendance. Although figures vary from election to election, citizens who are more closely tied to the social structures of the family and community are more likely to vote, sometimes at a percentage as much as fifteen to twenty points higher than those with low ties to the community (Miller and Shanks 1996, 101).

In Box 5.1 the group that demonstrates a lack of social involvement is the "Unplugged," who tend to be young and are much more likely to say they follow politics "hardly at all." They are much less likely to write to their local representatives or the newspaper, and they do not volunteer within the community. Because they move often, they do not feel connected to their communities. Not surprisingly, 68 percent of this group is not registered to vote.

Ironically, although degree of social involvement has fallen for many citizens, this concept also helps to explain why the drop among women going to the polls is less than for men. Pomper and Sernekos (1991) suggest women have two incentives to engage in voting: greater psychological solidarity with other women and a greater likelihood of attachments to the community. Carole Chaney and Jonathan Nagler compare this idea with an alternative political hypothesis—in the 1980s women saw greater differences between the two parties on issues that were important to them, which led fewer women to decline to vote when compared with men. Although women do have distinct policy preferences on social issues compared with men, these differences do not explain levels of turnout. Instead, the findings support Pomper and Sernekos—women express a greater degree of social connectedness with the community, which leads them to be more supportive of the activity of voting than men (Chaney and Nagler 1993).

Declining political efficacy is as important as weakened social involvement, accounting for 9 percent of the turnout decline in Table 5.4. "Political efficacy" is a term used by political scientists in two different senses. The first meaning refers to a sense of internal efficacy—the degree of confidence people have in their ability to understand and participate in politics. The second meaning refers to external efficacy—the sense people have that their political activity has some effect on what government actually does (Rosenstone and Hansen 1993, 23; Craig and Maggiotto 1992). Both types of efficacy are a prerequisite for a sense of psychological involvement with the political system.

As one measure of internal efficacy, the National Election Studies ask people whether they agree that "politics and government are so complicated that a person like me can't really understand what is going on." In

1960 about 60 percent agreed, whereas in the 1990s the figure has risen to three-quarters of those polled. Among likely nonvoters in Box 5.1, low levels of internal efficacy are especially evident among the "Don't Knows." They believe politics is difficult to understand, and they lack positive views about the political parties because of an almost total lack of knowledge about the parties. They are not sure whether the country is on the right track or not, as 42 percent had no opinion about that question. Not unexpectedly, 72 percent of the "Don't Knows" are unregistered.

Low levels of external efficacy are also found among the electorate. Nearly three-quarters of respondents in 1960 rejected the idea that "people like me don't have a say in what the government does," but by 1996 only 44 percent disagreed. Moreover, among the group of likely nonvoters in Box 5.1, 30 percent of the sample indicated feelings of low efficacy. About the only difference is between those with high and low amounts of political information. The "Irritables" are avid consumers of information and say they follow what is going on in politics more than any other group of nonvoters. But 65 percent of the "Irritables" believe the country has "pretty seriously gotten off on the wrong track." A second group, the "Alienated," displayed the most negative views of all five groups when stating their opinions about politicians, political institutions, and the importance of elections. Among this group, 39 percent took the view that it makes no real difference who is elected, the highest percentage of any of the groups. A profile of this group finds them disproportionately older and poorer than the rest of the nonvoters (see Box 5.1).

Mobilization by Political Parties

In Table 5.4 well over the half of the decline in turnout can be attributed to a decline in political party mobilization. As Rosenstone and Hansen suggest, a key aspect of participation is that people take part because someone "encourages or inspires" them to do so (Rosenstone and Hansen 1993, 161). Thus political parties affect turnout directly by contacting people to vote, and indirectly by choosing candidates who run competitive races, or in the case of third parties by selecting candidates who stress issues largely ignored by the major parties.

Critics make several charges against the parties in regard to mobilization. Many years ago the political parties in large cities encouraged political participation through energetic precinct captains, who registered those who were eligible (and some allegedly deceased) and provided transportation and child care on election day. Today help with child care or transportation to the polls is sporadic and is provided mostly by a few candidates rather than the parties. The chances of a party worker visiting a potential voter are only slightly better than an appearance by the Maytag repairman, as

National Election Studies data show that contact by party workers ranged from a low of 19 percent in 1990 to a high of 31 percent in 1982. On average, then, the Democratic and Republican parties personally contact one out of every four Americans to promote the candidates and the election. This contact does make a difference, however, as those who are reached by the parties in presidential years are about 8 percent more likely to vote; in nonpresidential years the figure is 10.4 percent (Rosenstone and Hansen 1993, 172).

Advances in technology, combined with the parties' limited resources, have led parties to restructure their mobilization efforts. To reach the voters, parties now emphasize contacting those most likely to vote: those with more income and a college education, as well as long-term community residents. After the 1960s, the parties determined that the most cost-effective way to reach this audience was through mass appeals over television and radio rather than personal contact. In particular, parties give much less attention to contacting potential voters at the stages of registering to vote and conducting the party canvass. Large-scale funds are only allocated to voter registration on rare occasions such as in 1984, when Ronald Reagan did not face a primary election opponent and Republicans could afford to spend $4 million to register 2 million voters. From 1988 to 1992, Republicans registered close to 2 million voters, whereas Democrats were only able to sign 200,000 voters (Barnes 1992, 1896). Since the passage of the National Voter Registration Act, the parties have appeared content to leave voter registration efforts largely in the hands of the states. Although the parties once relied on personal contact through door-to-door canvassing to determine likely party supporters, today they find it less costly to buy computer software that not only tracks party voting in recent elections but also provides a social and economic profile of the area through census data.

Party mobilization efforts are also enhanced by candidates who run exciting and competitive races or energize specific groups. In four elections beginning with 1960 the presidential candidates were separated by less than three percentage points in the final Gallup poll: 1960 (Kennedy-Nixon), 1968 (Humphrey-Nixon), 1976 (Carter-Ford), and 1980 (Carter-Reagan). In the excitement of a dead-heat race, citizens are 3 percent more likely to vote (Rosenstone and Hansen 1993, 181). A candidate who articulates group interests increases participation among group members. For example, the difference in turnout between blacks and whites for the 1972–1980 period was greater than 10 percent. When Jessie Jackson ran as a presidential candidate in 1984 and 1988, the gap narrowed to slightly more than 5 percent in 1984 and 7 percent in 1988 (Tate 1991). In 1992 no prominent black presidential candidate remained after Douglas Wilder, former governor of Virginia, dropped out at an early stage of the Democratic primaries. In that year the gap reverted back to nearly 10 percent.

Conversely, noncharismatic candidates contribute to low turnout. The 1988 race between Michael Dukakis and George Bush fell into this category, as humorist Mark Russell observed the candidates were so bland they exhibited all the consistency of white bread, and many termed the 1996 candidacy of Bob Dole charismatically challenged as well. Not surprisingly, the turnout figures for these two elections in Table 5.2, 50 and 49 percent respectively, are two of the lowest percentages in the post–World War II era.

Ironically, the presence of third-party candidates is a most effective way of attracting citizens to the polls. In 1968, George Wallace, running on the American Independent Party ticket, won 14 percent of the popular vote, and turnout reached 61 percent. At least a part of the 1992 upturn in participation resulted from third-party candidate Ross Perot. Among Perot supporters polled, 14 percent indicated they would not vote for either George Bush or Bill Clinton but would have stayed at home if Perot had not been on the ballot (Bohanan 1993, 32). If those 3 million voters had carried through on their pledge, turnout would have decreased about 1.5 percent.

Thus the "puzzle of participation" asks why there has been a decline in voter turnout since the 1960s, given both increasing levels of education and an easing of voter registration laws. Pieces of the puzzle include changes in education and voter registration, which increased participation beyond what it would have been otherwise but were not able to stem forces working in the other direction, such as declining social involvement and political efficacy. The largest piece of the puzzle comes from the decrease in mobilization efforts by the parties themselves. The parties changed from a retail strategy of selling through one-on-one personal contact to a wholesale strategy of impersonal selling through the mass media. An unintended impact of this strategy is that a "downsized" electorate undermines the victorious party's claim of representing the "will of the people."

Party Identification, Realignment, and the "New" Independent Voter

In a classic volume, *The Changing American Voter*, Nie, Verba, and Petrocik state that the decline in party identification and the subsequent rise in the number of independents constitutes the most dramatic political change in the 1960s and 1970s (Nie, Verba, and Petrocik 1979, 47). These "new" independents were not the indifferent or inattentive citizens described in voting behavior studies of the 1950s. They were persons whose education level and knowledge of politics were as high as or higher than partisans who were spurred to participate by an interest in issues or in specific candidates (Burnham 1970, 129–130; DeVries and Tarrance 1972; Pomper 1975, 34). To what extent has partisan identification actually declined? Is there an identifiable group of "new" independents? Or are they simply "hidden partisans" with views on the issues and candidates that differ little from party identifiers? Although divisions among political scientists on these issues remain, one useful approach is to distinguish between changes occurring in the *directional balance of partisanship* (that is, changes between Republicans and Democrats) and in the *strength of party identification* (the ratio of party identifiers to nonpartisans). Shifts of voters between the Republican and Democratic parties are a key element of what V. O. Key has called "secular realignment" (1959, 198). This shift in the partisan balance of power occurs over several elections and has several features: a shift in the regional bases of support for each of the parties; changes in the social and economic groups that support the two parties; the emergence of new social groups that are drawn to one or both parties; the emergence of a set of new issues that redraw the cleavage lines between the parties; and a rethinking by voters of their attachment to the parties (Sundquist 1983, chap. 4). Table 5.5 depicts variations in party identification among the potential electorate and indicates a number of trends.

Taking 1952 (the first year for which National Election Studies data are available) as a starting point and concentrating on "strong" and "weak" party identifiers in Table 5.5, in 1952 Democrats enjoyed a nineteen-point difference in party identification over Republicans. Democratic party identification peaked in 1964 with a twenty-seven-point difference, and the party's presidential candidate, Lyndon B. Johnson, received the largest electoral percentage margin in history. This triumph, however, was followed by eight years of division among the Democratic coalition, which was con-

TABLE 5.5 Party Identification, 1952–1996 (in percentages)

Year	Strong Dem.	Weak Dem.	Indep. Dem.	Indep. Indep.	Indep. Repub.	Weak Repub.	Strong Repub.	Apolit-ical
1952	22	25	10	6	7	14	14	3
1956	21	23	6	9	8	14	15	4
1960	20	25	6	10	7	14	16	2
1964	27	25	9	8	6	14	11	1
1968	20	25	10	11	9	15	10	1
1972	15	26	11	13	10	13	10	1
1976	15	25	12	15	10	14	9	1
1980	18	23	11	13	10	14	9	2
1984	17	20	11	11	12	15	12	2
1988	17	18	12	11	13	14	14	2
1992	18	18	14	12	12	14	11	1
1996	19	19	14	8	11	15	13	1

SOURCE: National Election Studies.

fronted with the Vietnam War, racial issues, and urban riots. Although the public elected Republican Richard Nixon to the presidency by a narrow margin in 1968 and by a landslide in 1972, throughout the 1970s the Democratic party retained a twelve- to eighteen-percentage-point difference in party identification over the Republicans. Since the 1980 election the GOP has gained ground, as between 25 to 28 percent claim Republican identification. Yet speculation about a new Republican majority emerging at the national level seemed to be quite premature, as in the 1996 election 38 percent identified with the Democratic party, compared with 28 percent for Republicans.

National party identification levels however, may hide important changes occurring in regions of the country. Among the nation's eligible electorate, change toward the Republican party has occurred most noticeably in one region: the South. In 1952 over two-thirds of the eligible voters in the South identified with the Democratic party. By George McGovern's candidacy in 1972, the number of self-identified Democrats in the South had shrunk to 42 percent, and by 1988 the two parties were virtually even, with 29 percent identifying with the Democrats and 30 percent with the GOP.

In terms of the *strength* of party identification (the ratio of party identifiers to nonpartisans), most people still identify with political parties, although party identification itself has declined. The "strong" and "weak" categories in Table 5.5 suggest that between 1952 and 1968 partisan identification ranged from 70 to 77 percent, with the highest figure occurring in 1964. After the 1968 election the range was 61 to 66 percent, with the highest levels of identification occurring in the 1996 election. If the average level of identification from 1952 to 1968 is compared with the average for 1972 to 1996, party identification has dropped 10 percentage points. Independent status has gained favor slightly, with several-percentage-point gains among Independent Democrats and Independent Republicans as well as Strong Republicans. Although Democrats saw an erosion in party identification after 1972, since that time party identification has steadied at slightly less than four in ten Americans.

The findings in Table 5.5 raise several important questions. Most importantly, given the decline in party identification, do parties still play the role of providing cues for their partisans? Are "Independent Republicans" or "Independent Democrats" truly independent, or are they hidden partisans? Finally, do the "Pure" Independents truly disdain the political parties, and do they have higher levels of education that lead them to scrutinize both the candidates and the issues? In the NES survey, respondents are asked whether in general they think of themselves as Republicans, Democrats, or Independents. If they choose independent status, a follow-up question asks whether they think of themselves as closer to the Republican or Democratic party. Only when they have twice declined to identify with either party are they classified as "Independent Independents" or "Pure" Independents.

Not unexpectedly, strong party identification is highly correlated with voting decisions. Among Strong Democrats in every election from 1952 to 1992 (except 1972), between 82 and 96 percent voted for the Democratic presidential candidate, whereas for Strong Republicans (with the exception of 1964) the figure was 4 percent or less supporting the Democratic candidate (Abramson, Aldrich, and Rohde 1995, 232–233).

As to whether "Independent" Republicans and Democrats are covert partisans, one line of analysis does not equate them with party identifiers, contending that the key elements of party identification are durability over time and the extent to which partisan feelings are bound with self-identity (Converse and Pierce 1985, 143). Although Independent "leaners" may exhibit partisan behavior due to the attractiveness of specific candidates and issues, they lack both the durability of attitudes and the psychological sense of belonging necessary for party identification. The conclusion of Miller and Shanks is succinct: "Independent 'leaners' or non-identifiers with party preferences, should not be confused with party identifiers, despite occasional treatment as such by other scholars" (1996, 127).

A second view of the voting practices and background of self-proclaimed independents questions whether people are as nonpartisan as they say they are, and questions any link between education and independent status. Bruce Keith and colleagues used questions about respondents' feelings toward the parties and past voting behavior to differentiate among the "Republican Independents," "Democratic Independents," and "Pure Independents." Regardless of their stated nonaffiliation, the views about the parties of Republican and Democratic "leaners" were almost identical to the responses of Weak Republicans or Weak Democrats (Keith et al. 1992, 96–103). Further, truly independent voters would not support the same political party year after year. When respondents to the National Election Survey were asked whether they "always" vote for the presidential candidate of the same party, for elections from 1952 to 1980, the averages were as follows: Strong Democrats (79 percent); Weak Democrats (54 percent); Independent Democrats (33 percent); Pure Independents (17 percent); Independent Republicans (31 percent); Weak Republicans (49 percent); and Strong Republicans (73 percent). These results, proceeding in a linear fashion from one pole to the other, would appear to validate the notion that independents are not wedded to one political party. Both Brody and Keith find problems with these results. By taking the respondents' answers about their votes in two adjacent elections, these studies found a number of "concealed partisans," that is, independents who had actually voted for the same party four and eight years previously but answered negatively when asked whether they had "always" voted for the same party (Brody 1991, 179–205; Keith et al. 1992, 106–107).

Higher levels of education do not seem to correlate with independent status. Instead, people with higher levels of education are less likely to be Pure Independents and more likely to be "leaners" (Keith et al. 1992, 129). Over time (from 1952 to 1988) the proportion of Pure Independents with less education (i.e., did not finish high school) increased, whereas the proportion of college educated decreased.

If we grant that the number of independents may be overstated in Table 5.5, why does independent status remain so popular? Using data from the University of Michigan Survey Research Center, Warren Miller found two important reasons: the impact of generational change and differences between voters and nonvoters. First, people become more partisan as they grow older. When the first wave of baby boomers (or those born between 1946 and 1964) reached voting age in the late 1960s, they formed a large part of the voting population. By 1972 those in their late teens and early twenties made up a third of the electorate. Breaking the electorate down by the year they became eligible to vote for president, and concentrating on those who turned eighteen in 1968, 1972, or 1976, Miller found either delay or a refusal to accept partisan status. In 1968, among those first eligible to vote, there were a greater number of nonpartisans than party identifiers. After 1976 there was an increase in partisan status among those first eligible to vote in the 1980s (Miller 1990, 101–103). This delay among those coming of voting age in the late 1960s and early 1970s substantially increased the number of nonpartisans.

A second reason for preferring independent status is evident when voters and nonvoters are compared. The change toward independent status has been far more dramatic among nonvoters. Confining the analysis to strong party identifiers and nonpartisans produces almost a wave effect in party identification. At the top of the wave from 1952 to 1964, University of Michigan data indicate that strong partisans (strong Republicans or strong Democrats) outnumbered those with no partisan preference by 39 percent to 7 percent. Voters did not emerge unscathed from the social upheaval from 1968 to 1976 however. A small trough occurred as the strong partisan category decreased to 30 percent, compared with 10 percent for nonpartisans. By the 1980s the wave reforms only slightly diminished from the 1952–1964 pattern, with 35 percent of voters claiming strong partisan preference to 8 percent no preference. Among nonvoters, however, the pattern is more like a wave that dissipates once it hits a seawall. In the 1952–1964 period, even nonvoters expressed strong partisanship with 26 percent in this category, compared with 8 percent in the nonpartisan category. During the 1968–1976 period this wave flattened dramatically, as the number expressing no party preference (19 percent) exceeded the number of strong partisans (16 percent). This trend continued through the 1980s, with 17 percent preferring nonpartisan status (Miller 1990, 106–107). The nonpartisan identification, therefore, occurred primarily among those who were apathetic about participating in the electoral process in the first place.

Third Parties and the Electorate

In the course of our nation's history, four types of third parties have arisen: economic protest parties (Greenbacks, Populists), ideological parties (Libertarians and Socialists), one-issue parties (including the Know-Nothings and Prohibitionists), and factional parties (including Theodore Roosevelt's Bull Moose Party in 1912 and the States' Rights Party in 1948) (Wilson 1983, 149–151). In the first part of this century, third-party candidates received more than 10 percent of the vote in two presidential elections: Teddy Roosevelt's 27.4 percent in 1912 and Robert LaFollette's 16.5 percent in 1924. Third parties find it difficult to maintain electoral support once the issues they raise are incorporated by one of the major parties.

Recently the number of self-proclaimed independent voters would seem to provide fertile ground for the reemergence of third parties, and significant third-party movements have grown since the 1960s. George Wallace appealed to an independent-minded populace in 1968 and garnered 13.5 percent of the vote. Similarly, although denying that he was out to establish a permanent third party in 1980, Representative John Anderson assembled a coalition of moderate Republicans, disenchanted Democrats, and independents that captured 6.6 percent of the presidential vote in 1980.

In 1992 industrialist Ross Perot raised the possibility of forging a bipartisan group of disaffected Republicans and Democrats, as well as those new to politics. Perot did get his name on the ballot in all fifty states. After dropping out and reentering the race in October, he garnered 19 percent of the vote in the general election. Perot established the Reform party in late 1995 as the vehicle to challenge the major parties. Before he could do that, he faced competition for his own party's nomination from former Colorado governor Richard Lamm. Although gaining the nomination, Perot was excluded from the presidential debates. His message was not as popular the second time around, and he received only 8.5 percent of the vote. The Reform party remains at best a potential model for a third party.

An evaluation of Ross Perot indicates that although he broke the mold in several ways regarding third-party activity, he also illustrates the difficulties of forging a new party coalition in the United States. First, the efforts of third parties focus largely on a candidate and his or her issues, and only secondarily on organization and continuing participation by activists. In this area the Perot record is mixed. Multimillionaire Perot headed an economic protest party that combined a populist message to the electorate ("I'm Ross. You're the Boss!") with stands on two major issues—the federal budget deficit and political reform—that successfully courted those who were fed up with "politics as usual." Theodore Lowi (1993) suggests that the term "Pied Piper" fits Perot because he marched people into an active role in politics, exercised centralized control over his original organization, United We Stand America, and then marched them back out again. There was no attempt to start at the bottom by running candidates for state or congressional elections after 1992.

If a third-party candidate withdraws from the race or is defeated, or a major party incorporates the third party's issues, the organizational momentum usually expires along with the candidate. In this area Perot's efforts fared slightly better. Despite the Republican and Democratic parties' increased attention to budget deficits and political reform, the candidate refused to simply "go away." Although his issues were taken up by the two major parties, United We Stand America chapters were formed in the fifty states to serve as a political network for Perot. With the subsequent transformation into the Reform party, Perot stated his intention to democratize the nomination process for 1996 by sending out 1.3 million ballots to individuals who either were registered members or had signed the Reform party's ballot-access petitions in the states. Some members had difficulties obtaining ballots, however, and only a small fraction of the ballots were returned, leading critics to charge that the process was manipulated by Perot.

Another formidable task for third parties is to attract independent voters who can form a durable base for the third party. Among the three types of independents specified previously (Pure, Republican, and Democratic) the range of opinion about the issues parallels the public at large (Keith et al. 1992, 166). Independents are not united on one issue or a set of issues to a greater degree than the public at large. A poll of Perot voters conducted by the Democratic Leadership Council found them only slightly more likely than Republicans or Democrats to cite "waste and spending" as Washington's major problem, and they were only slightly more likely to be critical of Congress (Berke 1993).

A final hurdle for third parties is that partisan affiliation remains the most stable predictor of the electorate's voting behavior. Table 5.5 indicates that partisan affiliation has gradually declined since 1960, but the division of the electorate between the two major parties is remarkably stable. Those who identify themselves with a political party seem to be quite consistent in supporting their party's candidates. Moreover, the fact that the Republican party was a minority party until 1994 did not prevent it from showing remarkable strength. Since 1952, Republicans had occupied the White House for sixteen years, without ever claiming the affiliation of more than 35 percent of the electorate.

Voting Behavior

Political scientists have long debated the impact of parties, candidates, and issues on the voting decision. The authors of the classic 1950s voting study *The American Voter* stressed the importance of party identification. They viewed party identification as a psychological or emotional attachment rather than a rational weighing of which party might serve the individual's self-interest. Because party identification was a part of the socialization process that includes such influences as parents, schooling, and religion, it was viewed as an "antecedent factor" relatively immune from change (Campbell et al. 1960, 137). In contrast, a competing conception contends that party identification allows citizens to make a quick assessment of candidates and issues, and to keep a kind of "running tally" of both parties' performance in office. Unless a competing candidate or issue is particularly attractive, the "standing decision" is to vote with the party (Fiorina 1977, 1981; Jackson 1975). This second concept suggests that occasionally three-way interaction between parties, candidates, and issues replaces people's structured view of the candidates and issues.

Both concepts of the role of party identification have their adherents, but for our purposes it is important to note that this variable has had the most impact on voting decisions in presidential elections since 1956, with the exception of the 1972 election (Gant and Luttbeg 1991, 63). Voter defections pose a particular problem for Democrats. Exit polls of voters shown in Table 5.6 indicate that in elections before 1996 the party's presidential candidates were fortunate to retain even three-quarters of the votes of self-proclaimed Democrats. Indeed, Jimmy Carter's figures were closer to two-thirds of Democratic voters in 1980. Republican voters demonstrated more loyalty to their party's nominee, as support levels of 90 percent or better were not unusual in the 1980s. Ross Perot's presence on the 1992 ballot resulted in significant defections among Republican voters, as 17 percent of them preferred the Texas business tycoon. Bill Clinton was also affected by Perot, as his vote among Democrats (77 percent) was lower than Michael Dukakis's in 1988.

Ideology and Social Groupings

One difficulty of using ideology in election analysis is that people are often asked in polls to identify themselves as liberal, moderate, or conservative. Any concept of ideology is thus self-designated, rather than derived from respondents' answers to a set of questions about issues that would allow respondents to be grouped into ideological categories. One unsurprising result is the popularity of the term "moderate," as 47 percent of the 1996 electorate chose this designation, compared with 33 percent choosing

TABLE 5.6 Presidential Voting by Groups (in percentages)

	1992			1996		
	Clinton	Bush	Perot	Clinton	Dole	Perot
All Voters	43	38	19	49	41	9
Party						
Democrats	77	10	13	84	10	5
Independents	38	32	30	43	35	17
Republicans	10	73	17	13	80	6
Ideology						
Liberals	68	14	18	78	11	7
Moderates	48	31	21	57	33	9
Conservatives	18	65	17	20	71	8
Region						
From the East	47	35	18	55	34	9
From the Midwest	42	37	21	48	41	10
From the South	42	43	16	46	46	7
From the West	44	34	22	48	40	8
Religion						
White Protestant	33	46	21	36	53	10
White born-again Christian	23	61	15	26	65	8
Catholic	44	36	20	53	37	9
Jewish	78	12	10	78	16	3
Gender						
Women	46	37	17	54	38	7
Men	41	38	21	43	44	10
Single women	51	34	15	62	28	7
Homemaker	36	45	19	46	43	9

(continues)

TABLE 5.6 *(continued)*

	1992			1996		
	Clinton	Bush	Perot	Clinton	Dole	Perot
Race						
Whites	39	41	20	43	46	9
African Americans	81	11	7	84	12	4
Hispanics/Latinos	62	25	14	72	21	6
Race/Region						
Whites in South	34	48	18	36	56	8
Family Income						
Under $15,000	59	23	18	59	28	11
$15,000–$29,999	45	35	20	53	36	9
$30,000–$49,999	41	38	21	48	40	10
$50,000–$74,999	40	42	18	47	45	7
$75,000 and over	36	48	16	44	48	7
Education						
Not a high school grad	55	28	17	59	28	11
High school grad	43	36	20	51	35	13
Some college	42	37	21	48	40	10
College grad	40	42	18	44	46	8
Postgraduate	49	36	15	52	40	5

NOTE: Income categories listed are for 1992.

SOURCE: Data for 1996 are from a Votex News Service exit poll of 16,627 voters. Data for 1992 are from a Votex Research and Surveys exit poll of 15,490 voters.

"conservative" and 20 percent "liberal." With nearly half of the electorate placing themselves firmly in the middle of the political spectrum, this self-proclaimed nonideological group was on the winning side in all elections except in 1988, where by the thinnest of margins they favored Michael Dukakis.

Political parties in the past conceived of elections in terms of building coalitions of groups. The contribution of any social group to an electoral coalition depends on the size of the group in the population, the extent to which it turns out to vote, and the group's loyalty to the political party. As we have already examined trends in turnout, we shall focus our attention on group size and loyalty. Several problems are associated with relying on groups to examine voting behavior, however. Since most voters belong to more than one group, will different group loyalties tend to reinforce each other or will "crosscutting loyalties" occur, as voters are pulled in different directions by conflicting group pressures? This problem is related to a second one: With the exception of race, and to a lesser extent geographic region, the standard categories of religion, gender, social class, and age have been less important predictors in recent elections. Comparing the Democratic "New Deal" coalition with subsequent voting behavior illustrates this phenomenon.

As noted in Chapter 2, Democrats constructed the New Deal coalition based on economic condition and history. Those who were relatively disadvantaged—the working class (both union and nonunion), the poor, and those with lower levels of formal education—supported the Democrats. The coalition also included religious minorities, specifically Catholics and Jews. Jews made up only a small portion (4 percent) of the electorate, but they were solidly behind Roosevelt. Their presence in large cities helped tip the balance in states in which urban and rural votes were evenly matched. Blacks moved away from the GOP, the party of Lincoln, in favor of the social programs Democrats began during the New Deal.

By the early 1960s, changes among social classes, along with shifts in regional support, had undermined the New Deal coalition. Initially many members of the working class (including union members) and Catholics were immigrants, but their descendants sought and gained middle-class status. Since 1976 white Catholics have been as likely to be middle class as white Protestants (Abramson, Aldrich, and Rohde 1995, 158–160). But after 1976 no Democratic presidential nominee has received over 54 percent of the Catholic vote. Although the percentage of working-age Americans belonging to unions decreased, those who remained in union jobs saw their earnings increase substantially. The 1980 and 1984 elections marked the highest level of union support for the Republicans, as Ronald Reagan received 44 percent and 46 percent of their votes respectively.

Another factor that greatly diminished the New Deal coalition was a confluence of race and region. As the Democratic party became identified with civil rights legislation, the proportion of blacks and Hispanics supporting the party grew, with a subsequent decline in support by whites, particularly in the South. The divergence in the white vote between the 1964 and 1968 elections is particularly striking. In Lyndon Johnson's 1964 landslide election, the 65 percent of whites who were willing to go "all the way with LBJ" were complemented by a massive 96 percent of black voters. Hubert Humphrey, facing a three-candidate race in 1968, retained over 90 percent of the black vote but slumped to only 43 percent of the white vote. Since then no Democratic presidential candidate has attracted a majority of white votes. In the 1992 and 1996 elections, according to Table 5.6, candidates George Bush and Bob Dole maintained slender 2 and 3 percent pluralities among white voters. Thus the strong majorities given Clinton by black voters (who constituted 10 percent of all 1996 voters) and Hispanics (5 percent of all voters) were major elements in both his victories. Hispanic voters have traditionally given the Democratic nominee 60 percent of their vote or more, with the exception of 1980, when the figure dipped to 59 percent (Carmines and Stimson 1989).

When region is added to the voting equation, white southerners' desertion of the Democratic party is even more dramatic. In 1976 native southerner Jimmy Carter could not attract a majority of voters from this region. Republican presidential candidates drew 60 percent or more of the vote among white southerners through the 1980s. Even the presence of former Arkansas governor Bill Clinton and former Tennessee senator Albert Gore at the head of the Democratic ticket in 1992 and again in 1996 could not reverse the trend. In those two elections only slightly more than a third of southern whites endorsed the Democratic ticket. In addition, the 1992 exit poll cited in Table 5.6 found only four out of ten white southerners voting for the Democratic congressional candidate, and only one-third usually thinking of themselves as Democrats ("Ethnocultural Patterns" 1993). The decline in support among southern whites for the Democratic party races continued through 1998, as only 35 percent chose the party's candidates in House races that year ("A Look at Voting Patterns" 1998).

Prior to 1980, polls found few differences in presidential voting between men and women. In 1976, for example, a *New York Times* exit poll found men and women each giving Jimmy Carter 50 percent of the vote. Through the 1980s, however, a gap occurred between men and women in the degree of support for the Republican candidate. Reagan drew 55 percent of male voters in 1980, but only 47 percent of female voters, for a "gap" of 8 percent. For the remaining elections the gap for the Republican candidate ranged from 7 percent in 1988 to 1 percent in 1992. In general, men were more likely than women to vote for the Republican candidate in the elections of the 1980s. Even greater gender differences are evident between male and female college graduates. The greatest gap, seventeen points, occurred in 1980 as Ronald Reagan garnered nearly 60 percent of male college graduates, but only 42 percent of female college graduates.

Although women were less supportive of the GOP nominee in the 1980s, two caveats are necessary about a "gender gap." First, as with any group, voting patterns among women are not monolithic. The greatest differences are evident between the categories of homemakers and unmarried women. Homemakers voted consistently for Republican candidates from 1984 to 1992, whereas unmarried women provided major support for the Democratic presidential ticket, even giving Walter Mondale a slim 1 percent plurality of their vote during Reagan's lopsided victory in 1984. A second caveat is that either a majority of women (or a plurality of women in races with three candidates) must favor the Democratic presidential candidate for any gap to lead to election victory. Despite receiving less support from women than men in 1980–1988, the Republican candidate received a plurality of support from *both* women and men. In 1992 and 1996 a plurality of women selected the Democratic candidate; the vote among men, however, was quite close in both elections, favoring Clinton over Bush in 1992 by a slim 3 percent margin, but Bob Dole over Clinton by a narrow 1 percent margin in 1996.

In regard to age, the voting behavior of both older and younger Americans reveals a more complex pattern in recent years. At the presidential level, for the three elections in the 1980s those sixty and older firmly supported the Republican nominee. Only in 1992 and 1996 did a majority of seniors cast ballots for the Democratic nominee, Bill Clinton. On the other hand, if the younger vote is expanded to include those under thirty, the pattern is inconsistent, favoring Carter by a slim margin in 1980, giving solid support to Reagan and Bush in 1984 and 1988, and switching to Clinton in 1992 and 1996.

Certainly one factor that has a major impact on political attitudes is degree of religious commitment (Wald 1992; Leege and Kellstedt 1993). Since 1980, white Evangelical Christians have given the Republican nominee between 61 and 81 percent of the vote. In the 1992 and 1996 elections Ross Perot did not gain a greater percentage of votes from Evangelical Christians than any other group in the electorate, but his presence was still sufficient to lower the support given by this group to George Bush and Bob Dole to the 60 percent range. White Protestants' support of Republican nominees has ranged from 46 percent in the three-way 1992 race to 72 percent for Ronald Reagan in 1984. Since 1980 the Catholic vote has been a swing vote, supporting Republican presidential candidates in the 1980s by 50 to 55 percent margins, but returning to the Democratic fold in the 1992 and 1996 elections. Voting patterns become even more complex as the various ways in which religion, race, and region interconnect are considered. For example, Evangelical Christians are more likely to be found in the South, thereby heightening regional support for Republicans. On the other hand, a factor that decreases the level of support by Protestants for GOP candidates is that most blacks are Protestant, and a large majority of black voters usually vote for Democrats.

In sum, the Republican coalition in the 1980s, ranked in order of the degree of support, consisted of white born-again Christians, white southerners, those with incomes of over $75,000, independents, moderates, men, and first-time voters. In 1992, Bill Clinton's victory was based on heavy support from traditional Democratic groups, including blacks, Hispanics, Jews, and those with low incomes. In that election Clinton demonstrated an ability to reassemble some parts of the New Deal coalition, such as union households (55 percent), the elderly (50 percent), and Catholics (44 percent). In addition he secured the support of women (46 percent), moderates (48 percent) and those with middle incomes (41 percent). While Democratic party officials pointed with pride to the groups that favored Clinton, car bumper stickers gleefully pointed to the 57 percent of the votes that were "Anti-Clinton." Compared with 1992, Clinton increased his margins by 6 to 9 percentage points in 1996 among Catholics, women, moderates, and those with middle incomes, while receiving 2 percent less of the elderly vote. Whether this constitutes a durable coalition or is simply a reaction to the candidate is open to debate.

Role of Issues

In early studies of the importance of issues in elections, Campbell and colleagues came to a pessimistic conclusion. To qualify as an "issue-oriented electorate," voters must hold opinions on key issues, must be aware of what government is doing about the main issues, and must believe the major parties have different stances on these issues. In 1956 only a quarter to a third of the electorate could meet these qualifications (Campbell et al. 1960, 168–187). In election surveys conducted since 1972, Paul Abramson and colleagues found voters meeting the first two criteria: More than 80 percent of those polled expressed an opinion on key issues, whereas 66 percent of the respondents could identify the candidates' views on the issues. Wider variation occurred in the ability to determine the differences between the candidates on these issues, ranging from one-third of those polled in 1976 to two-thirds in 1984 and 1992 (Abramson, Aldrich, and Rohde 1995, 179–183). The varying results may be due to the political visibility of the candidates. In 1984 the electorate had four years to absorb the views of incumbent Ronald Reagan; Democratic challenger Walter Mondale had served as vice president from 1977 to 1981. George Bush's four years as vice president provided voters a similar opportunity in 1992. Conversely, 1976 offered two lesser-known candidates. Gerald Ford had been in office only two years, and Jimmy Carter suffered from lack of name identification, as was evident at one presidential primary rally when he was introduced as "Jimmy Walker," a brand of liquor.

Another factor that affects the importance of issues is candidates' greater comfort with bringing certain types of issues to the attention of the electorate than others. Carmines and Stimson distinguish between "easy" and "hard" issues. Easy issues are more likely to be symbolic rather than technical, and to deal with policy goals rather than means. The voters' response to such issues is likely to be an ingrained or "gut" response rather than a careful weighing of the nuances of the issue. Issues such as abortion, the death penalty, and desegregation fall into this category. The hard issues are more technical and complex, increasing the electorate's difficulty of understanding or deciding upon such issues (Carmines and Stimson 1980). In the 1988 election, for example, Republicans feared that Michael Dukakis would exploit the savings and loan scandal, which saw numerous savings and loan associations go out of business after making unsound or illegal loans, with the government left to pick up the tab on the federally insured loans. After the election, when asked why he had not seized upon this issue, Dukakis blamed the lack of a visual—his campaign could not find a way to boil down the issue for an effective thirty-second campaign spot.

Surveys suggest that issues have come to play a more important role in voting decisions in recent elections, but questions remain about the time frame in which voters employ issues. Are issues used in a retrospective manner? That is, do voters use the current election as a referendum on what the incumbent party accomplished in the past four years? Do voters employ prospective judgment—attempting to evaluate the issues and promises candidates make for the next four years? Or is some combination of retrospective and prospective judgment relied on?

One method of answering these questions is to focus on the most important issue or problem as seen by the electorate. As Table 5.7 indicates, since 1976 some aspect of the economy (including unemployment, inflation, and government spending) has been cited as the most important problem. Many scholars find voters exercising retrospective judgment on what has happened to the economy, particularly in the ten months before the election (Fiorina 1981; Kiewiet 1983, 154–158; Beck 1991; Lewis-Beck 1985, 1988). The public is inundated with information on this subject by the media, but most often the focus is short-term, primarily on what has happened in the year before the election. The table provides a summary of the overall income gain or loss in the election year, after inflation is factored out. In the last two columns of the table the Gallup poll seeks a prospective judgment in asking voters, "Looking ahead for the next few years, which party do

TABLE 5.7   Key Issues and Voting Patterns, 1952–1996

Year	Most Important Issue	% Cited	Election Year % Change in Real Disposable Income per Capita	Party Best for Most Important Issue; % Saying Dem.	Repub.
1952	Korean War	N.L.	1.1	15	36
1956	Keeping peace	N.L.	2.7	25	33
1960	Keeping peace	N.L.	0	25	29
1964	Race relations/	N.L.	5.5	49	23
	Vietnam	N.L.		45	22
1968	Vietnam	51	3.1	29	34
1972	Vietnam	27	3.0	29	39
1976	Economy/jobs	62	2.6	43	23
1980	Economy/jobs	76	−0.1	32	35
1984	Economy/jobs	30	5.5	37	39
1988	Economy/jobs	45	2.5	33	38
1992	Economy/jobs	68	1.3	45	36
1996	Economy/jobs	40	2.8	41	31

SOURCES: *Gallup Report*, October 1984, 20–22; "Trend on Party Best Able to Handle Most Important Problem," *Gallup Opinion Index*, October 1988, 8; Leslie McAneny, "Voters See Democratic Party 'Best for Prosperity,'" *Gallup Poll Monthly*, October 1992, 26–27; Lydia Saad, "Economy Still Top Concern," *Gallup Poll Monthly*, September 1996, 10; U.S. Bureau of the Census, *Survey of Current Business*, April 1993, S1; *Gallup Poll Monthly*, August 1996, 3–4; U.S. Bureau of the Census, *Survey of Current Business*, April 1997, D6.

you think *will* do the best job on the issue most important to you?" In 1952 and 1956 international issues were most important, the economy was relatively prosperous, and the electorate felt Republicans would do the best job in the future. Conversely in 1960, although "keeping peace" was deemed most important, the economy was stagnating and the electorate saw little difference in the ability of the parties to handle their most important issue. The election outcome reflected voter ambiguity, as John Kennedy won by the narrowest of margins. By 1980 the economy was the most important issue by a wide margin; income levels after inflation had decreased slightly, and over 60 percent gave Jimmy Carter a "poor" rating in handling the issue. Ronald Reagan subsequently defeated Carter in a landslide. In 1996, with the change in income after inflation at close to 3 percent, and the Democratic party viewed as best to handle inflation, Clinton was reelected by a substantial margin.

The necessity of combining retrospective and prospective judgments is evident in the 1988 and 1992 elections. The Reagan administration received a "poor" rating in managing the economy from 56 percent of respondents, yet George Bush was not sent into early political retirement.

One apparent reason is that in the prospective judgment of future behavior in Table 5.7, the Republican party still maintained a slight lead over the Democrats. Prospective judgments also entered the 1992 presidential election. Almost three-quarters of those polled expressed dissatisfaction with the way things were going in the United States, with the result that even incumbent George Bush called himself "the candidate of change" (Hugick and McAneny 1992, 3). Similarly, in Table 5.7 over two-thirds of the electorate in 1992 saw the economy as the key issue, whereas 97 percent of Clinton supporters and 89 percent of Perot supporters described the national economy as "not good" or "poor."

One final factor is that voter perspectives may change when the analysis is shifted to House and Senate elections. The electorate tends to be less aware of the actions of Congress, resulting in more difficulty in evaluating past actions. Brad Lockerbie (1991a, 1991b) finds that voters tend to look more to the future when making congressional voting decisions, an effect that is independent from both party identification and retrospective evaluations.

Value Clusters and the Electorate

Given the electorate's self-described independence, the decreased reliability of group membership in predicting voting behavior, and the difficulty of distinguishing issue influence from candidate influences, one other method of understanding voting behavior is to divide the electorate according to the values they hold, or "value clusters." Norman Ornstein and colleagues first took into account such basic social and political values as the degree of tolerance or intolerance toward civil liberties and free speech, beliefs about social justice questions such as welfare, and attitudes about government size and effectiveness (Ornstein, Kohut, and McCarthy 1988, 8–11). Such personal factors as degree of religious faith, degree of financial pressure felt by individuals, and alienation toward government were added, resulting in an electorate divided into ten groups. Exploring these groupings can produce a better understanding of the difficulties parties have in forming winning coalitions. The four core groups for the Democratic party found in Table 5.8 are the "Seculars," the "New Democrats," the "New Deal Democrats," and the "Partisan Poor." In the moderate center are the "New Economy Independents," the "Embittered," and those unlikely to vote, the "Bystanders." Conversely, for the Republicans the core groups are the "Enterprisers" and the "Moralists," whereas the "Libertarians" are more tentative in their support for the GOP.

The parties find it difficult to utilize values to appeal to their core supporters, as well as voters who lean toward one party or see themselves as Independents. A common tactic of both parties is to appropriate rhetoric with "populist" overtones. As William Schneider states, populism "has two

TABLE 5.8 The Electorate and Voting Preferences by Value Groups

"The Not So Left"	"The Detached Center"	"The Divided Right"
Seculars 7% of adult population; 9% of likely voters *Who They Are:* Mostly white, educated, affluent, low religious faith. *Key Attitudes:* This group is driven by social issues and embraces the "liberal" label. They are progovernment and proenvironment. Distrustful of business. *Democratic Presidential Preference:* 1996, 90% (Perot 6%)	**New Economy Independents** 14% of adult population; 10% of likely voters *Who They Are:* Mostly female, high school graduates financially pressured. *Key Attitudes:* Values tend to conflict (e.g., anti-government and proenvironment). *Democratic Presidential Preference:* 1996, 53% (Perot 16%)	**Enterprisers** 12% of adult population; 19% of likely voters *Who They Are:* Mostly white, affluent, well educated. *Key Attitudes:* Strongly probusiness, antigovernment. Anti-welfare. *Republican Presidential Voting:* 1988, 96%; 1992, 69%; 1996, 88% (Perot 3%)
New Democrats 12% of adult population; 12% of likely voters *Who They Are:* White, average education, with many Catholics and Evangelicals. *Key Attitudes:* They are progovernment and probusiness. Socially tolerant on issues such as abortion. *Democratic Presidential Preference:* 1996, 86% (Perot 4%)	**Embittered** 6% of adult population; 5% of likely voters *Who They Are:* Low income and education, religious, socially intolerant, one in five is black, one in three has a child under eighteen. *Key Attitudes:* Distrust of government, politicians, and corporations. Religious and socially intolerant. *Democratic Presidential Preference:* 1996, 45% (Perot 11%)	**Moralists** 15% of adult population; 18% of likely voters *Who They Are:* White, middle age, middle income, religious (mostly Evangelicals), socially conservative. *Key Attitudes:* Socially conservative—favor the death penalty and school prayer. They are anti-big business and big government; militaristic. *Republican Presidential Preference:* 1988, 98%; 1992, 62%; 1996, 66% (Perot 7%)

New Deal Democrats
8% of adult population; 10% of likely voters
Who They Are: Older, religious, pro-America, pro-union, below average education and income.
Key Attitudes: Conservative on racial and welfare issues, do not trust politicians or businesspeople. Moderately tolerant, pro-American.
Democratic Presidential Preference: 1996, 74% (Perot 12%)

Partisan Poor
9% of adult population; 10% of likely voters
Who They Are: Very poor, disadvantaged, a third live in the South. Very religious and socially conservative.
Key Attitudes: Believe government should spend more to help poor people but oppose tax increases.
Democratic Presidential Preference: 1996, 92% (Perot 3%)

Bystanders
10% of adult population; 0% of likely voters
Who They Are: Very young, poorly educated, low income.
Key Attitudes: Opt out of the political process or are not eligible to vote. Only claimed commitment is environmentalism.

Libertarians
7% of adult population; 7% of likely voters
Who They Are: Affluent, white, mostly male, highly educated, low religious faith.
Key Attitudes: Antigovernment and anti-socialwelfare, liberal on social issues. Cynical about politicians.
Republican Presidential Preference: 1996, 34% (Perot 12%)

SOURCE: The Pew Research Center for the People & the Press, "Voter Typology: Dole Fails with Populists, GOP Moderates; Clinton Unites Democrats, Gains Working Class Independents." Available at: <www.people-press.org>.

faces: economically liberal and socially conservative" (1992). Both of the faces are antielitist. Republicans accuse Democrats of personifying the "cultural elite," of which the greatest transgressors are the "Hollywood elite" or the "limousine liberals." Conversely, Democrats refer to the "fat-cat Republicans and their rich friends." Beyond the name calling, the parties seek to frame the issues so that voters must decide which poses the greater threat—economic insecurity or cultural anxiety. In the 1968 and 1972 elections the GOP relied on social issues as a "wedge" to split the Democratic party. Richard Nixon successfully employed a law-and-order appeal, racial backlash, and patriotism. The slogan of the three As (acid, amnesty, and abortion) was applied to Democratic presidential candidates, neutralizing any appeal to economic populism (Schneider 1992). In 1976, Jimmy Carter was able to reflect voters' feelings about economic pressures unleashed by the 1973 Arab oil embargo and to portray himself in common and noncommon terms as a "peanut farmer *and* a nuclear engineer." However, the economy's poor performance provided an opening for Republicans in 1980. Ronald Reagan combined economic and social populism with his program of across-the-board tax cuts and getting the government "off your backs and out of your pockets." This message was aimed at two value clusters— the Libertarians, who are nominally Republican, and the Seculars in the Democratic party. The strategy was successful with Libertarians, and among Seculars the rate of defection to the GOP ranged from 24 to 34 percent.

With a healthy economy in 1988, George Bush's campaign was able to focus once again on cultural anxiety. It used such symbols as the pledge of allegiance, the death penalty, furloughs of criminals, and "card carrying membership" in the American Civil Liberties Union (ACLU) to paint Michael Dukakis as unrepresentative of key American values (Schneider 1992).

In 1992 the GOP experienced difficulty maintaining the strategy that secured Republican control of the White House for twenty out of twenty-four years between 1968 and 1992. The major problem was keeping the peace between the Moralists and the Enterprisers. Both groups had given Republicans over 90 percent of their vote in the presidential elections of the 1980s. The main differences between the two groups involved issues of personal freedom. Enterprisers tend to take a moderate stance on such issues; for example, 38 percent of this group think laws should be changed to make it more difficult for a woman to get an abortion, compared with 44 percent of the nation (Times Mirror Center 1990, 74). Conversely, Moralists are strongly anti-abortion and tend to support leaders like evangelist Pat Robertson. Although his bid for the 1988 presidential nomination was defeated, Robertson kept up the pressure with a 1991 pledge to have a "working majority" of the Republican party under the control of "pro-family Christians" within five years (King 1993). At the 1992 GOP national convention, supporters of what former national chairman Lee Atwater called the "big tent" notion of the party, in which a diverse range of views could be voiced, were in the minority. Presidential candidate Pat Buchanan proclaimed that the fight for the Republican party was a "cultural war," even a "religious war . . . for the soul of America." Republican National Committee chairman Rich Bond attempted to be antielitist but only raised questions when he stated that "we are America. Those other people are not America" (Shepard 1992). The result of the infighting, as indicated in Table 5.8, was a substantial drop in support for George Bush by *both* Moralists (62 percent of their vote) and Enterprisers (69 percent). The Perot candidacy, with its emphasis on running government like a business, was attractive to Enterprisers, and he received 21 percent of their vote. By 1996 the Enterprisers' flirtation with Perot was over. Dole's emphasis on a 15 percent tax cut and economic growth attracted 88 percent of their vote, whereas Perot plunged to 3 percent. One out of three Moralists believed that Dole was not deeply committed to their agenda, and he won only 66 percent of their vote.

In 1992, Bill Clinton was able to express the value concerns of the core Democrats and one Democratic leaning group, whether the issue was social justice (Seculars), the deficit (New Deal Democrats), the environment (Seculars), or economic pressure (Partisan Poor and New Economy Independents). By receiving two-thirds or more of each group's vote, Clinton built the values coalition necessary to capture the presidency. However, the 66 percent support that the New Deal Democrats gave Clinton was the lowest of any Democratic core group; Ross Perot received 17 percent of their vote, the most support given to him by any of the Democratic core groups.

The Clinton administration used several strategies in 1996, appealing to the four groupings in the Democratic Party and also to Independents and to some Republicans as well. The most important element is what was called the "triangulation strategy." The goal was to move Clinton to the center between more liberal congressional Democrats and more conservative congressional Republicans. Clinton wanted to take away the Republicans' ability to use social issues such as crime, the family, schools, and welfare as "wedge" issues to chip away parts of the Democratic coalition. On the one hand, Clinton moved to the right as he declared in his State of the Union speech that "the era of big government was over," signed a welfare reform bill that imposed time limits on recipients, supported mandatory uniforms for schools, endorsed a "V" chip in televisions so that parents could screen out violent programs, and eventually supported a seven-year plan to balance the budget. On the other hand, his emphasis on the role of government in maintaining such social welfare programs as Social Security, Medicare, and Medicaid gained him solid support among the Seculars (90 percent) and the Partisan Poor (92 percent).

Congressional elections in 1998 demonstrated Republican difficulties in relying too heavily on issues central to the Moralists. Before that election, as he neared the end of a four-year investigation of President Clinton, Special Prosecutor Kenneth Starr advised the House Judiciary Committee that "substantial and credible" evidence existed to impeach (i.e., indict) the president on a series of charges ranging from perjury before a grand jury to obstructing Starr's investigation. In a brief televised statement Clinton did finally admit to an "inappropriate relationship" with a former White House intern Monica Lewinsky. The House Judiciary Committee scheduled impeachment hearings to begin shortly after the election.

For Republicans, a central question was whether to make Clinton's difficulties a major theme in a congressional election, hoping to motivate that key constituency of Moralists to turn out. Or would this strategy backfire among Enterprisers and those groups in the political center? A Gallup poll one month before the election showed Americans opposing impeachment by a margin of 53 percent to 43 percent ("53% Oppose Impeachment Hearings" 1998). A lackluster session of Congress, however, gave Republicans few issues to which they could "point with pride."

Surprising the political experts, the Democrats gained five seats in the House (the first time the president's party had gained seats in a midterm election since 1934), and stayed even in the Senate. Yet the results of the election should be viewed within the context of few compelling issues to attract voters, decreased media coverage, and low turnout. The Republican hope that the Clinton-Lewinksy matter would dominate the election was realized only in media coverage. Election analyst Robert Lichter found the networks aired six stories about the Lewinsky scandal for every one about electoral politics, and coverage of the elections decreased by 73 percent in 1998 when compared with 1994 (Berke 1998). Not surprisingly, turnout declined to 36.1 percent, the lowest in fifty-six years. Whereas a better than expected turnout rate of 22 percent for Republicans helped them take control of Congress in 1994, an 18 percent turnout in 1998 contributed to a loss of seats. The scandal did not energize the Moralists, as exit polls indicated participation by members of the religious right declined from 17 percent of voters in 1994 to 13 percent in 1998. Democrats experienced a smaller, 2 percent decline compared with 1994 (from 18.9 to 16.8).

Within that smaller core of Democratic party identifiers, blacks made up a larger share. Blacks again voted overwhelmingly Democratic (89 percent), and their votes were pivotal in a number of races.

The presidential scandal entered the battle only indirectly, as Voter News Service exit polls indicated that the five most important issues were education (19 percent), moral and ethical standards (19 percent), the economy/jobs (14 percent), Social Security (12 percent), and taxes (11 percent). Although those who emphasized moral and ethical standards as the most important issue chose Republicans overwhelmingly (85 percent), those who cited education, the economy, and Social Security as key issues voted for Democrats by margins of 60 percent or greater ("Exit Poll" 1998). In the short term, Democrats refocused voters on social issues such as education and Social Security, where they are traditionally strong.

At both the national and state levels, candidates who stressed moderation prevailed. This tactic was used successfully by winners in three key gubernatorial races: Democrat Grey Davis in California, and Republicans George W. Bush in Texas and Jeb Bush in Florida, sons of former president George Bush.

In sum, both Republicans and Democrats face substantial problems holding their core constituencies together. Some Republicans believe the key to future electoral success is to select candidates who can reestablish a working relationship between the Enterprisers and the Moralists. Other Republicans believe that in the absence of a major recession, the GOP should continue to stress social values in the campaign to regain the presidency.

For Democrats, the key problem is disagreement among core groups over social programs and the means to finance such programs. The New Deal Democrats, Partisan Poor, and Seculars want to be able to turn to government for such benefits as housing for the elderly, Social Security, veterans benefits, school lunches, day care, and college loans. Strong agreement is expressed with the statement that "government should be there when you find yourself in a situation," that is, one that cannot be handled by an individual. Yet they also firmly agree about the dangers of "big government," which is nevertheless necessary to provide such programs. All three groups support the notion that "government does not care much about the little guy." Few in the three value clusters express support for raising taxes to pay for the programs they want expanded.

For the Democrats who gained office in 1992 due to economic anxiety, their stewardship of the economy was the major factor in retaining the presidency in 1996. As the economic expansion set new records for longevity, Democratic candidates found the dual tasks of maintaining economic security and stemming cultural anxiety to be daunting.

Ticket Splitting

Throughout American history, until the mid-1960s, a majority of voters (60 to 80 percent) voted a straight ticket (DeVries and Tarrance 1972, 31). As a result, from 1880 to 1956 only 17 percent of the states simultaneously elected governors and senators of opposite parties. Since the mid-1960s voting patterns have shifted dramatically. When the Gallup poll now asks whether respondents voted for candidates of different parties anywhere on the ballot, about 60 percent in presidential years answer affirmatively. The results can be observed at the ballot box: Between 1960 and 1992, 40 percent of the states holding presidential and gubernatorial elections split the two offices between the two parties.

Table 5.9 illustrates similar trends for presidential and congressional voting. Before 1968, from 12 to 15 percent of voters split their tickets for these two offices. Between 1972 and 1994 the range was 22 percent to 30 percent; only in the 1996 election did the figure drop to 17 percent. A further breakdown of the data in the table would find few differences with voters as a whole in terms of gender, education, profession, and ideology. However, political party identification, race, and region are significantly related to splitting one's vote. Among Independents an average of 29 percent from 1972 to 1996 reported selecting a Republican presidential candidate and a Democratic member of Congress, whereas for Republicans the average was 22 percent and for Democrats 14 percent. Less split-ticket voting where identification with the parties is the strongest has been validated at the national and state levels in numerous studies (Brown and Wright 1992; Beck et al. 1992). Given blacks' propensity to support the Democratic party, less ticket splitting would be expected among them, and over this period an average of 5 percent of blacks recorded a GOP presidential vote and Democratic congressional vote. Not surprisingly, more southerners than northerners were attracted to this type of split ticket, with a regional average of 26 percent, compared with 16 percent for voters outside the South. Split-ticket voting is also more prevalent when strong third-party candidates are on the ballot. Ross Perot's 19 percent of the vote in 1992 ensured a larger number of ticket

TABLE 5.9   Split-Ticket Voting, 1952–1996 (in percentages)

Year	Democratic Pres./Dem. Congress	Democratic Pres./Repub. Congress	Republican Pres./Dem. Congress	Republican Pres./Repub. Congress
1952	39	2	10	49
1956	39	2	13	45
1960	45	4	10	41
1964	59	9	6	26
1968	40	7	11	42
1972	31	5	25	40
1976	42	9	16	34
1980	35	8	20	38
1984	36	6	20	39
1988	40	7	18	34
1992	48	10	12	30
1996	44	13	4	39

SOURCE: National Election Studies.

splitters, whereas in 1996 one national exit poll showed that of those who split their presidential and congressional choices, almost one-half voted for third-party candidate Ross Perot (Nelson 1997, 75).

There is no shortage of possible explanations for split-ticket voting, but all of them face the task of accounting for two types of divided government— Republican presidents and Democrats controlling Congress, and more recently the electorate's choice of a Democratic president and a GOP-controlled House. Whereas one line of reasoning contends that voters do not purposely create divided government (Petrocik and Doherty 1996), three other explanations not only stress that rational voters intentionally seek divided government but that in doing so they take into account the political parties' stance on the issues. Under Morris Fiorina's "policy balancing" notion the electorate perceives both parties to be on the ideological fringe of the political spectrum. The president's views are seen as having more prominence in policymaking than in Congress. In order to achieve moderate policy outcomes, the electorate "seems to behave as if it were balancing the policies or ideologies of opposing parties by placing them in control of different institutions" (Fiorina 1992, 73). In testing this idea, one study found that six measures of ideology and national issues were strongly connected to voters' presidential choices, but only one of the measures was related to choices for the House (Jacobson 1990b). Former House Speaker Tip O'Neill's statement that "all politics is local" seems to apply. House elections hinge more on local concerns and the quality of constituent service that a member performs (Born 1994).

In contrast, Gary Jacobson's "different expectations" concept assumes that rational voters want the best of all worlds. For the president who is expected to deliver public goods to all citizens, the Republican ideology of low taxes, less government spending, strong defense, and economic growth fits the voters' preferences. At the congressional level voters prefer that the program cuts needed to reduce spending be made in some other district than their own. As Jacobson (1990b, 119) states:

> Offered two presidential candidates, voters choose the one they think more likely to keep taxes low, and defense strong and govern competently. Offered two House candidates, voters choose the one they think more likely to deliver local benefits and protect their favorite spending.

Jacobson contends that Republican congressional candidates benefited greatly from several factors in the early 1990s, including redistricting, which added seats in the South and West, where the party is the strongest, and the creation of "majority-minority" seats in the South, which concentrated black Democratic votes into fewer districts (Jacobson and Kim 1996). Once Republicans gained control of both houses of Congress, and appeared ready to shut down the government in order to implement some of the policies contained the Contract with America, voters selected the presidential candidate most likely to preserve social programs such as Medicare and Social Security, and a Republican Congress to focus on cutting both taxes and government spending (Jacobson 1997, 155–156). Support for Jacobson's thesis has been found in several studies (Alvarez and Schousen 1993; Zupan 1991).

A third explanation asserts that voters are aware of existing ideological cleavages in the parties. Democratic members of Congress have been able to win in conservative states and districts by running apart from their party's presidential candidate, who is often more liberal than voters (Frymer, Kim, and Bimes 1997, 196). Voters can therefore make ideologically consistent choices by voting for the Republican presidential candidate and Democratic members of Congress. Thus GOP wins in 1994 were not due to voters' preferences for partisan balance but resulted from the inability of Democratic congressional candidates to separate themselves ideologically from the label given to the national party.

In sum, then, although ticket splitting has increased, the data also reveal a remarkable degree of party durability; in key presidential and congressional races only 15 to 25 percent will divide their choices. In seeking to account for ticket splitting, the most empirical support exists for Gary Jacobson's "different expectations" concept. The variety of ways in which votes can be divided, however, as well as the presence of third-party candidates, continue to complicate the search for an explanation.

Conclusion: The Changing Electorate

Various forms of political participation have remained steady over the last twenty years, with the exception of voting, where rates of participation have declined. Higher levels of income and less restrictive voter registration laws are factors associated with higher levels of turnout, but they have been swamped by such factors as greater social mobility and a younger population base.

Despite an increase in the number of people claiming "independent" status, voters continue to rally around the candidates of the two major parties. Party identification still remains a key predictor of how the electorate will vote, whereas splits within social and economic groups make the use of group membership less reliable as a voting predictor than in the past. Political scientists have also grouped voters by the divisions over values within the parties and have examined the problems this causes in building durable coalitions. In the next chapter we shall focus on the role of money in political campaigns.

6

Campaign Finance

During election periods hardly a week goes by without allegations of a candidate's violating campaign finance laws, and heated denials by the accused. Election financing is an important topic, but it is often discussed in terms that are difficult for the average citizen to understand. Whether intended or not, the combination of large amounts of money and the barrage of technical terms such as "federal" and "nonfederal" accounts, as well as "independent expenditures," produces in many citizens a "MEGO effect"—my eyes glaze over. To minimize this effect, our focus will be on four issues. The first issue is the effect of campaign contributions on representative government. Are campaign costs rising so rapidly that election outcomes are skewed toward those who can afford generous campaign contributions? In short, does the role of money in campaigns make a mockery of representative government? The answer to that question depends on whether influence in the nation's Capitol is viewed as unilateral (from donor to decisionmaker only) or bilateral (a two-way flow of influence).

A second issue is the goals reformers have in designing and implementing campaign finance laws. What are these goals, and are they internally consistent with one another? How have the goals been modified or negated by decisions of the courts and the Federal Election Commission (FEC)?

A third issue is the importance of campaign finance law for candidates, parties, and interest groups. For candidates, the finance laws are of critical importance in determining who runs for public office, the campaign strategy that is used, and who gets elected. More recent innovations such as soft money and issue advocacy ads provide new opportunities for parties and interest groups, but a firestorm of criticism can arise if the public perceives them as mechanisms allowing improper access to decisionmakers.

The final issue is campaign finance reform, a subject about which much is said but little is done. Several broad approaches to reform and their potential consequences are explored. Disagreement on how to modify existing law is again linked to a clash of goals among reformers, the courts, and the public.

Campaign Finance and Public Decisionmaking

Given the many charges of campaign finance abuse after each election, it is not surprising that most Americans view the role of money in politics as a *unilateral* or one-way application of influence. Funds flow from the individual or interest group to the decisionmaker for the purpose of improperly influencing public sector decisions. Philip Stern, whose book *The Best Congress Money Can Buy* reflects this view, suggests "the line between a campaign contribution and a bribe is only, as one senator put it, 'a hair's breadth'" (1988, 18). The assumption is that contributions drive the agenda of decisionmakers, assuring that donors' issues are discussed and, more often than not, decided according to the preferences of moneyed interests. Thus critics contend that existing methods of campaign finance strike at the very heart of representative government. The key principle, as stated by reform advocate Senator Russ Feingold (R–Wis.), is that "principal input should come from the people back home. . . . Money cuts the link between the representative and the represented" (Shulte and Enda 1997). Accepting the unilateral view of the role in money in politics leads to a call for dramatic changes in the way that campaigns are financed. Reducing the role of money in politics, it is assumed, will do much to restore that severed link between the representative and the represented.

A second view, which is the perspective adopted in this chapter, is that contributing money is a *bilateral* or exchange relationship (Sorauf 1992, 60–64; Schlozman and Tierney 1986; Keleher 1996). Campaign donors seek information, access, and influence on both current and future public policies. Legislators, in addition to using campaign donations to maximize constituent vote totals at the next election, have other goals, including using interest group members to lobby other congressional members to support a member's bill or using the legislator's upcoming vote to cause the interest group to modify its stance on an issue. As Frank Sorauf (1992, 63–64) describes the process:

> It is not only a transferring of goods or services for something of equal value. It is also a mutual relationship in which the actions, goals, and strategies of one participant interact with those of the other. The sum of all the exchanges creates a market that defines alternative options, a range of "prices," and the viable and negotiable terms of individual exchanges.

Although scholars know the general goals of both groups and candidates, the lack of knowledge about the specifics of alternative options, or the range of "prices," leads to a more cautious evaluation of campaign reform efforts. Candidates and groups will still seek to maintain an equal bargaining relationship and will use loopholes or unintended consequences of reforms to negotiate a new "price." Although campaign reform may be able to temporarily modify the most outrageous abuses of the system, expecting reform legislation to restore faith in representative government places too high a burden on the reform vehicle.

Campaign Finance Laws: History, Goals, and the Courts

The means by which money is raised and how it is spent in political campaigns have been issues since the beginning the Republic. At that time, campaign financing was handled by the candidates themselves, one major expense being the provision of whisky to increase turnout on election day. With the arrival of Jacksonian democracy in 1828, costs increased as the electorate broadened, and elements of modern campaigning such as parades and speeches at mass meetings were introduced. To pay for the campaigns, the Democratic party began to assess government workers, who in the period before civil service laws owed their positions to the patronage provided by the party machine. In the business expansion that occurred after the Civil War, wealthy individuals became a major financial source. In 1888 the Republican national chairman raised about 40 percent of the cost of the presidential campaign from manufacturers in his home state of Pennsylvania. The party's chair in 1896, Mark Hanna, made the process more systematic by assessing banks and corporations based on their financial worth (Mutch 1988, xvi–xvii). Several early attempts by Congress to deal with these excesses included the 1907 Tillman Act, which prohibited banks or corporations from contributing to candidates for federal office, and the 1910 Publicity Act and later amendments, which required disclosure of campaign receipts and expenditures after the election. Expenditures were limited to $5,000 for House races and $10,000 for Senate campaigns.

When a Supreme Court decision weakened the acts, Congress tried again with the Federal Corrupt Practices Act of 1925, which reenacted campaign disclosure provisions and raised spending limits for Senate races in larger states to $25,000. As Herbert Alexander points out, candidates needed to report only spending that was made with their "knowledge or consent" (1992), thus encouraging candidates to maximize ignorance about the activities of their committees. Few bothered to disclose the sums raised by their committees while donors avoided individual contribution limits by spreading the funds among multiple campaign committees. Such precautions may have been unnecessary, as no reports exist of any prosecutions under the act.

Understanding the goals of campaign reform legislation passed by Congress in recent years, the Federal Election Commission's interpretation of those laws, and Supreme Court rulings in this area is essential to any attempt to evaluate the current system or the numerous proposals to reform that system. The 1974 Federal Election Campaign Act Amendments and subsequent amendments had three overriding goals: to establish greater equality in political campaigns, to protect the integrity of the electoral system, and to increase participation in the political system by candidates, individual citizens, and political parties (Corrado 1992, 13–15).

Greater Equality in the Political System

In 1972 fifty-one millionaires contributed a total of $6 million to political campaigns, capped by W. Clement Stone's $2 million gift to Richard Nixon's campaign. Executives from twenty-one corporations were convicted of illegal $100,000 contributions. These sums raised questions of whether "fat cats" could buy access to key decisionmakers or even sway their votes in exchange for a sizable contribution. Even if blatant "vote buying" did not always occur, large contributions were seen as a form of "multiple voting" in which individuals and groups sought influence beyond the political system's central premise of "one person, one vote."

In response, the 1974 amendments to the Federal Election Campaign Act of 1971 (FECA) imposed strict limits on contributions by individuals and PACs, which are outlined in Table 6.1. The Federal Election Commission defines "federal expenditures" (or more commonly termed "hard" funds) as contributions used for "cash, equipment, or services which go directly to a candidate's campaign committee for use at its discretion." Once a candidate formally declares for a federal office, individuals can donate $1,000 apiece to a candidate's primary, runoff, and general election campaigns. The total cap is $25,000 on all federal campaigns during an election cycle,

TABLE 6.1   Federal Contribution Limits

Contribution	By a Person	By a Political Action Committee
To a candidate	$1,000 per election	$5,000 per election
To a political party (national committee)	$20,000 per election	$15,000 per year
To a political action committee	$5,000 per year	$5,000 per year
Overall limit	$25,000	No limit

SOURCE: Brooks Jackson, "Financing the 1996 Campaign: The Law of the Jungle," in Larry J. Sabato, ed., *Toward the Millennium* (Boston, Mass.: Allyn and Bacon, 1977). Copyright 1997 by Allyn and Bacon. Reprinted by permission.

of which no more than $5,000 may go to state parties, and not more than $20,000 to national parties. Similarly, PACs are limited to $5,000 apiece in direct contributions for any primary, runoff, and general election races, but they may give that amount to as many candidates as they want. Parties could spend $30,000 on House races, and $.02 times the voting-age population of a state for Senate elections. Further, to ensure that wealthier candidates did not bury opponents in an avalanche of spending, the amounts that a candidate could spend on his or her own campaign were limited. Finally, to equalize the resources available in presidential campaigns, public financing was established in which private contributions of $250 or less would be matched on a dollar-per-dollar basis by public funds.

Several of these provisions were quickly challenged in the case of *Buckley v. Valeo* (1976). The 1976 case raised a key constitutional issue: Does the First Amendment protect only the right to speak? Or is giving money to a campaign a form of protected speech? In a split decision the Court established the principle that contributing campaign funds is a form of speech protected by the First Amendment. The central purpose of the FECA, to prevent the real or imagined coercive effects of large contributions on candidates' actions once in office, was accepted by the justices. Thus provisions such as the $1,000 limit on individual contributions and $25,000 in total contributions did not significantly undermine the potential for "robust and effective" discussion of the issues and candidates, and left individuals free to effectively advocate their ideas through monetary contributions. Moreover, the restriction on contributions was narrowly targeted to an area in which corruption was most likely to occur: the exchange of money for a member's future vote.

However, the Court took a negative view of several other limits imposed by the 1974 amendments. Restrictions on using a candidate's own money or family money in campaigns imposed "significantly more severe restrictions" on protected freedoms of political expression and association and were struck down. "The candidate," the Court asserted, "no less than any other person, has a First Amendment right to engage in the discussion of public issues and to vigorously and tirelessly advocate his own election" (Lockard and Murphy 1980, 209–210). Moreover, the Court pointed out that a candidate spending his or her own money would be *less* likely to be influenced by campaign donations, thus helping to accomplish a second reform goal, that is, protecting the integrity of the political system.

Yet another issue raised in the case dealt with independent spending. Could individuals and groups engage in unlimited spending to promote a candidate as long as the money was not contributed directly to the campaign? In addressing this issue, the Court established the framework for "nonfederal expenditures" (or more commonly termed "soft" funds), which are funds raised outside the constraints of federal law but are spent on activities meant to influence the outcome of federal elections (Corrado 1997, 147). The Court stated that capping the amount individuals spent independently of candidates restricts the First Amendment right to engage in "vigorous advocacy" of ideas. As long as persons or groups do not "in express terms advocate" the election or defeat of a candidate, they can spend as much as they want. In a footnote the court defined the concept of "express advocacy" to mean using such terms as "vote for or against," "elect," "Smith for Congress," or "defeat." Groups could conduct "issue advocacy" campaigns and severely criticize a candidate's view of specific issues, as long as they avoided the "magic words" specified by the Court.

Improving the Integrity of the Political System

The second goal would be implemented by mandating a full and public disclosure of the funds raised and spent. Each candidate was required to register one central campaign committee, and that committee was held responsible for filing timely reports of campaign spending. The law operated under the premise that "sunlight is the best disinfectant." Because campaign committees knew the news media and hence the public would closely examine their campaign reports, the chances of spending irregularities would decrease. The law also assumes that information flowing to the public increases their knowledge of campaign finance practices, and allows for a more informed choice among the candidates. However, a substantial gap exists between the premise of the law and actual practice. Even among the "attentive public," who pay close attention to politics, information about campaign finance is scattered, is often provided well after the election, and is difficult to put in perspective. By the 1996 election, however, the Federal Election Commission provided a comprehensive website, and several independent sites were available to assist interested citizens. An evaluation of these sites in provided in Box 6.1.

Increased Participation in the Political System

A third goal of campaign finance reform was to increase participation in the political system by candidates, individual voters, and political parties. Ceilings on spending by presidential candidates were established in each state for the purpose of encouraging less well known individuals to run for president and to provide voters with a wider range of choices in presidential primaries. In the 1976 and 1978 campaigns, however, the intended effect was not accomplished. Voter participation was lower, and the limits on campaigns meant that candidates were less willing to spend on activities such as grassroots campaigning or party-building activities. Parties argued that they needed more financial resources to participate effectively in fed-

---

BOX 6.1   Campaign Finance Information Sites

Several sites offer ongoing information about campaign finance. Among the most important sites are the following:

1. Federal Election Commission <http://www.fec.gov>
   Prior to the 1996 election the FEC site was not well organized and was slow to provide detailed information. More recently the site has provided timely press releases as well as detailed information on candidate expenditures, PAC spending, soft money, and national party committee spending.
2. FEC Info <http://www.tray.com/fecinfo/>
   Nonpartisan federal candidate campaign finance information is provided by the previous webmaster of the Federal Election Commission's web page. Includes soft money database, presidential, House and Senate candidate fund-raising information.
3. Center for Public Integrity <http://www.publicintegrity.org>
   The site is a combination of political science and investigative journalism, for the purpose of encouraging educated debate on the issues. Includes assets held by candidates, honorarium information, and Indiana state campaign finance information.
4. Citizens Research Foundation <http://www.usc.edu/dept/CRF>
   CRF is a nonprofit organization committed to broadening public knowledge of political financing and election reform. The site provides access to recent publications, court decisions, legislation, initiatives, and research about political finance.

SOURCE: Adapted from "Enforcing Campaign Reform—Available Info," Center House Bulletin, *Center for the Study of the Presidency* (Fall 1996): 8.

---

eral and state elections. Congress responded in 1979 with revisions to the FECA that increased the flow of soft money. Expenditures for such "party-building" activities as voter registration, turnout drives, and grassroots activities (e.g., bumper stickers and yard signs) were exempted. The funds could also be used to pay for a portion of a party's overhead and administrative expenses. The parties needed only to establish "reasonable accounting systems" to determine what part of an activity should be paid for by such funds. Although the 1979 amendment specifically prohibited the use of soft money in broadcast advertising, later Federal Election Commission rulings allowed such spending if party themes or symbols were stressed, rather than a specific candidate. Common Cause petitioned the FEC to ban soft money in 1984, and as a result of a lawsuit filed by the group the Federal Election Commission determined in 1991 that parties must disclose soft money donations.

The Supreme Court eliminated one potential roadblock in the quest for soft money in the case of *Colorado Republican Federal Campaign Committee v. Federal Election Commission,* decided in June 1996. Nearly a decade earlier, Representative Timothy Wirth sought the Democratic party's nomination for a Colorado Senate seat. Before the Republicans chose a candidate, the state Republican party ran radio ads and printed fliers attacking Wirth's record. When the Federal Election Commission attempted to apply this spending to the overall limit in senatorial campaigns, the state Republican party argued it should be free to contribute any amount, just like political action committees, as long as it did not coordinate its efforts with the candidate. The Supreme Court agreed. "We do not see how a Constitution that grants to individuals, candidates and ordinary political committees the right to make unlimited independent expenditures could deny the right to political parties," wrote Justices Stephen Breyer, Sandra Day O'Conner, and David Souter (*Colorado Republican Federal Campaign Committee v. Federal Election Commission,* 1996). Three other justices in a concurring opinion were willing to go even further. Justices Antonin Scalia, Anthony Kennedy, and William Rhenquist stated that *any* limits on political party spending, whether coordinated with the candidate or not, violated the First Amendment's guarantee of freedom of speech. Justice Clarence Thomas urged fellow members to reverse *Buckley v. Valeo,* stating that contribution limits "infringe as directly and as seriously upon freedom of political expression as do expenditure limits" (*Colorado Republican Federal Campaign Committee v. Federal Election Commission,* 1996).

The Court's decision was important for several reasons. First, its willingness to protect political contributions as a form of speech increased the difficulty of enacting campaign reform in the Congress. More importantly, the parties were now free to spend unlimited amounts in the general election. New ground could be broken in the area of independent expenditures, and issue advocacy campaigns accelerated.

In sum, this section has suggested that reform advocates and the courts emphasize different values in the area of campaign finance. In reviewing legislation, the Supreme Court determined that the reformers' first goal of increased political equality must often yield to the value of freedom of speech. The Court's wider interpretation of the concept of speech set the stage for increased independent spending and issue advocacy campaigns. With an understanding of the goals of reformers and how the courts have modified finance laws, attention can be turned to trends in campaign finance.

Skyrocketing Campaign Costs or Underfunded Campaigns?

When the amounts expended for all offices are considered (Table 6.2), the rise in costs is dramatic. Over $4 billion was spent for political activities in 1996, and costs rose twenty-three times between 1960 and 1996. The 1980s

TABLE 6.2   Total Campaign Expenditures for All Offices, and Presidential
Offices in Presidential Years, 1960–1996 (in millions of dollars)

	All Offices		Presidential Office	
Year	Actual	Inflation Adjusted	Actual	Inflation Adjusted
1960	175	175	30.0	30.0
1964	200	191	60.0	57.3
1968	300	255	100.0	85.1
1972	425	301	138.0	97.7
1976	540	281	160.0	83.2
1980	1,200	431	275.0	98.8
1984	1,800	513	325.0	92.6
1988	2,700	676	500.0	125.1
1992	3,220	679	550.0	116.0
1996	4,000	761	700.0	130.0

NOTE: The figures in the category "all offices" include expenditures for ballot propositions.
The inflation-adjusted figures are derived from the consumer price indexes (yearly averages)
with 1960 as the base year.
SOURCES: Herbert E. Alexander and Anthony Corrado, *Financing the 1992 Election* (Ar-
monk, N.Y.: Sharpe, 1995), 6, and table 2.2. Reprinted by permission of M. E. Sharpe, Inc.,
Armonk, N.Y. 10504. "All offices" figure for 1996 is a *National Journal* estimate from
Jonathan Ruach, "Blow It Up," *National Journal*, March 29, 1997, 604; the "presidential of-
fice" figure is an estimate from the Citizens' Research Foundation.

saw a massive escalation of costs, with a 122 percent rise in 1980, followed
by 50 percent increases in both 1984 and 1988. In contrast, the 1990s show
relative restraint, with cost increases remaining below 25 percent.

The inflation-adjusted figures in Table 6.2 provide a broader context for
evaluation. The average increase for the 1960–1996 period was 20 percent
per year, not an unreasonable figure given the importance of media buys for
campaigns and the rising costs for all kinds of television advertising.

Frank Sorauf (1992) contends that charges of overspending on campaigns is one of the major "myths" of campaign finance. Former House
Speaker Newt Gingrich also called modern politics "underfunded" (Carney
1996b, 1521). One study finds that spending in congressional elections
comes to about $3 per eligible voter, with the total approximating one-half
of what the nation spent on potato chips in a year (Smith 1995). Moreover,
in an era when about of half of voters cannot identify their representative
in Congress, advocates contend that money is a proxy for information.
Whether the message is in the form of direct ads, advocacy ads, or independent expenditures, any increase in the number of messages leads to a
more informed electorate.

Critics of the current system quickly respond that the quality of information is the issue rather than the quantity. If the content is simply hurling

charges and countercharges, the result is a less enlightened electorate and lower participation rates. The impact of negative advertising on participation is considered in Chapter 7; but certainly the nation's rapid transition into an "information society" can ill afford to skimp on the distribution of political information.

Changing Sources of Campaign Finance: The Soft Money Revolution and the Parties

The major change that has taken place since 1980 is the increased importance of soft money in campaigns. As previously noted, "federal expenditures" or "hard" funds are given directly to a candidate's campaign committee, whereas "nonfederal expenditures" or "soft" money is meant to influence the outcome of elections. But the funds are not given directly to the candidate, and the spending cannot directly advocate voting for a candidate (Corrado 1997, 147).

Table 6.3 shows that since the 1980s, on average, Democrats have raised about half the hard money sums raised by Republicans. A part of the gap is due to the success of the Republican party in generating funds from small donors, who are defined as those giving $200 or less. During the 1980s the Republican committees were the innovators, and by the beginning of the decade they had developed over 2 million names for direct mail solicitations. Although the cost of generating names is high, and most of the mail never produces a reply, those who do respond positively can usually be counted on for future donations. Thus from 1991 to 1996 FEC records show the Republican National Committee gathered $198 million in donations under $200, more than double the Democratic National Committee's figure of $94 million.

The trend most evident in the table is the explosion in "soft" money or "nonfederal expenditures." Soft money accounted for only 16 percent of

TABLE 6.3   Party Hard and Soft Money Expenditures, 1991–1998
(in millions of dollars)

	Hard Money			Soft Money		
	Democrats	*Republicans*	*Total*	*Democrats*	*Republicans*	*Total*
1991–1992	171.9	256.1	428.0	32.9	46.2	79.1
1993–1994	137.8	234.7	372.5	50.4	48.4	98.8
1995–1996	214.3	408.5	622.8	121.8	149.7	271.5
1997–1998[a]	105.5	177.5	283.0	78.8	93.7	172.5

[a] Through October 14, 1998.
SOURCE: Federal Election Commission. Available at <www.fec.gov>.

party money expenditures in 1991–1992, but four years later the percentage jumped to 30 percent. Similarly, the amounts of soft money collected by both parties expanded nearly fourfold during the same period. Democrats, who had been badly outspent in this area in previous elections, increased soft money contributions to $121.8 million in 1996. Yet they continued to lag behind Republicans, whose coffers swelled to $149.7 million.

The rise in soft money is important for two reasons. First, its early use had a significantly positive effect in revitalizing many state parties from a state of atrophy in the early 1980s. Second, the national political parties have used these funds to indirectly assist congressional and presidential races. In doing so, many observers insist, they have made the strict regulations on direct contributions to candidates meaningless.

Republicans were the first to see the national implications of soft money, as in 1980 Reagan operatives took control of these funds in a few key states such as Texas and Ohio in order to stress key themes of the Reagan campaign. Initially the soft money amounts were rather low, with about $1.6 million spent on Reagan's behalf in 1980 (Alexander and Corrado 1995, 242). By the end of the 1980s, however, the $15 million in soft funds flowing to candidates of both parties was significant enough that Common Cause filed a lawsuit. Even though the lawsuit resulted in a subsequent FEC requirement in 1991 that parties disclose soft money contributions and expenditures, tracking how these funds are actually used is very difficult. Although party officials contend that the "money is spent on Mom and apple pie stuff" (Donovan 1993, 1198), a liberal interpretation of the law means the funds are employed for a wide range of activities. In one election the Democratic National Committee used the funds for the following (in descending order): 39 percent of the funds went toward administrative costs (such as sending campaign operatives and political consultants to assist in state races), coordinated campaigns (sharing costs for phone banks, door-to-door canvassing, etc.), generic media purchases ("Vote Democratic" campaign spots), transfers of money to state and local candidates, and "building funds" used to purchase recording facilities and computers.

Any evaluation of the phenomenon of soft money finds significant benefits and costs. First, one major benefit is the impact of soft funds on state parties. The money greatly assisted the state parties in revitalizing their organizations and moving into the era of modern campaigning. Computers were bought and software designed that allowed instant access to lists of party activists and voters (Adamy 1984; Jacobson 1985–1986; Herrnson 1988; Dwyre 1994b). Second, soft money can be seen as a natural reaction to the current system. If the amounts that can be given to candidates directly are unrealistically low, it is not surprising to see donors flock to this legal method (Donovan 1993, 1197).

Two of the most important costs that soft money imposes on the political system are found in the difficulty of tracking the money, and the contention that the funds are "fat cat" money designed to restore the unique access and influence of wealthy individual, corporate, and union donors. As to the first cost, only with great difficulty can one implement the advice allegedly given during the Watergate scandal by secret source "Deep Throat" to two *Washington Post* reporters: "Follow the money!" Broad definitions of how the money can be used leads to ingenious interpretations. Few can top the former chair of the Democratic Congressional Campaign Committee, who upon learning that building-fund expenses (including the cost of constructing the party's national headquarters) could be paid for by soft funds, ordered the furniture in the headquarters to be bolted to the floor to qualify as part of the "building" (Dwyre 1996, 411). When vague definitions are combined with the federal, state, and local avenues through which soft money can flow, this category of funds is more likely to provide continued employment for campaign finance specialists than enlightenment for the average citizen.

A second major cost is the contention that soft money is "fat cat" money. The Center for Responsive Politics, a nonpartisan research group, found that 50 percent of the soft money in the 1992 election came in the form of checks larger than $20,000 (Donovan 1993, 1196). Moreover, between 1992 and 1996 three corporations and two unions gave more than $1 million in soft money, thus reaching the amounts that spurred campaign reform efforts in the 1970s.

Finance Laws and Presidential Campaigns

The degree to which campaign finance law shapes election campaigns—who runs for the presidency, when they run, the amounts that are spent, and most importantly who gets the party's nomination—is difficult to overstate. Related issues include the mounting costs and the rigors of the "invisible primary," the rise of entrepreneurial candidates, and the implications for candidates of political parties being used as a conduit for soft money in presidential elections.

Since 1992 one of the major trends in "who runs" in recent elections has been the emergence of what Anthony Corrado (1997, 140) has termed the "entrepreneurial candidate" who is willing to forgo public financing and commit vast personal amounts to the presidential race. Entrepreneurial candidates have several initial advantages. They can focus on the message of the campaign and not be diverted by fund-raising responsibilities. The campaign can hire the best personnel and does not lack resources to buy crucial airtime. Candidates can promote messages they believe in rather than modify them to gain contributors. Once they attain stature and name recognition, the option exists for future elections of utilizing the more traditional route of public financing.

The prototype for entrepreneurial candidates is independent candidate Ross Perot, who in 1992 provided $63.3 million of his own money (and 93 percent of the campaign's funding) to obtain 19 percent of the vote. Considerable modification of the self-financing strategy occurred in 1996, however. Perot used $7–9 million of personal funds to get his party, the Reform party, organized and qualified for the ballot in most states. Because of his previous vote total, Perot qualified for $29 million in public funds in 1996, but the Federal Election Commission determined it was Perot the "Independent" who qualified for the funds and not the Reform party, which did not exist in 1992. After former Colorado governor Dick Lamm announced he would seek the Reform party nomination, Perot retained the nomination and stayed within the guidelines to receive public funding. The 8 percent of the vote that he received in 1996 assures the Reform party of a place on the ballot in most states in 2000, as well as 50 percent of the public funds given to the major-party candidates.

Assuming the role of entrepreneurial hopefuls for the GOP nomination in 1996 were Malcolm S. (Steve) Forbes and tire manufacturer Maurice (Morrey) Taylor, who loaned their campaigns $37.5 million (90 percent of the total receipts), and $6.5 million (99.9 percent of receipts) respectively. Both candidates spent huge sums for the number of votes received ($408 for each Forbe vote and $725 for Taylor in the pivotal Iowa caucus) and provide striking contrasts in the degree to which the use of personal money can garner public acceptance. Forbes finished first only in Delaware and Arizona, but his theme of "hope, opportunity, and growth" resonated with Republican primary election voters, and his call for a 15 percent "flat tax" was later incorporated into candidate Bob Dole's call for tax cuts. Taylor's message did not catch on with early primary voters. Presidential primary races now resemble congressional and state races. Personal wealth is playing a greater role in determining who can credibly run for office, who can saturate the airwaves with their message, and which issues come to play a central role in the election.

Candidates who chose the traditional route of public funding were limited in 1996 to $37.09 million for the primary elections and an equal amount for the general election. Of that, $30.91 million was allocated for various campaign costs, plus an additional 20 percent for the costs of fundraising. Moreover, federal candidates agreed to spending limits within each state. For Republican hopefuls such as Senator Phil Gramm (R–Tex.) and Lamar Alexander, campaign law created the formidable obstacle of what Republican consultant Stuart Stevens terms the "invisible primary" (Jackson 1997, 230). The invisible primary occurs in the year before the first scheduled primary in New Hampshire. In 1996 the first federal matching funds did not become available until January, but campaign experts estimated that to be competitive, candidates had to raise at least $20 million in 1995 in order to build strong campaign organizations in fifty states and buy media to gain name recognition. Raising that amount more quickly with $5,000 infusions from PACs is a tempting strategy. Because PACs prefer to wait for a front-runner to emerge, both Gramm and Alexander raised less than $1 million from this source. If, for example, a campaign's goal is to have 10,000 donors give the maximum $1,000, only half of the $20 million needed would be generated. How realistic is a goal of 10,000 contributors? The Bush campaign in 1992 did convince 18,000 donors to give the maximum, but George Bush was the incumbent president, which eased the burden of fund-raising considerably. Although 1988 Republican candidate Pat Robertson demonstrated that it was possible to raise $30.9 million largely in small donations, few candidates could match his extensive direct mailing list. In Phil Gramm's case, the $20 million goal in 1995 was reached by transferring funds from his senatorial campaign committee and spending long hours making phone calls. Lamar Alexander spent a third of his time in fund-raising activities but fell short of the mark by raising only $14 million. Both candidates met their match in Bob Dole, who collected $23 million during the invisible primary.

At the general election stage, campaign finance law has a major effect on candidates' strategy, particularly for challengers. If the challenger spends heavily in the early primary states to lock up the nomination, funds for the rest of prenomination period can be tight. Such was the case for Bob Dole, who by the end of April was perilously close to the $37.09 million limit. Staff reductions, as well as all kinds of creative accounting techniques, were used to avoid exceeding the limit, including a "yard sale" at which items ranging from two-way radios to VCRs were sold raise $1.2 million. Thus Dole could afford no television advertising between April and the nomination at the end of August (Jackson 1997, 236). The Dole message was not totally closed out, however, as his media consultants also designed the Republican party's issue advocacy ads paid for by soft money. Conversely, if the incumbent has no serious challengers within the party, the flexibility exists to preserve most of the prenomination money for the general election period or to spend selectively based on the perceived strength of the challengers. The Clinton campaign followed the latter strategy and had $20 million left to spend during the time the Dole campaign had no funds for its own ads.

Federal election law allows each party to spend about $12 million in coordinated activities to promote their presidential candidates. These sums, however, represent only a small fraction of the money that parties can pour into the campaigns. The use of soft funds for "party-building" activities and issue advocacy ads, along with the use of independent expenditures, all greatly enhance the role the national parties play in presidential elections.

At the national level a rough division of labor exists, with the Republican National Committee (RNC) and Democratic National Committee (DNC) concentrating on raising funds for general party-building activities and for presidential campaigning while both parties' National Congressional Committees focus on House and Senate races.

Fund-raising is clearly "job 1" for both parties, and their level of success is evident in Table 6.4. For Republicans, the 1996 total amounts spent by all of the national committees grew by 115 percent compared to 1992; Democrats were just as successful with a 113 percent increase over the period. As for the actual sums raised, the pattern we have observed is that Republicans are far more skillful at mobilizing support than are Democrats. Table 6.4 shows that in 1991–1992 only a small gap separated the RNC and DNC in soft money fund-raising. Both parties made this a priority in 1996, taking in nearly triple their amounts of 1992, and Democrats trailed the GOP by only $14 million. The infamous "spending gap" did not disappear, however; it simply shifted to the area of hard funds, where the RNC outspent its Democratic counterpart by $87 million.

To generate the sums displayed in Table 6.4, the parties resorted to fund-raising extravaganzas such as the RNC black-tie dinner in January 1996 that netted a record $16 million dollars and the DNC national presidential gala that provided $12 million in one night. Of course not all of that money is available to support candidates; the old adage that "it takes money to make money" applies to the parties as well. Haley Barbour, the chair of the Republican National Committee, estimated that $61 million was spent on fund-raising in 1996 alone. Particularly costly were direct mail solicitations to small donors (Jackson 1997, 243).

Although soft funds allowed the national parties to play a greater role in campaigns, the massive amounts involved raised some disturbing questions. How were the funds raised? How was the money that was transferred to presidential campaigns or to the state level eventually spent? Did the use of soft money in issue ads simply push the envelope in distinguishing between hard and soft spending, or did it effectively break any existing boundaries between the two? Just as important as the way in which sums are raised and spent by the national parties is the degree to which campaign law heightens the role of national parties in campaigns. Due to the Court decisions and FEC interpretations previously discussed, the parties are important not only as a source of finance but as a strategic player. The national committees must coordinate their efforts not only with candidates but with state parties to take full advantage of the ambiguity in the law when funds are transferred between levels in our federal system.

TABLE 6.4 National Party Disbursements, 1991–1992 and 1995–1996[a] (in millions of dollars)

	1995–1996	1991–1992		1995–1996	1991–1992
Republican National Committee (RNC)			Democratic National Committee (DNC)		
Federal (hard)	193.0	81.9	Federal (hard)	105.6	65.0
Nonfederal (soft)	114.9	33.6	Nonfederal (soft)	100.4	28.3
National Republican Senatorial Committee (NRSC)			Democratic Senatorial Campaign Committee (DSCC)		
Federal (hard)	66.0	71.3	Federal (hard)	30.8	25.5
Nonfederal (soft)	29.3	7.7	Nonfederal (soft)	14.1	0.5
National Republican Congressional Committee (NRCC)			Democratic Congressional Campaign Committee (DCCC)		
Federal (hard)	73.6	34.3	Federal (hard)	26.4	12.6
Nonfederal (soft)	28.7	6.2	Nonfederal (soft)	11.8	4.0

[a] Does not include transfers among listed committees.
SOURCE: Federal Election Commission. Available at: <www.fec.gov>.

The legal ambiguities of soft money afford the parties tremendous flexibility and a greater presence in national campaigns, but the vagueness in the law can be a two-edged sword for parties and their politicians. A good example of the two-edged nature of soft money can be found in the experiences of the Clinton administration and the Democratic National Committee in the 1996 campaign. Still smarting from the Republican takeover of the Congress in 1994 and fearing a Republican sweep in 1996, Clinton vowed to dramatically increase the party's soft money funds. On a memo from his chief fund-raiser, the president wrote that he was "ready to start overnights (sleep overs in the Lincoln Bedroom) right away" and ordered the fund-raiser to "get other names at $100,000 or more, $50,000 or more" (Mitchell 1997).

When reports of the White House "sleep overs" surfaced in the press after the election, the public perceived a connection between the contributions and later political favors. In his 1992 book *Putting People First* the president termed it deplorable when "political action committees, industry lobbies and cliques of $100,000 donors buy access to Congress and the White House." Yet in 1996 he found it necessary to state at one point that "the Lincoln bedroom was never 'sold'" ("President's Remarks" 1997). Moreover, both President Clinton and Vice President Gore acknowledged contacting soft money donors on White House phones, but Gore claimed his calls were legal because they were made on a Democratic National Committee telephone calling card.

In their attempt to maximize fund-raising, the White House and the Democratic Party failed to exercise adequate oversight over who the donors were. Congressional hearings were held in response to allegations that the People's Republic of China, hoping to influence American politicians, funded middlemen who then gave soft money contributions to the DNC. Although the committee did not reach any solid conclusions about foreign influence on the election, the DNC elected to return over $3.6 million of funds from "suspicious" sources ("Democratic Party Returns More Suspect Donations" 1997). Moreover, in 1997 alone the Democratic party spent $11 million defending itself in investigations into its fund-raising, adding substantially to the party's debt burden ("Campaign Finance Legal Fight Buries Democratic Party in Debt" 1997).

Just as controversial are questions about how soft money is used. The first strategy of both national parties is to convert as much soft money into hard as possible, since "hard" money is a precious commodity right before the general election. Although this switch is legal, in a number of instances in 1996 the DNC did not seek permission from individuals before making the conversion into hard money. As a result, at least sixty-two people were in technical violation of the law that forbids giving over $25,000 in hard money over the two-year election cycle (Van Atta 1997). Thus the Democratic National Committee risked alienating core supporters in the scramble to raise and convert soft funds.

Having national or state parties pay as many presidential campaign bills as possible is a second strategy. To do this, the candidates must make the case that their appearance is not to promote their election but to strengthen the party or support another candidate. When George Bush addressed Unity 88 conferences in Denver, Cincinnati, and Atlanta in 1988, the tab was picked up by national and state parties. The Federal Election Commission decided the president had stepped over the line when his speech referred to the profound "choice our nation will make this November," and it fined the Bush-Quayle Committee (Fritsch 1996).

Yet another major use for party soft money is to purchase issue advocacy ads. The first step in this "follow the money" saga is the transfer of money to state party coffers. For example, DNC and Clinton strategists budgeted $42.4 million in soft money for Clinton issue ads; of that amount at least $32 million (and perhaps as much as $41.6 million) was transferred to state party committees for this purpose (Abramson and Wayne 1997). In one case the Pennsylvania Democratic Party, which had $200,000 in debts from the 1994 election, received $2.8 million over a six-month period. The RNC also spent $30.5 million on issue advocacy ads in 1996, with $18 million going for Bob Dole ads. At the second stage, the money arrives at the state level with specific instructions on which media consultants should get the contract to produce the ads. The Pennsylvania Democratic Party paid $2.7 million to the media consulting firm of Squier, Knapp & Ochs Communications (Barnes 1996b). Not surprisingly, the favored media consultants were the same ones the presidential candidates used—Bob Squier for Bill Clinton and the DNC, and Don Sipple and Mike Murphy for Bob Dole. Sipple and Murphy even recycled parts of Dole presidential campaign ads for use in the state-level efforts.

Once the ads are produced, state parties are instructed by the media consultant on where and when to run the ads. A disclaimer is added at the end of the advertisement, "authorized and paid for by the state party of . . . ," but other than approval before broadcast, the state parties play almost no role in the production or placement of the ads (Barnes 1996b, 1041). The reason for this elaborate transfer mechanism is the need to conserve resources. Both parties interpreted the law to mean that only 35 percent of the cost of an issue ad could be paid for with soft funds if either national committee directly bought the airtime. However if either the RNC or DNC transferred funds to the state level for that group to buy the airtime, from 50 to 78 percent of an ad's cost could come from soft money, depending on the state (Jackson 1997, 245).

The Clinton strategy for the soft funds disregarded the conventional wisdom that few people pay attention to politics sixteen months before the election. Democratic issue advocacy ads ran three times a week in such key electoral college states as California, Pennsylvania, Florida, and Ohio. By election time the Democrats had spent $85 million to create what a key campaign strategist called a "fully advertised" presidency.

If issue ads are crafted by the media consultants of the presidential candidates, feature the name, face, and program of the candidate, are paid for by national committee funds transferred to the state level, and are placed on the air according to instructions from the media consultant of the national party committee, has the barrier between hard and soft money been effectively broken? Media consultants cling to the exact wording of the Buckley decision and avoid using such terms as "support" or "vote for." Instead, the ads employ such terms as "the president's plan" or "tell President Clinton" prominently in the ads. Yet the candidates realize that campaign law creates a kind of legal fiction. Bob Dole was very candid when he was asked about generic or issue advertising before a television hookup of American Broadcasting Corporation television affiliates: "It doesn't say Bob Dole for President. . . . It never mentions the word I'm—it never says I'm running for president. I hope that's fairly obvious, since I'm the only one in the picture" (Jackson 1997, 239). Auditors from the Federal Election Commission found the fiction to be illegal, charging that the Clinton and Dole campaigns both benefited from issue advertising paid for by their political parties and that the value of the ads should have counted against their spending totals. Their recommendation, that the Dole and Clinton campaigns be asked to repay $17.7 million and $7 million respectively, was never implemented (Abramson 1998).

In sum, the parties have taken considerable risks and have demonstrated great tenacity in pursuing soft funds. The depth of the parties' dependence on such funds is suggested by the editorial cartoon in Figure 6.1. Due to the continuous escalation of soft money spending and the view that this money guts existing regulations on spending, changes in soft money rules are a centerpiece of many campaign reform proposals.

Congressional Races

The basic trends in congressional campaign spending can be seen in Table 6.5. Comparing the 1979–1980 and the 1995–1996 cycles, the amount spent on campaigns rose from $239 million to $765.3 million. House races show the greatest increase in magnitude, as the amounts in 1995–1996 were three and a half times that of the earliest figures. For House races in two cycles (1983–1984 and 1993–1994) candidates got a break, as costs declined slightly. The Senate showed more variation, with total spending registering less in three cycles. The amounts spent in the 1995–1996 Senate races declined, for example, even though there were a record number of

FIGURE 6.1 "They Always Come Running" by Steve Breen. © 1997 by Copley News Service.

open seats. In part this retreat in spending levels is explained by a large number of seats in small-population states, where campaign spending patterns are usually less than in the more populated states. Republican House and Senate campaigns increased spending by 12.7 percent in 1996, whereas spending by Democrats remained unchanged from 1994 levels (Federal Election Commission 1996). Examining the figures in terms of inflation-adjusted dollars, however, alters the conception of surging campaign costs. House races in four of the election cycles registered declines of 0.7 percent to 7.4 percent.

The two years in which increases of 50 percent or more occurred in House contests need to be placed in context. Both the 1981–1982 and the 1991–1992 cycles were elections in which candidates faced changes wrought by congressional redistricting. In the worst case, two incumbents could be placed in the same district, inviting an escalation of costs as the seasoned fund-raisers square off. At best an incumbent could be faced with voters who are unfamiliar with one's name and record, which also raises campaign costs. Accentuating the change for the 1991–1992 cycle, a number of states in the South and West responded to pressure from the Justice Department by creating districts in which minorities composed a majority of the voting population. The explosion in the number of House candidates, from 1,370 in 1990 to 2,041 in 1992, was a major reason for the dramatic increase in costs. But in the Senate, redistricting does not occur. What, then, accounts for the 35 and 51 percent increases in costs in the 1981–1982 and 1991–1992 cycles? In both time periods the number of open seats increased dramatically, as did the number of Senate aspirants, for example, climbing from 151 in 1989–1990 to 249 in 1991–1992. The funds invested by the larger number of candidates account for much of the increase in these two cycles.

Although it is possible to apply inflation-adjusted dollars to the cold aggregate figures in Table 6.5 and argue that the costs of campaigning have not gotten out of hand, candidates view the reality of fund-raising quite differently. In 1994 jubilant Republican freshmen flocked to Washington, D.C., only to be told by party leaders that to prepare for the next election they had to generate $100,000 in funds in their first year ($200,000 if they were in a very competitive election). Given the average amounts raised for Senate seats ($4.3 million) and House seats ($643,000), the question became how to generate the $14,000 and $6,200 a week needed for the Senate and House contests respectively. Although large fund-raisers provide part of the resources, a portion of the money must be generated though a process many candidates find both difficult and distasteful, "cold calling" or "dialing for dollars." To avoid violating the federal law prohibiting fund-raising solicitations on federal property, Republicans, for example, are frequent visitors to Suite 2 at the National Republican Congressional

TABLE 6.5   Total Spending by Candidates in All Congressional Races, 1979–1998[a]

Election Cycle	Number of Candidates	Total $s Spent	Senate $s	House $s	Percentage Change from Previous Election		Average Dollars Raised	
					Senate	House	Senate	House
1979–1980	–	239.0	102.9	136.0	–	–	1,079,000	148,000
1981–1982	2,240	342.4	138.4	204.0	+34.5	+50.0	1,771,000	223,000
1983–1984	2,036	374.1	170.5	203.6	+23.2	-0.2	2,274,000	241,000
1985–1986	1,873	450.9	211.6	239.3	+24.1	+17.5	2,722,000	280,000
1987–1988	1,792	457.7	201.2	256.5	-4.9	+ 7.2	2,649,000	282,000
1989–1990	1,759	446.3	180.4	265.8	-10.3	+ 3.6	2,662,000	308,000
1991–1992	2,950	678.3	271.6	406.7	+50.6	+53.0	3,900,000	544,000
1993–1994	2,376	725.2	319.0	406.2	+17.4	-0.1	4,600,000	516,000
1995–1996	2,605	765.3	287.5	477.8	-9.9	+17.6	4,300,000	643,000
1997–1998[a]	1,747	780.7	312.9	468.7	+16.0	-5.0	2,580,000	338,000

[a] Through October 14, 1998.

SOURCES: Herbert E. Alexander and Anthony Corrado, *Financing the 1992 Election* (Armonk, N.Y.: Sharpe, 1995), table 7.1, p. 178. Reprinted by permission from M. E. Sharpe, Inc. Armonk, N.Y. 10504. 1993–1994 and 1995–1996 data are from Federal Election Commission, "Congressional Fundraising Up Again in 1996," April 14, 1997, available at <www.fec.gov/press/canye96.htm> and "Party Fundraising Slows for 98 Elections," October 29, 1998, available at <www.fec.golv/press/pregsum.htm>.

Committee headquarters, where they line up business cards from PACs, philosophical allies, and others and then start dialing to make their pitch for dollars. Former senator Paul Simon notes that visitors to the Capitol are often disappointed to see few members on the floor; the reality is that "there are more senators on the telephones, trying to raise money, than there are on the floor of the United States Senate" (Barton 1996, A22).

Who Provides the Funds?

Congressional campaign funding comes from three main sources. First, contrary to public perception, individuals rather than well-heeled groups provide most of the funds for congressional campaigns. Second, despite limitations imposed by federal law, groups have found ways to magnify their influence through both direct means such as bundling and indirect means such as soft money. Third, the amounts that political parties give directly to candidates are very small. But by acting as a conduit for soft money and through spending made "on behalf of" candidates, the parties have influence on campaign finance beyond that suggested by the meager amounts they contribute directly to candidates.

Individuals are by far the largest source of funds for congressional campaigns. As noted in Table 6.6, they provided nearly two-thirds of the funds for Senate races and over one-half of the money for House contests in 1996. In the Senate from 1974 to 1990, donations from individuals declined from 76 percent of the total in 1974 to 65 percent in 1990. Since that time, this source of donations has remained relatively steady, with individuals supplying 61 to 66 percent of all funds. A similar pattern occurred in the House from 1974 to 1990, with individuals providing 73 percent of all funds in 1974 but 45 percent in 1990. Since that time, the amount of funds coming from individuals has slowly increased, as the amount received from PACs has dropped off.

Although contributions are limited to $1,000 per election under campaign finance law, no shortage of innovation exists in magnifying the influence of each donation, as individuals in effect "bundle" their contributions. This is done through donors who evidently have such strong family bonds that their aunts and uncles, in-laws, and even children are known to give $1,000 on the same day to the same candidate. When the checks are delivered in one group, or "bundle," careful note is made of the individual responsible for such a substantial infusion of money to the campaign effort.

In Table 6.6, PACs reached their highest proportion of funds provided in 1988. In that year they accounted for 43 percent of House funds and 26 percent of Senate contributions. Since that time, the share of PAC-generated funds has dropped slightly to 35 percent of funds for House races and 18

TABLE 6.6   Sources of Contributions to Congressional General Election
Campaigns, 1974–1998

Year	_Percentage of House Funds Raised from_				
	Individuals	_Parties_[a]	_PACs_	_Candidates_	_Unknown_
1974	73	4	17	6	n.a.
1976	59	8	23	9	n.a.
1978	61	5	25	9	n.a.
1980	67[c]	4	29	n.a.	n.a.
1982	63[c]	6	31	n.a.	n.a.
1984	51	3	39	6	n.a.
1986	52	2	39	7	n.a.
1988	49	2	43	6	n.a.
1990	45	1	42	6	6
1992	49	<1	38	9	4
1994	52	<1	37	8	3
1996	55	<1	35	7	3
1998[b]	54	<1	35	6	4

Year	_Percentage of Senate Funds Raised from_				
	Individuals	_Parties_[a]	_PACs_	_Candidates_	_Unknown_
1974	76	6	11	1	6
1976	69	4	15	12	n.a.
1978	76	2	14	8	n.a.
1980	77[c]	2	21	n.a.	n.a.
1982	81[c]	1	18	n.a.	n.a.
1984	68	1	25	6	n.a.
1986	68	1	25	6	n.a.
1988	67	1	26	6	n.a.
1990	65	<1	23	5	7
1992	66	<1	25	5	5
1994	61	<1	16	20	3
1996	64	<1	19	13	4
1998	63	<1	18	11	7

[a] Does not include party expenditures "on behalf of" candidates.
[b] Through October 14, 1998.
[c] Includes candidates' contributions to their own campaigns, loans, and transfers.
SOURCES: 1974–1986 percentages are from Gary C. Jacobson, _The Politics of Congressional Elections,_ 3d ed. (New York: HarperCollins, 1992), 65. 1988–1998 percentages are from Federal Election Commission, "Financial Activity of General Election Coingressional Candidates, 1988–1998." (Washington, D.C.: Federal Election Commission, 1998). Available at: <www.fec.gov>. Federal Election Commission, "Financial Activity of General Election of Congressional Candidates—House," available at: <www.fec.gov/finance/hse30/ng.htm>. Federal Election Commission, "Financial Activity of General Election Congressional Candidates—Senate 1988–1996," available at <www/fec.gov/finance/sen30/ng.htm>.

percent for the Senate. Some of the major PAC contributors will be discussed in Chapter 8. Our focus here is on how groups use techniques such as bundling to extend their influence and how members of Congress have created their own leadership PACs to gain leverage over an unwieldy Congress.

The practice of bundling can also consist of having people give their individual contribution to an interest group rather than to the candidate directly. Legally, the interest group representative is simply presenting the collected or "bundled" individual checks to the candidate, but an unstated implication is that the interest group should receive credit for raising the funds. EMILY's List, a political network for Democratic women who support abortion rights, is an ardent supporter of bundling. The group believes that raising funds early is the key to political success for women, and its name is an acronym—Early Money Is Like Yeast (it makes dough rise). The group argues strongly that the practice must be retained, as candidates must know the money is coming from concerned women and other supporters of the group's goals. EMILY's List argues that bundling is a crucial vehicle through which reform-minded women can in turn be elected to Congress.

Key lawmakers in Congress also employ "leadership PACs" as a tool for gaining some leverage over members who are increasingly beholden to neither party nor leadership. Senate majority leader Trent Lott's New Republican Majority Fund gave $1.3 million to forty-three GOP Senate and House candidates in 1996; House representative Dick Armey's Majority Leader's Fund weighed in with $1.6 million in receipts (Wayne 1997a). Not to be outdone, former Speaker Newt Gingrich's fund-raising innovation was the "Incumbent Protection Fund." Members made payments to the fund based on seniority, and the money was redistributed to members in tight races. Gingrich distributed nearly $2 million to House members in 1996 from his own campaign money and his Monday Morning PAC (Wayne 1997b).

One other use of PACs makes it very difficult to track the exact amount spent on congressional races because millions of dollars go unreported through state-based political action committees, or "backdoor PACs." Members of Congress establish the state PACs for the stated purpose of helping state and local candidates. Weaker state party organizations created a vacuum that congressional members' state PACs were happy to fill. Candidates cannot use state PACs to pay for their own campaign-related activities, but many "party-building" activities are permitted, such as paying for travel expenses and cellular phone services, or even providing cash incentives to activists who turn out voters. Although these organizations do help rebuild state parties, the line between permitted party-building activities and campaign law violation is very thin. If the state parties pay for a plane ride home and a pancake breakfast for a member, the campaign receives no money directly, but the added exposure is beneficial to the member's re-election chances (Carney 1996a, 468).

One example of a backdoor PAC, which raised legal and ethical questions about how far to stretch the party-building notion, is GOPAC, formerly headed by Newt Gingrich. GOPAC was originally funded by establishing six tax-exempt foundations, including the Abraham Lincoln Opportunity Foundation and the Progress and Freedom Foundation. The latter foundation sponsored a weekly cable television program that beamed a college course taught by Gingrich, Renewing American Civilization, by satellite to one hundred sites across the country. Beginning with the 1989–1990 election cycle, GOPAC contributed millions of dollars to state and local candidates for the avowed goal of eventually winning a House Republican majority. The strategy of having a "farm team" of seasoned state-level candidates who subsequently run for national office was validated in 1994, when Republicans gained control of both houses of Congress. Thirty-three Republicans elected that year were GOPAC alumni.

A subsequent House Ethics Subcommittee investigation of GOPAC activities focused on how the money was raised more than on who received it. The Ethics Subcommittee report stated that Gingrich should have known the information given on GOPAC's state-level activities was "inaccurate, incomplete, and unrealistic" but concluded that the former Speaker did not intentionally mislead the subcommittee. Because Gingrich failed to get proper legal advice in arranging financing for his foundations and because his actions did not "reflect credibly on the House of Representatives," he was fined $300,000. Although the case served as a warning to members of Congress about the hazards of financing through tax-exempt foundations, it did not establish any clear guidelines as to what is appropriate spending by federal candidates at the state level, and what is not. The lack of clarity also hinders enforcement of election laws by many state officials, who see congressional member–controlled state PACs as falling under the responsibility of the Federal Election Commission.

Political Parties and Congressional Campaign Finance

Political parties play an important role in campaign finance because their contributions are more likely to fund nonincumbent candidates when compared to individuals or PACs. The result should be more competition for public office. The four party organizations charged with distributing party funds to congressional candidates, often termed the "Hill Committees," include the Democratic Senatorial Campaign Committee (DSCC), the Democratic Congressional Campaign Committee (DCCC), the National Republican Senatorial Committee (NRSC), and the National Republican Congressional Committee (NRCC). When direct contributions to candidates are considered, the political parties are a minuscule source of funds for congressional candidates. As shown in Table 6.6, both parties provided 6 percent of funds for House candidates in 1982, and 2 percent for Senate hopefuls in 1980. Since that time, as shown in Table 6.7, direct contributions to congressional candidates have varied from $1.5 million to $3.7 million. Given the escalation of campaign costs, these funds currently do not even provide 1 percent of congressional campaign expenditures.

In addition to the direct spending defined above, the parties can draw limited amounts from their hard money accounts for two other types of expenditures: "coordinated" and "independent." Coordinated expenditures are also known as "on-behalf-of" spending, or in FEC jargon as "441a(d)" expenditures. The limit for these funds is based on a formula adjusted for inflation. Under this form, parties may seek a candidate's input on how best to use the funds, but the party retains ultimate control over the actual expenditures.

Independent expenditures, the result of the Colorado Republican Federal Campaign Committee case previously discussed, allow party organizations that do not coordinate their activities with candidates to engage in unlimited spending. Both "on-behalf-of" and independent expenditures give the

TABLE 6.7   Political Party Spending in Congressional Elections, 1986–1998 (in millions of dollars)

	1986	1988	1990	1992	1994	1996	1998[a]
Democrats							
Contributions	1.7	1.7	1.5	1.9	2.2	2.2	0.7
"on-behalf-of" spending	9.0	17.9	8.7	28.0	21.1	22.6	6.7
Independent expenditures	–	–	–	–	–	1.5	0.4
Total	10.7	19.6	10.2	29.9	23.3	26.3	7.8
Republicans							
Contributions	3.4	3.4	2.9	3.0	2.8	3.7	1.6
"on-behalf-of" spending	14.3	22.7	10.7	33.8	20.4	31.0	4.3
Independent expenditures	–	–	–	–	–	10.0	–
Total	17.7	26.1	13.6	36.8	23.2	44.7	5.9
Grand total	28.4	45.7	23.8	66.7	46.5	71.0	13.7

[a] Through October 14, 1998.

SOURCE: Federal Election Commission, "Fundraising Escalates for Political Party Committees," October 27, 1998. Available at: <www.fec.gov/press/ptypre98.htm>.

parties far more leverage than simply handing over the cash. Thus a rough indicator of the parties' electoral influence is their ability to increase the proportion of money going to the coordinated and independent expenditures categories. The figures in Table 6.7 repeat a familiar theme—in every year except 1994, Republican Hill Committees spent substantially more to promote their candidates than did their Democratic counterparts. Comparing 1988 to 1992 shows that both parties were able to increase their coordinated spending by over $10 million, but neither party was able to keep up this pace in 1996. Republicans allocated nearly $3 million less in coordinated expenses, but this was partially compensated for by $10 million in the new category of independent spending. Democrats, however, designated $5.4 million less in coordinated funds and generated only $1.5 million in independent expenditures.

When all three types of party expenditures (direct, coordinated, and independent) are taken together, the parties only accounted for 10 percent of all money spent on congressional elections in 1992 and 9 percent in 1996. Party funds may be limited in amount, but the parties should be able to promote competition in campaigns because they are more likely to give to nonincumbents than are individuals or PACs (Dwyre 1994b; Sorauf 1992, 217). Given limited resources, parties should maximize the number of seats by giving to challengers in closely contested races in which a cash infusion could make the difference; marginal challengers are a less wise investment (Jacobson 1980, 1985–1986; Kernell 1986). Parties are not always able to follow this rational strategy in practice, due to informational, political, and campaign finance constraints. Parties often lack perfect information about which candidates will prove to be competitive, and they will inevitably give to some who are not strong challengers. Moreover, a political constraint facing parties is that incumbents seldom feel safe no matter what their previous margin of victory was, so funds are provided to maintain rapport with key officeholders. A final factor affecting party strategy is the incentives provided by campaign finance laws. In the 1991–1992 and 1995–1996 cycles, Republican congressional committees raised greater amounts of hard funds, which they distributed to competitive challengers. With fewer hard dollars available, Democrats conserved that resource in a strategy similar to a shell game at a county fair. They chose to use a greater portion of their soft money for administrative expenses, and then under obscure provisions of the law were required to contribute to nonfederal candidates as well. With over a half million dollars going to 241 state and local candidates in thirty states during the 1991–1992 cycle, Democrats spent only 55 percent of congressional soft money on competitive candidates (Dwyre 1996, 413–414). Party money is still more likely to foster competition in elections, when compared with contributions by individuals and

PACs, but political realities and electoral law have required Democratic congressional committees to modify a purely rational strategy.

State Legislative Races

Because a number of states do not systematically gather campaign finance data, and the reporting of figures from those states that do collect data is often not timely, generalizations are difficult. In only a few states, such as Indiana, is information on state races computerized and readily available to researchers. The National Conference of State Legislatures groups legislatures into three types based on length of the session, salaries, and size of staff. "Professional" legislatures work full-time, pay high salaries, and have a large staff; at the opposite end, "citizen" legislatures are part-time, have low pay, and require a small staff; "hybrid" legislatures fall in between. In states with professional legislatures, such as California, Illinois, Massachusetts, New York, and Pennsylvania, campaign costs have escalated the most. California, which pays legislators $72,000 per year, has seen the average cost of state house races rise from $93,000 in 1978 to $229,000 in 1986 to $512,000 in 1990. By 1996 average spending had risen to over $600,000, which places the state races on a par with the $643,000 average in 1996 spent for a U.S. House seat. The $2 million spent by Tom Hayden for an assembly seat was once thought to be an untouchable record, but recent spending patterns have placed it in jeopardy. Greater variation in campaign costs is found in states with hybrid legislatures. Washington State, which pays its legislators $28,800 per year, had five races that topped $225,000 in 1990; in contrast, the cost for gaining a Senate seat in Colorado is between $30,000 and $40,000, and House seats run closer to $20,000 (Rosenthal 1996, 119). Among citizen legislatures the costs are much more reasonable. In Maine, spending for Senate seats ranges from $20,000 to $30,000, whereas House campaigns run between $4,000 to $5,000. States such as New Hampshire, Wyoming, and New Mexico are bargains, as expenditures tend to average several thousand dollars. However, a member's compensation is also in the bargain category, as Wyoming legislators are paid $125 per day for a twenty-six-day session. In New Mexico, lawmakers are paid no salary for the thirty-one-day session but receive $133 per day for expenses.

With campaign finance reform stalled at the national level, experimentation is occurring at the state level. Several states, including Wisconsin and Minnesota, began regulating campaign spending in the late 1970s. Beginning in the early 1990s, interest groups such as Common Cause, the U.S. Public Interest Research Group (U.S. PIRG), and the League of Women Voters used state initiative and referendum processes to enact strict contribution limits in such diverse states as Florida, Arkansas, Nevada, California, Colorado, Missouri, Montana, and Oregon. Most of these states based their legislation on a model put forward by U.S. PIRG, and limit contributions to $100 or less. California has a range of $100 to $500, depending on the office. Arkansas, Oregon, and Arkansas add an incentive: An individual who gives to a candidate who agrees to the $100 contribution limit gets a credit on his or her state income tax of $50 or less. The state of Maine has recently joined the handful of states that not only limit donations but provide public funds to candidates who accept spending limits.

A governor's race in Minnesota is a textbook example of how state campaign spending limits and public financing can accomplish the goal of increasing participation in the political system by candidates, citizens, and parties. The state's reform law limited campaign spending to $2.1 million per candidate in 1998, and provided a public subsidy if a candidate received 5 percent of the primary vote. Former professional wrestler Jessie "The Body" Ventura, running as the Reform party candidate, qualified for the subsidy with 10 percent of the primary vote. Although the two major-party candidates, the mayor of St. Paul and the son of the late Hubert Humphrey, claimed substantial advantages in name visibility and fund-raising, the spending limits meant that they could not flood the airwaves with ads. To a greater extent the candidates were forced into relying on televised debates to define themselves to the electorate, and Ventura's candor and antiestablishment remarks appealed to voters. Running on about $400,000, Ventura used irreverent ads featuring the theme from the television show *Shaft*. Ventura posed first as an action figure battling "Evil Special Interest Man" and then as Rodin's sculpture *The Thinker* ("Campaign Finance Reform" 1998). Although some of the Hollywood techniques common to professional wrestling helped him win that race and become Governor "the Mind" Ventura, it was the institutional reforms of spending limits and public financing that made it possible for him to get his message to the public. The lively race spurred public participation as well, as 59.1 percent of Minnesota's electorate voted, the highest turnout rate in the nation that year.

National Reform Proposals

Reform of campaign finance is continually on the congressional agenda. Finding a proposal that can attract the sixty votes necessary in the Senate to close off a filibuster and bring a measure to a floor vote is a difficult task indeed. In the following section we explore three broad approaches to campaign reform, evaluating each in light of the goals of campaign reform discussed earlier in this chapter.

Disclosure Only

This proposal would strip away the existing limits of $1,000 and $5,000 on individuals and groups, and require timely reporting of expenditures. The key value here is that prompt disclosure of contributions, rather than limits on donations, is the best way to limit the influence of political money. This perspective is based on three assumptions. The first assumption is that too little is spent on political campaigns, not too much. The second assumption is that current restrictions are not working; like water flowing downhill, individuals and groups find many ways to circumvent spending limits. The third assumption is that soft money and independent spending are important sources of finance because current laws hold down donations by individuals.

Opponents of disclosure reject all three of the assumptions made by its supporters. First, they believe that, although money spent in campaigns is indeed small compared to sums used in advertising commercial products, as long as the emphasis remains on attacking one's opponent, any proposal that encourages greater spending is unlikely to increase voter understanding of either issues or candidates.

Second, regarding the charge that campaign laws are ineffective, just because some candidates are able to evade the intent of the law does not mean that all attempts to stem such spending should be abandoned. Regarding the the third assumption that soft money and independent expenditures would be less important sources of funds if current restrictions on individuals were removed, Ellen Miller, former director of the Center for Responsive Politics, contends that less than one-quarter of 1 percent of the American public makes a campaign contribution of $200 or more (Clines 1997). Removing the restrictions is unlikely to result in a flowering of political contributions from the average citizen. Instead, with any spending limits abolished, candidates will search for ever larger contributions, in a competitive spiral much like an arms race. Finally, this approach would require candidates to hire additional expertise to meet the strict deadlines for filing reports.

Comprehensive Reform Packages

Although new reform proposals of massive complexity spring up continuously, this section focuses on the three reform proposals outlined in Table 6.8. The three measures, which are useful in illustrating key areas of agreement and disagreement among reformers, are the McCain-Feingold bill, introduced by Senators John McCain (R–Ariz.) and Russ Feingold (D–Wis.); a proposal by scholars Norman Ornstein and Thomas E. Mann; and a proposal from the Citizens Research Foundation (CRF), a nonpartisan research

TABLE 6.8   Three Approaches to Campaign Finance Reform

	McCain-Feingold	Ornstein-Mann	Citizens Research Foundation
Voluntary spending limits	Senate: $1.5 to $8.25 million per election. House: $600,000 per election cycle. Limits may be exceeded if opponent exceeds them.	No provisions	House and Senate: No spending limits. Presidential: Retains current limits.
Contributions	Individuals and PACs may give $1,000 in the primary and $1,000 in general elections. No candidate may raise more than 20 percent of the spending limit from PACs in House races and 25 percent in Senate races.	Individuals may give $2,500 or $3,000 in primary and in general election. Individuals may give $25,000 to candidates and $25,000 more to parties. Small donations encouraged by a 100 percent tax credit on the first $100. Present law governs PAC donations.	Individuals may contribute $3,000 per candidate per election, with total contributions limited to $100,000. PACs are limited to $6,000 per election. There is no overall limit on the amount candidates can collect from PACs.
Sources of contributions	House and Senate: 60 percent of all individual contributions must come from in-state residents. Bundling of multiple contributions by PACs are essentially prohibited. Overall limit of contributions is raised from $25,000 to $30,000.	Small in-state contributions encouraged by television vouchers.	No distinction between in-state and out-of-state contributions.
Soft money	Banned by requiring national parties to raise and spend only "hard money." Requires all election-year spending, including by state and local parties that could affect federal elections (including for registration and to get out the vote), to be paid in hard funds. Bars federal officeholders and candidates from raising unregulated contributions.	Prohibits national parties from raising and using soft money.	Prohibits funneling soft money to state and local committees, and federal candidates from soliciting such funds.

Independent expenditures	Requires prompt reporting and permits candidates to exceed spending limits to reply to attack advertisements. Holds that an independent expenditure is not independent if the person making the expenditure has raised money for the candidate or has used the same consultant as the candidate.	No provisions, but parties would no longer need to use them because existing limits on how much a party could spend to help candidates would be repealed.	No limits on party contributions. Should decrease issue advocacy ads. Labor unions and corporations must pay for issue advocacy campaigns out of voluntary contributions, not general funds.
Public financing or other assistance	Senate candidates complying with spending limits, if they have raised 10 percent of state spending limit, qualify for thirty minutes of free, prime-time television on stations in their state. Complying House and Senate candidates may also purchase television time at 50 percent of the lowest rate. Senate candidates may send two statewide mailings at third-class, non-profit rates. House candidates may send three districtwide mailings at that rate.	Creates a "broadcast bank" of minutes or radio and television time, to be used in increments of sixty seconds or longer, with the candidate required to be in the ad. Candidates also get vouchers of $100 or less for each $25,000 they raise in in-state contributions.	Partial public funding of congressional elections by increasing income-tax checkoff to $5 and indexing the checkoff to inflation. Participating candidates must agree to contribute or lend no more than $50,000 to their own campaign.

SOURCES: The McCain-Feingold and Ornstein-Mann proposals are from Adam Clymer, "Four Possible Routes Toward Campaign Reform," *New York Times*, April 6, 1997. © 1997 by the *New York Times*. Reprinted with permission. The Citizens Research Foundation proposal is from Citizens Research Foundation, "New Realities, New Thinking: Report of the Task Force on Campaign Reform," available at <www.usc.edu>.

group founded by a key scholar of campaign finance, Herbert Alexander. In addition, as a number of states have enacted reforms, both the actual benefits and the unintended consequences of several state reforms will be noted.

Voluntary Spending Limits and Incentives. Because of the Buckley decision, which protects campaign contributions as a form of speech, federal restrictions on spending by candidates are voluntary in most reform measures. The McCain-Feingold bill uses a complex formula that in general sets Senate spending limits at $1.5 million to $8.25 million (depending on a state's population), and $600,000 per election cycle in the House. The limits are flexible, allowing a candidate to exceed any limit if his or her opponent does so. To encourage candidates to keep within the limits, various incentives are included in the proposals, such as lower postage rates for mailings and, most importantly, favorable rates for purchasing television advertising. In the latter category, McCain-Feingold requires television stations to provide both "free" or discounted airtime, whereas Ornstein-Mann focuses on a "broadcast bank" that provides minutes of airtime based on how closely a candidate follows the fund-raising rules.

The broadcast industry actively opposed the provisions for "free" or discounted airtime. Indeed, the opposition was so strong that a revised McCain-Feingold bill dropped the airtime provisions in a bid for more support. The sections that would limit spending by candidates are a major sticking point among reformers as well, as Ornstein-Mann has no candidate spending limit, and the Citizens Research Foundation proposal retains current spending limits only for presidential campaigns. The absence of restrictions on spending is due to the belief that such limits adversely affect competition. A spending cap hinders challengers because they must use more resources than incumbents to make their name and message known to voters. One study of successful challengers between 1978 and 1994 found that in the House by 1994 two-thirds were above the McCain-Feingold proposed limit (with average spending of $738,000), whereas in the Senate 65 percent of successful challengers were over the limit (Janofsky 1996).

Individual and Group Contributions. Should contributions from individuals and groups be increased or decreased? Addressing this hotly contested issue, the McCain-Feingold proposal retains the current $1,000 limit on individuals but would dramatically reduce the amount PACs could donate from $5,000 per election to $1,000. The proposal reflects a unilateral view of the relationship between politics and money, that the focus on the needs of a member's constituents can only be restored by reducing the availability of group funds in politics.

Critics of this approach point out that campaign costs have risen dramatically but the amount that individual and groups may give has not been indexed for inflation, remaining the same today as in 1974. Moreover, the lowered amounts of the McCain-Feingold bill punish challengers at a most crucial time, when considerable "seed money" is needed in order to secure the nomination. For this reason the Ornstein-Mann proposal boosts individual contribution limits to $3,000, and the Citizens' Research Foundation would allow up to $100,000 to be spent at the "seed money" stage.

At the state level, contribution limits of $100 on both candidates and PACs have been enacted in states as diverse as Arkansas, California, Colorado, Missouri, and Oregon. In the 1996 Oregon primaries, the law had the intended effect, as 80 percent of contributions came from individuals, and 20 percent from PACs, a reversal of 1992 percentages (Carney 1997, 111). Yet the state contribution limits had a less desirable effect in several states—dramatically increased independent expenditures. Wisconsin, which strictly limits contributions from individuals, PACs, and parties, found that independent expenditures mushroomed from $225,970 in the 1987–1988 election cycle to more than $1 million in the 1993–1994 cycle. In Washington State the growth was even more dramatic, from $19,689 in 1991–1992 to $236,570 just two years later (Carney 1997, 113). To bypass contribution limits, the Washington State trial lawyers PAC split itself into several different PACs and continued to donate. A final difficult hurdle is that most of the state laws enacting limits are being challenged in the federal courts. How the precedents set in federal cases previously discussed will eventually apply to state laws remains to be seen.

Sources of Contributions.   Reflecting the assumption that money raised closer to home is "good money" because it better reflects the needs of the district or state and reduces the influence of Washington power brokers, the McCain-Feingold bill requires 60 percent of all funds in House and Senate races to be gathered from within the state. Other plans focus on incentives to encourage in-state fund-raising, such as providing vouchers for television. Norman Ornstein and Tom Mann assume a more moderate position by encouraging in-state contributions through the provision of television time.

Yet restricting out-of-state money raises constitutional issues. If contributions are a form of protected speech, would limiting the ability of someone in Pennsylvania to contribute to a California race be analogous to restricting an individual's right to speak in another state? Moreover, if an incumbent has a powerful in-state network of financial interests, would such a restriction effectively curtail the challenger's ability to mount a competitive campaign? Women, minorities, and candidates with a strong ideology may find it imperative to gain funds from outside their state. Candidates from smaller states and poorer districts would likewise be disadvantaged. For these reasons no such limits are found in the Citizens' Research Foundation proposal.

Bundling is yet another source of contributions that divides reform groups. The McCain-Feingold bill would effectively ban the practice by not allowing multiple contributions collected by PACs, corporations, and unions. Advocates argue that bundling effectively negates the limits on individuals and groups by delivering their checks as a unit. Other reformers such as Ornstein-Mann are hesitant to ban the practice, and the CRF measure merely requires that bundling be reported. In this instance the reluctance is due to the use that groups such as EMILY's List make of bundling.

Soft Money and Independent Expenditures. Due to developments in recent years, many see soft money as the area in most urgent need of reform. Indeed, some reform advocates believe that if comprehensive campaign reform cannot be achieved, a ban on soft money should be the interim priority. This consensus is reflected in Table 6.8, as all three proposals ban the practice. Yet soft money and independent expenditures are inextricably linked. Three potential consequences of banning soft money are (1) a weakening of the role of political parties, (2) a corresponding rise in independent expenditures, and (3) decreased accountability for the money spent in campaigns. A soft money ban would deprive the parties of resources that have been successfully used for party-building activities. Moreover, banning the use of soft funds would ultimately weaken the reformers' goal of accountability in the political system. Political parties must report their soft money expenditures. Although following this money trail is difficult, newspaper reports and congressional investigations do provide some measure of accountability for questionable funding practices by political leaders. If the soft funds option were unavailable, interest groups and wealthy individuals would likely assume a more dominant role in campaigns. None of the multitude of individuals and groups currently have to report the sums spent in the categories of independent expenditures or issue advocacy ads.

The McCain-Feingold approach does tighten the definition of independent expenditures, and it provides a mechanism for allowing candidates to exceed the spending level in order to respond to negative attacks. But this proposal cannot tighten the definition very much, given the Supreme Court's tendency to view limits on independent expenditures as a violation of First Amendment freedoms. Barring a major change in the philosophy of the Supreme Court justices, any attempt to tightly regulate this area is likely to be among the first provisions to be struck down by the Court.

Public Finance

Although full public funding of congressional campaigns remains the long-term goal of some reform groups, the concept faces serious difficulties. Among the problems that must be overcome are congressional opposition, lukewarm public opinion, and questions about whether reform will accomplish the goal of making elections more competitive. Evidence on this question will also be gathered from state-level reforms, although the results are far from clear-cut.

Typically the minority party in Congress has been less willing to support public financing, on the premise that greater sums must be raised to overcome an incumbent's advantage. Yet another problem is finding the necessary funds for public financing in an era in which the rhetoric of budget cutting is given greater priority. The system of tax checkoffs that provide funds for presidential elections has seen a drop in participation, from an average of 27 percent in the 1970s to less than 20 percent in the 1990s (Sorauf 1992, 142). The tax checkoff was raised to $3 to try to keep the presidential fund solvent for 1996. Increasing the tax checkoff to $5 to extend public financing to the congressional level would bring in at most $120 million per election cycle for congressional races, far short of the $200–$300 million estimates of costs for public funding of congressional races (Alexander and Corrado 1995, 269; Jost 1996, 128). Key members of Congress also believe that raising funds should be the responsibility of the candidate rather than the taxpayer. An outspoken opponent is the current Senate majority leader, Trent Lott (R–Miss.), who sees public financing as "food stamps for politicians" (Clymer 1997).

Decreased participation in the tax checkoff is mirrored in polling results about public finance. Although 36 percent of Gallup respondents were "very dissatisfied" and 22 percent "somewhat dissatisfied" with campaign finance laws (Gallup 1996b, 37), reaction to public financing is mixed at best and depends on how the question is worded. When asked about "public financing" without any explanation of the term, citizens appear confused on the concept, as 49 percent of those questioned by an ABC News/Washington Post poll were undecided, compared to 20 percent in favor and 31 percent opposed (Sorauf 1992, 145–146). Only when the concept is presented in very general terms is there widespread agreement. When the Gallup poll asked over time whether it is a "good idea" to "provide a fixed amount of money" for presidential and congressional elections, 65 percent responded positively (Gallup 1996a, 42). If more details are provided on the concept, public response is slightly negative. When Gallup worded the question, for example, as favoring "a new campaign finance system" in which "federal campaigns are funded by the government, and contributions from individuals and private groups are banned," 52 percent disagreed (Gallup 1996b, 37).

A final concern is the impact of public financing on electoral outcomes. Would taxpayer financing accomplish the goal of increasing competition in congressional elections? Gary Jacobson's seminal work on congressional financing finds that the spending done by incumbents yields a much smaller return for each extra dollar spent compared to challenger spending (Jacobson 1978, 1980, 1985, 1990). Given this advantage that extra spending by challengers generates, any attempt to restrict that ability through limits on contributions or public financing would actually decrease competition. A contrary view is provided by a study that applied four different models of public financing to congressional elections. Public financing would increase competitiveness in congressional elections, particularly if the public money were available at higher rather than lower funding levels (Goidel and Gross 1996, 139). The lessons from two state programs provide support for both conceptions. Minnesota and Wisconsin have extensive experience with public financing, having introduced programs in 1976 and 1977 respectively. The Minnesota experience indicates that providing taxpayer dollars does assist challengers and would provide even more support if the amounts of public funding were increased (Donnay and Ramsden 1995). Evidence from Wisconsin stipulates that public financing does not increase competition; instead, the overall strategic environment, and not just the question of fund-raising, influenced the decision about whether to run (Mayer and Wood 1995). Frank Sorauf (1992, 57) provides an apt summary of the difficulties concerning public financing and competition, as well as campaign finance reform in general: "The complexity of the subject defeats all but the experts, and even they do not easily come to consensus judgments."

Conclusion

This chapter has concentrated on the values that guided campaign reform efforts, the laws that resulted, and the courts' interpretation of such laws. As campaign finance law evolved, it initially allowed the national parties to transfer funds to strengthen state and local party organizations. Today national candidates primarily view campaign finance provisions as a means by which they can indirectly spend more than the law prescribes.

Public perception of soft money abuses increased the pressure on Congress to enact meaningful campaign finance reform. Before major changes in the law can occur, several ongoing problems must be overcome. As Fred Wertheimer, former chair of Common Cause suggests, rather than a heated clash between Republican and Democratic ideology, what prevails in Washington, D.C., is an "incumbency party." Members of both parties are reluctant to part with the fund-raising benefits that the current system provides and to adopt a system whose electoral consequences would be vast and difficult to predict.

This chapter suggests that the relationship between money and politics is not merely a unilateral one in which PAC contributions corrupt politicians, but a bilateral relationship in which members of Congress utilize interest groups not only to fund campaigns but as resources to successfully enact their own programs. Successful reforms must take this relationship into account.

Although groups may agree on the broad goals of reform, such as increasing competition in elections, they disagree heartily on which specific provisions will best implement these goals. Over the years different versions of the McCain-Feingold proposal have received the most publicity; in the first quarter of 1997 alone fifty-seven different campaign finance measures were introduced into Congress.

In past years campaign finance reform has fallen short of the sixty votes needed to break a filibuster and bring a bill to the Senate floor. In the future, political scandals and public indignation may compel the Congress and the president to overcome their differences on campaign reform and enact legislation. If this occurs, two outcomes seem certain: The measure will have unanticipated consequences that call for further reforms, and the measure will have a difficult time before a Supreme Court that is increasingly inclined to view political contributions as a protected form of speech.

7

Parties and Campaigns

An Altered Role

As a significant shift occurred in the 1970s toward candidate-centered campaigning via the media, questions arose about the role of political parties in campaigns. This chapter will explore the uneasy alliance between the parties and the candidates in the campaign arena, looking at five areas in particular. First, political scientists changed their view of the impact of campaigns from having little effect to the notion that candidates can be "sold" like products to a more balanced view of what campaigns can accomplish. Second, the parties have completed the transition outlined in Chapter 2 from having a peripheral role to being an intermediary in campaigns. Third, the role of professionals in campaign organizations is now even more crucial, with duties ranging from designing the structure of the organization to making decisions about strategy. Fourth, the types of messages the candidates present are changing, and now include a proliferation of "negative" campaign commercials. Fifth, candidates are using innovations in technology to get their messages across, ranging from cable television to the Internet.

The Purposes and Impacts of Campaigns

From a candidate's point of view the purpose of campaigns is simple: Spend enormous sums of money and blanket the airwaves with your message in order to obtain or keep political office. For the society campaigns are as much a means of producing political stability as producing political change. Consensus is reached on what programs are legitimate, as well as on providing an orderly succession to office. Campaigns fill a range of needs for individuals, including watching commercials to see what issues are important, signaling political activists to become involved, and making fun of people at conventions wearing elephant noses or donkey ears (Gronbeck 1987, 141–147).

Research over the past fifty years reveals a substantial difference between what office-seekers intend campaigns to do and their actual impact on the citizenry. In the late 1940s and early 1950s researchers developed a "limited effects model" of political mass communication. Campaign messages were broad, aimed at many groups. People gained most of their political information from family, friends, and coworkers, who shared the same social and economic status. The impact of all these messages was to reinforce existing party preferences. Thus the major impact of campaigns was to increase turnout. Occasionally campaigns would produce minor changes in voters' preferences, but conversion to the opposing party or candidate occurred very rarely (Lazarsfeld, Berelson, and Gaudet 1948; Berelson, Lazarsfeld, and McPhee 1954). Political scientists employing rational choice models from economics also downplayed the impact of campaigns. This theory suggests that the central goal of politicians is to maximize votes. Because most Americans are moderate, politicians move toward the political center as well, and a primary purpose of the campaign effort is to blur the differences between the candidates. Other factors have greater impact on election outcomes, such as the president's approval rating and the state of the economy shortly before the election (Tufte 1975).

By the late 1970s the work of Dan Nimmo and Robert Savage was instrumental in emphasizing the significance of campaigns. Nimmo's book *The Political Persuaders* (1970) outlined a "field theory of campaign effects." The mass media (particularly television) are important in changing the field or context in which people view politics. Campaigns should target those with low involvement in politics because they are more susceptible to images of a strong leader onto which people can project their own needs or wants. Indeed Nimmo and Savage (1976) were concerned that television would be so powerful a tool in manufacturing candidate images that campaigns would be all style and no substance.

Although the debate among political scientists about the impact of campaigns remains heated, the notion that campaigns can sell candidates like soap is not favored. Whenever a campaign successfully uses a technique to influence voters in the short term, opponents eventually mimic or counteract the technique. It is more accurate to say that campaigns can have a major effect, provided that the candidates propose a set of themes with widespread appeal ("broadcasting") and then tailor those themes to specific audiences ("narrowcasting"). By personalizing their messages, office seekers distinguish themselves from one another and offer a skeptical electorate a reason to vote for them (Baer 1995, 61).

The Changing Roles of Parties in Campaigns

Parties as Political Machines

The role that political parties play in campaigns has undergone vast changes during the last one hundred years. During the nineteenth century, political parties offered a series of incentives to candidates that helped parties dominate the political system and exercise great influence over the lives of ordinary citizens. Economic incentives, in the form of social services, were provided by local party officials. Through the patronage system party leaders filled government positions with party loyalists. The party thereby controlled municipal jobs, public works projects such as street repair, and distributions of food and clothing to the poor. The social and psychological incentives that were offered were also important, particularly for immigrant families. Often the party provided the only means of social mobility for families frozen out of the mainstream culture by their ethnic background. Social activities ranging from picnics to dances were available though party-sponsored social and athletic clubs.

Local party organizations completely controlled the electoral process. At the recruitment stage, candidate selection was dominated by the infamous "smoke-filled room" in which party leaders realistically evaluated the candidates and chose the ones who demonstrated the greatest potential. Even with the arrival of the direct primary in numerous states in the early 1900s, party bosses would specify a ticket of party-endorsed candidates and then actively campaign for the ticket. The direct primary expanded participation by the electorate and provided an avenue for maverick candidates to challenge party bosses and occasionally win.

National party committees played a major role in campaign management. With a monopoly over campaign contributions, national committees publicized their party's position on the issues and scheduled politicians with national reputations to speak at rallies. Local party organizations handled detail work such as providing information about voting patterns, registering people to vote, and making sure citizens got to the polls to pull the lever for the correct party. To assist the candidates the national party provided a "campaign textbook," a four- to five-hundred-page document containing tips on organizing the campaign, statistical tables of voting patterns, and any scandals brewing within the opposing party (Herrnson 1990, 15).

Parties in Decline/Parties as Peripheral Institutions

The system that prevailed in the 1960s and 1970s centered around candidates, with parties relegated to peripheral positions. Parties declined because many of the methods used to recruit candidates and win votes in the past no longer worked. The parties had counted on their control of positions in city government to attract of steady stream of recruits into the system. One of the most important legal reforms advocated by the Progressive movement was a merit system of government. In many cities, competence rather than party loyalty became the criterion for filling positions. The merit system also caused the parties to lose control of distributing social services. When receiving a Christmas turkey or having a pothole filled did not depend on voting for the winning party, the parties lost a powerful economic incentive. To handle other citizen complaints about government, some cities designated an ombudsman to act as an intermediary, a role formerly filled by the parties.

A transformation in the culture meant that what the parties once provided as social and psychological incentives were now obtainable by other means. For immigrant or minority groups, sports or entertainment appeared to provide greater social mobility than the political parties. Radio, television, and the movies provided entertainment, although with far less personal involvement than a door-to-door campaign. Going to the movies or attending a sporting event proved to be much more popular than taking in a party-sponsored dance or mass rally. Candidates sought to bypass local party organizations and establish a personal link with the voter. Although "reach out and touch someone" was the telephone company's slogan at the time, candidates tried to accomplish the same thing by using the marketing tools of advertising in their campaign messages.

Implementation of a direct primary had important consequences for the parties. Many local and state parties no longer endorsed candidates before the primary, taking away the incentive to work one's way up through the party in return for the party's support in the primary. Weak parties shared recruitment functions with issue-oriented interest groups, notably labor, business, and civic groups. Over time the changes in recruitment patterns were felt at the presidential level. Ronald Reagan's challenge to incumbent president Gerald Ford in 1976 was the closest since Eisenhower battled Taft in 1952. As mavericks and outsiders made significant inroads into the Democratic party, the 1972 presidential nomination of George McGovern and 1976 nomination of Jimmy Carter went to men who achieved prominence without the help of party kingmakers. Both Ronald Reagan and Jimmy Carter ran personalized campaigns and were relatively new to traditional party organizations; both candidates employed professional campaign consultants. By the early 1980s professional consultants had become bigger power brokers in some states than party chairpersons.

The Parties Respond: National Parties as Intermediaries

No longer content to be largely ignored by candidates and professional consultants, national and state parties sought to play a more active role in the electoral area beginning in the early 1980s. Paul Herrnson suggests that the parties' current role in elections is broker or intermediary, much like a stockbroker or a real estate agent. The parties must convince interest groups, PACs, and consultants that their "stock" of useful advice and other resources should be valued and accepted in recruiting candidates, campaigning for office, and increasing party voting (Herrnson 1988, 47). The national parties have emerged to offer "one-stop" campaign services, with the parties more heavily involved in five areas: recruiting candidates, managing campaigns, fund-raising, implementing strategy, and voter turnout programs.

The area of recruitment is still largely the responsibility of the individual. For House and Senate seats the national party committees are involved on a selective basis, working with local party officials to encourage candidates in elections that are either very competitive or uncontested. Parties have undertaken both passive and active recruitment efforts. Passive recruiting simply seeks to make individuals aware of election opportunities. It is done through newsletters and "training colleges" for candidates and managers on such subjects as fund-raising and use of the media. Both the Republican National Committee and the Democratic National Committee give particular emphasis to making opportunities known to women and minorities, including such programs as the RNC Women's Outreach Program and the DNC Eleanor Roosevelt Program (Herrnson 1988, 49). The programs are low-key and the participants usually receive a small stipend for their participation. In active recruiting the parties usually search for candidates to run for the House and Senate. If an announced candidate is viewed by the party as a disaster waiting to occur, negative recruitment may be subtly employed to discourage the person from running, perhaps by showing him or her discouraging polling results. The Republican National Committee has actively sought out and supported candidates since the early 1980s, but has been hampered by a series of turf battles with state and local party activists. Party rules now require the National Committee to obtain the permission of the state chairperson and state party delegation before providing any assistance. The Democratic National Committee was slower to send people into the field to do active recruiting (Sabato 1988; Gibson, Frendreis, and Vertz 1989; Frendreis, Gibson, and Vertz 1990).

The area of campaign management is still dominated by individual campaigns, but parties are attempting to play a larger role. Some congressional candidates are shocked by the prices charged by prestigious campaign management firms. For them the Republican party has bought large "blocks" of services from prestigious firms and makes the services available to candidates for less than market cost. Moreover, in 1986 the party began the Republican Campaign Academy, where candidates are instructed in the latest campaign techniques by leading political consultants and media persons (Herrnson 1988, 57). The academy is an attempt to maintain an ongoing relationship with political professionals in order to ensure that their expertise remains available to a wide range of the party's candidates.

Although the national parties give much assistance to congressional office seekers, they do not ignore state office seekers. The Republican National Committee (RNC) has developed programs to provide professional staff, data processing services, cash grants, and consulting services for fund-raising, campaigning, and media. By 1988 the RNC was distributing more than $2 million per year to state legislative candidates. With a later start and fewer resources, the Democrats under Chair Paul Kirk (1985–1989) concentrated their efforts in sixteen key states. A Democratic Party Election Force consisting of a full-time political operative and a fund-raiser for each state was paid for by the Democratic National Committee (DNC). John Bibby points out several differences between Republican and Democratic efforts to aid state parties. The GOP operation is a national party effort carried out in conjunction with state parties. In contrast, the Democratic approach is more of a partnership between national groups (the DNC and the Democratic Senatorial and Congressional Campaign Committees), state parties, and nonparty groups such as the American Federation of State, County, and Municipal Employees (Bibby 1990, 35).

Regarding the third area, fund-raising, the ability of the national parties to use the states as a conduit to raise funds to support national candidates was a major theme in Chapter 6. In addition, state parties have not neglected efforts to help state candidates. Table 7.1 provides an overview of such efforts. The pattern is that of Democratic party organizers scrambling to emulate their more organized GOP counterparts. Over nine out of ten Republicans at the state level could count on party assistance in fund-raising efforts. Some evidence exists of an even larger gap between the parties in fund-raising techniques and abilities. For example, a television commercial run by the California Republican Party in the 1980s announced that the Democrats were always attacking President Reagan. The party wanted to know voters' opinion of how the president was doing. A "hot line" was

TABLE 7.1   Assistance Provided by State Parties to Candidates for State Office

Assistance/Service Provided	Republican %	Democratic %
Campaign seminars	100	76
Fund-raising assistance	95	63
Financial contributions	90	70
Polling	78	50
Media consulting	75	46
Coordinating PAC contributions	52	31

SOURCE: John Bibby, "Party Organization at the State Level," in L. Sandy Maisel, ed., *The Parties Respond* (Boulder: Westview, 1990), 29.

set up to tabulate opinions and send them to the president. The call cost $2, and the money would help elect Republican candidates. Thousands of calls came in, not all of which were complimentary. In the San Francisco area, 31 percent of the callers rated the president only fair or poor, whereas in Los Angeles the figure was 22 percent. No matter what the caller's party identification was, a $2 contribution was made to the Republican party, with the money automatically collected by the phone company. California Democrats were not amused (Nelson 1984).

Parties also seek to offer expertise in a fourth area—implementing the overall campaign strategy, including broadcasting the candidate's message. Party assistance includes a range of services, from critiquing a campaign organization to offering the party's television and radio production facilities. For example, the National Republican Congressional Committee's (NRCC) media center produced 245 television commercials and 173 radio commercials for approximately fifty candidates, whereas the Democratic Congressional Campaign Committee (DCCC) was responsible for about seven hundred television spots and five hundred radio spots for 115 Democratic contestants (Herrnson 1988, 57). The parties usually target this kind of comprehensive assistance to challengers in competitive districts. Although candidates are free to ignore or even disparage the advice and the services of the party, doing so could jeopardize their access to services later on in the campaign.

Finally, it is the party's role to increase the number of party faithful who vote on election day. To fulfill this role parties run their own advertising campaigns and voter registration drives. In the early 1980s the Republican party's ad campaign focused on the need to provide a Republican Congress to pass President Reagan's legislation. One 1980 Republican National Committee spot parodied the former Speaker of the House, Tip O'Neill. A portly, white-haired legislator driving down the road is reminded by his aide that the vehicle is nearly out of gas. The legislator makes several denials and the car passes several gas stations; then the vehicle quits. When the actor cries, "Hey! We're out of gas!" the announcer proclaims, "The Democrats are out of gas! Vote Republican for a change!" Change did come—in the form of a recession in 1982. Then the RNC ran a radio spot in which a catchy country-western tune encouraged voters to "stay the course, my friend." The Democratic National Committee responded in 1982 with a television spot in which an elephant (substituting for the proverbial bull) wanders into a china shop and dramatically tramples everything in sight, including china marked "Social Security" and "Jobs." Contending that Republicans have made a "real mess of things," the announcer asserts, "Democrats stand for fairness." Subsequent spots proclaimed, "It's not fair! It's Republican." For 1994 the National Republican Congressional Committee produced a series of commercials stating that it was time to "bring down the curtain" on fifty years of Democratic control of the House.

Since the 1980s, the parties have gradually expanded their electoral activities and have assumed the role of broker. This process is not without setbacks, however. During an economic downturn between 1989 and 1992 both parties suffered financial shortfalls that slowed their efforts to recruit and support candidates. The Democratic Congressional Campaign Committee faced $1.6 million in debt and key staff turnovers while the National Republican Senatorial Committee laid off its entire political division, including the director and a half dozen regional directors (Kenworthy 1989, 1991). Although the parties attempt to make their presence known in campaigns, their efforts can be frustrated by downturns in the economy.

The Candidate: Recruitment and Motivation

What motivates a person to cross the threshold from being interested to becoming a candidate? Is it concern for a particular issue, or is it self-aggrandizement? Researchers studying the "why" of candidacy have taken a sociological approach, a psychological approach, and a structural approach. Assuming that background, particularly occupational background, facilitates entry into public office, researchers have classified public officials according to occupation, educational experience, and their fathers' occupational status. It is assumed that certain occupations and social backgrounds carry with them a socialization process that influences individuals to run for political office. Donald Matthews (1960) concludes that a particular type of social environment produces a candidate. Matthews maintains that given a background of position, wealth, security, and a family tradition of activism, a candidate will emerge. This perspective applies quite well to the Kennedys, the Rockefellers, the Roosevelts, and the Bushes.

But this theory attributes less political ambition to women and minorities because they tend to have lower education and income levels, and their socialization process places less value on aspiring to or holding public office. Only women who are "countersocialized" are activated politically. For example, potential female office seekers might come from families in which the mother is politically active, is employed outside the home, or volunteers in a nonpartisan interest group (Sapiro 1983; Sapiro and Farah 1980; Fowlkes 1984).

Data collected on the characteristics of people in public office indicate that they certainly do not typify the population at large. Table 7.2 provides a sample of the background of members of Congress in one term in the 1980s, as well as in the last year of Democratic control of Congress in the early 1990s, and in a recent year when Republicans controlled both houses

TABLE 7.2 Selected Profiles of Members of Congress

	1981–1982		1993–1994		1997–1998	
	House	Senate	House	Senate	House	Senate
Political Party						
Democrats	242	46	258	57	207	45
Republicans	192	53	176	43	227	55
Independents	1	–	1	–	1	–
Gender						
Men	416	96	387	94	384	91
Women	19	2	48	6	51	9
Race[a]						
Whites	410	97	374	96	377	96
Blacks	18	0	39	1	37	1
Hispanics	4	0	17	0	18	–
Asians	3	3	5	2	3	2
Native Americans	–	–	–	1	–	1
Religion						
Protestants	270	72	255	59	259	57
Roman Catholics	118	16	118	23	127	24
Jews	27	6	32	10	25	10
Others	20	6	30	8	24	9
Profession[b]						
Law	186	57	181	58	172	53
Business/banking	117	23	131	27	181	33
Education	42	5	66	12	74	13
Public service	37	2	86	12	100	26
Agriculture	20	5	19	5	22	8
Journalism	16	2	24	8	12	9
Medicine	3	1	6	0	12	2
Clergy	3	0	2	1	1	1
Law enforcement	0	0	10	0	10	–
Real estate	n.l.	n.l.	27	4	23	5
Military	0	1	0	1	1	1
Aeronautics	0	1	2	1	1	1
Others[c]	11	0	7	0	23	1

[a] Nonvoting delegates have not been included in the totals.
[b] Members with more than one occupation have all of them listed, resulting in totals higher than total membership. N.l. means the profession is not listed as the major profession.
[c] Category of "other occupations" includes actor/entertainer, artistic/creative, engineering, health care, labor officials, professional sports, technical/trade.

SOURCES: Republished with permission of Congressional Quarterly Inc., 1414 22nd St. NW, Washington DC, 20037. "Characteristics of the 97th Congress," *Congressional Almanac* 1981; Phil Duncan, "Looking Beyond Gridlock," *Congressional Quarterly Weekly Reports,* Supplement to No. 3, January 16, 1993; Allan Freedman, "Lawyers Take a Back in the 105th Congress," Congressional Quarterly Weekly Report, January 4, 1997. Reproduced by permission of the publisher via copyright clearance center.

of Congress. In the table, a disproportionately large number of members come from the middle or upper social classes, and from such professions as law, business, or education. The two parties do attract members from different occupations. When Republicans gained control of the Congress in the mid-1990s, the number of members with a business or banking background increased to such an extent that by 1997 this category outweighed the number of lawyers in the House for the first time since *Congressional Quarterly* began to keep track of occupations in 1953 (Freedman 1997, 27). In terms of race and gender, the two Congresses in the 1990s included more diversity. The number of black members in the House doubled between 1981 and 1994. Starting from a very small base, Hispanic members were four times the number in 1981. The numbers for both groups in the House seemed to plateau in the mid-1990s. A record number of women were motivated to run, and fifty-one obtained public office in the House in 1997, and nine in the Senate. Are countersocialization processes at work? More recent research on women political activists at state party conventions shows that having a politically active mother is only marginally related to seeking public office, whereas belonging to interest groups (such as business or women's rights groups) and working outside the home are strongly related to running for office. Although women do exhibit less political ambition than men, the "ambition gap" has narrowed over time (Fowlkes, Perkins, and Rinehart 1979; Clark, Hadley, and Darcy 1989, 203; Constantini 1990, 751). One study of Arizona state and local officials finds that only 25 percent of women express political ambition in their first or second term, but by the third or fourth term the figure increases to 42 percent. Men with higher incomes and education may approach political ambition with an "up or out" attitude. If they do not immediately run for a higher office, they may return to the private sector. Women, with less challenging opportunities available outside public office, begin to enjoy their success and decide to seek higher office at a later stage (Burt-Way and Kelly 1992, 19).

A second approach to understanding why certain people decide to run for public office is psychological—the individual's personality traits and personal ambitions. Joseph Schlesinger (1966) believes that personal ambition both motivates people to seek office and determines what level of office they seek: "Ambition lies at the heart of politics." Schlesinger identified three degrees of ambition: (1) *discrete* ambition, whereby the officeholder aspires only to a local office and then retires; (2) *static* ambition, whereby an officeholder seeks a particular office and wants to make a career in it; and (3) *progressive* ambition, whereby an officeholder's current position is viewed simply as a stepping-stone to higher office. Because of the high turnover among state legislators who do not move on to other offices, this group exhibits more discrete, limited political ambitions. Those who progressively seek higher office—including Bob Dole and Bill Clinton—lie at the other end of the scale. Bob Dole entered politics as a member of the House in 1960, and by 1968 he was elected to the Senate. Dole moved up the political ladder quickly, accepting an additional position as chairperson of the Republican party in 1971. Dole was moved aside to make room for George Bush as GOP chair in 1973. By 1976, Dole had rebounded to serve as Gerald Ford's vice presidential running mate, although he was not a particularly popular candidate, due in part to his razor-sharp comments aimed at the opposition. In the Senate, Dole became Senate majority leader in 1985, served as minority leader from 1987 to 1994, and regained the majority leader position in 1995. In his presidential bids, Dole lost badly in the 1980 primary but did slightly better in losing to George Bush in 1988. A more organized campaign gained him the GOP presidential nomination in 1996.

Bill Clinton also demonstrated progressive ambition. After receiving a Rhodes Scholarship and graduating from Yale Law School, he became a law professor at the University of Arkansas. Narrowly defeated in a 1974 congressional race, he was elected attorney general in 1976. Next he sought the governor's office and at the age of thirty-two became the nation's youngest governor—as well as the youngest to lose that office two years later. He regained the governorship in 1982 and held it until his successful run for the presidency in 1992.

Some researchers have tried to analyze the intensity of Democratic and Republican candidates' career commitment to politics. Are Democrats more likely than Republicans to perceive their candidacy for public office as a stepping-stone in their political career? Jeff Fishel found that Democrats and Republicans do differ significantly in their levels of personal ambition; Democrats were much more likely to view their candidacies as stepping-stones (1971, 35):

> Because the differences between Democratic and Republican challengers cannot be explained by the higher social status of Republicans, nor by a greater degree of social mobility among Democrats one is left with an unfashionably simple conclusion: Democrats, as Democrats, are simply more careerist in their orientation to politics than are Republicans.

A third approach to understanding why people become candidates emphasizes political opportunities. The structural approach contends that personal political ambitions are molded by the "opportunity structure" presented to the office seeker. Running for office is perceived as a risk, with the magnitude of the risk partially determined by the structural characteristics of the electoral system. What Boss Plunket of New York's Tammany Hall said many years ago about graft also applies to ambition: "I seen my opportunities and I took 'em!" Sometimes opportunities for political candidacy and electoral success are beyond the control of the individual. Structural factors, such as the size of the election district, the degree of party competition within that district, and the presence of an incumbent, affect one's chances for moving up the political ladder. "The theory rests on the idea that office-seekers attempt to behave in a rational manner in selecting among alternative offices," explains Gordon Black. "Rather than being driven by excessive ambition, they tend to develop ambition slowly as a result of their changing circumstances" (Black 1972, 145). For example, a political novice's decision to run against an incumbent is a very difficult one. The incumbent, due to position, staff, and public recognition, usually enjoys enormous financial and personnel advantages over all challengers. The great majority of incumbents who seek reelection are successful; 90 percent of the incumbent House members up for reelection in midterm elections during the period 1958–1970 were successful, whereas for elections from 1986 to 1990 the reelection rate averaged an astounding 97 percent. The structural approach, therefore, emphasizes an individual's immediate circumstances at the time of the decision to seek office, rather than personal background or personality. Ambition is believed to develop in relation to political opportunities (Fowler and McClure 1989). For example, large districts require large campaign expenditures, there is usually more intraparty competition, and the possibilities are more limited.

Another important factor affecting one's chances for election is the relative strength of the parties in the district. Obviously, there are more political opportunities for a candidate in a "safe" district (where one's party usually wins) than for a candidate in a more competitive district.

None of these three approaches claims to offer a total explanation. James David Barber (1965) suggests an approach that combines personal ambition, opportunity, and resources. He points out that all three elements should be considered in decisions to seek public office, and he suggests that potential candidates must give an affirmative answer to the following questions:

1. Do I want it? (ambition)
2. Can I do it? (resources)
3. Do they want me? (opportunity)

Noting that these factors are interrelated, Barber says that if any one of them is missing, the prospective candidate usually will not enter an election race.

Campaign Organization and Decisionmaking: Specialization of Labor

As candidates try to maximize their chances to win, they no longer put much stock in party loyalty, bumper stickers, or handshaking. In trying to get the greatest return for their time and money, candidates have sought the specialists and their professional techniques. Unlike the amateurs of the past, candidates must now surround themselves with professional managers, statisticians, pollsters, advertising specialists, and lawyers.

Specialization and division of labor have become key principles in campaign organization for most major offices. The next section deals with the parts of the organization that have primary responsibility for the three central tasks of the campaign: the collection of information, the decisionmaking processes about the campaign's key issues and themes, and the means by which the campaign messages will be disseminated.

The Role of Campaign Consultants

Figure 7.1 displays the structure for one model of an "ideal" campaign organization to accomplish these tasks. Although the purpose of campaigns is mass persuasion, campaigns are increasingly specialized in their organization and operation. Political consultants or "handlers" play a central role in political campaigns. Consultants are needed for research (issue and opponent research), advertising, fund-raising, and polling. Increasingly, campaigns are relying on two concepts: *geodemographics,* gathering information about specific segments of the electorate, and *narrowcasting,* choosing specific issues that appeal most to each group and then disseminating that information primarily to that group.

Information Needs: Research

Research consultants gather information to provide the candidate with a candid profile of his or her district. This, in turn, suggests guidelines for making key strategy decisions. More specifically, information must be gathered about the social, economic, and political makeup of the district or the state, as well as the past record of both the opponent and the candidate. Although the lists vary, issue and opponent research must provide the candidate information on a minimum of five factors:

1. voting behavior patterns such as voter turnout, ticket splitting, and party competition
2. demographics—racial, income, educational, occupational, age, and residential characteristics
3. party affiliation—strength of the voters' party identification and participation in party organizations and activities
4. issue position and concerns—the candidate's own priorities and issue stands
5. profile of the opposition—group support, issue positions, skills, strengths and weaknesses with the voters, and advertising tactics

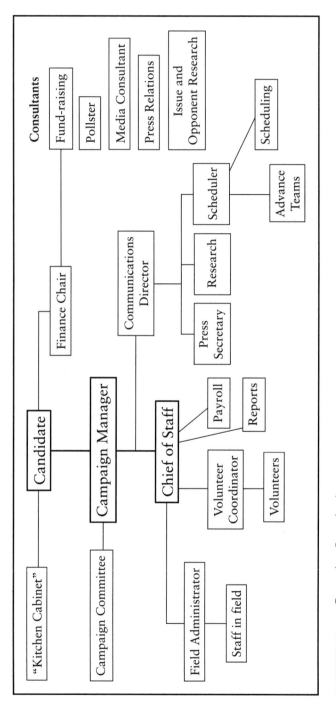

FIGURE 7.1   Campaign Organization

Statistics of past elections are important in predicting future voting behavior, identifying the relative strength of party registration in a particular district, and determining voter turnout levels. Election statistics—voter turnout, registration lists, and candidate totals—are available from county, municipal, state, and federal governments.

In addition to voting data, research provides candidates information about geodemographics. Feeding an enormous amount of detailed statistical information into a computer, the campaign can quickly learn the various income groupings, ethnic groups, housing styles, and social classes that make up the candidate's constituency (Robbin 1989). Clusters or "groupings" of several hundred households can be identified, such as "Roseanne's neighbors," a mix of urban, white, middle-class, backyard, single-family dwellings. Demographic characteristics suggest possible issues of concern to voters. A district with a large proportion of aged citizens would undoubtedly be interested in federal health care policies for the aged. Similarly, districts with low per capita income would be more concerned with job opportunities and social welfare benefits. Demographic information pertaining to city blocks, census tracts, standard metropolitan statistical areas (S.M.S.A.), and states is available from the U.S. Bureau of the Census through its TIGER (Topologically Integrated Geographic Encoding and Referencing) system, and the data can be readily adapted to many computer systems.

Information Needs: Public Opinion

Polling, or survey research, is the most common means of gathering up-to-date information about the electorate. Candidates for public office rely on their polling firm to identify voter priorities and preferences, assess voter expectations of the officeholder, and measure voter familiarity with the candidates and issues. Indeed, the polling firm plays such an important role in the organization that candidates are often accused of being driven by polling numbers rather than principle.

Pollsters offer five different types of polls, often presented to the candidate in the form of a package. The *benchmark poll* is the basic planning document for the campaign, as it contains important issues to stress during the campaign; how to campaign among various groups; where to place the campaign's geographic focus; candidate personality information (including which personality factors to stress in advertising); how much emphasis needs to be given to familiarizing people with the candidate's name; what is known and unknown about the candidate's past record; potential areas of appeal that might increase the number of vote switchers; which voters are undecided—their characteristics and issue preferences; the characteristics and issue preferences of ticket splitters; and the media that each voter group utilizes most often. Often this poll will be quite large, ranging from 1,500 to 2,000 respondents. For presidential and senatorial candidates benchmark polls are often completed up to two years before the election. On the basis of benchmark polling, potential contenders may not even enter the race. As a result of the U.S.-led victory in the Persian Gulf War, George Bush enjoyed a 89 percent public approval rating in spring of 1991—a Gallup poll record ("Bush Job Performance Trend" 1992). Such strong numbers persuaded several prominent Democratic presidential hopefuls to skip the 1992 race, including Jessie Jackson, House majority leader Richard Gephardt, Senator Bill Bradley, and Senator Jay Rockefeller.

Benchmark polls help candidates develop their themes and sharpen their images, but to determine whether these messages are getting though to the electorate candidates use *trend* polls. These follow-up surveys act as a kind of "report card" for candidates by probing more deeply into a narrower range of subjects. Trend polls have a smaller sample size, often five hundred respondents, and may be carried out as often as once a month.

Early in the history of election surveys, in 1948, pollsters predicted that Thomas Dewey, rather than Harry Truman, would win the presidential election. This specific error was largely due to the pollsters' failure to detect a last-minute shift in the preference of the electorate because of the time delay between asking the question and publishing the results. To avoid such surprises, *tracking* polls are used the last two to four weeks of the campaign. To detect shifts in voter sentiment, one hundred to two hundred likely voters are called each night. They are asked very specific questions about changes in their perceptions of the issues and the candidates (Traugott and Lavrakas 1996, 17–18). The sample size is small enough to raise questions about its validity; however, a type of "moving average" is used. The first three nights' results are added up. From that point, as each new night's results come in, the oldest night's results are dropped (Sabato 1981, 76). To process this information more efficiently, senatorial and congressional campaigns with sufficient financial resources use a computer-aided telephone interviewing system (CATI). Interviewers can directly enter responses into the computer, allowing immediate compilation of responses.

Focus groups are a basic tool used by polling organizations. Such groups are not a random sample but usually consist of ten to twenty people who are chosen to represent the target groups the campaign is trying to influence. The questions are often open-ended to uncover more deeply embedded responses that might be missed by questions designed by pollsters. Potential commercials are screened by focus groups. Pretesting may tell the campaign which ads will not work, rather than which ones are the best.

The polls used by candidates have a strategic purpose as well; they try to find out how the public will respond to political trends that grab the headlines. Whether the top story is a presidential scandal involving an intern or a shutdown of many government services as the Congress and the president battle over budgetary matters, polling information is critical to determine whether the headlines are of real concern to constituents (and thus can affect reelection chances) or if their impact is confined "inside the Beltway" (i.e., to Washington, D.C.).

Pollsters can also use public opinion results as a strategic weapon. Announcing the results of candidate preference polls almost automatically gets coverage in newspapers, radio, and television. Dramatizing one candidate's standing may also effectively knock an opponent from the race, since a poor showing tends to demoralize volunteers and discourage potential contributors. In September 1996, when the polls showed that Bob Dole lagged far behind Bill Clinton in voter popularity, his fund-raising efforts were seriously hampered. The big contributors who usually give to both candidates to ensure a friendly reception by the victor, felt no need to support a sure loser.

Polls have been criticized for both the methods they use and the undesirable effects they can have on election outcomes. Several reasons exist for healthy skepticism about poll results. Interest groups give polls a bad name by relying on thinly disguised SUGs, or "selling under the guise of polling." Questions are heavily biased toward the group's point of view, for the purpose of obtaining a contribution with the "poll" return.

Ethical questions are also raised about "push polling" (also called negative persuasion phoning, or negative canvassing). The Dole campaign used this technique successfully in the New Hampshire primary and the Iowa caucus in 1996. Prospective voters were called and asked who they would be voting for. If the response was other than Dole, the voter was given a series of negative statements of questionable validity about the other candidate. At the end of the call the voter was again asked who his or her choice would now be. Although the practice has been denounced by organizations of professional pollsters, it helped derail the campaigns of Steve Forbes and Lamar Alexander in Iowa and New Hampshire.

Responsible pollsters face two more basic problems. The first issue is that telemarketers inundate Americans with so many obnoxious phone calls that it is difficult to find people who will take the fifteen or twenty minutes necessary for the average phone poll. The American Association for Public Opinion reports that as many as eight phone calls are necessary for a completed survey, forcing pollsters to assume that the minority willing to take part is still representative of the general public. A second problem is that the rise of instant and overnight polls forces respondents to make snap judgments on complex issues, whereas considerable information and time are necessary to form a stable opinion. As a result, polls may show either contradictory results or a volatile public opinion that is heavily dependent on the next round of news bulletins and candidate statements. For this reason James Fishkin (1995) advocates the "deliberative poll," in which a representative group of citizens are gathered and given information, with discussions occurring before individuals are polled. Although this technique can supply a missing component within public opinion, an artificial element is introduced into the process as campaigns take place amid heated political battles in which few citizens have the time or energy to undertake the kind of deliberation Fishkin advocates.

Polls have been criticized for exerting several undesirable influences on elections. One is the so-called bandwagon effect, which occurs when citizens desire to vote for the predicted winner. On the opposite side of the coin is the underdog effect, which leads a voter to support a candidate precisely because he or she is trailing in the polls. Although several reasons for questioning both the accuracy and the purpose of polls have been noted, they are still widely read, quoted, and believed by politicians and the public.

Campaign and Media Consultants: Crafting and Broadcasting the Message

Often one consultant formulates the grand strategy for the campaign and is responsible for keeping the candidate focused and "on message." Major national candidate consultants often share the media spotlight with their clients. James Carville filled the major consultant role in the 1992 Clinton campaign. Carville was known as the "Ragin' Cajun," reflecting both his Louisiana upbringing and his rather direct and forceful manner of communication. After several years as a self-described "failure" as a political consultant, he managed several successful Democratic campaigns between 1986 and 1991, including a Pennsylvania special election for Harris Wofford in 1991. Carville's "rule 1" is "never lose sight of what's botherin' people at the local K-Mart" (Grady 1992). That issue was health care, and Carville devised the following campaign slogans: "It's time to take care of our own" and "if the criminal has a right to a lawyer, the working family has a right to a doctor." Carville's approach is that the most important factor in campaign strategy is candidate definition; *what* the candidate communicates is more important than *how* the message is communicated. To be successful the candidate must "get on the offensive, define yourself, tell people what the election is about, stay on it, and stay tenaciously focused" (Raskin 1992, 28). Although the slogan became the source of endless parody, the large banner Carville placed in the 1992 campaign war room—It's the economy, stupid—emphasized the importance of that issue. Carville did not fit the political consultant stereotype, favoring blue jeans and running shoes, ordering the same 7:30 A.M. breakfast at Your Mama's Cafe in Little Rock, and serving only as an unofficial adviser after the campaign, paraphrasing Groucho Marx's statement that he "wouldn't live in any country whose government would hire me" (Grady 1992).

Carville's replacement in 1996 was Dick Morris, who had worked for Bill Clinton in his Arkansas campaigns and for key Republicans such as Senator Jesse Helms (R–N.C.) and Senate majority leader Trent Lott (R–Miss.). As the chief campaign strategist in 1995 and much of 1996, Morris refined a theme Clinton used in 1992 when he described himself as a "third-way" candidate. As discussed in Chapter 5, Morris's "triangulation strategy" successfully situated Clinton between more conservative congressional Republicans and more liberal congressional Democrats. Ultimately Morris was forced to resign in the fall before the election because of an adulterous affair that made the front pages of the tabloids.

Among Republicans, Ralph Reed is an example of the influence that consultants can exercise. As head of the Christian Coalition for eight years, Reed transformed that group into one of the most potent forces in Republican politics. His working relationship with other conservative groups led him to establish the Century Strategies consulting firm in 1997. Within two weeks he was besieged with calls from hundreds of potential clients, including nine potential GOP presidential candidates for the 2000 election. Unlike traditional campaign managers, Reed works only with candidates who share his culturally conservative convictions. Starting with Senate and gubernatorial candidates, his goal is to build a set of candidates who can capture the presidency, in the process becoming not the "IBM" but the "Microsoft" of consultants (Berke 1997). Thus before Reed considers working with a candidate, he requires the voting history of the district, the amount of money raised, and the campaign plan. In essence, potential clients must audition to see if they meet *his* standards.

In formulating campaign strategy, consultants utilize the results from research and initial polling to determine the key themes for the campaign. Although the candidate may have position papers on many issues, emphasizing too many issues simply confuses voters. In general, the consultant may recommend emphasizing substantive *positional* issues, such as economic reform, tax reform, or health care. In contrast, *valence* issues focus on personal qualities such as leadership, compassion, and integrity (Salmore and Salmore 1989, 112–113). From these two types of issues four strategies emerge:

1. Emphasize positional issues and try to increase the electorate's perceptions of the differences between the candidates.
2. Begin with a positional issue but stress your candidate's ability to deal with the issue because of the candidate's personal qualities.
3. Stress valence issues and the superiority of your candidate's personal qualities.

4. Stress valence issues but underline the inadequacy of the opponent's personal qualities.

With the second strategy, what begins as a positional issue may end up as a valence issue if a candidate places the most emphasis on his or her personal qualities. If the third strategy is chosen, because few candidates will admit to a lack of virtuous qualities, the campaign often revolves around which candidate best exemplifies the desired quality. By 1996, given the number of questionable occurrences in the Clinton White House, including allegations of presidential affairs, improprieties in the White House Travel Office (Travelgate), FBI files ending up in the White House (Filegate), and allegations of campaign finance violations, the Dole campaign stressed valence issues. Dole's campaign theme was "A better man for a better America." When these charges about Clinton's character did not resonate with the voters, an exasperated Dole exclaimed, "Where's the outrage?" Clinton's strategists deemphasized the presidency as a place for moral leadership. As a positional issue, their campaign theme, "building a bridge toward the twenty-first century," provided few details on where the bridge led. Yet the theme did stress differences between the two men in terms of age and vision. Combined with an economy that showed continued improvement during Clinton's first term, the voters rewarded the incumbent.

Media Consultants

Media consultants, who have previous experience in either advertising or television production, are a vital part of a candidate's team. In 1984, for example, Ronald Reagan's campaign assembled the "Tuesday team" to design the reelection spots. The group was headed by James Travis, president of Della Femina, Travisan Advertising Agency. Other team members included Phil Dusenberry (who produced ads for Pepsi), Ron Travisano (who created the singing cat ads for Meow Mix), and Hal Riney (who designed ads for Old Milwaukee Beer, Gallo Wines, and Saturn cars). The team used lush spots of family reunions, parades, and weddings to push the Reagan administration's "morning again in America" theme. Proving that media advising is an inexact science, techniques and themes that work well in selling one candidate do not always transfer to another candidate. The Bush campaign in 1992 created the "November company," consisting of executives who had no experience in the political arena but whose impressive list of clients included BMW, Pontiac, Budweiser, Burger King, Kraft Foods, Stanley Tools, and (appropriately for a political campaign) Milk of Magnesia (Wines 1992). Given a $40 million advertising budget, the spots created by the group were not considered hard-hitting enough by most observers (Berke 1992a). Similarly, Hal Riney was hired by Ross Perot in 1992 to produce campaign ads. However, the volatile candidate dismissed not only the spots but the firm as well.

The advertising background of many media consultants and the tactics they use raise charges of creating false candidate images, as well as distorting the issues and candidate preferences, in short, marketing the candidate like a box of cereal or a deodorant. Some critics of the consultants complain that voters are being entertained and duped rather than informed. They believe that the purpose of the short TV spot is to sell the voter an illusion, to move the voter to act without analyzing the material presented, to "con" the voter psychologically. Most consultants responsible for the commercials reply that they do not fabricate a message. Democratic consultant Tony Schwartz (1973, 93) contends that the most successful political commercials are "similar to Rorschach patterns. They do not tell the viewer anything. They surface his feelings and provide a context for him to express those feelings." He prefers the term "partipulation" to "manipulation." Voters must be willing to participate in their own manipulation by bringing certain emotional feelings and reactions to a particular commercial. As to informing the voter about what a candidate will do about an issue, Schwartz (1985) contends that listing a candidate's stands on the issues will confuse voters, but they can evaluate a candidate's feelings about an issue.

Although consultants' ethical standards may be questionable, analysis has shown that organizations that include professionals generally fare better at the polls, for both national and local offices. Winners in state legislative races reported that their organizations were of fundamental importance; by contrast, the losers in those elections were not sure about the importance of good organizations. The victors in these elections also paid much more attention to political advisers than did their defeated opponents.

As previously noted, narrowcasting is employed to transmit messages that will appeal to specific groups supporting the candidate. Consultants must select the media that will most efficiently accomplish this task, and they generally rely on seven types of communication: (1) television spots and programs, (2) radio spots and programs, (3) newspaper ads and fliers, (4) interactive technologies, (5) printed material, (6) display advertising, and (7) direct mailings.

Television.   Television remains the most important source of information about candidates, as shown in Table 7.3. Indeed, 46 percent of Americans reported regularly watching newsmagazine shows (such as *60 Minutes* or *20/20*), with 30 percent regularly watching CNN. Television is also the main source of first impressions about candidates. A Times Mirror poll found that 62 percent first learned about candidates through television advertisements (Times Mirror Center 1992b, 48–49). Interestingly, several types of TV political programs—editorials, talk shows, educational programs, documentaries, and specials—rank as more influential sources of information than talks with friends, contacts with candidates, or discussions with party workers or one's own family. Newspaper editorials are more influential than television editorials or talk shows. Radio newscasts are ranked higher than political brochures, billboards, or magazine stories.

Congressional campaigns are increasingly dominated by spending on television, as that medium accounted for almost half of Senate expenditures and a third of House candidates' budget for the election. In large, populous states such as California it is not unusual for candidates to spend up to two-thirds of their funds on television (Luntz 1988, 82). Media consultants find television is particularly useful in conveying a compressed twenty-, thirty-, or sixty-second message to large audiences because it gives the viewer the illusion of immediacy as well as a sense of involvement in the audiovisual presentation. As Napolitan (1971, 48–49) states:

> Television has an inherent mobility. It moves. It captures time and makes a record of it. . . . A still photograph or a printed word is static, it does not move forward or backward. Furthermore, it takes a much more willful effort to ignore that which stimulates two of our senses than that which strikes only one. In other words, that which I see and hear involves me more than what I just see. Once I am involved, I become a participant and add something of myself to what I see and hear. I add my own impressions and attitudes. I have become part of a circle of communication.

TABLE 7.3   Information Sources About National Candidates (in percentages)

Year	Television	Newspaper	Radio	Talk Radio	Magazines	Talked to Other People	Internet
1952	51	79	70	n.a.	40	27	n.a.
1956	74	69	45	n.a.	31	28	n.a.
1960	87	80	42	n.a.	41	33	n.a.
1964	89	79	48	n.a.	39	31	n.a.
1968	89	75	41	n.a.	36	33	n.a.
1972	88	57	43	n.a.	33	32	n.a.
1976	89	73	45	n.a.	48	37	n.a.
1980	86	71	47	n.a.	35	36	n.a.
1984	86	77	45	n.a.	35	32	n.a.
1988	n.a.	64	31	n.a.	25	29	n.a.
1992	89	65	37	n.a.	23	37	n.a.
1996	76	58	40	38	34	29	6

SOURCE: National Election Studies.

Although audio and visual messages in television advertising do work together, one Republican pollster finds that 80 to 90 percent of what people retain from television are the *visual* images (Napolitan 1971, 48–49). Thus how a person looks on television, or even the backgrounds that are utilized, is often more important than the stated audio message. During the 1984 election CBS correspondent Leslie Stahl reported on federal programs to aid disabled persons. While showing footage of President Reagan greeting groups at the White House and at various locations, Stahl's comments emphasized the lack of government action in this area. Within minutes Ronald Reagan's White House communications director, Michael Deaver, called, complimenting the reporter on the best four-and-a-half-minute political commercial produced to date for the president. Under Deaver's rule that "the visual beats the verbal," the imagery would be remembered long after the commentary was forgotten (Smith 1988, 413–414; Graber 1989, 202–203).

Network and independent television stations remain the medium of choice for political advertising. The cost of television campaigning may seem exorbitant, but it needs to be considered in terms of the cost per home reached. For presidential candidates in 1996, a thirty-second prime-time commercial on one of the top five networks ranged from over $400,000 to $500,000. For statewide candidates, a thirty-second or sixty-second spot on the top-rated show can vary greatly according to the size of the market. The sum of $30,000 would only buy thirty seconds in Los Angeles, whereas sixty seconds in Chicago costs roughly $15,000, compared to $6,000 in Minneapolis (Meyer and Porado 1990, 42; Luntz 1988, 82).

To cut costs, candidates are increasingly turning to the ten-second spot, which runs for about half the price of the thirty-second spot but only allows time for about twenty words. Critics worry that the compressed time period does not allow for much more than name calling. In California's 1992 primary election, Republican senatorial candidate Bruce Herschensohn used his ten seconds to state, "I'm Bruce Herschensohn. My opponent, Tom Campbell, was the only Republican congressman opposing the 1990 anticrime bill. He's liberal and wrong." Tom Cambell (pushing the envelope with an extended twenty-nine-word reply) responded, "Bruce Herschensohn is lying. Tom Campbell voted to extend the death penalty to 27 crimes, and was named 'Legislator of the Year' by the California Fraternal Order of Police" (Kolbert 1992b). Some consultants contend that the ten-second spot fits an age of decreasing attention spans and can convey significant political information.

Cable television, which is found in about 75 percent of households in major metropolitan areas, offers several benefits to candidates engaged in narrowcasting. Many channels are targeted to specific audiences with channels for general news, financial news, sports, and popular music. Candidates find it easier to buy a spot in a specific time period, and for less money. Moreover, research on cable subscribers finds that they are more likely to vote, to be involved in political fundraising, and to work actively for a political candidate. Since 1988 cable television has been used extensively in presidential contests. One major drawback to cable was its exclusion from national ratings services, making it difficult to verify which segments of the audience watch cable. However, since the first national ratings appeared in 1993, media consultants have increasingly looked to cable television as a narrowcast medium.

Radio.   Radio is found in 99 percent of American homes, 95 percent of cars, and in 61 percent of workplaces. For local elections, radio is one of the two major means used by candidates, along with television. Radio advertising offers several benefits to candidate advertising when compared with television. First, the audience for radio is more interested in local politics and has more knowledge of it than television viewers (Becker and Dunwoody 1982, 214–215, 218).

Second, radio stations offer programs that appeal to narrow, homogeneous segments of the population, ranging from classical music to continuous news broadcasts to alternative rock. This segmenting of listeners allows candidates to tailor their messages to specific audiences, knowing that segments of the population who may strongly oppose the message are unlikely to be listening. Indeed, some professionals argue that in certain commuter markets in which people spend much time in their cars, such as Southern California, radio ads can be more effective than television ads.

Radio also functions as an effective vehicle for negative advertising. Spots aired during drive-time commutes that bash an opponent resonate with the public, who are already angry at being stuck in traffic. Further, what was once thought to be a disadvantage of radio—that it does not provide a strong visual image to accompany the message—allows candidates to make negative attacks without becoming too closely associated with the attack. Such ads are difficult for the opposition to keep up with because of the large number of radio stations in any market (Kolbert 1992a).

Finally, radio has several advantages in terms of costs. Because less technical and expensive production equipment is required, a high-quality spot can be produced for about $750–$1,000 (South 1992, 30). Candidates can quickly and inexpensively respond to a recent event, the latest polling results, or an opponent's last-minute campaign attacks. Moreover, airing radio spots is much less expensive, although, as with television, the cost of radio time varies. A sixty-second spot on the number one–rated station in New York City can cost $900; in Topeka, Kansas, a similar spot may cost $50.

More recently, some political consultants have questioned several of radio's benefits. Listeners are shifting to FM stations that favor "more music and less talk." In this format, however, political commercials constitute more of an intrusion. The splintering of rock 'n' roll formats into "micro-differentiated stations" has led to the radio version of "grazing" (a practice originated by television viewers, wherein viewers exhibit such dexterity in changing channels with the remote control that it rivals a fast-paced video game) (Wolff 1989, 34). Those buying radio advertisements are no longer ensured that specific demographic segments will identify with a station. Finally, technological changes have lowered the cost of video production and editing equipment, thereby diminishing this traditional advantage of radio.

Ironically, although media advisers spend more time and money on electronic media advertising, some critics question the utility of the advertising that is run. Research on the effectiveness of television advertising finds that it has the greatest impact on low-level, nonpartisan, and state races (Swinyard and Coney 1978). When voters know little about the candidates, television ads convey the message more effectively than the news. Massive media spending to disseminate the message, however, does not directly translate into votes. Particularly in high interest–high visibility races, voters receive substantial cues from other sources. Moreover, incumbency has proved to be a more important (if not the single most important) factor in determining election success.

Newspapers. Those who use newspapers as their source of information have higher levels of education, which in turn is linked to a greater knowledge of politics and a greater likelihood of voting in elections (Becker and Whitney 1980, 110; Becker and Dunwoody 1982, 214). This medium is therefore better than television for disseminating in-depth information on the candidates' background and issue positions, as well as for "get-out-the-vote" campaigns. Newspaper readers are more likely to make up their minds earlier about the candidates or the issues, and they are much less likely to change their decisions.

More recently, however, questions have been raised about whether newspapers are declining as a source of information. More than 78 percent of the adult public reported reading a newspaper just about every day in the 1970s, compared to 62 percent in the 1990s. When the question becomes more specific—Did you get a chance to read a newspaper yesterday?—only 48 percent responded affirmatively (Times Mirror Center 1992b, 49). Of those under thirty-five, only 24 percent responded affirmatively.

Voters rate newspaper editorials as more influential in their decision-making than television editorials. Yet it is important to differentiate between national and local races. Little evidence exists of the ability of editorials to influence voter behavior at the presidential level, but their influence is likely to be greater at the state and local levels (Dunham 1991, 66).

Republican campaign consultant Frank Luntz contends that newspaper ads do not have much of an impact, even among those who claim to read the newspaper daily (Luntz 1988,109). One difficulty is that to get the most mileage out of a newspaper ad, candidates are cautioned that it must be "different." A typical daily newspaper includes at least three hundred ads, all competing for the reader's attention. The candidate's ad must catch the reader's eye as he or she proceeds to the comics or the sports section. Good artwork, "catchy" headlines, and large ads are necessary to attract attention. The cost of such advertisements varies with the newspaper's circulation, the size of the ad, and its location in the newspaper. Newspaper ads vary in price from $1,000 per page in medium-sized newspapers to $56,700 for a full-page ad in the Sunday *New York Times.*

Interactive Technology: Not Ready for Prime Time? Opinions differ as to whether the Internet and related technologies will play a major role in campaigns. Campaign finance law prevents the president and members of Congress from using their official government-financed home pages to solicit funds (or to pursue any other election purposes) within sixty days of an election, including providing links to any other websites that could provide that information (Klotz 1997, 483). Going on-line provides a means for third-party or less well funded candidates to reach a larger number of voters. For example, GOP presidential candidate Phil Gramm's website recorded 197,000 hits, or visits, for an investment of $8,000, about eight times the number of potential voters that could be reached if the same amount were spent on first-class mail (Just 1997, 100). Although the cost per voter reached is low, for a number of web pages the amount of information provided about political issues is low as well. A study of the home pages of forty-five Senate candidates in 1996 found they ranged from providing no information to two typewritten pages (28 percent), three to ten pages (44 percent), to more than ten pages (28 percent) (Klotz 1997, 483–484).

As with any new medium, media advisers experienced difficulties in providing visitors with a meaningful interactive experience. GOP candidate Steve Forbes's home page, featuring a "flat tax calculator" did provide the amount of tax that would be paid under the candidate's flat tax proposal once visitors supplied their income and number of personal exemptions and dependents. Other home pages, however, would win few awards for innovation. Bill Clinton's home page used an "Electoral College computer" that added up the number of votes once a visitor predicted which candidate would win each state, and Bob Dole's home page printed out a campaign flier with the visitor's name prominently displayed as a supporter of the candidate.

Of those seeking information on-line, studies have found a bias toward higher levels of income and education, in part due to limitations of access to computers and to Internet providers (Birdsell 1996, 33). Thus about 12 percent of the voting-age population received political or policy news from on-line services in 1996, whereas 4 percent used the Internet or commercial services (Pew Research Center 1996, 4). Not surprisingly, a profile of this group finds them to be largely white and male, as well as younger and more politically knowledgeable than the general population. The number of those seeking political and policy news was small, but they were very active, as one in three took part in both public opinion polls and on-line discussions about the election. There is little evidence that interactive technologies are supplanting the more traditional sources of information, as on-line users were seeking additional information not available from other sources and were attracted by the convenience of the Internet. One-third of Internet users, for example, sought information about congressional races, whereas one-fourth were looking for news about local races (Pew Research Center 1996, 15).

As for the quality of information conveyed, the Internet represents an unregulated market for information and news, where the vast quantity of data available results in wide variation in quality. Finding desired sites is the first problem. When keywords are typed into the available search engines (e.g., Alta Vista, Yahoo, Lycos), the results may be hundreds or even thousands of possibilities. Moreover, the old adage "Let the buyer beware" certainly applies to the Internet, given the ability to post items anonymously and the lack of identification from many individuals and groups posting messages or establishing web pages. In 1996 for example, a group obtained a web address that was very close to Bob Dole's home page, and produced an official-looking site that was actually a parody of the Dole campaign. A final problem is that the high levels of education and knowledge possessed by on-line users increases their chances of being disappointed by the results of the web pages. Only about a quarter of those who sought on-line information found it to be "very useful," whereas two-thirds described it as "somewhat useful" (Pew Research Center 1996, 19).

In sum, one view is that the current state of on-line development is analogous to the early use of television in campaigns. Once media advisers learned how to use television's strengths to disseminate information, it became an indispensable medium. Others believe the disparity between the volume and quality of information, as well as the difficulty of providing a meaningful interactive experience, will confine on-line use to political junkies and policy activists.

The Campaign Manager

Campaign organizations vary in size from a group of three or four who are trying to elect a friend to a minor office to a team of thousands who work in a presidential campaign. Whatever the size or complexity of the organization, the basic task remains the same: to coordinate the efforts of the three groups of campaign workers—the professionals, the party workers, and the nonparty volunteers. The person primarily responsible for this task is the campaign manager.

The professional campaign manager of today differs from past managers in two distinct ways: the relationship with the party organization and the sophistication of the skills employed. The traditional campaign manager, who had many years of party experience, relied heavily on the organization and the skills of party workers for the traditional vote-getting procedures—door knocking, canvassing, and personal voter contact in the precincts. The professional, however, operates largely from an established, private, profit-making firm that is relatively independent of the political party.

The professional campaign manager also differs from the traditional one in his or her personal background, which will determine the skills the professional uses. The professional is well versed in marketing, public relations, and communications rather than door knocking and backroom dealing. By the early 1970s, David Rosenbloom (1973, 67) found that over two-thirds of campaign managers had a background in public relations, advertising, journalism, or radio and television; only 11 percent came from a traditional political party or campaign staff position.

Although a campaign manager is likely to work for candidates of a single party, a campaign manager views campaigns from a business perspective rather than a party perspective. Bill Roberts, of the Spencer-Roberts team, emphasized this at a meeting sponsored by the Republican National Committee (Rosenbloom 1973, 104): "As a Campaign manager, your sole purpose is to win. There is absolutely no other goal. You are not trying to prove a cause or sell a philosophy. You are trying to win a campaign in the most expeditious manner possible, using every legal and moral way to do so."

As Roberts suggests, the unofficial cliché of campaign managers is that "all is fair in love and war." Thus in a symposium one year after the 1996 election, Clinton senior strategist George Stephanopoulos acknowledged seeking strategic advantage by demanding that presidential debates be held in early and mid-October so that the debates would be a "nonevent"—they would have no impact on the outcome of the election. Yet the decisions of campaign managers often make it difficult to draw a line between ethical and unethical behavior. At the same symposium, Dole campaign manager Scott Reed was asked why the campaign continued to run an advertisement that was shown to be "demonstrably false." Although Reed regretted airing a spot that was wrong to begin with, to acknowledge error when his candidate was so far behind would have been perceived as a further sign of weakness (Germond and Whitcover 1997).

The illustration of campaign organization presented in Figure 7.1 gives the impression of a well-run, hierarchical structure with clear lines of authority. Far from being a well-oiled machine, a campaign is an exercise in frenzy, or as one consultant described it, "a Marx Brothers movie without a laugh track." Actual responsibilities may not be reflected on the chart, and day-to-day decisionmaking in the organization is fluid. In the Clinton campaign, for example, key decisions about how much soft money would be needed, where it should be raised, and how it should be allocated were made by White House deputy chief of staff Harold Ickes. To coordinate Clinton's themes and messages for the day, campaign consultant Dick Morris would have a conference call every weekday morning with Ickes, deputy campaign manager and communications director Ann Lewis, White House communications director Donald Baer, presidential press secretary Michael McCurry, White House political affairs director Doug Sosnik, senior strategy adviser George Stephanopoulos, and pollster Mark Penn. Weekly strategy meetings would include fifteen to twenty other high-ranking campaign officials and would review weekly changes in the polling data and the efforts of the Clinton reelection committee and the Democratic National Committee, and even examine proposed scripts for future television spots (Barnes 1996a, 1569–1570). From the chaos inherent in most campaigns, these twenty-five members were able to bring sufficient order to accomplish Bill Clinton's reelection in 1996.

The Impact of Negative Campaigning

When Independent candidate Pat Buchanan indicated in 1992 that he would not criticize Vice President Dan Quayle because he did not want to be accused of "child abuse," or when George Bush's campaign press secretary described Independent candidate Ross Perot as having a wingspan with his ears that exceeded his total height, the opening salvos of negative campaigning had been fired. Not surprisingly, the public perception is that negative campaigns are on the rise. About half of the respondents in one poll of registered voters found that most of the commercials they viewed attacked a candidate, and 40 percent claimed current campaigns are more negative than those of a decade ago (Rothenberg 1990b). Studies by academics suggest a more complex picture. A study of 379 prominent campaign spots from 1952 to 1996 found 54 percent to be negative, with nominating campaigns slightly more negative than general elections (57 percent to 53 percent), and Republican spots more negative than Democratic spots (60 percent to 48 percent) (West 1997, 58). In analyzing 1984 GOP senatorial spots, for example, Payne and Baukus (1988, 165) found attack ads to be predominant among incumbents and challengers. Regional variation was evident, as southern GOP candidates made the greatest use of this tactic, followed by the Midwest, West, and North.

Although perceptions of negative ads are on the increase, agreement on what constitutes "negative campaign ads" or a "negative campaign" is not as great. What is negative to one partisan is simply "getting out the facts" to another partisan. Karen Johnson-Cartee and Gary Copeland (1991, 38–51) provide a more useful definition by breaking the concept of negative ads into three parts: direct attack ads, direct comparison ads, and implied comparison ads. *Direct attack* ads, as the name implies, have as their sole purpose attacking the opposition. The ad is structured to imply that the opponent is inferior. Consultants advocating this type of ad believe that part of the electorate votes *against* one candidate rather than *for* the opponent. The direct attack has always been a mainstay of our nation's political history. In 1832, Representative John Livingston called his opponent "utterly corrupt" and added this summation: "He shines and stinks like a rotten mackerel by moonlight!" In 1884, on learning that Democratic candidate Grover Cleveland had fathered an illegitimate son, youngsters were encouraged to attend Cleveland's rallies to chant "Ma! Ma! Where's my Pa!" In 1944 opponents of youthful presidential candidate Thomas E. Dewey said he ran for office by "throwing his diaper into the ring." George Smathers defeated Senator Claude Pepper in the 1950 Florida senatorial primary race by absurd but sensational-sounding charges, calling Pepper "a shameless EXTROVERT" who "practices NEPOTISM with his sister-in-law" and has "a sister who was once a THESPIAN!" (Moody 1992).

More recent attack ads display only slightly greater subtlety. In the 1990 California gubernatorial race, Dianne Feinstein's campaign broadcast a spot that showed her Republican opponent, Senator Pete Wilson, being wheeled into the Senate on a stretcher to cast a critical budget vote. The announcer quoted the comments of Republican leader Bob Dole: "Wilson was under heavy sedation. They rolled him in on the floor. I said vote 'yes'; he voted 'yes.' We rolled Wilson out again. He does better under sedation." The announcer then asked voters to imagine what the Democratic leader of the State Assembly and the legislature would do to a Wilson governorship ("Dole Was Kidding" 1990).

Because direct attack messages do not provide any kind of comparison, they run the greatest risk of backfiring on the sponsor if the public finds the message to be in bad taste. By placing the ad in a humorous context, Feinstein's campaign hoped to lessen the possibility of a backlash, but the candidate was defeated.

In contrast, the *direct comparison* spot contrasts the candidates' records, experience, or positions on the issues, for the purpose of claiming superiority over the opponent (Johnson-Cartee and Copeland 1991, 42). The ad uses inductive logic in offering a few specific bits of information and asking the viewer to draw a broad conclusion about a candidate's superiority. As one example, a 1996 spot produced by the Democratic National Committee began with Bob Dole proclaiming, "We sent him the first balanced budget in a generation. He vetoed it. We're going to veto Bill Clinton." The announcer then continued, "The facts? The President proposes a balanced budget protecting Medicare, education, the environment. But Dole is voting no. The President cuts taxes for 40 million Americans. Dole votes no. The President bans assault weapons; demands work for welfare while protecting kids. Dole says no to the Clinton plans. It's time to say yes to the Clinton plans—yes to America's families" (West 1997, 32).

Implied comparison ads, the third type, are not negative in the sense of the words used, but in the conclusion that the viewer draws from the comparison. Two classic examples are the 1964 "Daisy Ad" and the 1984 "Bear Ad." For the Johnson campaign in 1964, Democratic advertising consultant Tony Schwartz designed a spot that had a powerful impact on viewers. A small girl in a field of flowers is plucking petals from a daisy. She counts the petals and reaches "nine." Then she is startled, and the camera zooms in for an extreme close-up of her pupil. A man's voice off-screen begins a countdown, and when he reaches "zero," an atomic explosion fills the screen. Over the distinctive mushroom cloud, President Johnson's voice proclaims: "These are the stakes—to make a world in which all of God's children can live, or to go into the dark. We must either love each other, or we must die." The announcer then urges viewers to vote for President Johnson on November 4 because "the stakes are too high for you to stay home" (Schwartz 1973, 93–96; Diamond and Bates 1992, 124). The Democrats ran the ad only once, but network news programs subsequently aired it. Tony Schwartz explained that the commercial had such an impact because it "*evoked* a deep feeling in many people that Goldwater might actually use nuclear weapons. This mistrust was not in the *Daisy* spot. It was in the people who viewed the commercial. The stimuli of the film and sound evoked these feelings and allowed people to express what they inherently believed" (Schwartz 1973, 93).

Provoking a similar reaction was the goal of three ads run by Republicans in 1998. Although the spots avoided direct mention of President Clinton's sex scandal, the indirect reference sought such a comparison. In "The Denial" the President is shown as he misleads the public by stating he did not have "sexual relations" with Monica Lewinsky. The announcer states, "Remember, it's your choice. For balance. Vote Republican" ("Angle of G.O.P. Attack" 1998). A second spot, "The Question," asks, "In every election there is a big question to think about. This year, the question is, should we reward Bill Clinton?" The final spot, "The Answer," features a dialogue between two women: Woman 1: "What did you tell your kids?"

Woman 2: "I didn't know what to say." Woman 1: "It's wrong. For seven months he lied to us." The spots hoped to underscore Clinton's perceived weakness as a moral leader when compared to Republican congressional candidates.

For the student of campaigns, negative spots raise several important questions: How effective are negative ads? How can candidates respond to this tactic? Most importantly, does the emphasis on negative spots increase voter alienation and lead to decreasing participation in elections?

As to the effectiveness of such campaigns, as Tony Schwartz indicated, the greatest limitation is that a spot must evoke an emotional feeling the voter can identify with. In the case of the Republican ads, although many Americans abhorred Clinton's behavior in office, they did not buy the implied comparison with the moral virtue of Republican congressional candidates. If the intended comparison is accepted, negative ads are effective. Even if voters say they dislike negative advertising, they tend to retain the negative message better, and to act on it. One survey of six southern states found that 65 percent of respondents did not favor the use of such ads, but two-thirds were able to remember specific negative ads (Johnson-Cartee and Copeland 1991, 11). Similarly, positive ads may require five to ten viewings before the message registers, whereas a negative commercial makes an impact after one or two viewings (Guskind and Hagstrom 1988, 2787). If the voters find the attack to be credible, usually for a week or two a candidate running the negative spot will see a small decline in voter approval, but in the long term voters forget the source of the spot while retaining its negative content (Pfau and Kenski 1990, 158; May 1988; Hagstrom and Guskind 1986). In the 1992 Democratic senatorial primary in New York, for example, former vice presidential candidate Geraldine Ferraro was comfortably ahead in the polls until opponents raised questions about ties between organized crime and both Ferraro and her husband. Over the long term the ads had the desired effect, as observers agreed the ads were a major reason that Ferraro lost the nomination in a very close election.

If negative ads are so effective, how can candidates respond? The best defense may be an inoculation campaign, combined with refutational preemption. Although these terms may sound like a combined press release from the public health service and the military, the inoculation concept attempts to raise a threat in order to motivate the viewer to defend against the attack. Simultaneously, the refutation provides material in a supportive environment to ward off the attack (Pfau and Kenski 1990, 75; Pfau and Burgoon 1988). In his 1988 reelection bid incumbent congressman Wayne Owens of Utah ran an early spot in which a rather matronly looking actress (who actually did happen to be Wayne Owens's neighbor) shakes her finger at the camera and scolds, "Shame on you boys for calling Wayne Owens a big spender! I've been his neighbor for years. The man is *cheap!*" After extolling his many thrifty virtues, she concludes, "You boys ought to start telling the truth, and *stop fibbing!*" In this case the symbol of an elderly relative or friend who speaks one's mind provides credibility to both raise the threat (opponents are going to start lying) and provide the refutation (the reasons he is not a "big spender"). Research has shown that inoculation must be started early to be effective, and that the effect is likely to help the candidate much later in the race. Television is a particularly appropriate medium for inoculation spots because the viewers tend to be passive and thus more receptive to the message (Cundy 1986; Kern 1989).

One short-term check on negative ads is that they do run in cycles. Given a constant diet of negative ads, voters may express increased dissatisfaction with the tone of the election. When negative campaign ads become *the* focus of the election, candidates will abruptly switch tactics. Polls taken for Representative Ron Wyden (D–Ore.), for example, who ran for a Senate seat in a 1996 special election, indicated that voters' primary concern was the negative tone of the election. Wyden had relied on negative campaigning in the past but began having himself introduced at campaign events with a song recorded by Bing Crosby and the Andrews Sisters: "*Ac-cent-tchu-ate the positive . . . E-lim-in-ate the negative*" (Elving 1996, 440). Wyden continued this theme through the campaign.

As to whether an abundance of negativity in campaigns drives voters from the polls, the studies to date are inconclusive. Stephen Ansolabehere and Shanto Iyengar (1995) contend that negative campaigns do have a measurable effect on both turnout and political efficacy. Advertising can mobilize or demobilize voters, depending on the type of messages that are transmitted. A major difficulty is isolating the impact of campaign ads on the voter from the effect of other influences. To accomplish this, a control group that saw no political advertisements was compared to groups that saw actual campaign spots that candidates aired, as well as the authors' professionally produced fictional ads that used actual candidates' names. They found that exposure to positive ads increased intention to vote by 2.3 percent, whereas viewing negative ads reduced it by 4.6 percent (Ansolabehere and Iyengar 1995, 104–105; Ansolabehere et al. 1994, 835). The greatest impact occurred with nonpartisans, who are likely to have a more pessimistic view of politics in the first place. For partisans, the greatest effect was on deciding which candidate to vote for rather than whether to vote (Ansolabehere and Iyengar 1995, 110–112). A similar effect was observed on political efficacy, Among those who saw the negative ads there were 5.2 percent fewer people who felt that their vote counted, compared with the control group.

The effect of negative ads on voter turnout and political efficacy is still under debate, however. One study determined that campaigns based on negative advertising do not have a major effect on decreasing political trust (Martinez and Delegal 1990). Another critique targets Ansolabehere and Iyengar, contending that negative ads have very little effect on turnout. When these spots are broken down into issue attacks and character attacks, Finkel and Greer (1998, 577) find that ads that target issues decrease participation slightly, character attacks mobilize voters slightly, and the net effect is very small. Although the finding that attacking character actually entices more voters seems counterintuitive, one explanation is that these spots give more information to voters, and the new data are given greater weight. The spots provide stronger emotional reasons to participate (Lau 1985). The electorate not only responds by voting against the target of attacks, but a candidate's supporters respond by seeking more information to offset the flood of negative images. In sum, it may be both convenient and satisfying to blame lower turnout in part on the use of negative ads, but conclusive statements about their impact must await further study.

Evaluating the Media and the Candidates

The relationship between the media and the candidates has always been one of interdependence, combined with mutual suspicion and antagonism. Two of the complaints traditionally lodged against the electronic and printed media are that they operate with a distinct conservative or liberal bias, favoring one party over the other, and that they have undue influence on election outcomes.

Historically, all candidates have complained about an unfair or biased press. During President Kennedy's administration the White House would cancel its subscription for short periods to papers that had fallen into disfavor. After losing the gubernatorial race in California in 1962, Richard Nixon lambasted the press for unfair coverage: "You won't have Nixon to kick around anymore because, gentlemen, this is my last press conference" (Facts on File 1962, 390). Vice presidents have often been given the task of criticizing the media. During the Nixon administration Vice President Spiro Agnew attacked the "instant analysis and querulous criticism" of network commentators who had been elected by no one. His counterpart in the Bush administration, Dan Quayle, decried the "liberal media elite," who selected and interpreted the issues presented to the nation. At rallies, Bush would hold up a bumper sticker reading "Annoy the media: Re-elect Bush," while GOP crowds would chant "tell the truth" to reporters.

The second complaint is that the "big" names in journalism set the themes, decide the issues, and even overwhelm the candidates' messages with their own presence. Of course, correspondents and columnists do play a significant role in interpreting political events and in analyzing candidates. Some critics believe that because 98 percent of all American homes have television sets, the media can mold public opinion, shape voter preferences, single out their own preferred candidates, and create an aura among voters that their chosen candidate is the nation's favorite politician. Other critics believe that the major problem is the blurring of the lines between entertainment and news reporting and the resulting celebrity status of many journalists. The crush of media covering the New Hampshire presidential primary caused *Washington Post* reporter Howard Kurtz to ask, "Was the presidential primary about New Hampshire, or was it about Dan Rather, Tom Brokaw, Peter Jennings, Larry King, Mary Matalin, Tim Russert, Cokie Roberts, Bernard Shaw, Don Imus, Fred Barnes, Chris Matthews, and a few hundred of their closest friends?" (Owen 1997, 215). Moreover, the proliferation of political commentary on such shows as *Crossfire* or *The Capital Gang* means that more emphasis is given to what commentators think than to what politicians say.

Those who support the media claim its ability to change votes or perceptions of issues is limited. The media's position is that it reports, and doesn't create, the news. As ABC reporter Sam Donaldson states, "When we cover the candidates, we cover their campaigns as they outline them" (Hertzgaard 1988, 36). In this view voters are also seen as individuals who have their own predispositions and opinions, not as vacuums waiting to be filled by journalists or television newscasters. This view argues that voters screen out most material that conflicts with their own views, listen selectively, and evaluate the content of the message. From this perspective, the media simply convey cues to an already predisposed audience, so that voter opinions are not altered but simply reinforced and stabilized.

Although candidates believe that fewer of their messages are being reported and that the media grossly distort the tone and context of those that are conveyed, what is different in recent years is the ability of candidates to do something about it. The change is best summarized in the headline of one article: "If You Can't Beat 'Em, Bypass 'Em!" (Balz 1992). Office seekers actively avoid spontaneous and challenging formats such as debates or appearances on NBC's *Meet the Press* or CBS's *Face the Nation*. The number of presidential press conferences has declined over the past fifteen years, and network coverage of such events is sporadic. Instead, office seekers attempt to transmit their messages directly to the electorate, unfiltered by the media, for example, by using the Internet and appearing on talk radio shows. Another method is the "message of the day." The campaign limits the ability of reporters to choose from among many messages by determining one message or theme to emphasize. The candidate repeats only that message—leaving the media the option of using that message or having nothing to report. Members of Congress also use technology provided by political parties to bypass the national networks. Incumbents can speak on key issues at the television studios of the Republican and Democratic headquarters. Video press releases are transmitted directly to local television stations and can be used on nightly news broadcasts.

The media, in turn, react to the candidates' attempts to control reporting of their messages by deemphasizing coverage of political events. Believing that a sense of drama is necessary to gain ratings, the media follow the old adage "if it bleeds, it leads!" Thus crime and natural disasters receive prominent coverage. To add a sense of drama to coverage of political events, the media focus on the "horse race" aspects of elections and play an "expectations game" using the polls, paying too much attention to who is ahead in the polls at the moment (West 1997, 72–74). CNN and *USA Today* even provide daily tracking polls of presidential candidates' popularity. Conversely, they give too little attention to the content of an office seeker's message or how the programs proposed will affect the daily life of average citizens. In the electronic media, coverage of substance is usually reduced to ten-second or thirty-second "sound bites" in which politicians must use catchy phrases or slogans designed to grab the viewer's attention. CBS News became so concerned about ten-second sound bites that it directed reporters to use thirty-second clips of candidates' speeches. The network relaxed this requirement when if found that politicians were so accustomed to speaking in ten-second bites that they said nothing of substance in the remaining twenty seconds. Moreover, in the "expectations game" media use the results of early polls to project the percentage of the vote a presidential candidate needs in each primary election to remain viable. Candidates who do not meet media expectations are quickly designated to an "also ran" category.

One final complaint about the media is that not enough has been done to analyze the content of candidates' negative advertising and to alert the electorate about which charges have validity and which do not. This charge was aired in the early 1980s by political scientist Larry Sabato and repeated after the 1988 election by columnists such as David Broder (Sabato 1981; Broder 1989). Since the 1988 election major newspapers such as the *Washington Post* and the *New York Times* have analyzed national spots while regional papers have examined state races. One survey of newspapers and television stations found that 65 percent of newspapers and 44 percent of television stations conducted ad watches (West 1997, 100).

Some of the "ad watches" merely comment on the factual accuracy of an ad, whereas others comment on the strategy behind the ad. For example, a 1992 Bill Clinton spot put forward a plan to create 8 million new jobs. The *New York Times* described both the images on the screen and the script of the spot. Assessing the accuracy of the spot, a reporter expressed doubt that the plan could be sold to Congress but indicated that it could work under the right economic conditions. A "scorecard" section in the article analyzed the visual setting for the commercial, as well as who the spot might appeal to—Democrats who voted for Ronald Reagan and George Bush in past elections but were concerned about the state of the economy (Berke 1992b).

This newspaper analysis has had both positive and negative effects. On the positive side the analysis decreases the likelihood of outrageously false advertisements. Some candidates now regularly document their claims, giving the source for the statement much like footnotes in a text. However, media attempts to inform voters can run into the law of unintended consequences. For example, when viewers were shown a CNN ad watch, they developed greater sympathy for the candidate who was being scrutinized by reporters. The effect was most evident among nonpartisans. The combination of repeating the negative content of the ad and singling out the ad for criticism violated the media's norm of fairness and increased levels of alienation and cynicism among Independents (Ansolabehere and Iyengar 1995, 139–141).

A second effect is that the media become incorporated into a candidate's advertising. If a newspaper declares a spot to be distorted or misleading, political consultants charged up with the entrepreneurial spirit are likely to seize upon those words for *their* candidate's next spot, attempting to put the prestige of the newspaper behind their candidate. If both candidates can use statements from the same or different newspapers to attack each other's credibility, voter confusion may simply increase.

A final difficulty is that television advertising evokes strong emotional feelings and images, often without mentioning the opponent's name. Newspapers must then attempt the very difficult task of analyzing vivid television images in cold print, knowing that the public is more likely to retain the initial image of the ad rather than the subsequent analysis (West 1997, 96; Rothenberg 1990a).

Conclusion: Parties and Campaign Politics: An Altered Balance

In this chapter we have examined the three campaign roles that political parties play. During the period of rule by political bosses, party organization dominated candidates' campaigns. By the 1950s many candidates mounted independent operations, raising both the money and the personnel necessary for the campaign. Since the 1980s the political parties have staged a comeback of sorts, operating as an intermediary by providing such services as campaign schools and broadcasting facilities. Although showing more signs of life, parties must still compete for influence, with both the experts hired by the campaigns and interest groups.

A successful candidate today generally combines traditional and new methods of campaigning; a party organization, when it is available, can be an important source of personal contact with the voters—through door knocking, canvassing, and telephoning. Consultants, despite their public denouncements of party structure, still rely on party organization when it is advantageous. They are available for party employment and generally align themselves with one or another party by working exclusively for its candidates.

Negative campaigns constitute a substantial portion of political advertising, and such tactics have the effect of lowering participation in the political system, especially among Independents. Negative campaigning may be viewed as the advertising the citizenry "loves to hate" because at the same time that the public denounces such advertising it also relies on it to evaluate the worst that can be said about a candidate.

In the tumultuous relationship between the media and contestants for public office, candidates have mastered how to bypass the media and present their views more directly to the public, using methods ranging from the Internet to the "message of the day." As to the media's ability to exercise undue influence over the electorate, the media's primary impact is to reinforce rather than overturn existing political attitudes.

Interest groups (discussed in the next chapter) provide substantial competition for parties because groups have mastered the new technology in order to raise substantial amounts of money, contact voters, and directly influence Washington politics, much to the chagrin of both parties. Clearly, the present is an uncomfortable period of transition for parties, candidates, and professionals in campaign politics.

8

Political Campaigns and Interest Groups

From Electoral Campaigns to Advocacy Campaigns

The distance between political campaigns run largely by and for political parties and political campaigns run largely by and for interest groups was bridged in the early 1990s. The political campaign that symbolized the merging of the two types of campaigns was President Clinton's unsuccessful health care reform efforts in 1993–1994. Obviously, many important elements of modern campaigns had been used in both types of campaigns in many previous years, but the nearly complete merging of the types of campaigns was indicative of a new style of interest group politics based on the election campaign model described in the two previous chapters. That new style of interest group campaign can be called the "total war" model. It has raised the stakes of interest group conflict significantly, as well as the costs.

Interest groups are frequent participants in the election game as well, playing two distinct roles. First, groups have come to dominate direct policy-making processes in many states as over the decades they have discovered the advantages of initiative and referendum in the advancement of their policy objectives. These I&R elections have become more frequent in many states, especially in the West. Each year hundreds of campaigns are contested among thousands of interest groups to influence an ever growing range of public policies. Second, as the 1994, 1996, and 1998 elections demonstrated, groups have become increasingly powerful political actors in election campaigns in support of political parties and their candidates. Groups such as the AFL-CIO have reasserted their once powerful contribution to the Democratic party, and the Christian Coalition has emerged as the Right's (and the

Republican party's) organizational equivalent to Big Labor. Additionally, dozens of other groups joined the electoral battles and made significant contributions. In this chapter we will discuss the range of interest group strategies and tactics as they have been applied in electoral campaigns.

The "Total War" Campaign of Health Care Reform

The political "war" over health care reform was one of the defining moments in recent American political history. It was defining because it clearly established the previously suspected fact that interest groups could successfully withstand the power of a determined president and all the political resources he could muster in a direct showdown on a policy issue. It was also defining in the sense that the outcomes of the issue war echoed throughout the nation and changed the course of American political party history by officially ending the New Deal era and giving Republicans control of Congress for the first time in almost fifty years.

The issue of health care reform had been raised to the status of a potential major issue in the 1990 U.S. Senate race in Pennsylvania. The underdog Democratic candidate turned to health care as his issue and won a dramatic victory. A year later, as Bill Clinton planned for his campaign to win the Democratic party presidential nomination, the potential of health care was acknowledged as powerful. After the general election campaign against the incumbent president, George Bush, health care grew to be the top new domestic program in the new Clinton administration. The battle over health care reform in 1993–1994 marked the formal beginning of the era of massive interest group participation in the "new style" of political campaigns. Interest groups had participated in various issue campaigns previously, but never with the intensity, commitment of resources, and wide range of strategies and tactics found in the health care reform effort.

Certainly, interest groups and movements have been periodic participants in some of the great political campaigns of American history. The abolitionist movement was active in the formation of the new Republican party in the 1850s and vitally important in Abraham Lincoln's successful presidential campaign in 1860. Decades later, the suffrage movement tried to affect a series of elections in its efforts to secure the vote for women. Prohibitionists triumphed in the early twentieth century with their drive to ban alcoholic beverages. More recently, many movements, including those of feminists, environmentalists, political reformers, and "pro-choice" and "pro-life" groups, have been active in a wide range of political campaigns. Some of these campaigns have been interest group campaigns focusing on a specific legislative goal and containing a grassroots component. Others focused on political election campaigns as groups sought to elect friends of their cause to various public offices. Finally, interest groups have sometimes gone directly to the public in election campaigns to enact "direct legislation" using the tools of initiative, referendum, and even recall.

Clearly, interest groups frequently used campaigns to achieve their political objectives. But something different occurred in 1993–1994. For the first time, interest groups mobilized enormous resources to fight complete political campaigns on a national level. The campaigns were nearly identical in almost every aspect to the campaigns waged by successful presidential candidates such as Ronald Reagan and Bill Clinton. They had nearly unlimited resources to utilize; they recruited personnel from party campaigns to lend their expertise; they used highly centralized organizational structures and "war rooms" to coordinate the various participants; and they unleashed the multiple channels of modern communications media from television advertising to the Internet to battle for the favor of American public opinion. In the 1998 elections, dozens of interest groups spent a reported total of at least $260 million in television and radio advertisements, according to the Annenberg Public Policy Center, to advance their political agendas or to support or oppose particular candidates. Sixty-seven groups were identified as sponsoring such ads in the 1998 elections (*New York Times* 1998i).

The line between interest groups and political parties has been blurred by recent events. Increasingly, major interests use the techniques of modern election campaigns and they share the same personnel, who offer their expertise to parties, candidates, and interest groups. Of course, there are still differences between political parties and interest groups. Parties seek to win elections and govern. They use issues to put together strategies to win and occupy political offices. Periodic elections and campaigns make up the parties' main arena. Interest groups, on the other hand, seek to impact public policy, and thus elections are just one of several types of campaigns that groups may use in order to achieve their policy objectives.

In this book, we suggest that political campaigns have become the bridge between parties and interest groups. This chapter discusses the nature of interest group participation in modern campaigns. Chapter 9 will present the major points of traditional interest group lobbying in noncampaign venues, and Chapter 10 will discuss the internal aspects of interest groups, such as formation, maintenance, leadership, and membership, which operate to support campaigns.

The Greatest Interest Group Campaign in American History?

In terms of the range of resources expended and the number of strategies and tactics employed, many political observers have anointed the 1993–

1994 health care reform effort as the "greatest interest group battle in American political history. More importantly, given the fact that interest group politics have emerged in its most complete and most expensive forms in the United States, one could then logically argue that it was the greatest such battle in world history" (Johnson and Broder 1996).

The issue, health care reform, emerged from the 1991 special Senate election in Pennsylvania. Democratic candidate Harris Wofford used the issue to win a stunning victory. Since Wofford's campaign advisers, James Carville and Paul Begala, went on to become strategists for the 1992 Clinton presidential campaign, it was not surprising that Bill Clinton grasped health care reform as one of his central themes. Relatively soon after the Clinton administration settled into the White House, the new president appointed his wife, Hillary Rodham Clinton, coordinator of the administration's health care reforms. Later, both supporters and detractors agreed that appointing the First Lady as the administration's leader on this crucial issue was a fundamental mistake that opposing interest groups utilized in their successful campaign to kill the reforms.

The *New York Times* declared that "Clinton's health care plan was the very centerpiece of his Presidency—'our most urgent priority' as [Clinton] told Congress in a grand unveiling of the plan in September 1993" (*New York Times* 1996c). As is well-known, the reform initiative died in the late summer of 1994 after being assaulted by a powerful coalition of interest groups. When health care reform was declared the Clinton administration's top priority, it attracted a particularly large number of opponents operating with an impressive range of political objectives—not the least being the destruction of the Clinton presidency. The success of the antireform interest group coalition also had a significant impact on American political party history, since it set the stage for the 1994 House and Senate elections and the destruction of the Democratic party majorities in Congress.

The demise of the reforms proposed by Clinton did not mark the end of the health care war. It raged throughout 1995 and 1996 in various forms and returned in 1997 in the budget deficit debates and efforts to cut billions of dollars from the Medicare program. One group, the National Coalition on Health Care, took out *New York Times* ads in October 1997 warning that health care costs could rise nearly 90 percent in the coming decade and could prevent families from retiring comfortably or sending a child to college. The ad urged readers to join the coalition in calling for health care reform or to get additional information by visiting its website. The battle continued into 1998 as the issue changed to controlling some of the problems that have emerged as more and more Americans come under the health insurance system administered by health maintenance organizations (HMOs). Insurance companies and their allies spent $60 million in the first half of 1998 while their opponents (medical organizations, trial lawyers, unions, and consumer groups) spent $14 million. Another $11 million was spent on media advertising against managed-care legislation; additional millions were made in campaign contributions to opponents of the reform legislation. During the same period, tobacco companies spent about $40 million to kill legislation to raise cigarette taxes to curb teenage smoking ("Opponents of Health-Care Reform" 1998).

Interest Groups Seek to Mold Public Opinion in Media Campaigns

"Appeals to the masses" are used frequently by interest groups as supporting tactics for broader lobbying campaigns. An appeal to the masses is generally the tactic of large, wealthy groups and is based on a paid mass media campaign using extensive television commercials and major newspaper advertising. However, even the weakest groups can seek to mold public opinion by appeals to gain the attention of "free media."

Groups can use mass media campaigns to pursue four major objectives: group maintenance, public goodwill, defensive strategy, and offensive strategy. Many media appeals contain coupons to send to the lobbying targets such as senators, representatives, or bureaucrats, and other coupons that ask the reader to send money to the group to support future efforts. Some groups have significantly increased their membership bases during such media campaigns. Various liberal groups greatly increased their membership during the Nixon impeachment process in the 1970s and the Robert Bork Supreme Court nomination process in the late 1980s. Another internal goal related to maintenance is providing evidence to existing members that the group is effectively representing them in the public policy process. Just having a high visibility media presence can help insulate interest group leadership from membership complaints.

The other three objectives relate directly to the policymaking process. A particular media campaign can have an offensive or a defensive strategic orientation or may be building a foundation for future media campaigns. "Goodwill" campaigns lay such a foundation for future lobbying. Mobil Oil has run numerous goodwill campaigns over the years. Many of these ads have nothing to do with Mobil's lobbying agenda. They urge such actions as parents getting inoculations for their children or citizens acting more responsibly within their communities.

A 1997 Mobil Oil *New York Times* ad is a perfect example of the goodwill type of media effort. Its title, "Why Not Seek Quality?" alludes to an award that the Mobil Corporation had received from the National Association of Television Program Executives Educational Foundation. The award recognized Mobil's significant contribution to education through television. The ad also notes Mobil's long-standing sponsorship of *Masterpiece Theater* and public television in general. This is a fine example of media communications that are intended to generate goodwill and do not refer to a larger political agenda.

Many goodwill ads are presented by interests seeking to refurbish somewhat tarnished images. Philip Morris, a giant corporation that produces a wide range of products, including Miller Beer, Kraft Foods, and tobacco products, bought a double-page ad in the *New York Times Magazine* titled "Helping the Helpers: Victim Services." The ad addresses domestic violence and contains information on services to victims of domestic abuse. It should be noted that goodwill media ads are relatively rare, since most groups prefer to spend their scarce resources in defending gains already made or seeking new legislative goals.

A majority of issue advocacy ads in recent years seem to be defensive. This may be a function of the style of politics operating in the United States since the late 1970s—a politics with little chance of new taxes or budgets for new programs and lots of attacks on existing programs to help cut the persistent federal budget deficits. An excellent example of defensive media is an ad sponsored by the Pharmaceutical Research and Manufacturers of America, which appeared in the *Washington Post*. Two-thirds of the ad is a single sentence: "Prescription drug price increases are the lowest in over 20 years." This is a clear-cut effort to defend the industry against charges of excessive profits and price increases. The National Council of Senior Citizens tried a subliminal kind of ad that appeared in the *New York Times* in the summer of 1997. Displayed in bold print was the following: "If you want to know what Medicare 'means-testing' really means, read between the lines." Set in smaller print between the lines of the above message is: "higher Medicare premiums; two tiered health care; less retirement security; huge administrative costs; a threat to privacy; and everyone loses." That ad is subtle compared to another *New York Times* ad run by the National Employment Law Project stating, in huge type, "They're chomping at the MINIMUM WAGE . . . Stop the new attack."

Offensive ads are attack ads seeking to change some aspect of American society or politics or to pass a new law to that effect. A sixteen-organization coalition (including the American Lung Association, Defenders of Wildlife, the Sierra Club, and Zero Population Growth) took out a full-page ad in the *New York Times* addressed to President Clinton and Vice President Gore. The ad was titled "Listen to the Truth. Not the Fairy Tales" and urged the president and his environmentalist vice president to support proposed Environmental Protection Agency–updated clean air health standards and reject the counter arguments of "big polluters."

Figures 8.1–8.3 are three examples of effective advocacy ads placed in the national media. One is an ad for the American Civil Liberties Union's campaign to defend the First Amendment and to oppose proposals in Congress to make the burning of the American flag illegal. The second ad is part of an anti-tobacco campaign. This ad, from the Campaign for Tobacco-Free Kids, seeks to frame the debate over tobacco as a matter of protecting children from smoking, a goal virtually all American citizens can agree on. The final ad is from the American Forest & Paper Association. This ad states that the American Forest & Paper Association has high standards of environmental protection and that members of the group who cannot support these standards are asked to leave. Each of these advertisements illustrates the general idea of advocacy ads: Associate the group (or the cause) with a value that appeals to a large number of Americans—in these examples, defending the First Amendment, protecting the health of children, and protecting the environment.

Media campaigns can be very expensive strategies for interest groups. A full-page ad in a national newspaper or a newsmagazine costs thousands of dollars. In September 1987 real estate multimillionaire Donald Trump spent over $94,000 for full-page political advertisements in the *New York Times,* the *Washington Post,* and the *Boston Globe,* arguing that America's allies should pay a fair share of their defense costs (Ryan, Swanson, and Buchholz 1987). The high cost of media advertising makes it a tool of business lobbies or rich, well-established lobbies like the National Rifle Association or the American Medical Association.

After the Republicans took control of Congress following the 1994 elections, part of the GOP agenda was a sharp reduction or even elimination of funding for Public Broadcasting. A liberal group, People for the American Way, sent out a packet in 1995 to stir up grassroots opposition to Republican plans to cut back such funding. "Yes! I want to stand up for Public Broadcasting! I am outraged by Newt Gingrich's leadership of the Right-Wing campaign to willfully distort public broadcasting's proud record of accomplishment. It is time to stand up to the censors." A request for a donation was followed by three clip-out messages addressed to "my representatives in Congress." A typical "postcard" stated: "Dear Senator Orrin G. Hatch, I am writing to express my deep personal concern about the American Family Association's vicious and distorted attack on public television. I urge you to oppose all efforts by Speaker Gingrich to pull the plug on PBS."

Often an interest group or, better still, a coalition pursues a coordinated media campaign in a variety of media in order to target a range of audiences. These audiences could include national opinion leaders, issue activists, corporate employees, stockholders, regional audiences, Congress, labor unions, and academics. To reach these targets, a coalition may place

Let me ask you something... Does freedom mean you have the right to burn the flag?

The U.S. Supreme Court says yes, under the First Amendment to the Constitution. But Congress doesn't like the Court's decision, and is only a few votes away from changing the Constitution to permit the government to punish people who use the flag to express dissent. It's not only flag burning they mean to punish; they want to make it a crime to "desecrate" the flag. That means that anyone who shows disrespect for the flag could be prosecuted and put in prison.

But isn't Congress showing disrespect for the flag by trying to destroy our right of free speech? Free speech, after all, is what the flag represents. Countries like China imprison people who disrespect their flag, but in the U.S. we're proud of our tolerance for dissent. Congress is pretending to honor the flag. But as it prepares to unravel our right to free speech, Congress desecrates what the flag means and what millions of Americans have died to defend.

If you are for the Constitution and freedoms it protects, shouldn't you be against the "flag amendment?" Think about it. Use our web page and write to your Senator today.

Ira Glasser
Executive Director of the American Civil Liberties Union
125 Broad Street
New York, New York 10004
www.aclu.org

FIGURE 8.1   ACLU Ad

FIGURE 8.2   Campaign for Tobacco-Free Kids Ad

We've set tough standards for our members.

• Promptly reforest harvested areas

• Protect water quality

• Protect wildlife habitat

• Practice sustainable forestry standards that
have been endorsed by leading conservation
groups like The Conservation Fund

We have an expert review panel made up of
leading conservation organizations.

High standards. But 130 member companies
of the American Forest & Paper Association
agreed to abide by them.

And the 15 companies that refused?

They were asked to leave the organization.

Just like that.

We've learned that America's forests are a resource
that must constantly be nurtured and renewed.

There is no compromise on that.

The American Forest & Paper Association.
Showing the World a Higher Standard.

FIGURE 8.3   American Forest & Paper Association Ad

its ads in college newspapers, regional trade publications, specific magazines, and different types of newspapers. For example, national newspapers such as the *New York Times, Wall Street Journal,* and *Washington Post* may be included because their subscribers include people and businesses across the nation as well as many libraries in addition to their city and regional audiences. Even a one-day campaign would cost hundreds of thousands of dollars! When the pharmaceutical industry launched a massive media campaign in 1993 defending its drug prices and denying any linkage to rising health costs, it took out full-page ads on the same day in forty different newspapers. The cost of the ads was reported to be more than $500,000. Other interests target elite public opinion in Washington, D.C., by placing ads in small-circulation political journals such as *Roll Call,* the *National Journal,* and the *Congressional Quarterly.* In 1990, the Mexican government sponsored a media campaign costing at least $1 million that was designed to combat American "confusion" about Mexico's role in combating illegal drugs (*Los Angeles Times* 1990).

Grassroots Interest Group Issue Campaigns

The objective of many interest group ads is to enhance grassroots campaigns. In most of these ads the political targets are clearly identified by cut-out coupons or letters included in the ad to be sent directly to the targets. Another way to accomplish this is to have the coupons or "fill in the blank with your name" letters sent to the interest group offices and be "bundled" there for delivery to the targeted officials.

Many lobbying campaigns with broad-based strategies and tactics in recent years have required resources from "outside the beltway." The beltway refers to the highway that encircles Washington, D.C. It is the symbolic barrier separating "insider Washington politics" from politics found in the rest of the nation. Such "outreach lobbying" is often called "grassroots lobbying." The standard definition of grassroots lobbying is mobilizing supporters on the subnational levels of American politics to put pressure on targets at the national level.

Liberal interest groups such as labor unions, public interest groups such as environmentalists, and political reform groups such as Common Cause pioneered the development of grassroots lobbying in the 1960s and 1970s. Ironically, conservative interest groups refined the practices and made grassroots lobbying a major part of modern political campaigning. What corporate America added to the technique was money—lots and lots of money. With the infusion of money came the professional campaign consultants, the Washington, D.C., and New York City PR (public relations) and media firms, and the various technologies such as direct mail and computers that have become the standard in the profession of grassroots campaign management.

Some have argued that grassroots lobbying campaigns are much more effective than traditional lobbying efforts, which are described in the following chapter. No less an authority than former Senate majority leader and 1996 Republican presidential candidate Robert Dole has suggested that the combination of money and mail from constituents will probably equal a lobbying victory. Senator John Danforth noted that when letter-writing and newspaper ad campaigns are organized, "members of the Congress of the United States crumble like cookies" (*Salt Lake Tribune* 1984a).

Grassroots campaigning may be effective or ineffective. Effective grassroots campaigns are natural and spontaneous. A lobby wants such a campaign to be perceived as thousands of concerned citizens (preferably voting constituents) communicating their political desires to their elected representatives. Ineffective grassroots lobbying is called "Astroturf lobbying" because it is clearly artificial. Enhanced communications capabilities have brought grassroots lobbying to the forefront in contemporary lobbying campaigns. Activating grassroots members or sympathizers can be accomplished quite easily with computers.

Lobbies can activate either "rifle" or "shotgun" styles of grassroots campaigns. As the names imply, the two types of campaign differ in terms of the number of communications activated by the group. The rifle tactic is to pinpoint a target and then bring specific resources to the target. This approach involves relatively few people to activate it. The shotgun approach relies on activating large numbers of communications. A typical shotgunning campaign is centered around either mass mailings or media ads urging a group's membership or the public to blanket Congress with letters or phone calls. An effective campaign can generate millions of communications to the Congress over a very short period of time. Several such campaigns can operate at the same time and may well generate millions of messages to Congress in a day. In a classic campaign run by the banking lobby in the early 1980s Congress was inundated by a massive grassroots letter- and postcard-writing campaign that totaled over 22 million letters and postcards (*Statistics of the Week* 1983, 720).

The following are some classic examples of grassroots lobbying as it has been perfected by corporate America:

- Coca-Cola urged its stockholders to join its Civic Action Network (CAN) and recruited over 50,000 stockholder-grassroots activists.
- The American Bankers Association, one of the heavyweight

lobbying groups, in 1983 orchestrated an estimated 22 million postcards, letters, and mailgrams to force Congress to cancel a requirement that banks and other financial institutions withhold income taxes on interest and dividends.

- Delta Airlines in 1997 distributed messages to its passengers on their food trays and frequent fliers in the monthly mailings urging them to "call or fax your U.S. congressional representatives today at 202-224-3121" to oppose congressional efforts to raise taxes on air travel and frequent flier miles.

- The National Restaurant Association in 1998 flew in 150 restauranteurs from forty states to meet with congresspersons to try to kill a drunk driving bill that the association believed could have a financial impact on their businesses. Mom-and-pop beer and liquor stores were also sending faxes and making phone calls to their congresspersons.

There are a variety of ways interest groups can "help" connect a grass-roots constituent with a government official. After being contacted by the group by telephone, the constituent can fax his or her letterhead with signature to the group and the group's message can be inserted on the letterhead and then sent to the government official. If the group determines the constituent has a clear and desirable message to communicate, the group can immediately connect him or her to the Washington, D.C., office of the official using "patch-through" technologies. Some are asked if they would like the group to write a letter for them. Groups use different styles of stationery, envelopes, and stamps to make the letters appear as individual as possible. Sometimes "key constituents" (or "grasstops") are singled out by interest groups because of their prominence in the home districts of important congressional members. They are brought to Washington, D.C. (usually at the expense of the group) for personal visits with their representatives.

The most effective grassroots campaigns are as personal and individualistic as possible. Congressional staff screen all incoming mail, and personal letters receive more attention than mimeographed postcards. Letters from "important people" and letters with unusually interesting arguments may be brought to the attention of members of Congress. Letters from groups that come into contact with the representative may be brought to his or her desk as well.

"Patch-through" technology has also greatly facilitated the lobbyist's task of linking the public to the politician. One such computer program selects names and phone numbers from a database, makes a phone call to the name, delivers a prerecorded message about pending legislation, and then connects listeners to the office of their members of Congress. When used by one interest group, the program had a 25 percent success rate. If that seems low, it is much higher than the success rate of direct mail efforts.

Fax communications are another tool of successful grassroots campaigns and have also become the preferred method of internal rapid communications in many interest groups. Faxes can be generated one at a time by individuals, or "astro faxes" can be ground out by a computer and dozens of fax machines. One computer fax system can generate as many as 10,000 fax messages a day (Browning 1994, 2450).

Among new technologies that have contributed to the enhancement of grassroots lobbying are desktop publishing, shortwave radio, citizen access television, computer-supported fax networks, independent video production, and computer billboards. The Internet has become increasingly popular for lobbying communications. Groups set up a web page and members and other activists can "pull up the page" and receive instant communications. The group's page address can be communicated to potential viewers in print or television ads or by in-house publications. More and more interest groups are now including their website addresses in their advertising and their direct mail. By late 1998, web pages had become a "sign of seriousness" in that almost all the serious lobbies had them. The more sophisticated the web pages were, the more seriously the lobby was taken as a major player in the interest group game. Hill and Hughes (1998) studied the use of the Internet by interest groups and noted that many groups were using it for a wide variety of objectives, for example, posting group testimonies, conducting public meetings, posting in-house information, announcing legal actions, communicating to politicians, indicating support for sympathetic politicians, recruiting new members, fund-raising, communications to and from members, and links to allied groups. The mean size of the websites studied was 82 pages, but the largest had 652 pages!

The expanded use of the Internet by interest groups has been dramatic in the late 1990s. For example, various electric power interest groups took out a multipage ad in the *New York Times* in June 1997 and emphasized their websites: American Public Power Association (<www.appanet.org>); Edison Electric Institute (<www.eei.org>); Electric Power Research Institute (<www.epri.com>); Gas Research Institute (<www.gri.org>); National Energy Information Center (<www.eia.doe.gov>); and National Rural Electric Cooperative Association (<www.nreca.org>).

Manipulation of the news media to bring about a grassroots effect is yet another successful grassroots tactic. The goal is to generate newspaper editorials supporting the group's political position and put pressure on politicians dependent on the future support of the media in upcoming campaigns. Editorials appear to be particularly effective in "low salience issue" campaigns and in legislative (rather than executive) campaigns. A variety of tactics are effective in this area. A group can go for high-prestige newspapers such a the *New York Times, Wall Street Journal,* or a handful of other such newspapers. Sometimes the support of a paper such as the *New York Times* or *Washington Post* may be sufficient to tilt the political balance in favor of an issue. The alternative tactic is to try to "tidal wave" key members of Congress with a series of editorial-page statements on the issue from newspapers in their home districts or states. One lobby that has used the editorial-page tactic is the liberal free speech lobby, People for the American Way.

In 1998, computer software giant Microsoft was having some political and legal problems in Washington, D.C., and several state capitals. The firm's media and lobbying strategy plan was leaked to the press and allegedly included using of many of its supporters in key states to write letters to the editors of local newspapers and generating as much local media support as possible. Some of the letters and other media pieces were to be commissioned by the company's PR firm and sent to local supporters for submission to the media. One round of articles was to coincide with the oral arguments before the U.S. Court of Appeals.

The humble telephone remains a mainstay of many grassroots lobbying operations. Common Cause, for example, uses direct mail, in-house magazines, and a telephone network to activate its troops for grassroots campaigns. Common Cause's Washington, D.C., headquarters calls coordinators in selected congressional districts across the country, who in turn contact several other Common Cause members, who each contact other members and so on down the action alert "communications tree."

The technology, now dated, that made interest groups very aware of the tremendous potential of grassroots lobbying was direct mail. Richard Viguerie founded the technology in the late 1970s and provided conservative groups with a tremendous fund-raising tool and helped create a wide range of such groups. Today, almost every group in the nation uses some form of direct mail. The typical established citizen receives dozens of fund-raising letters and appeals, ranging from environmentalists to senior citizens. Most Americans probably receive in any given year dozens of "appeals packets" from interest groups. Since many groups share their membership lists, the more groups and magazines you subscribe to, the more such direct mail you will probably find in your mailbox.

Fine-tuning direct mail is not a casual operation. Everything that goes into the communications package is tested and retested: the size of the envelopes, the color of the paper, the type size and style, the number of pages, and the personal touches that are added to the letter, such as the recipient's name and address or the signature of the person who is supposed to have signed the letter. The content is also tested and refined to make it as powerful a selling mechanism as possible. A well-designed appeal can raise millions of dollars, whereas a poorly designed one can threaten the group's survival.

The central motivation of direct mail is fear. Frightening events or prospective events and political actors are used to frighten the recipient into joining the group or at least providing money to avoid the prospective bad outcome. Following the Republican takeover of Congress in 1995, liberal groups featured Newt Gingrich as the object of fear; conservatives presented a future negatively impacted by Ted Kennedy or Bill and Hillary Clinton. The sudden resignation of Newt Gingrich after the 1998 elections left the Democrats without an opponent to attack in their direct mail campaigns. Direct mail frequently uses emotions, including "outrage, fear, guilt, pity or self-interest" (*New York Times* 1995c).

Groups combine direct mail, media ads, and some of the new communications technologies of the last several decades to maximize the possibility of getting the message to the grassroots target. Some groups began using toll-free telephone numbers for the public to call and request information on issues the groups were supporting. During the Clinton administration's health care reform crusade in 1993–1994, the American Medical Association ran its number for information on the association's health care plan. Tobacco company Philip Morris hired a Washington polling firm to generate mailgrams in opposition to a proposed law banning smoking on airline flights. The firm called smokers and read them a script that included a prewritten mailgram. The caller asked smokers if they would consent to having the mailgram sent to their state's senator on the smoker's behalf. If they received an affirmative reply, a mailgram was sent at Philip Morris's expense.

Letter-writing campaigns are the most common grassroots campaigns. The most effective ones use individually written letters or produce a huge flood of orchestrated mail. The targets of letter-writing campaigns, politicians and bureaucrats, frequently are so swamped by mail that they note only the quantity and quality of the letters. Huge deliveries of such mail may influence politicians who have not made up their minds on an issue or those who face a particularly difficult reelection campaign.

Another very frequently used grassroots political tactic to influence public policy is the boycott. It can be used by both powerful and weak groups, but it is particularly useful for groups without the traditional routes of access. Various boycotts in recent decades have been successful, including United Farm Workers boycotts against grape growers in California during the 1960s and 1970s; a boycott of Colorado by civil rights groups protesting a state law undermining "gay civil rights"; and the boycott of the state of Arizona by civil rights groups after that state decided not to observe Martin Luther King's birthday as a state holiday.

Boycotting involves asking supporters of some group or cause to avoid purchasing products from a company or industry being boycotted or to refuse to visit a boycotted state and thus reduce state income from tourism, conventions, or normal commerce. Appeals for a boycott turn up in the most unlikely places. Recently, a comicbook store in Utah distributed a boycott request bookmark to all its youthful customers. Its message was, "Don't! Buy! Thai! Stop Child Sex Tourism in Thailand" "Our weapon of choice is BOYCOTT. We want Americans to boycott anything made or manufactured in Thailand. . . . And the only thing that will stop it is the loss of money." The appeal closed with a reference to a website maintained by the boycott effort.

Boycotts have become more and more popular in recent years. In fact, there is a magazine that details various boycotts around the nation, the *Boycott Quarterly*. Dozens of boycotts have been organized by various groups, and some of them have been continuing for years. A political boycott can be successful if it accomplishes its main task of gaining media attention for the group and its cause and ultimately moves public opinion in its support. All three of the boycotts noted above were able to do this, but the vast majority of boycotts fail. A famous 1970s boycott failure was a boycott of states that had failed to ratify the Equal Rights Amendment, led by various feminist groups including the National Organization of Women (NOW). Despite tremendous efforts to enforce that boycott and the loss of many millions of dollars in business in three key states, the legislatures targeted never ratified the amendment.

Interest Group Campaigns Against Parties and Candidates

In most election years, some major political interest groups seek to defeat specific candidates in an effort to secure more favorable treatment for legislation they support. Organized labor did just that during the 1996 elections by targeting for defeat almost three dozen freshmen Republican members of the House of Representatives. Groups that declare war on a political party must carry out their threats of defeating their enemy or be able to withstand a hostile legislative environment dominated by their enemies. Sometimes the existing environment is so hostile that even if groups fail to defeat their enemies, the outcomes could not be any worse than already exist. Such was the attitude of organized labor and many environmentalists in the 1996 elections.

Groups may use an electoral retaliation strategy, which to be effective must be based on some evidence that a group can reward or punish a candidate in elections. Several lobbies have been perceived by politicians as being able to defeat their opponents. The National Rifle Association, the anti-abortion movement, the Moral Majority and National Conservative Political Action Committee (the late NCPAC), environmentalists, organized labor, and the Christian Coalition have all been given credit for defeating senators and house members in elections since the 1970s. Part of the myth of retribution lies in the groups not being shy about claiming credit for whatever victories may occur in an election. In the crucial 1994 congressional elections, liberal Democrat after Democrat was defeated, and the Christian Coalition claimed credit. Interest groups need to "deliver the vote" for or against a specific candidate. In 1998, however, the Christian Coalition was unable to deliver the votes to defeat Democratic candidates for Congress, and the group's status dropped as a result of this perceived failure. The National Rifle Association claimed a great election victory in 1994 with the "defeat of 32 anti-gun politicians." *Campaigns and Elections* magazine declared that the NRA had "a lot more to do with the November [1994] elections than most pundits realized." According to its own count, the NRA spent money on twenty races. Nine of the ten NRA-backed candidates won in 1994; six of the eleven targeted candidates were defeated (O'Leary 1994, 32).

Organized labor has had difficulty delivering its vote as more and more of its membership gain middle-class income and identify with the values of the Republican party. For example, it has been estimated that about one-third of the National Education Association's nearly 2 million members are Republicans. However, the proportion of labor families who voted in the 1998 elections rose sharply, as did the percentage voting for Democratic candidates. Organized labor's favorite political party ended up with more seats in the House of Representatives than it has had since the 1992 elections.

In general elections, interest groups have an impact in terms of the range of services they can offer a favored candidate. Giants such as the AFL-CIO, AARP, women's organizations, the Christian Coalition, and single-issue groups can conduct voter registration campaigns, and "get out the vote" telephone efforts that can be invaluable to a candidate. The American Medical Association, beginning in the early 1980s, has made available to endorsed candidates the services of any of six national pollsters—a service that was been very popular with many national candidates. A variant of traditional election-day strategies is the development of endorsement lists or candidate ratings. Many groups publish their ratings and some of the most effective groups get a great deal of media attention when they announce their "dirty dozen," "heroes and zeroes," and "warriors for small business." Nearly a hundred groups rate the Congress yearly on a selected range of issues.

The largest lobby in the United States for small businesses—the National Federation of Independent Business (NFIB)—puts together its ratings each year by polling the group's 600,000 members about the stands the membership wants the group to take on issues before Congress. The polling information is then sent to congressional offices. Just prior to a crucial vote on one of the group's priority issues, a special green-edged postcard is sent to members of Congress warning them that the vote will be part of the NFIB's next report card. Approximately thirty votes have constituted the NFIB ratings. To each member of Congress receiving a 70 percent or higher rating on the report card, the NFIB awards a small pewter trophy inscribed with the words "Guardian of Small Business." The NFIB will also launch a media campaign in the politician's home district or state announcing the award. In recent years, about a third of the House and half of the Senate have received such awards. Finally, the NFIB has a PAC that contributes hundreds of thousands of dollars each year to deserving congressional candidates. A 70 percent rating entitles an incumbent to the group's endorsement, as well as a monetary contribution if the race warrants it. Conversely, any incumbent with a score of less than 40 percent may see his or her challenger receiving such a PAC contribution from the NFIB (*Salt Lake Tribune* 1984b).

Many interest group ratings are of little importance to the typical member of Congress. Most Republicans from rural or agricultural states are not concerned over a low rating from the AFL-CIO; in fact, a bad labor rating is usually a plus in conservative districts. However, strong ratings from labor and ethnic lobbies are very important to big city–based Democratic candidates. In the 1994 elections, for example, conservative U.S. senator Orrin Hatch (R–Utah) received zero ratings from gays and lesbians, some environmentalist groups, and Ralph Nader's Public Citizen, and a rating of 8 from the National Education Association. On the other hand, Hatch got 100s from a promilitary group, conservatives, a pro–private property association, and the Christian Coalition. One group, the Watchdogs of the Treasury, gave Senator Hatch a 103 rating that was based on extra bonus points for his record. Will any of these ratings have an impact on Hatch's next election? Certainly people trying to find out if Senator Hatch shares their preferences in a particular policy area can find some of that information in these ratings, but no discernible relationship exists between any of Hatch's low ratings and any future electoral problems (*Deseret News* 1994).

Interest Group Efforts in Party Campaigns

Interest groups have participated in political party election campaigns throughout much of this nation's political history. The history of the

Republican party in the pre–Civil War period of the 1850s was largely a history of various antislavery groups helping to elect Republicans to office in an effort to destroy slavery. The once powerful political machines that controlled many of America's major cities in the late nineteenth century operated effectively by working with a wide variety of interest groups—some business and others ethnic or religious in nature. However, our focus is on what political scientists and historians call the New Deal party system, which began with the election of Franklin D. Roosevelt in 1932 and continued at least to the 1960s. During this period emerged the present pattern of interest group involvement in traditional party election campaigns.

The image problems that both Democratic and Republican parties have faced in recent campaigns highlights the extent of interest group participation in modern party campaigns. The Democratic party had a severe political image problem in the middle and late 1980s. Many viewed the party as captive to a number of powerful interest groups; various public opinion polls indicated that this subservient relationship—real or imagined—was costing the party votes in presidential campaigns. Any list of groups and movements that appeared to have a stranglehold over the Democratic party would include first organized labor and specifically the AFL-CIO. The giant labor confederation emerged from its battles with American business in the first three decades of this century as a powerful force in American politics based on the number of members it organized and the money it could raise and spend in political campaigns. Gradually, it came to align itself with the Democratic party of Roosevelt and Truman (1933–1953), and by the 1960s it had become the foundation of the party. Organized labor had become the core of the party because the party never spent resources developing its own viable structure for campaign support, fund-raising, or even volunteer administration. Whenever the Democratic party needed money, it turned to labor; when it needed volunteers in a specific campaign, it turned to labor; and when it needed administrative support such as computers, the unions would offer their computers to the party. In fact, it was not in the interest of the unions for the Democratic party to develop its own independent resource base in these areas, since any enhancement of the party's resources would only result in a lessening of the political power of the unions in the party. Union power in the Democratic party had become so great by the 1970s that a number of seats were reserved for union representatives in the key Democratic party committees.

Other groups or movements have also been perceived by many as having extraordinary influence and access in the Democratic party. One such group is the "education lobby." Represented by the powerful National Education Association (NEA), an educational professional group, teachers and school administrators have become frequent participants in Democratic councils and conventions. Significant parts of the women's movement have also signed on with the Democratic party in recent decades, as have groups representing gays and lesbians and their political interests. All of these groups or movements became visible in Democratic party activities and came to symbolize to some the party's power core. Republicans successfully portrayed the party as the captive of these powerful interests, which represent policy agendas outside the mainstream of American politics. It was not until the twin successes of the presidential victories in 1992 and 1996 that the party was able to shift the public's attention away from these charges of interest group domination.

The Republican party has had similar image problems. Since the beginning of the New Deal system in 1932, the interest that many felt dominated the Republicans was "big business." With the Democrats "in the pocket" of organized labor, the Republicans continued their predepression probusiness orientation. But their probusiness orientation was not the interest group relationship that has caused the party some political damage in recent years. The GOP has become the party of choice of "fundamentalist Christians," and thus organizations such as Jerry Fallwell's Moral Majority and Ralph Reed's Christian Coalition became powerful actors inside Republican political circles. The 1995 Christian Coalition campaign in support of Republican House Speaker Newt Gingrich's Contract with America spent more than $1 million on a lobbying campaign through phone banks, fax networks, satellite television, computerized bulletin boards, talk radio, and direct mail (*New York Times* 1995a).

Many within the party worried that this religious identification could be as dangerous for the GOP as identifications that the Democrats developed. Like the relationship between the Democratic party and organized labor (and militant women's groups as well as gay and lesbian groups), the symbiotic relationship between the GOP and fundamentalist Christians has been a mixed blessing. Since the 1970s, fundamentalist Christians have been escalating their activities in support of Republican candidates for public offices. The resources that interest groups bring to a political party and its political election campaigns are, first and foremost, voters and dollars. Both labor and fundamentalist Christians have claimed the ability to bring large numbers of voters to party campaigns. The Christian Coalition and its nearly 2 million members claimed to be the decisive element when the Republicans unexpectedly captured the Congress in the 1994 elections. Studies indicated that fundamentalist or evangelical Christians accounted for 29 percent of the total GOP 1994 vote and, as a group, 75 percent of them voted for Republican congressional candidates that year (Hershey 1997, 222). Over 46 million pieces of pro-Republican literature were distributed by the Christian Coalition and its thousands of individual churches during the 1996 campaign. The conservative religious movement had one of the strongest pro-GOP votes during both the 1994 and 1996 elections. Labor's voting loyalty had been declining since the 1940s. During the 1990s, although most labor families voted Democratic, the general economic prosperity evident since the 1940s had moved many of these families into the middle class and toward the Republican party and its more conservative candidates.

For decades, the Democrats have relied on "big labor" to get out the vote—especially in states in which unions are very strong, such as in those in the Northeast. As noted previously, labor has been the financial godfather of Democratic party organizations and campaigns since the 1940s and the founding of the first political action committees under the then separate labor confederations. In fact, the party has relied on organized labor for nearly every aspect of its operation and has largely ignored possible alternative sources of support. Democrats' reluctance to computerize their party operations in the late 1980s was largely a result of labor reluctance to pay the bill, only for the party to discover it can perform as a party without labor. It was not unusual for AFL-CIO campaign specialists to lend their expertise to Democratic party campaigns in trouble as well as bring with them highly organized telephone "get out the vote" and volunteer operations.

Interest Groups, Political Parties, and Financial Support

Money is the second resource that interest groups bring to party campaigns. Modern political campaigns expend enormous amounts of money on the media, consultants, and technologies that have become part of almost every campaign level but the most rural or lowest levels. The national level of politics—presidential, congressional, and national party organizations—spent more than $2 billion in 1996 (Corrado 1997, 135). Additional tens of millions of dollars were spent on state- and local-level races in 1994. The money had to come from somewhere, and the parties and various interest groups went to new levels of inventiveness to raise these huge amounts of political campaign funds.

Since 1932 big business has filled the coffers of both major parties. The reason for giving money to both Republicans and Democrats is found in the long-term Democratic domination of the Congress. Between 1933 and 1994, the Democrats controlled the House of Representatives for all but four years (1947–1948 and 1953–1954) and the Senate for almost as many years. With the Democrats in control of the lawmaking branch of government, America's business community had to deal with them and finance their campaigns in order to get the access they desired. Big business strongly prefers to have Republicans in control of Congress but can usually work very nicely with Democrats, who may favor labor but understand that business campaign contributions come when Congress provides the legislation business wants. Many large soft money business contributions come from corporations and interest groups with serious political agendas before the federal government: tobacco, telecommunications, lawyers, and energy companies. The real test came in the 1996 congressional campaigns following the Republican capture of both houses of Congress in 1994. The triumphant Republicans threatened business with reduced access if they continued to give campaign money to the defeated Democrats, but still businesses hedged their bet by continuing to make such contributions—admittedly at a reduced level compared to the 1980s. Tobacco giant Philip Morris gave a total of $2 million in 1995–1996—$1.6 million to Republicans and $400,000 to the minority Democrats.

Corporate America actively supported the Republican party during the 1996 elections. One corporation gave $2.2 million in "soft money" to the GOP. Corporations were also active in financially supporting both the Republican and Democratic 1996 national party conventions. The GOP San Diego convention raised money from Microsoft, Philip Morris, Time Warner, and Lockheed Martin and AT&T—which gave nearly $2.7 million. The Amway Corporation came up with $1.3 million after it had given the party $2.5 million in 1994. The Amway money was used by the Republicans to buy television time on two cable networks (The Family Channel and USA Network), and for thirteen hours during their own convention, Republicans leaders favorably reported on themselves. Later that summer, the Democrats raised even more money than their rivals, with the largest contributions coming from Ameritech ($2.4 million), Motorola ($1 million), AT&T ($558,000), United Airlines ($432,000), and Kemper Securities ($339,000). Among the top ten convention-supporting interests that gave money to both parties were AT&T, Microsoft, United Airlines, and Philip Morris (Jackson 1997, 241). When the final totals were reported, the Republican convention was supported by over $11 million in private contributions; the Democratic convention received $21 million.

Under the leadership of the Chamber of Commerce, big business organized "The Coalition" to support Republicans in the 1996 elections. The coalition was an ad hoc group of thirty-three organizations to raise money and refute AFL-CIO attack ads. It financed a pair of issue campaigns through the media in a total of thirty-three congressional districts at a cost of $7 million. The other major GOP ally, the Christian Coalition, reportedly spent about $10 million to produce and distribute through its local church network almost 50 million pro-Republican "voter guides." The Christian Coalition also produced radio ads and organized an army of volunteers to aid the GOP (Corrado 1997, 164).

After the Republicans won control of the Congress in 1994, they bluntly told corporate America that if they expect access and favorable business legislation, they would have to "change their evil ways" of giving the majority of their PAC money to the Democrats and switch their contributions to the GOP. Prior to 1994, business PACs gave most of their money to Democrats in the Congress. After 1994, business PACs continued to support those Democrats who survived that election but greatly increased business PAC giving to Republican members of Congress.

Business and business lobbyists have continued to give huge amounts of money to both parties, since divided government (a Democratic president and a Republican Congress) requires access to both parties. A January 1996 Republican National Committee fund-raiser set a record for the organization by raising $16 million from business and their lobbyists. The Democratic party counterpart's fund-raiser raised $12 million in May of that year. Later, as the fund-raising scandal emerged during the 1996 campaign, tales to buying access to the president and selling nights in the Lincoln Bedroom were commonplace. It was noted that a $100,000 donation to the Democratic party would get the donor invitations to four annual events with the president or vice president and additional opportunities such as participation in official U.S. trade missions to foreign nations. Republicans offered corporate America similar types of access opportunities: $250,000 to the RNC got the donor lunch with Bob Dole and Newt Gingrich, but a donation of only $45,000 got a tasty breakfast with Speaker Gingrich (Jackson 1997, 243).

Labor union PACs continued their overwhelming support for Democratic candidates in the 1996 elections. In 1994, 96 percent of the labor PACs' nearly $41 million went to the Democrats. The AFL-CIO's $35 million campaign effort during the 1995–1996 election cycle was a mixture of media and services in support of the Democratic party. Reportedly, about two-thirds of that amount went for radio and television ads, with the rest being spent for organizing, "get out the vote" campaigns, and training political workers. Business made a halfhearted effort to directly counter labor advertising (about $5 million), but most of its 1996 financial support for Republican candidates went directly to the party in the form of soft money.

Interest group financing of political candidates and political parties exploded into the nation's consciousness during and after the 1996 general elections. The avalanche of revelations began when large sums of Indonesian corporate money were linked to donations to the Clinton presidential reelection campaign. Some foreign and domestic contributions totaling $1.5 million had to be returned to their donors. Later exposures indicated that the Clinton White House regularly invited major contributors to spend the night in various historic bedrooms.

Republicans in Congress showed that they knew how to raise money in huge amounts too. The *New York Times* reported in January 1997 that for $250,000 contributors got access to the party's private skybox, pictures with the presidential and vice presidential nominees, plus special assistance with political problems in Washington, D.C. These special donors, called "season ticket holders," had become the new peak standard of party fund providers. The old standard in the 1992 elections was a mere $100,000. In 1996 the GOP recorded seventy-five contributions of $250,000 or more and the Democrats a total of forty-five. The Republican list included Philip Morris ($2.5 million) and four other tobacco companies (an additional $2.8 million). Congress spent an enormous amount of time in 1996 writing the first major revision in telecommunications law in decades, and all parties to the 1996 law expected further major changes in 1997.

Another example of ties between interest groups, political parties, and public policy is found in the case of the giant agricultural corporation Archer Daniels Midland (ADM). ADM, its executives, and its PAC gave more than $1 million to both Republican and Democratic federal candidates in 1996. Those contributions bought access to key congressional decisionmakers on issues of major concern to ADM like the billions of dollars in ethanol subsidies it receives from the federal government. The companies that form the so-called China Lobby (the three hundred companies forming the United States–China Business Council) contributed more than $55 million to party campaigns in 1995–1996 ("Rights vs. Revenues" 1997).

The two major parties were prolific producers in the 1995–1996 fundraising cycle. The Democratic National Committee raised $229 million and the RNC raised $312 million—approximately a third of these amounts came from unlimited donations in the category of soft money. During the 1995–1996 cycle, the Democrats raised $345 million and the Republicans almost $555 million (Federal Election Commission 1997a).

Reportedly, Republican donation solicitations "strongly implied" that the money would help buy special access to top Republican congressional leaders. The GOP concentrated its appeals to those corporations and individuals having pending business before the Congress. One corporation gave the Republicans a check for $500,000 and noted that a lot of money buys a lot of access. A Republican National Committee January 1996 invitation to a fund-raising dinner promised those who gave $250,000 or more private meetings with Republican House chairpersons and lunch with Speaker Newt Gingrich and then Senate majority leader Bob Dole. A record $17 million was raised at that dinner. Another event offered to donors centered around the 1996 GOP national convention in San Diego. Along with the "regular" social benefits, donors were given the promise of "support personnel" in Washington, D.C., to help with any party-related request.

Interest Group Campaigns in
Initiatives and Referenda

The Progressive movement, which dominated the political agenda at the turn of the century, had a profound impact on the ability of interest groups to advance their agendas. Political parties were stripped of long held powers to nominate candidates for elections, and other reforms allowed citizens the power to initiate legislation, void existing laws, and even throw publicly elected officials out of office prior to the next election. All of these new procedures were enacted to promote democracy, but in the case of the direct democracy reforms (initiatives, referenda, and recalls) the power often was transferred from political parties to powerful interest groups.

These reforms originated largely in California under Progressive reformist Hiram Johnson and then gradually spread eastward across the nation before losing political steam at about the Mississippi River. The first state to pass an initiative law was South Dakota in 1898, but the first state to have an initiative election was Oregon in 1904. As of 1995, most of the states having "direct democracy" laws are found west of the Mississippi; the most active states in terms of ballot propositions are west of the Rocky Mountains, especially Washington, Oregon, and California. Twenty-four states have initiative provisions, but only six (Florida, Illinois, Maine, Massachusetts, Michigan, and Ohio) are east of the Mississippi River. Thirty-four states have referenda laws, fourteen of which are east of the Mississippi. One explanation for this difference lies in the stronger position of political parties in the East as opposed to the West and their ability to resist lawmaking initiatives while agreeing to the less powerful law approving referenda demands.

The golden age of ballot propositions occurred in the 1910s, when 269 appeared (and 98 passed) in the various states. Only ten propositions passed in the entire decade of the 1960s. In the 1990s, however, this record will certainly be surpassed with a projected 353 measures expected by the year 2000. In the 1950s, California passed only two propositions. By the 1980s, Los Angeles County ballots averaged about thirty state and local propositions per election. As soon as the dust settles from the current year's proposition campaigns, the signature collectors are already on their way to the malls to collect names for the next campaign and the vote two years later.

There were 235 propositions on the ballots in forty-one states and the District of Columbia in the 1998 general elections. Sixty-one were citizen-initiated proposals and the remainder were referred to the voters by state legislatures as referenda. In the 1998 I&R contest, the voters passed thirty-eight of the sixty-one citizen-initiated propositions, a 62 percent success rate. Over the last hundred years of such propositions, around 40 percent have won in an average election year.

An industry grew up to service the needs of the interest groups seeking to use direct democracy to further their political agendas. Firms were formed to provide campaign management skills, petitioning for signature collections, media strategies and production, and polling expertise. Later, additional expertise was required in the areas of litigation, direct mail fund-raising, and coalition building. There are three separate phases during which the industry must offer the right mix of services to interest groups: (1) qualifying, (2) campaigning, and (3) defending or challenging the results in the courts.

Increasingly, proposition litigation has become one of the most significant areas of interest group campaigning. Almost every major initiative that wins at the polls is routinely challenged in court, which is often the only real check on interest groups' direct law writing. Court battles are fought at every stage of the initiative process: proposition titling, measure wording, official descriptions in voter guides, qualifying procedures, and the constitutionality of successful propositions. Between 1960 and 1980, only three initiatives approved in California were not entirely or partially declared unconstitutional by state or federal courts (Butler and Ranney 1994).

Direct democracy (initiatives and referenda) is significant in about fifteen states. Between 1950 and 1992, California led all the states in having 127 measures on the ballot, followed by Oregon's 97 and North Dakota's 95. On the other end of the continuum, among those states with direct democracy provisions, Kentucky held none; New Mexico, two; and Wyoming, three. California is the state that uses direct democracy with the greatest frequency at the state and local levels of politics. In any given election, there are a dozen or so statewide initiatives as well as dozens of county and city initiatives. California could be called "an interest group playpen" in the sense that almost all the statewide initiatives are sponsored by major groups or coalitions of groups.

Progressive reforms severely weakened California political parties in their role as campaign resource providers in regular election campaigns; the frequent initiative campaigns increasingly came to look just like office-oriented campaigns. Special initiative-supporting companies were born in California to organize initiative campaigns. These campaign management firms provided all the campaign-related services previously offered by the two major parties: worker organization, strategies and tactics, communications, advertising and media campaigns, polling, and other such parts of modern campaigns. Thus two incentives for interest groups to use direct democracy were in place: enabling laws, dating from approximately 1905, and the private organizations that by the 1940s allowed groups to bypass parties and state government.

Why do interest groups find initiative campaigns to be an attractive strategy? The major advantage is that they can avoid the normal legislative process and literally write the exact law the group desires and then go out and make it law. They can avoid the uncertainty and compromise of the normal legislative process by going to the initiative campaign if they have the resources to pursue that path. Initiatives are also attractive to groups that have lost their issues in the legislative chambers, in the governor's office in terms of a veto, or even in the courts. Frequently an interest group can introduce a piece of legislation into the state legislature and have it emerge from the process as a new law that is very different from the law desired by the group. The initiative process allows interest groups to avoid this problem.

What resources are necessary for success in initiative campaigns? No single essential resource can guarantee success. Various types of groups have used very different combinations of resources in victorious initiative campaigns. Perhaps the single most useful resource is money. In an initiative campaign environment, money can buy almost every other key resource, including leadership, management skills, media strategies and production advice, and lots of media access. It can buy "volunteers" to work the petition tables in shopping malls to qualify an initiative for the ballot. Money can even buy respect for a group if an expensive public relations campaign is carefully crafted. Groups with money have a very significant advantage in the initiative campaign process. One study indicated that groups with the most money won more often than they lost, but it did not explain why some very underfinanced interests were able to win as well (Magleby 1998).

Even the poorest interest groups can mount successful initiative campaigns if they have alternative resources such as numbers, public sympathy, or special membership characteristics such as respect or celebrity status. For small, poor groups, the existence of preexisting public support or sympathy may be an essential resource. For large, financially weak groups, membership numbers may be decisive in the petition phase or in the decisionmaking election. Although it is easier for powerful groups to participate and achieve success in initiative campaigns, poorer and weaker groups have a chance to play the game.

In the 1996 November general elections, there were ninety-six statewide propositions on the ballot in twenty states. This broke the 1914 record of ninety initiatives. The all-time low, twelve, was recorded in 1968. An estimated $200 million was spent on these ballot propositions in 1996. The best-known of the 1996 propositions were the California initiatives that sought to overturn state laws on affirmative action and another that sought to legalize the medical use of marijuana. These attracted enormous media attention throughout the nation and also the anticipation that if they were successful in California, other groups would attempt them in other states. This is the "agenda-setting" role of initiatives. One interest group, U.S. Term Limits, spent more than $1 million supporting term limit measures in fourteen states. This group was supporting the requirement to identify whether or not candidates on future ballots support a constitutional amendment on congressional term limits.

Oregon voters had their typically crowded initiative ballot in 1996. A record twenty-three measures were on the ballot. One of the most interesting was an effort to prohibit the Oregon state legislature from changing voter-passed initiative laws for a period of five years. It was defeated, but five states as of 1992 had such provisions protecting this type of law from legislative change. By 1998 a different type of initiative law was drawing attention. Utah voters passed Prop 5, which provided for raising the winning vote percentage from a plurality to two-thirds for all initiatives dealing with hunting and the environment. In Colorado, a state law tightly controlling who can seek petition signatures for initiatives was recently passed by opponents of the initiative process, and it is heading for the U.S. Supreme Court for final approval.

Initiatives range from those with potentially profound impact on millions of Americans to those that impact only a handful of people. An example of the latter type was a measure on the Alaska state ballot in 1996 that banned hunting wolves, wolverines, foxes, or lynx on the same day that the hunter flies in an airplane. The purpose of this initiative was to prevent hunters from flying around the state, sighting an animal on the ground below, landing the plane, and then shooting it.

Interest groups must qualify an initiative in order for it to reach the ballot for a popular vote. The proposed law must be titled and the various details written. In these early steps, the interest must have legal or at least legislative knowledge. The next major step is the petition drive to obtain sufficient signatures from a state's voters to qualify the proposed initiative. The number of valid voter signatures required varies from state to state, from 2.7 percent of those voting in the previous general election in North Dakota to a high of 15 percent in Wyoming. The higher the threshold, the fewer the initiatives on the ballot. The most common threshold is 6 percent, as found in California and Oregon.

Both conservative and liberal interest groups have frequently used initiatives. During the 1970s and 1980s conservatives used the process to limit state and local governments' taxing power and to establish term limits. Environmentalist groups often used initiatives to limit corporate use of certain lands and to limit hunters. In general, voters tend to view propositions with general suspicion and tend to vote no if doubt exists. Thus the process tends to favor conservatives in their defense of the status quo.

The campaigns for some propositions have been quite inexpensive, whereas others rival the most expensive U.S. Senate and gubernatorial campaigns. A 1988 California initiative campaign financed by five insurance companies totaled $101 million. The same year saw $21 million (tobacco companies) and $8 million (National Rifle Association) campaigns in California. The 1998 California proposition dealing with Native American casinos recorded well over $100 million in total spending as Native American nations poured about $85 million into their effort and Las Vegas gambling interests spent over $45 million in an unsuccessful effort to protect the billions of dollars at stake in their industry. Some less controversial propositions can get by on shoestring budgets with almost no expenditures for media. These campaigns largely rely on free media for the communication of their supporting arguments to the voting public. These campaigns can succeed only if they are unopposed, and even in that case there is no guarantee of victory, since voters will vote against propositions they have heard little about.

Conclusion: The Role of Campaigns in Linking Political Parties and Interest Groups

Contemporary interest groups are frequent campaigners. They campaign in initiative and referendum campaigns as they seek to pass laws that they desire while bypassing state legislatures and other governmental institutions that may obstruct their goals. Media campaigns are also important tactics for many interest groups. They seek to establish reservoirs of goodwill in the public for future issue campaigns, present their defense of existing policies, or argue their demands for policy changes. Grassroots campaigns are run to supplement insider campaigns by professional lobbyists working in Washington, D.C., or the various state capitals. Grassroots efforts attempt to activate membership, selected publics, or the general public to exert pressure by forwarding supportive communications to the intended target—usually political but sometimes private organizations.

Many interest group campaigns proceed simultaneously. This is a major change in the general area of campaigns. At one time several years ago, the word "campaign" was understood (with the few exceptions from states such as California) to mean political party election campaigns. Now a campaign is more likely to mean an interest group campaign, since they seem to be part of every month of the year, unlike party campaigns, which are concentrated around our two-year cycle of fixed elections. The health care reform campaign, discussed at the beginning of this chapter, may be the greatest interest group issue campaign in American political history. But it is certainly not the last major issue campaign. It served as the model for other issue campaigns that followed it in the mid-1990s, and as the unofficial announcement that party-oriented campaigns and interest group campaigns had finally come together.

The next chapter discusses the "inside" tactics of interest group campaigns along with their major participants, the lobbyists, and Chapter 10 examines internal interest group characteristics such as leadership, money, and membership and how they can be converted to valuable political lobbying resources useful in issue and party campaigns.

9

Interest Group Lobbying

Campaigning Inside the Government

Lobbying in Washington, D.C., and the various state capitals and other local governments is usually personified by the lobbyist. The lobbyist is the person sitting up in the gallery of the House of Representatives or in the back of the committee meeting rooms. The lobbyist is also the association representative who helps draft forthcoming legislation for a state legislator and then testifies at committee hearings on the value of the proposed law. Lobbyists often symbolize the interest groups for which they work. Jack Valenti, adviser to former president Lyndon B. Johnson, has represented Hollywood in Washington for decades. He is the president of the Motion Pictures Association and one of the most powerful and best paid of all the association lobbyists in the capital.

The Lobbying Profession

What types of people become lobbyists? Former U.S. Senate majority leader and unsuccessful Republican 1996 presidential candidate Robert Dole became a lobbyist in 1997. Dole joined the Washington law firm of Verner, Liipfert, Bernard, McPherson, and Hand. His fourteen-room office suite is located a couple of blocks from the White House. Dole earned his estimated $600,000 1997 salary not by lobbying in the normal meaning of the word but by providing access and strategic advice to his clients. Dole was hired to help the firm erase its image as a "Democratic" law firm. The $6 million that it spent on lobbying fees (ranking third in the city) represented only 10 percent of its total business. Other former political heavyweights who joined Verner-Liipfert in recent years included Bob Dole's Democratic counterpart, former Senate majority leader George Mitchell, former Texas governor, Democrat Ann Richards, and former Texas senator and Treasury secretary Lloyd Bentsen.

Personal connections also play an important role for state-level lobbyists. In Utah, for example, the new lobbying firm of Foxley, Pignanelli, and Evans was formed in August 1997. Doug Foxley came from his own lobbying firm and a background as chairman of the Utah State Board of (Higher Education) Regents. Frank Pignanelli was a lobbyist for his corporation, Blue Cross–Blue Shield, and the former minority leader of the State House of Representatives. Charlie Evans was a colleague of Foxley in his previous lobbying firm after he had successfully managed the 1996 reelection campaign of Utah's very popular Republican governor, Mike Leavitt, and the 1994 reelection campaign of Republican U.S. senator Orrin Hatch. The new firm promised clients "the most comprehensive level of government relations available in Utah" ("Political Operatives" 1997).

The most visible lobbyists are voluntarily or involuntarily retired politicians or heavyweight political activists. But they do not represent the typical lobbyist. Lobbyists come from a wide variety of backgrounds and occupations. Some are long-term interest group activists; others are associational employees who may do association office work during most of the year and emerge as lobbyists during the short legislative sessions common in many states. Other come from a governmental background, not as high-profile elected officials but as "faceless staffers" from obscure committees or governmental offices. Lobbyists used to be stereotyped as overweight males smoking long cigars, but the Gucci shoes and expensive suits are still part of the image for both male and female lobbyists. Research on the state level indicates the emergence of women as lobbyists across the nation, and that pattern holds in Washington as well.

To be successful, a good lobbyist must have something to sell potential clients. Some sell subject matter expertise such as deep knowledge of a particular area, for example, the health care industry. Such knowledge can come from working in the industry or from governmental expertise gained as legislative staff on the health or tax writing committees. Others offer a deep understanding of the legislative process, policymakers of all types, or the political process. This is the type of knowledge offered by the Bob Doles of the lobbying world. They can crack the political maze by offering strategic advice and personal access. Other lawyer-lobbyists can offer advice on the legal process—an area of lobbying that has become very important for many interest groups. A final type of knowledge is communications. This sector is dominated by public relations and political communications specialists and has spread far beyond New York City's Madison Avenue to major cities across the nation.

The pool from which lobbyists emerge is largely located in Washington, D.C., or the various state capitals. Former government employees and elected officials make up a large part of the pool, as do the jack-of-all-trades lawyers and employees of trade associations, interest groups, and other such organizations. However, in recent years new professions such as public relations persons and accountants have become prominent in the lobbying field.

The *Washington Post* and the *National Journal* are excellent papers to read in order to understand the broad range of experts who make up the Washington, D.C., lobbying corps. With billions of dollars at stake for America's major corporations, many lobbyists may be employed and millions of dollars spent in lobbying campaigns; almost all involved will consider it money well spent. The well-reported 1997 Congress–White House budget deal produced dozens of such lobbying profiles. One of the nation's largest pension funds, the TIAA-CREF (which probably holds the money invested for your college professor's retirement), hired a corps of lobbyists to defend its tax-deductible status, including a former Republican member of the House, a former Bush chief legislative aide, and several heavyweights from the superlobbying firm of Hill and Knowlton. Despite this firepower, it lost the battle in 1997. Another lobbying battle in that budget deal involved internal medicine physicians and radiologists. The former were represented by the famous law/lobbyist firm of Patton Boggs, and the losing radiologists retained another powerful Washington, D.C., law firm, Mannatt, Phelps, and Phillips. Airline companies retained a significant part of the lobbying community in their battles among themselves over the airline ticket tax that generated over $33 billion in a five-year period. Delta (former Republican National Committee chair Haley Barbour), American (former Bush transportation secretary James Burnley IV and wife of Senate minority leader, Linda Daschle), and Southwest (several former congressmen and aides plus Fred McClure, President Bush's top legislative adviser) used both lobbyists and CEOs as well as passengers as grassroots lobbyists. Perhaps the most important battles (in terms of the billions of dollars on the table) were over efforts to cut more than $100 billion in Medicare spending in the budget over a five-year period. The American Association of Retired Persons (AARP) defeated various proposals, including a proposal to raise Medicare premiums on wealthier seniors, increase the age for eligibility, and charge a set fee for each home health care visit. One interest group, the American Hospital Association, was concerned over so many budget issues that it hired an all-star team of lobbyists including Christopher O'Neill, son of the former House Speaker, former GOP head Haley Barbour, and a host of former staff aides of top congressmen and senators.

Voluntarily and involuntarily retired (i.e., defeated in reelection attempts), politicians can become nearly perfect lobbyists. After all, they come to the job possessing the skills necessary for lobbying success: access to governmental decisionmakers, knowledge of the legislative process, political skills, and even knowledge of the law, since many are lawyers as well. Many former members of Congress have become permanent residents of the capital, and after they leave Congress, they seek alternative employment in order to avoid returning to their home state. One incentive has lured over two hundred former members of Congress to become lobbyists in Washington: money. One former congressman is reportedly earning almost $350,000 a year as a lobbyist for banking interests. Senator Bob Dole's $600,000 a year salary is a bit on the high side for such former members, but his resume is a bit better than others'. A Dole-type lobbyist is called a "rainmaker" in that his role is to find clients and let them "rain money" down on the law-lobbying firm. For example, former vice president Walter Mondale was nominated to be the U.S. ambassador to Japan in August 1997. Prior to that appointment, he rained more than a million dollars a year in billings on his law firm.

Not all of the former government officials who turn to lobbying come from the Congress or state legislatures. One of the most successful (and, incidentally, best compensated) is former Nixon administration secretary of state, Dr. Henry Kissinger, who so capitalized on his "special relationship" with the People's Republic of China that he has been called "China's single best lobbyist" by the *New York Times* (1996a). Maybe Kissinger is China's best lobbyist, but he is only one of many. Among the big names who lobby for the People's Republic of China are former Hong Kong governor Chris Patten, four other ex-secretaries of state (Alexander Haig, Cyrus Vance, George Schultz, and Lawrence Eagleburger), former secretary of defense Richard Cheney, former national security adviser Brent Scrowcroft, ex-Senate Republican leader Howard Baker, and two former U.S. trade representatives, Carla Hills and William Brock (Grady 1997).

Former officials such as Kissinger are often eagerly sought out by foreign interests who assume that such people have extraordinary access and influence (much as such people may in their own home nations). A classic example of this type of lobbyist was Michael Deaver, a former White House staff member in the Reagan administration who landed three very lucrative clients—South Korea, Canada, and Philip Morris International—soon after he left his job with Ronald Reagan. Personal connections are the essence of Korean domestic politics, and thus hiring Deaver was a logical move for the South Koreans. Later Philip Morris, seeking to gain entry into the very restrictive and very rich South Korean tobacco market, hired Deaver to represent it in South Korea.

Perhaps one of the major selling points such lobbyists have when they approach potential clients is the access they retain to their former places of employment. Deaver kept his White House access pass long after he moved to the private sector as a lobbyist. Former members of Congress have access to the floor of Congress, its gyms and restaurants, and other gathering sites off-limits to ordinary lobbyists. In the Utah state legislature in 1997, the leadership finally had to remind the lobbyists who flooded the House floor when a major vote was scheduled that they did not have voting rights after the media reported that some lobbyists were voting in voice votes in that chamber.

"Inside lobbyists," as the name implies, are informal lobbyists who are sitting members of a legislature or bureaucracy. An example of this type of hidden lobbyist would be all the lawyers or veterans who also sit in legislatures or governmental offices. In the 1980s, a majority of House and Senate members were veterans and always seemed to find money for veterans' causes. Although the number of veterans in Congress has declined in recent years, Congress finds it politically impossible to vote against veterans. Congress also has great difficulty passing laws that affect lawyers. Maybe the large numbers of former lawyers have something to do with those outcomes.

Inside lobbyists are frequently found in the executive branch. Both the Reagan and Clinton administrations had many issue activists representing a wide range of special interests. Many lobbyists volunteer their time with the incoming presidential transition teams that select members of the new administration. Not surprisingly, many interest group advocates show up in the new administration when the appointments are announced. So common is this pattern that hundreds of such examples can be noted in all recent administrations.

Other interests with significant inside lobbies have included farmers, small businesses, and lawyers. The 1997 budget battles included a demand by Alaskan seafood processors seeking to increase their tax deductions for the costs of feeding employees located at remote sites in Alaska. The seafood companies wanted the same type of tax consideration given years earlier to the offshore oil drilling companies that had supporters on the Senate Finance Committee. In 1995, Senator Frank Murkowski of Alaska was added to the tax writing committee and was able to introduce the equal tax break to the 1997 budget bill. For the first time, the seafood interest had an inside lobbyist.

Bureaucratic lobbyists are government lobbyists who lobby other parts of the government. In the White House, the presidential lobbying staff is called the Office of Congressional Liaison. These "liaison lobbyists" have become a powerful corps of hundreds of professional advocates with total lobbying budgets approaching $20 million. Approximately fifty liaisons lobby for the military before Congress, and another twenty-five represent the interests of the State Department. Many of these liaisons move on to the private sector after a few years of lobbying for the government.

Former bureaucrats and political appointees know the lobbying business because they are the targets of lobbying campaigns or help organize such campaigns to secure their objectives. Even more prized are former legislative staff members who possess many of the key lobbying skills: legislative and political skills, contacts, and, most importantly, subject matter expertise. The banking industry, for example, is always looking for experienced staff members from the Finance or Banking Committees and the pattern extends to almost every other congressional committee or governmental agency.

Some of the highest-paid lobbyists in Washington, D.C., and the major state capitals are "lawyer-lobbyists" such as Bob Dole. Affiliated with the most prestigious Washington and regional law firms, these people seldom participate in the direct contacts other lobbyists daily perform. Depending on the relevant laws, they resist registration as lobbyists by emphasizing the lawyer part of their hyphenated job title. Traditionally, many of Washington's most powerful law firms resisted putting significant resources in their lobbying sections. However, since the 1980s, more and more of the megafirms have hired more personnel as their lobbying billings have multiplied. Washington is awash with lawyers. The number of lawyers admitted to practice before the federal courts of the District of Columbia increased from just under 1,000 in 1950 to 61,000 in 1990. Many of these are lawyer-lobbyists. A good example of this type of lawyer-lobbyist is Robert Strauss, former chairman of the Democratic National Committee, former trade representative and ambassador to Russia, and his law firm, Akin, Gump, Strauss, Hauer, and Feld.

The elite of these lawyer-lobbyists are often called "superlawyers." Their experience and knowledge are eagerly sought after by interests of all types. The very best of these have worked in the White House or as cabinet members. They personify the "revolving door" of private lobbying: government service followed by very lucrative career lobbying. Salaries for some of these superlawyers may run into the millions of dollars on an annual basis. The best way to describe the rationale behind these huge salaries is to note that a single provision inserted into a tax bill can be worth billions of dollars to a given industry. One bit of advice by superlawyer Clark Clifford was estimated to have saved the DuPont family over $500 million in taxes. Clifford received a reported $1 million at the time—worth over $4 million at 1996 prices. Lobbyist Micheal Deaver was earning about $400,000 to $500,000 per client per year for his access and lobbying skills. Many wealthy corporations and some of the richer trade associations retain several of the city's major law firms and perhaps a half dozen or more lobbying firms as lobbyists to ensure the widest possible representation. Some specialize in one type of issue; others focus on one site of specialization such as the FCC or the Senate Finance Committee; others do PR, media, or grassroots lobbying. Expertise and access can be very expensive but are well worth the costs, given the stakes.

Lobbyists with especially refined communications skills are frequently based in the public relations industry that began on Madison Avenue in

New York City and later established firm foundations in Washington, D.C. Many of these PR–lobbying firms generate extensive billings from their work for foreign governments and interests. A full range of services in PR lobbying can be provided by firms with a mixture of press kits, direct mail, fact-finding trips, traditional lobbying, seminars, and media cultivation activities. Such services can run an interest easily into the seven-figure billing category. Many of the lobbyists who emerged from the Reagan White House come from public relations backgrounds.

The efforts of Hill and Knowlton, a public relations/lobbying firm, in support of the Kuwaiti government during the Gulf War in 1990–1991 represent the most famous PR and lobbying campaign in recent political history. After Iraq invaded Kuwait in 1990, the Kuwaiti government-in-exile contracted with Hill and Knowlton to increase support in the United States for the liberation of Kuwait. A front group was formed, Citizens for a Free Kuwait, financed almost entirely by the Kuwaiti government and paying Hill and Knowlton $11.5 million for its PR lobbying. The agency proved to be a key element in developing U.S. political and military support for Kuwait (Trento 1992).

Just like the law firm that hired Republican Bob Dole to open doors in the Republican-controlled Congress, the Republican-dominated "complete service firm" of Black, Manafort, Stone, and Kelly added a former Democratic party finance chairman in order to enhance its access with Democratic power holders. But the classically successful "Republican-Democratic" lobby is the firm of Wexler and Reynolds. Anne Wexler, a former assistant to President Jimmy Carter, joined with Nancy Clark Reynolds, a vice president and head of Bendix Corporation's Washington office (as well as a personal friend of President Reagan) to establish a lobbying firm that could work both sides of the aisle in Congress or the executive branch. Wexler and Reynolds offers almost every lobbying service a client could require.

Although the full-services lobbying giants have dozens of employees, many of the lobbyists listed in the Washington, D.C., telephone book (and at the state level) are very small, one- or two-person firms. These "niche firms" tend to specialize in a single industry or around a narrow issue. Specializing in a narrow field, having just a few clients, and having a close personal, often long-term relationship between clients and lobbyists makes these firms long-term actors and very "service oriented."

When an interest group, a trade association, or a coalition plans a campaign, it often approaches it from a variety of directions. There are many roads to success in Washington, D.C., politics. The more voices a cause can produce, the better its chance of success. A corporation engaged in such a campaign may work through its own lobbying team, several lobbying firms, or public relations firms and one or more trade associations. Many may also belong to broad peak associations such as the Chamber of Commerce or the National Association of Small Business. Giant corporations such as Ford and General Electric have double-digit law and consulting firms representing their interests (Soloman 1987). In "emergencies," these corporations go out and buy whatever needs to be bought in order to win a campaign. Broadcast television lobbying with its major trade association, the National Association of Broadcasters, and its ten major constituent groups, including the various television networks, had hired 174 registered lobbyists ranging from stars on the left such as former Texas governor Ann Richards to conservatives including former Republican National Committee chairman Haley Barbour and GOP superlobbyist Tom Korologos. CBS had retained the services of twenty-nine lobbyists (Safire 1997).

Haley Barbour is an interesting case of a person converting political party experience into lobbying clout and financial compensation. Barbour was a lobbyist before becoming the Republican party head for a four-year period during the first Clinton administration. He quit the party job in 1997 and returned to his old lobbying firm of Barbour, Griffith, and Rogers and brought with him thirteen new clients, who had been major Republican money contributors. These new clients nearly doubled the client list of his firm and included such big-spending interests as telecommunications, tobacco, trucking, Mercedes Benz, and Delta Airlines. Barbour, closely identified with the Gingrich-led, Republican-dominated Congress, has been described as one of the best access lobbyists in Washington, D.C. (Wayne 1997d).

Most of the tens of thousands of lobbyists working in Washington and the state capitals are employees of various interests. These are called "in-house" lobbyists. Big, powerful organizations are characterized by large, well-funded governmental relations or legislature liaison staffs. Some of these groups maintain a dozen or more lobbyists and additional staff to support their activities. Weaker organizations do not have permanent lobbying corps, but they often "double hat" their executive directors, who operate as a lobbyist when needed and take care of the association the rest of the time.

Amateur lobbyists are both the best and the worst of lobbyists. They can be very useful to grassroots campaigns because of their enthusiasm and dedication, or they can be disastrous because they are often uncontrolled and nonprofessional. Many cause-oriented groups (moral, religious, women's, and environmental issues) choose to use amateur lobbyists because of the nature of the groups or simply because they do not have the money to hire professional lobbyists. Amateur lobbyists can be effective if they possess special talents or resources. An interest group that brings amateur lobbyists from the home district of a member of Congress will probably have its message heard. The message will be communicated even more effectively if it is voiced by several prominent businesspeople who have contributed campaign funds in past elections. The greatest danger with amateur lobbyists is that they can wreck groundwork carefully prepared by the organization with their excessive enthusiasm and perhaps offensive tactics.

Accountants have entered the Washington, D.C., lobbying game in recent years. The special contribution of accountants to the lobbying game is their ability to produce data on the tax implications of many types of legislation. Price Waterhouse, with a Washington staff of 123, did tax law analysis for Hewlett-Packard. The "big six" accounting firms (Anderson & Co., Coopers & Lybrand, Deloitte & Touche, Earnst & Young, KPMG Peat Marwick, and Price Waterhouse) increasingly monitor tax legislation and regulatory actions, help put together coalitions, provide low-profile technical advice on lobbying, and even directly lobby Congress and the executive branch. Price Waterhouse has a legislative monitoring service with 150 clients. The service costs each client about $20,000 per year (Stone 1993).

Most professions have standards that govern training and ethics, yet traditionally there were no such standards for lobbyists. A lobbyist was anyone who said he was one; but in many cases he was not. Lobbying has slowly become more professional in its standards and training. In terms of formal educational standards and credentialing, George Washington University's Graduate Program in Political Management (with a lobbying subfield) is the current state-of-the-art program in Washington. The American League of Lobbyists (ALL) was formed, in part, to improve the image of lobbying as a profession. Books by Ronald Hrebenar and Clive Thomas (1987, 1992a, 1992b, 1993) have reported research indicating that lobbying at the state level has also become more professional in recent years as better-trained, better-educated, and higher-paid lobbyists have become more common in many states and the "contract" (i.e., professional, multiclient) lobbyist has emerged in almost all the larger states and in many of the smaller states as well. Another change that has modified the image of lobbying is the increase in the number of women lobbyists in both the nation's capital and many state capitals.

The Lobbyist's Role in Political Issue Campaigns

The job that a lobbyist does in a political issue campaign includes many different types of tasks. A lobbyist may be a contact person who exists to link his or her interest with the appropriate governmental decisionmakers, in essence, an access creator. Some lobbyists earn a very fine living based on the people they know and getting their clients' messages to those people.

For contact lobbyists, the quality of their contacts is often more valuable than the quantity of their contacts. Interest group campaign strategists are very rare, but they are very valuable. They put together the lobbying campaigns, negotiate the coalitions, and allocate the various group resources to maximize the prospects of success. The most numerous of all are the liaison lobbyists. As their name implies, they act as a intermediaries between interest groups and government. The liaison lobbyists attend meetings, listen to hearings and debates, and collect information about what is occurring in their assigned territory—be it Congress, the regulatory agencies, or the White House. If something of significance happens or could happen to their clients, the liaison or watchdog lobbyists alert them, may give recommendations for action, and wait for directives. Some may report daily on the broad range of activities they are monitoring; others have a specific list of concerns and just follow those events, such as bills with tax implications for a specific industry such as energy. Finally, the most common type of lobbyist, in terms of the public perception of the profession, is the advocate who spends time going from office to office visiting politicians and bureaucrats, presenting data and arguments on their issues, and testifying at committee hearings.

Like the never ending debate regarding the symbiotic relationship between celebrities and the media, a similar debate exists regarding the relationship between lobbyists on one side and politicians and bureaucrats on the other side. Each side uses the other to advance its own political goals. Lester Milbrath in his classic study of lobbying argues that politicians often use lobbyists in order to gain support for the politician's or bureaucrat's bill. Lobbyists often write major bills; more than one new law has passed the legislature in a form nearly identical to what the lobbyist wrote before the session (Milbrath 1963, 234). Also, many a speech given on the floor of a legislative chamber or in committee hearings was written by supporting lobbyists for the legislator. Like the media and celebrities, lobbyists and legislators have a mutually supportive relationship. Lobbyists provide valuable information of a technical and political nature without which legislators would find lawmaking a enormously more difficult task.

Lobbyists and Lobbying Campaign Tactics

The art (not yet the science) of lobbying is organized around a wide range of possible tactics that the group strategist or lobbyist can select from to accomplish the group's issue campaign objectives. Some of these tactics are largely external to the everyday activities found in Washington, D.C., or the various state capitals.

Before we turn to the tactics of influence, we need to discuss the groundwork that precedes the actual lobbying activities. The most fundamental of these preliminary activities is aimed at creating access for the group, its lobbyists, and its messages.

In the world of retail stores, the secret of success has been called "location, location, and location." In the world of successful lobbying, the secret of success may be "access, access, and access." With tens of thousands of lobbyists seeking to make their case, not all of them will have their chance or their best chance to communicate. Almost every interest group pursues an access-creating strategy to set the stage for future lobbying campaigns. Some of these access-creating activities seek to establish a personal relationship, if not friendship, between the lobbyists and the governmental officials who can affect the group's fortune. Others involve the utilization of money in the form of campaign contributions from interest group political action committees, seeking to reward politicians for past support and entice them to support the group's positions in the future.

One of the interesting outcomes from the 1997 congressional hearings on the Clinton 1996 campaign funding scandals was a series of frank observations from governmental officials and lobbyists about the issue of access. Clinton's attorney general, Janet Reno, sent a letter to the House Judiciary Committee stating that the courts and U.S. law do not regard access (the opportunity to meet with governmental officials) as being the same as a job offer, a government contract, or a policy decision. The Reno conclusion was nicely summarized in a newspaper's headline: "Reno Says It's Legal to Sell Access" (1997). One businessman, Roger Tamraz, admitted giving $300,000 to the Democratic party during the 1996 elections to get access to federal decisionmakers to seek support for his proposal to build an oil pipeline in the Caspian Sea area. The Clinton administration never gave its permission despite his meeting with the president and his staff. Tamraz mentioned at the hearing that he should have given $600,000 instead of $300,000. But doubling the amount would not guarantee success; money can buy access (which he got) but does not guarantee results. Nelson Polsby, a prominent political scientist at the University of California–Berkeley, once remarked that "money buys access. So what?" (*New York Times* 1997c). Polsby notes that access is protected by the First Amendment to the Constitution (freedom to petition for the redress of grievances) and the courts have ruled that political contributions are a form of political speech and thus protected by the First Amendment's freedom of speech provisions. Access to politicians is granted as a result of many factors and only some of them are based on money or campaign contributions. Some access is granted on the basis of power or simply residence in the home constituency, old friendships, union leadership, organizational or issue group affiliations, and many other potential relationships.

It is important to distinguish between access-creating money politics and an old-fashioned bribe. In the late 1800s, a typical pattern of interest group–legislator behavior involved the direct (perhaps under the table in the form of cash-stuffed envelopes) exchange of money for laws. Political bosses such as William M. Tweed of New York's Tammany Hall political machine controlled a delegation of New York State legislators who were "for sale" for $100 to $5,000, depending on the issue (Thayer 1973, 37). Direct bribery was a standard tactic for many lobbyists a hundred years ago. Relatively few cases of interest group–legislature bribery have occurred in the last fifty years, and the use of direct bribes is considered to be one of the few tactics that lead to nearly certain disaster.

It has been noted that people in power lust not only for money but for other "vices" as well. It used to be the case that the way to a legislator's heart was through his stomach. Interest groups sponsored very expensive dinners and wined and dined their prospective targets. But in recent years, public and media attention and changing laws and legislative rules have significantly reduced these opportunities. Other groups sponsored golf or tennis tournaments or just played in them in order to meet and befriend political decisionmakers. Changing tastes have elevated and reduced the values of these access-creating activities. Golf used to be the preferred sport of lobbyists, since it had several advantages: It was expensive and exclusive and thus prestigious. It also had the advantage of being an all-day event, which allowed lobbyists to establish firmer ties with their political counterparts. However, by the 1980s, tennis began to replace golf as the preferred lobbyist sport because it was a much shorter game and could be handled over a lunch break or a couple of hours before or after work. One of Washington's most successful lobbyists noted that every PR and lobbying firm had a tennis-playing lobbyist and club memberships. Jack Valenti, head of the Motion Picture Association, had a half dozen tennis club memberships. As one Washington tennis pro noted, "Once you get to know people on the court, you can get through on the telephone without going through six or seven intermediaries" (Gamarekian 1983). Other groups use tickets to sporting events (tickets to Washington Redskins football games are very valuable) and entertainment events such as touring Broadway productions to create their access. The general rule for these access-creating events is that no lobbying business is to be discussed on the course or the courts. That can be done later after the access has been firmly established.

Today money is transferred from interest groups to politicians when a political action committee (PAC) makes a legal contribution to a candidate's campaign committee. These are not "bribes" for past or future votes, but concrete expressions of an organization's support for past and future efforts and its desire to maintain access established over the years. Tables 9.1 and 9.2 summarize the top ten PAC contributors to federal candidates in the 1995–1996 and 1997–1998 campaign cycles. These two tables show the diversity of interests that provide large contributions to federal candi-

TABLE 9.1   Top Ten PAC Contributors to Federal Campaigns, 1995–1996

Contributor	Total Donated
1. Philip Morris	$2,741,659
2. AT&T	$2,130,045
3. Trial Lawyers Assoc.	$2,106,325
4. Teamsters Union	$2,097,410
5. Laborers Union	$1,938,250
6. Electrical Workers Union	$1,821,710
7. RJR Nabisco	$1,765,306
8. National Education Assoc.	$1,661,960
9. American Medical Assoc.	$1,633,530
10. Am. Fed. of State, Co., Mun. Employees	$1,616,125

SOURCE: Federal Election Commission, January 1, 1995–June 30, 1996.

dates. Among the largest are PACs representing big companies, labor unions, lawyers, doctors, teachers, local government employees, home-builders, and automobile dealers. Some groups, such as the Trial Lawyers Association, gave large contributions in both election cycles. Other groups gave large contributions in response to a particular issue that was under consideration, for example, AT&T's contributions in connection with changes in telecommunications law. Of course, interest groups may also give money to political parties, in the form of "soft money" contributions, rather than to individual candidates. Table 9.3 shows the biggest soft money donors to the major parties in the 1997–1998 election cycle.

TABLE 9.2   Top Ten PAC Contributors to Federal Campaigns, 1997–1998

Contributor	Total Donated
1. Trial Lawyers Assoc.	$1,730,300
2. Am. Fed. of State, Co., Mun. Employees	$1,617,150
3. Electrical Workers Union	$1,422,145
4. Realtors PAC	$1,268,718
5. Nat. Assoc. of Homebuilders	$1,258,240
6. American Fed. of Teachers	$1,229,650
7. American Medical Assoc.	$1,184,601
8. Automobile Dealers Assoc.	$1,159,675
9. United Automobile Workers	$1,140,710
10. United Parcel Service	$1,094,120

SOURCE: Federal Election Commission, January 1, 1997–June 30, 1998. Report issued on September 24, 1998.

TABLE 9.3   Biggest Soft Money Donors to Political Parties, 1997–1998

Contributors to Republicans	Total Donated	To Democrats
1. Philip Morris	$1,800,000	$417,000
2. Amway Corp. and owners	$1,300,000	$0
3. RJR Nabisco (tobacco/food)	$568,850	$132,572
4. AT&T	$564,503	$280,240
Contributors to Democrats	Total Donated	To Republicans
1. Loral Space and Communications	$871,000	$0
2. Peter Buttenwieser (education)	$720,000	$0
3. Communication Workers of America	$561,250	$0
4. Williams & Bailey (law firm)	$410,000	$0

SOURCES: Federal Election Commission and Center for Responsive Politics, January 1, 1997–October 1, 1998.

Table 9.4 traces the growth in the number of PACs active at the federal level since 1974. The number of federal PACs has increased dramatically over time, with the number peaking at nearly 4,200 PACs in 1990. By 1998, the total had declined slightly to 3,762. Of course, only a small percentage of PACs are "major players" in the money-for-access game. For example, in 1996 roughly 14 percent of all PACs made more than 75 percent of the total contributions to federal candidates. Table 9.4 also shows an increase in the types of PACs. The number of PACs grew in all categories, but corporate and nonconnected (or "ideological") PACs grew most dramatically. The money given by PACs to federal candidates varied across these categories. In 1996, for example, corporate PACs gave $78 million, trade associations gave $60 million, labor unions gave $48 million, and ideological PACs gave $24 million.

Lobbyists who are ready to assist legislators when they need help will gain future access. Some lobbyists have sufficient access and influence with existing legislative leaders to be of assistance in helping new legislators gain

TABLE 9.4   PAC Growth Between 1974 and 1998, Selected Years

Date	Corporate	Labor	Trade	Nonconnected	Total
1974	89	201	318	–	608
1980	1,206	297	576	374	2,551
1985	1,710	388	695	1,003	3,992
1990	1,795	346	774	1,062	4,172
1995	1,674	334	815	1,020	4,016
1997	1,602	332	826	953	3,975
1998	1,565	325	820	897	3,762

NOTE: "Total" includes a small number of PACs from two additional categories, "cooperative" and "corporations without stock."
SOURCE: Federal Election Commission, "Semi-Annual Federal PAC Count," July 21, 1998.

assignments to desired committees. Because committees and subcommittees are often the decisive sites for the addition or subtraction of a single critical phrase or even a single word, such tactics can often prove to be invaluable to lobbyists. Such an outcome occurred in the 1998 federal budget bill, which emerged with a well-hidden clause committing the federal government to pay any legal judgments against it arising from continuing litigation on the failed savings and loan companies. Experts estimate that this one clause may cost the taxpayers of the United States up to $50 billion.

Celebrity lobbying also creates access for some interest groups. Groups that have trouble getting a hearing for their political demands may secure a celebrity to gain access to the decisionmaking system. The Hollywood A-list superstars (and even some of the lesser B-list ministars) can be recruited into a cause and brought to Washington, D.C., for hearings and media events. Among the stars who have lobbied in recent years have been Richard Gere (Tibet), Sally Fields (farm families), Charlton Heston (gun rights), Morgan Fairchild (environment), Martin Sheen (homelessness), Melanie Griffith (arts), Susan Sarandon (arts), Christopher Reeve (marine conservation), Quincy Jones (TV production rights), Sting (South American rain forest), Jane Fonda (Nature Conservancy), Billy Joel (Nature Conservancy), Barbara Streisand (women's rights and environment), and Michael Keaton (polluted rivers). These "celebrity lobbyists" have great ability to get media attention for a cause.

One environmentalist group, Earth Justice Legal Defense Fund (the former Sierra Club Legal Defense Fund), ran a celebrity ad in the *New York Times Magazine* in 1997 featuring actor Mel Gibson standing under the word "conspiracy," playing on the name of Gibson's 1997 movie. The ad promotes the Earth Justice Fund's recent successes and urges people to contact the group for help in environmentalist issues. Such a celebrity got the organization much more attention than it could have elicited with just a straight advocacy ad.

Beginning in 1995, many interest groups have had to turn to coalitions and contract lobbyists to establish access with the new Republican-controlled Congress. Broader coalition will have many more contacts with a wider range of politicians and bureaucrats than a single interest group. Sometimes even a multigroup coalition has insufficient access and the private sector may have to be hired to generate more access. Some private lobbying firms have added a specialization in coalition building for access creation and lobbying.

Lobby Campaigns in Terms of Information Presentations

A lobbyist has a variety of types of information that can be combined into a presentation in support of his or her organization's campaign. The information a lobbyist uses can be political, emotional, or rational. Statistics generated by the group can be presented to support an argument; political information, often in the form of public opinion, is frequently summarized in polling data or media commentaries. The lobbyist may also draw on scientific studies. Whatever the nature of the appeal, it must be communicated to the appropriate political decisionmakers; it is the lobbyist's job to decide which targets are the appropriate ones and how the data are to be communicated.

The first decision is targeting. The conventional wisdom of lobbying suggests that contacts with staff may be as useful as discussions with the politicians themselves. Key staff members often exercise an extraordinary influence over their political masters on certain types of issues. One lobbying study from several decades ago indicated that most lobbyists in Washington, D.C., lobbied the politicians' staffs more than the politicians themselves (Milbrath 1963, 216). Staff members are involved in every major step in the legislative process—from the initial research to the final vote roundups. However a lobbyist is determined to lobby the elected representatives themselves, which ones make the best targets? Experienced lobbyists suggest lobbying friends first; pursue the doubtful and ignore the known opponents. Bypassing opposition members reduces the probability of their becoming involved in the campaign, although not eliminating it.

The successful lobbying visit is pretty individualistic as each lobbyist has a unique style, but there is general agreement about the key elements. The conventional wisdom of lobbying emphasizes the need for a personal presentation set up as a formal appointment if possible; the need to be confident and knowledgeable on the issue; the requirement to be fair and honest in presenting arguments; the necessity for brevity; the need to request a specific action such as supporting a particular provision in committee; and the importance of leaving a summary fact sheet for later use by the political official. Other useful rules for lobbyists include (1) never ever lie because being caught reduces your credibility to zero, (2) try to link your issue either to the politician's home district in a positive manner or to some general political principle that may transcend local-level politics, and (3) never ever threaten politicians, unless your group is able to put such threats into reality (Milbrath 1963, 223–225).

Testifying at hearings and placing your group's arguments in the public record of the debate is a standard means of communication. Hearings on a given bill can be one-sided, since the committee leadership may already have made up its collective mind on a given issue, but these presentations serve a valuable purpose for many interest groups. Participation in formal hearings gives legitimacy to interest groups and allows them to be part of the debate and provide group leadership, with opportunities to play to its own membership. Additionally, hearings may be covered by the news media, giving the group much greater dissemination of its arguments.

Washington, D.C., is home to dozens of major research organizations called think tanks. One of the early major liberal think tanks was the Brookings Institute; it was joined by the conservative Heritage Foundation in 1973. In an environment in which "information equals power," many think tanks are sponsored by interest groups or work closely with them. During the first half of the Reagan administration, the Heritage Foundation produced hundreds of books, monographs, and analytical papers plus a monthly foreign policy and defense newsletter and a quarterly journal on policymaking. During Reagan's first term, the Heritage Foundation was quite important, as its policy recommendations were used by conservative Republicans in drawing up their action agendas to undo decades of liberal Democratic rule. It also was a significant intellectual influence on the Gingrich Republican revolution's agenda, the "contract with America." Various liberal interest groups such as the Progressive Policy Institute quickly entered the policy debates when the Clinton administration began its transition team policy discussions in late 1992 and early 1993.

Interest groups also seek to dominate staff and committee members when a major study commission is selected to study an emerging policy area. If a group can dominate such a committee, the issue can be framed in a very favorable way to protect the group's political objectives. Sometimes, it is argued, the membership of such study committees is selected to favor a specific policy recommendation. One of the best examples of stacking a study committee was the 1997 federal gambling study commission put together by President Clinton. Opponents of legalized gambling argued that members of the committee were stacked in favor of supporting continued gambling. As more and more political issues have been framed in much more sophisticated analytical forms, research and study committees play more important roles.

Polling data is another form of information that an interest group can use to frame the political discussion. Few groups can afford to do their own polling, but more groups are contracting out for survey research and focus-group analysis. The Health Insurance Association of America's "Harry and Louise" television ads were based on focus groups and research on how people felt about the proposed Clinton health care reforms in 1993–1994. In the same battle, the Pharmaceutical Manufacturers Association hired a pollster to research regularly the public's image of the drug companies. Discovering public ignorance about the role of the drug companies in developing new drugs, the association first ran some unsuccessful ads on the subject of the drug companies' research successes. Later polling encouraged the organization to shift its ad subjects to discussions of specific diseases and related drugs. These ads cost the group more than $32 million during the 1994–1995 period but were cheap when the group considered the financial costs of possible increased governmental regulations and restrictions (Barnes 1995).

Another way interest groups can influence an upcoming debate is to secure membership on a governmental advisory committee. There are well over 1,000 different federal advisory committees, commissions, councils boards, and panels. These committees advise the federal government in virtually every area of policymaking and span a wide range of subjects. Some multi-interest groups such as the AFL-CIO and major corporations such as AT&T serve on these boards. Diversity balancing is often a requirement for membership on such advisory committees. The previously mentioned federal advisory committee on gambling was much delayed as President Clinton apparently sought a Native American who had no public positions on legalized gambling but was favorable to continued gambling. A Native American was important, since so much of the nation's gambling is now conducted in reservation casinos.

Advisory committee membership is important to interest groups for a variety of reasons. First, the groups can use them to firm up their relationships with key governmental decisionmakers. Second, such memberships allow the groups to have a role in "framing the issue" and establishing a foundation of information upon which early recommendations for policies are based. Finally, membership on such committees legitimizes the member groups as "players" in the coming debate and enhances their role in later legislative debates.

Restrictions on Lobbying in the Federal Government

Until the late 1990s, there were no effective federal laws that regulated lobbying. Effective regulation of lobbying has been nearly impossible, given Supreme Court interpretations of the First Amendment as it has applied to the concept of "political speech." The First Amendment guarantees the people the right to freedom of speech and the right "to petition the Government for redress of grievances." Tension between the constitutional rights of freedom of speech and petition and the desire to control or at least bring into the open some of the excesses of the lobbying process have made the implementation of effective lobby laws a very difficult task.

Other than outright bribery, until very recently no lobbying techniques have been prohibited on the federal level. Given First Amendment concerns, almost all reformers have tried to increase public information about lobbying activities rather than prohibit or restrict any specific activities.

Prior to 1935, no laws restricted lobbying. In the 1930s, Congress passed several fragmented and inadequate pieces of legislation in response to specific scandals by public utility holding companies and the maritime industry. The electric power industry, known as the "Power Trust," was one of the most powerful interests in the 1930s. An early grassroots campaign aimed at the Congress generated more than 5 million letters to members of Congress opposing utility holding company legislation. That piece of legislation, the Public Utilities Holding Company Act of 1935, included within its various provisions a requirement for anyone employed or retained by a registered holding company to file reports with the Securities and Exchange Commission before attempting to influence Congress, the SEC, or the Federal Power Commission. This was the first piece of Congressional legislation to restrict lobbying in any manner. A scandal in the shipping industry regarding the lobbying practices of that industry as it attempted to influence a maritime subsidy bill resulted a lobby registration provision in the Merchant Marine Act of 1936. Shipping companies and shipyards receiving governmental subsidies had to report their income, expenses (including lobbying expenses), and interests on a monthly basis. The information generated by these requirements was considered confidential and was not made public until the passage of the Public Information Act of 1966.

The Foreign Agents Registration Act of 1938, or the McCormack Act, was an attempt to register anyone representing a foreign government or organization in the dangerous period just prior to World War II. The goal was to direct public attention to agents of foreign governments and attempt to neutralize foreign propaganda. The act was not effective to begin with and declined in effectiveness significantly with subsequent amendments over the years. Lawyers, for example, were exempted if they engaged in routine legal activities for their foreign clients. Consequently, many of the lawyer-lobbyists working in Washington, D.C., never registered, since they defined themselves as lawyers and not lobbyists.

In 1946, Congress passed as part of a general reorganization act the Federal Regulation of Lobbying Act—a comprehensive piece of legislation to cover lobbying of Congress. It required the registration of any person who was hired by someone else for the principal purpose of lobbying Congress and the submission of quarterly financial reports of lobbying expenditures. The Supreme Court ruled that the act is applicable only to (1) persons or organizations whose principal purpose is to influence legislation and (2) direct communications with congressmen on pending or proposed legislation.

The weaknesses of the 1946 law were legion. Many lobbyists never registered under its provisions, claiming that their principal purpose was not lobbying. Others did not register because they used their own money and did not "receive money for lobbying." Grassroots or indirect lobbying was not mentioned in the act and thus was unregulated. Groups could spend millions of dollars on grassroots campaigns and not report a dime. The law focused on lobbying members of Congress, and thus lobbying their personal staff, the executive branch, or the staff of congressional committees was not covered by the law. The reporting of expenditures was left up to the lobbyists, and many simply reported no lobbying expenses. And, finally, the act had no real investigation or enforcement provisions.

In 1995, Congress finally gave in to demands for reform and passed two provisions that impact lobbying. The first restricts gifts from lobbyists. New rules bar House and Senate members from accepting gifts, meals, and trips except from family members and friends. The Senate allows gifts valued at less than $50, with $100 total limits from a single source in a year. The House allows no gifts of any value from a lobbyist. There are exceptions in the rules, such as allowing trips and attendance at events that are connected to lawmakers' official duties, for example, throwing out the first ball at a baseball game. The exception for trips may be a big loophole in that it allows all-expenses-paid trips that are associated with fact finding or official duties such as "to speak on Congress" before a convention. International trips are limited to seven days and domestic trips to four days, excluding travel time. These changes could be the first steps toward effectively reducing the role of money in creating access. The style of lobbying in Washington has changed dramatically: Full-course dinners for members of Congress bought by lobbyists are now illegal, but stand-up buffets are legal (Schmidt 1996).

In 1995, Congress also repealed the 1946 Federal Regulation of Lobbying Act and replaced it with the Lobby Restrictions Act. Many of the 1946 loopholes were closed, but lobbying by religious groups resulted in grassroots lobbying and lobbying by religious groups being exempted from the provisions of the new law. The new law now covers all lobbyists who seek to influence Congress, congressional staff, and policymaking officials of the executive branch including the president, top White House officials, cabinet secretaries and their deputies, and independent agency administrators and their assistants. Representatives of U.S. subsidies of a foreign-owned company and lawyer-lobbyists for foreign entities are required to register.

Killing the grassroots reporting requirement and exempting religious groups from the reporting requirement may turn out to be fatal flaws in the new lobby law. Another significant provision that was killed would have established an enforcement agency. Attempts were made to ban key U.S. government personnel from ever becoming lobbyists for foreign interests. This failed, but a reform was passed and, for the first time, there were reporting and registration requirements on lobbyists in our nation's capital.

The only other laws that affect lobbying pertain to financial restrictions regarding contributions to federal campaigns. The Federal Campaign Act of 1971 banned group donations to general presidential campaigns unless funneled through political action committees, beginning with the 1976 presidential election. Since 1989, House and Senate rules have banned earnings from honoraria usually obtained by speaking before interest groups.

The 1978 Ethics in Government Act limits most ex–federal executive branch officials from lobbying on matters they had worked with in their federal jobs. Another provision banned senior governmental officials from lobbying their former agency or federal department for one year. None of these restrictions apply to former members of Congress. Therefore, when ex-senator Robert Dole joined a major Washington, D.C., lobbying firm in 1997, he was careful to say that he was not a lobbyist but merely offered strategic advice to his clients. Dole did not have to be so careful since even as a lobbyist he would not be in violation of the law as a former senator.

Judicial Lobbying Campaigns

Interest groups have been using the courts and judicial lobbying with great success since the 1940s, when the National Association for the Advancement of Colored People turned to judicial remedies in the face of legislative refusal to address the issue of segregation in America. Today, hundreds of groups are ready and able to play the "courts card" if they lose legislative, bureaucratic, or electoral battles. Judicial lobbying is a strategy available to big and small groups alike, but it requires very specific skills and resources or at least access to such resources. Groups with few resources can follow a minimum-resource strategy and groups with great resources can play all the cards in the judicial lobbying hand.

Interest groups use indirect judicial lobbying to set the stage for later direct lobbying. Groups try to influence judicial opinion by helping to frame upcoming issues in ways favorable to the group's interest. Tactics useful in legislative and executive branch lobbying do not work well in judicial lobbying. Picketing a federal courthouse has been illegal since the 1950s. Grassroots campaigns do not seem to be effective either, since judges never acknowledge reading communications on upcoming issues. Letter writing does happen and, particularly on the issue of abortion, many have tried to influence the courts in recent decades, but this does not seem to have influenced any key decisions (Vose 1958).

One particularly useful indirect tactic has centered around efforts to influence the selection of federal and state judges. Two presidential elections, the 1980 and 1996 elections, had such appointment focuses. In the 1980 election, many liberal groups were concerned with possible court appointments by conservative Republican Ronald Reagan. By the end of the Reagan administration in 1989, more than half of the 750 federal judges were Reagan appointees. After the Democrats won the White House under Clinton in the 1992 elections, many liberal interest groups were very hopeful of greatly influencing the federal judiciary with Clinton's appointments. Many of these groups were disappointed when President Clinton placed more emphasis on gender and ethnicity than on liberal ideology. Additionally, many liberal groups complained that the Clinton selection process was so slow that many judicial positions remained vacant for far too long. Part of the reason behind dozens of judicial vacancies in the Clinton second term was a Republican strategy that sought to delay and kill as many of the nominations as possible and hope that a Republican president in 2001 could fill the vacancies with judges favorable to conservative interest groups. Given that the impeachment process captured the attention of the Clinton White House in 1998, the Republicans' judicial strategy might be a successful one.

Federal judges are appointed by the president with the advice and consent of the Senate, producing a selection process that involves legislators, political parties, and pressure groups. Prior to the 1980s, the politics of federal judicial nominations were low-key. However, liberal interest groups mobilizing to kill the Bork nomination in 1989 and to challenge but lose on the Thomas nomination produced a conservative counterreaction and almost guaranteed future conservative opposition to a Democratic president's liberal or moderate judicial nominations. The 1987 Bork Supreme Court nomination came close to the idea of total interest group issue war that we discussed in connection with the health care reform battle later in 1993–1994. A large number of groups, 185 of them, opposed the nomination and fought the fifty-three pro-Bork groups with a range of tactics unseen in previous court nominations.

After an issue reaches some form of decision or nondecision in the legislative or executive branches, losing interest groups often try to bring it to the courts for another type of outcome. We have already discussed the idea of shaping the potential debate as a form of indirect lobbying. This can be done by writing articles favoring the group's position on an issue in leading law journals and legal periodicals. Such articles also demonstrate intellectual support for political proposals not yet accepted in legal decisions. Women's groups placed a series of favorable articles in journals prior to significant sex discrimination cases being decided in the 1970s.

Direct judicial lobbying usually involves sponsoring litigation or filing an amicus brief. Litigation sponsorship seeks to obtain court decisions supporting the group's goals. Such litigation requires significant legal resources and can be very expensive, with group costs perhaps running over $1 million for a case that goes to the Supreme Court. But anyone engaging in judicial lobbying must know that nothing seems to happen quickly in the judicial process. Some cases can take years to reach the Supreme Court. The case involving term limits passed by California voters in 1990 finally reached the federal appeals court in 1997 and will probably be appealed to the Supreme Court. However, even if a group can win a case at the highest levels, it must be prepared to protect its victory in follow-up or compliance cases. Judicial political campaigns require long-term commitment and the resources to stay in the campaign for years and perhaps decades. The NAACP began bringing civil rights and antidiscrimination cases to the courts in the 1940s and is still bringing such cases to the courts as the century ends.

Group sponsorship of litigation is very expensive and time-consuming. Public interest law firms, such as the National Women's Law Center and the Mountain States Legal Foundation, are designed to litigate their issues in the courts. Sponsoring litigation can produce favorable precedents and maybe even establish constitutional rights such as the right to privacy, as in the abortion cases. Another political goal of sponsoring litigation is to threaten opponents with a long, expensive court case in hopes that they will agree to the group's demands without going to court.

Although a given group may want to initiate a specific interest group legal campaign, the group must have the access to the legal and political expertise needed to be successful in such an environment. Expertise may be found in the group's staff or membership, or perhaps it can be donated to the group from interested outsiders such as law professors at a university law school. If the group has sufficient financial resources, it can buy the expertise it needs on the open market. Interest groups must also have "standing" in order to bring an issue to the courts. A real person must prove that he or she is injured by a particular law or policy. When President Clinton exercised his newly acquired line item veto in 1997, judicial experts reported that it would be very difficult for groups to bring the vetoes to the courts, since such vetoes would not produce many people with standing for a possible suit. Prior to the 1960s, rules of standing were quite restrictive; they were liberalized in the 1960s and 1970s but restricted again as the courts became more conservative in the 1980s.

For many interest groups, the easiest way to participate in a judicial lobbying campaign is to become a "friend of the court," an amicus curiae. An amicus brief consists of written arguments submitted to the court in support of one of the two sides in a case. A group needs permission from one of the parties or the court in order to file an amicus brief, but, in general, most groups are happy to have the support of additional groups in a judicial case, since numbers may show broad-based support for a group's claims. It has become a commonplace strategy to file amicus curiae briefs. About a third of interest groups appear to sponsor litigation and slightly more file amicus briefs (Walker 1983). Interest group litigation has boomed in recent decades for many reasons; one of the most important seems to be the willingness of foundations to fund such strategies by interest groups on both the left and the right (Berry 1984, 11).

A class action lawsuit allows a large group of "similarly situated" plaintiffs to combine similar suits into a single suit to bring to the courts for action. Among the most significant of such suits have been *Brown v. Topeka Board of Education* (1954), which desegregated public schools; *Roe v. Wade* (1973), which permitted abortion; and many consumer protection or environmentalist cases. As David Berger, one of the lawyers who frequently uses class action suits, has noted, "The class action is the greatest, most effective legal engine to remedy mass wrongs" (*New York Times* 1988). In recent years the federal courts have made such suits more difficult to file with new requirements that have increased the expense and time needed to qualify such suits. Some courts even require each person in a class (say, consumers who bought a certain product) to be notified and asked for permission to be represented in court. The Reagan administration was particularly hostile to class action suits, and the number of such cases in federal courts dropped significantly in the late 1980s.

The range of groups that use the courts to advance their political agenda is quite broad. They have expanded far beyond the traditional sponsors of business and labor and a few civil rights groups to thousands of new groups representing nearly every interest in society in one form or another.

Whereas conservatives may complain about activist liberal courts undermining the traditional powers of the legislative and executive branches, liberal groups complain about conservative judicial activism when policy outcomes tend to undermine their political goals. As the third branch of government, the courts are clearly major actors in the policymaking process of the 1990s. They have always been political actors, as they make political choices that can benefit one group more than another.

A new interest entered the judicial lobbying game in the late 1980s. Led by fundamentalist Christian law firms such as Liberty Counsel, Becket Fund for Religious Liberty, the American Center for Law and Justice (ACLJ), the American Family Association Law Center, the Christian Legal Society Center for Law and Religious Freedom, the Rutherford Institute, and the Western Center for Law and Religious Freedom, Christian views have been presented in a wide variety of suits on issues. Some of these Christian litigating law firms came out of the anti-abortion movement and other moral crusades of our era. Some are sponsored by major political actors such as the ACLJ, which is the legal arm of Pat Robertson's Christian Coalition. Christian law firms began with amicus briefs and later sponsored their own suits, which reached the Supreme Court. Among the victories they have won are decisions on issues of abortion protests, rights of student religious groups to meet on school campuses, and financial aid for students in religious schools. One of these Christian public law firms largely funded Paula Jones's civil lawsuit against President Clinton, which produced the presidential testimony that formed the basis for the impeachment charges against Bill Clinton.

When does it make sense for an interest group to choose judicial lobbying? Almost any group may participate in indirect lobbying (amicus briefs and opinion formation efforts) because the costs are low. Far fewer groups have the resources to do direct judicial lobbying. When judicial lobbying is combined with other traditional forms of lobbying to make a "total issue war campaign," the number of groups that have those resources is smaller still. Prior to the 1980s, judicial lobbying was often the last resort of groups that had lost in the traditional arenas of politics. But recently, many interest groups think about judicial lobbying as their first tactic in particular political situations. Thus judicial lobbying may be the last tactic of the weak; it can also be the first tactic of the strong and powerful and maybe even the weak as well.

Conclusion

The lobbyist is the most visible participant in lobbying campaigns. He or she is the representative of the interest as it contacts elected and appointed representatives with the group's political requests or demands. The strategies and tactics of direct lobbying are many, but they usually begin with the creation of access. After access is established, the key weapon is information in the forms of data or opinion. But no matter how skilled the individual lobbyist, his or her prospects for lobbying success depend on the resources of the group or groups behind the lobbyist. This concludes our analysis of modern political campaigns. We now turn to the political, economic, and social resources of interest groups and consider how they enhance or detract from groups' political campaigns.

10

Interest Group Politics

Building Campaign Power on Organizational Strength

In this chapter we examine interest groups themselves and aspects of their identity, resources, leadership, and other attributes that will help us understand how these organizational characteristics fuel the political activities that affect public policy decisionmaking.

Let us begin with some simple definitions. Over the years interest groups have been called trusts, vested interests, special interests, single interest groups, and pressure groups. These names carry certain unsavory connotations; even the more neutral term "lobby" has some negative baggage. We define political interest groups as groups based on one or more shared attitudes and making political claims on other groups or organizations in the society (Truman 1971). From this definition come two characteristics that are important to our understanding of interest group politics. First, groups are composed of individuals (or other organizations) who share some common characteristics and/or interests. Second, some groups choose to become involved in the political process and seek to have an impact on public policy.

Social and political movements that seek social change but have not formed into lasting organizations may be called preinterest groups. Social movements arise from the unfulfilled demands of a group of people and are persistent, organized expressions of collective behavior differing from fads, riots, or panics. Herbert Blumer defines social movements as developing by "acquiring organization and form, a body of customs and traditions, established leadership, an enduring division of labor, social rules and social values" (1951, 199). Some social movements may evolve into political interest groups with a well-defined membership, regular funding, permanent staff, and knowledge of how to operate within the political system.

Freeman (1983) views social action in terms of a continuum from contagious spontaneity and lack of structure (a crowd or a riot) to social movements having some structure to well-organized interest groups. Movements may have elaborate ideologies that argue their political agendas, and they often rely on unorthodox politics to advance their cause. Normal politics does not offer an effective set of tactics for movements. The postwar era has seen several movements, including the civil rights movement, the women's rights movement, the antiwar movement, the anti–nuclear weapons and power movements, the abortion rights movements (both for and against), animal and children's rights movements, and environmentalist concerns. Failed movements gradually disappear; successful movements often evolve into powerful interest groups.

Interest groups interact with political parties but are very different types of political organizations. Both parties and interest groups operate as communications conduits between citizens and government; parties seek to capture government, whereas interest groups want government to give them certain governmental policies. Parties live for elections, are highly regulated by state laws, and are broad-based coalitions of individuals who want to win elections. Interest groups want policy outcomes and are the least regulated organizations in the nation.

Not all potential interest groups exist at any given moment. So-called potential groups are groups of people who are not organized, and many are not effectively represented, for example, children. There are several organizations that claim to represent children in the political process and hundreds, if not thousands, of groups that may at one time or another purport to represent the interests of children. The reality is that when the interests of children come into conflict with other established interests in our society, the lobbying power of children is far weaker. All is not lost, however, for many potential groups. Sometimes circumstances come into being that allow their interests to become well represented in the political process. Prior to the 1960s senior citizens were largely unrepresented but now can select among a number of organizations, including the National Council of Senior Citizens and the American Association of Retired Persons (AARP), the nation's largest interest group in terms of membership numbers. AARP went from 1 million members in 1967 to over 33 million members in 1995. Another group that was largely unrepresented in the 1960s consisted of fundamentalist, "born again" Christians. The Moral Majority was founded by Rev. Jerry Falwell and claimed hundreds of thousands of members and millions of dollars in revenue before it disappeared in the late 1980s. Another fundamentalist "entrepreneur," Pat Robertson, created the Christian Coalition, which became a major player in Republican and conservative politics during the Reagan and Bush administrations. Today it effectively represents the political agenda of this sector. The fundamentalist Christian

Right could become organized in such numbers (possible 30 to 60 million people) that it surpasses even the senior citizens' lobby.

Lately many journalists have divided political interest groups into two broad types: self-oriented groups and public interest groups. Self-oriented groups seek to achieve some policy goal that will directly benefit their own membership. These are the "selfish" groups and are viewed by journalists as not being particularly interested in the impact of their political agenda on the broader public. Public interest groups (PIGs) pursue goals that may not benefit their membership directly but will be enjoyed by the general public. Many such groups seek policies that will never specifically benefit their membership. A classic example is the liberal group of highly educated professionals who seek to abolish the death penalty in criminal cases. Other public interest groups, such as Common Cause, Ralph Nader's consumer organization, and many environmentalist groups, pursue objectives that they believe will benefit the public in a general sense. Many interest groups now claim to be public interest groups, but, in reality, many of these groups are really self-oriented in their political goals and their funding sources.

A founding father, James Madison, was one of the first to write about interest groups and their effect on American politics. Madison's essay in *The Federalist Papers,* no. 10, noted his concern about the negative influence of groups (factions). Madison's factions were preinterest groups characterized by their temporary nature, but his concerns apply easily to contemporary interest group politics. He defined factions in a negative way by arguing that they were "adverse to the rights of citizens or . . . the interests of the community." No matter how Madison felt about these factions, he recognized that they were inherent to the nature of a democracy and impossible to eliminate. What Madison tried to do was to create in the new federal government's Constitution a set of mechanisms that could control the negative effects of factions. One such mechanism was a republican form of government in which no single faction could control political decisionmaking.

Another early political analyst was Alexis de Tocqueville, a French citizen who wrote of Americans' tendency to join together in interest groups when participating in domestic politics, which differed from the style of politics found in Europe at that time. "Whenever at the head of some new undertaking you see government in France, or a man of rank in England, in the United States you will be sure to find an association." De Tocqueville also concluded that "in no country in the world has the principle of association been more successfully used, or applied to a greater multitude of objects, than in America" (de Tocqueville [1835–1836] 1956). Studies by political scientists in the post–World War II era concluded that this tendency persisted. Compared to citizens in other selected democracies such as Great Britain, Germany, Italy, and Mexico, Americans were more likely to have interest group memberships and use them for political activities (Almond and Verba 1963).

"The exact number of interest groups operating in the United States is unknown." On the national level, the *Encyclopedia of Associations* (1996) has listed over 22,000 national nonprofit organizations. The largest category of groups is, as expected, business groups (17 percent). Political groups had the greatest growth in terms of numbers of new groups formed since 1980. Business, agricultural-environmentalist, social welfare, health, educational-cultural groups, and hobby groups have all added five hundred or more new groups since 1980. Labor unions and Greek letter societies are the only two categories that lost numbers. It should be noted that the summary of national groups includes many organizations that never become actively involved in normal patterns of politics. How many of the 22,000-plus groups are frequently active is simply unknown at this time. We do know that several thousand of these groups registered with Congress under the provisions of the 1946 Lobby Registration Act.

A major change in the American interest group pattern has been the continuing trend among groups to move their headquarters to Washington, D.C. Jack Walker's sample of national-level interest groups discovered that half of the groups had been founded since 1945 and that the nation's capital was the home of most of them. In 1960, Washington, D.C., was home for 67 percent of the nation's voluntary associations; by 1980 it was home to over 88 percent of voluntary associations (Walker 1983). By 1995, the National Trade and Professional Associations of the United States counted 7,400 national associations with headquarters in Washington, D.C. ("A Nation" 1995). A walk around the northwest quadrant of that city would reveal building after building of offices for one to dozens of groups or associations.

A clearer picture is emerging of the number of groups at the state level as a result of lobby registration laws that various states have enacted, especially California. One interesting finding is the numerical domination of businesses, banks, and economic groups among the state-level registrants. The number of local-level groups is impossible to determine because of the ephemeral nature of many of them. Many deal with specific local problems and may be founded and dissolved within the same calendar year. Finally, there are almost no reporting requirements for local-level groups in the United States. Despite these problems, it has been estimated that over 200,000 different organizations exist at the state and local levels of American politics.

What Causes Interest Groups to Form?

Political interest groups appear in American history in waves, specifically four major waves (Truman 1971, 30): First, the period between 1830 and

1860, when the first great national organizations were created, such as the Grange farm group. Second, the 1880s, when many new national groups emerged from the industrialization process, such as the American Federation of Labor. Third, the 1900–1920 era, when the largest number of powerful organizations were founded, including the U.S. Chamber of Commerce, the American Medical Association (AMA), the NAACP, the American Farm Bureau, and the American Cancer Society. Fourth, the years between 1960 and 1990, when the explosion of many specialized groups reflected the growing micro-nature of interest group in recent decades.

What forces are necessary for such large numbers of interest groups to be created in certain decades and not others? Wilson (1995) suggests that communications revolutions have been a major factor. In most of these eras, new communication technologies facilitated the ability of groups to seek new members and connect them to politics. Telegraphs, telephones, railroads, radio, national magazines, television, computers, faxes, and Internet web pages make such communications easier. Another important factor has been the changing the role of government, particularly its attempt to regulate business activity, which forced business to organize to counterprotect itself. Other factors include the increasing division of labor, particularly in economic sectors, and the growing heterogeneity of the American population. Wilson argues that periods of great social unrest and social movements are also associated with periods of interest group growth.

Truman (1971) and Salisbury (1969) have offered a disturbance theory suggesting that interest groups arise from the increased complexity of society and a systemic drive to achieve equilibrium. As society inevitably becomes more complex and specialized, more specialized groups and interests form associations to articulate their needs (Salisbury 1969). Until recent decades, a broad umbrella organization such as the National Association of Broadcasters could effectively represent the general interests of the communications industry, but dozens of spin-off organizations have emerged to represent the many new technologies, such as cable and satellite television and Internet interests. A second version of this theoretical perspective suggests that disturbances undermine the political power relationships among various sectors of society, which are "disturbed" or altered by various forces, including technical innovation, international events, societal changes, new legislation, governmental decisions, the formation of new interest groups, and business cycles. The disturbance creates new advantaged and disadvantaged groups; the latter may seek to restore equilibrium by organizing in an effort to convert their immobilized resources into political influence. For example, groups representing men emerged in the 1990s to counter various women's groups such as the National Organization of Women (NOW), which had become a powerful lobbying force affecting many political, social, and economic issues as well as laws impacting employment, marriage, and many other issues.

Neither perspective of disturbance theory offers a complete explanation on how groups are created. The equilibrium theory suggests a cyclical pattern of membership in groups; although this was true of agricultural groups and labor unions, it was not the case for professional or technical associations. Specialization does not explain why agricultural groups were almost all general farm organizations, such as the Grange or Farm Union, and does not explain why specialist crop associations are relatively modern. So we have to look to another theory. Salisbury (1969) offers another theory to explain group formation, entrepreneurial theory (or exchange theory), which suggests that the organizer is the key element in terms of why new groups are formed at a given moment of history. Consumer and environmentalist groups are often the products of such entrepreneurs. We will discuss this theory later in this chapter.

Political Science and Group Theory

The focus on interest groups as a part of political science began in the first decade of the twentieth century. Arthur F. Bentley's 1908 book *The Process of Government* was the first major work to use groups as a central theme for understanding American politics. Previous organizing structures had been based on the Constitution or how public laws were made in governmental institutions (Bentley 1949). Bentley argued that groups were the key unit for studying American society and politics. In fact, Bentley concluded that groups explained American politics in entirety. With David Truman's *The Governmental Process,* published after World War II, political science rediscovered Bentley's focus on groups (Truman 1971). At that time social science, in general, was searching for a theory to explain many of the events of World War II in a different, modern way. Truman's group focus was positive, portraying groups as essential elements of a modern democracy. Earl Latham's *The Group Basis of Politics* argued that groups struggled in legislatures and that the balance of power among the various participating groups was reflected in the laws enacted or killed (Latham 1952). Latham introduced the concept of governmental units as interest groups themselves, and subsequent researchers have broadened the concept of interest group politics to include the tens of thousands of American governments not only as sites for interest group battles but as demanding interest themselves.

From these early works on group theory emerged two broad theories that tried to explain political power in American society in a group framework. Elitist theorists such as E. E. Schattschneider and C. Wright Mills argued that a relatively small elite controlled politics in the United States and manipulated the important decisions. Schattschneider pointed to an "upper-class bias" of business domination in our American political system (Schattschneider 1975). C. Wright Mills's *The Power Elite* also perceived a small group of elites controlling real power in America (Mills 1956). The second theory, pluralist theory, began with Robert Dahl's *Who Governs?* It emphasized the importance of groups in policy decisionmaking (Dahl 1961). Dahl saw power not concentrated in the hands of the elite but in a complex assortment of groups and governmental officials and structures. Dahl's image of political power crossed social and economic class lines and was moderated by a pattern of multiple memberships, which made for broader participation in the decisionmaking processes. This pluralist theory came to be (and still is) the dominant model in political science for explaining the nature of American political power. Rational choice theory from economics has also become an important model used in researching interest group politics. The most important work from this perspective was Mancur Olson's *The Logic of Collective Action,* which has driven much of the research in recent decades on internal group politics, leadership, and membership (Olson 1965).

Leadership and Interest Group Power

High-quality leadership is an essential ingredient in the long-term success of a lobbying organization. Many organizational failures can be attributed to the crucial problem of inept leadership. The success or failure of leadership often depends on the situation. One leader may be successful in one organization and a compete failure in a different organization. The late Cesar Chavez, charismatic leader of the United Farm Workers, was a very successful union organizer, but he was over his head as an administrator. Most interest group leaders are manager-lobbyists lacking charismatic or entrepreneurial skills. These leaders have to manage a budget and a staff and organize for a occasional lobbying victory or two.

The reality of many complex organizations is that paid staff members dominate the elected leadership. Some associations have huge staffs numbering hundreds of people and filling floors of offices in major Washington, D.C., buildings. The National Rifle Association (NRA) and AARP have their own impressive buildings. The NRA's Washington, D.C., staff includes nearly five hundred persons, and the National Chamber of Commerce has over 1,200 employees in its Washington, D.C., office, including eleven lobbyists and about forty persons who support them with research.

Staff members can have an important impact on an organization's policies and lobbying strategies. Robert Michel's "iron law of oligarchy" argues that the larger the organization, generally the larger and more specialized the staff. As an organization becomes better established, it becomes more conservative in its policies and tactics as it seeks organizational security. The staff is not selected from the general membership, since expertise not found among the membership is required for many staff jobs. Michel suggests that group-elected leadership, the general membership, and the staff often are driven by different motivations and goals and that this may cause serious problems in many organizations (Michel 1962). One charge often heard in these situations is that the leadership has lost touch with the membership. Recent cases of this have occurred in the labor movement and the NRA. In the AFL-CIO, George Meany, a former plumber, was the longtime leader. However, Lane Kirkland, a graduate of Georgetown University's School of Foreign Affairs and the U.S. Merchant Marine Academy, was his successor. The AFL-CIO's secretary-treasurer, chief organizer, and head lobbyist were all lawyers. Kirkland, then seventy-three years old, was denied another term as AFL-CIO president in 1995. He was replaced by John Sweeney, president of the aggressive Service Employees union; Linda Chavez-Thompson became secretary-treasurer. Sweeney purged the AFL-CIO board and appointed new members so that twenty of its fifty-seven members were female, black, or Hispanic. Sweeney was only the fifth person to be president of the AFL-CIO dating back to 1881 (Victor 1995).

Is the staff of a large organization always more conservative and concerned about security than the general membership? Or, conversely, does a large organization have a staff that is more committed to the political goals of the organization than is the membership? The evidence is mixed and good examples of each can be presented. The staff of the National Council of Churches (NCC) has been far more radical in its support for guerrilla wars and social revolution in Africa and welfare and social policy reforms than its generally conservative membership. One explanation for this is the very low pay many NCC staff members receive: Part of their compensation is paid in the form of policy actions. The huge and relatively low-paid AFL-CIO staff, headquartered in Washington, D.C., is more liberal than the increasingly conservative rank-and-file union member, and the American Civil Liberties Union's (ACLU) leadership and staff are much more liberal than its average member. Another explanation for this pattern is that maintenance of the rank-and-file membership and organization is done at the grassroots level, leaving the national level relatively free to pursue its own politics. The NRA, on the other hand, has been waging a civil war for decades, its ideologically hardcore member-zealots constantly attacking the staff for being too cautious and conservative in its defense of the Second Amendment and gun rights. Some lobbies (e.g., the ones mentioned above) are well organized and well-off, but the majority of lobbies have small budgets and very small staffs (Wilson 1995, 224). Margaret Fisk, editor of the massive *Encyclopedia of Associations,* warns individuals interested in corresponding with the listed voluntary associations that many are essentially one-person operations (*Encyclopedia of Associations* 1996, 1140). Many public interest groups are very small operations. Berry (1977) discovered that only half the public interest groups he studied had one or more full-time staff members.

The degree of democracy in the leadership selection and policymaking processes of interest groups can impact their ability to achieve their political goals. Since America requires democracy in almost every decisionmaking process, nearly every interest group must at least try to portray itself as democratic. This does not mean that all groups are democratic. Wilson suggests that the least democratic organizations are those that rely heavily on material benefits (such as labor unions or some business groups), since those groups have members who are satisfied with the outcomes but not the process (Wilson 1995). The Teamsters Union is a classic example of an organization with nondemocratic leadership selection processes. Even the federally supervised election in 1996 was voided in 1997 for campaign finance irregularities.

The other two types of benefit organizations, solidary and purposive, seem to be more democratic. Apparently these organizations require high levels of membership participation. Solidary organization must use leadership posts as incentives in exchange for extra contributions. Purposive organizations, such as Common Cause, tend to be democratic in their leadership selection processes and policy decisionmaking largely because this seems to be important to the membership. Yearly, the League of Women Voters and the American Civil Liberties Union provide for membership input into the agenda that sets decisionmaking.

Regimes often experience crises as they make a transition from one political leader to another, and so do interest groups. Just as Yugoslavia collapsed following the death of longtime leader Josip Tito, the United Mine Workers never recovered from the death of its great leader, John L. Lewis. Successor after successor was unable to provide the union with honest, effective leadership, and the plight of union members continued to deteriorate. The United Farm Workers was never able to replace the charismatic Cesar Chavez after he died in 1994. Of course, there are many groups that have not only survived leadership successions but have prospered. Common Cause survived the leadership crisis that occurred when its founder, John Gardner, retired in 1977. Successors Nan Waterman, Archibald Cox, Fred Wertheimer, and Ann McBride provided more than adequate leadership, and the organization regained its former levels of influence.

Interest groups of all types may be vulnerable to leadership problems. But in terms of external threats, the purposive groups are the most vulnerable of all. Purposive groups are particularly vulnerable to changes in the political environment because often they cannot survive either success or failure. If a group is seeking to raise highway speed limits, what happens to the group after the government allows states to raise their speed limits to any level they choose? If a group supports welfare reform and it happens, what happens to the group? If a group is an environmental group that opposes a particular threat to the environment (a road through a wilderness area) and the group is unable to stop its construction, can the group convince the membership to support it if it chooses a new cause to defend?

Sometimes a group can turn a failure into an internal group maintenance success. Many of the liberal groups that attempted to keep Clarence Thomas off the Supreme Court were able to use the defeat in their direct mail solicitation campaigns and gain new members and money for future campaigns. An earlier successful campaign that defeated the Robert Bork nomination to the Supreme Court brought millions of dollars and hundreds of thousands of new members to liberal groups.

A group's leadership must decide how the group is to be structured. Key to this decision is matching the group's resources, including membership, to its political objectives and lobbying goals. The group may choose between a federated structure and a unitary structure. A federated association is an organization made up of other organizations. The National Association of Manufacturers (NAM) includes 13,000 member companies. The National Association of Broadcasters comprises many corporations and the major networks (ABC, CBS, and NBC). Many trade associations have corporations as their major members. And finally, almost all the coalitions that are created for a specific issue battle are largely composed of constituent companies, interest groups, and trade associations. Federations by their very design usually have members at the local level and are often organized by "federating" local organizations into a national federation with headquarters in Washington, D.C. As a result of this organization at the state and local levels, federated groups have the ability to do grassroots lobbying on their own.

A unitary group locates its organization in Washington, D.C., and has little (if any) organization at state and local levels. Some groups have state and local organizations, but they have no power and simply exist for the convenience of the national group. Common Cause started out as a purely unitary group and then added state chapters. It gave those chapters some independence to make their own policy decisions with national-level guidance after the local activists demanded more self-determination.

Federated associations are generally more effective in grassroots lobbying efforts, but they are also much more difficult to coordinate and lead in cohesive national campaigns. Unitary organizations, as a result of their national-level organization, are more effective in Washington lobbying because they can speak with a single voice, but they have limited grassroots capability unless they pay for it (Hall 1969, 136–140).

An important resource for many interest groups is the proportion of potential members who are enrolled as members in the group. A high proportion gives the group legitimacy as the "spokesperson" for the interest. A low proportion or many groups having a fraction of the membership pool calls into question the credibility of a group's claim to represent the interest. American interest groups represent a smaller proportion of the potential membership compared to interest groups in Europe, where large umbrella groups are common. Labor unions now represent less than 20 percent of the nonfarm working force. The American Medical Association represents only 36 percent of the 500,000 American physicians; the American Bar Association, only 45 percent of the nation's lawyers; and the American Association of University Professors, less than 20 percent of the professors. The three major veterans' organizations (the American Legion, Disabled American Veterans, and Veterans of Foreign Wars) only represent one-sixth of the nation's 28 million veterans. Consequently, it is difficult for many of these "peak associations" to speak as true representatives of given interest sectors.

Although having high proportions of potential memberships is an asset for an interest group, in today's world it is also important for a group's survival to establish its niche and unique benefit in competition with other groups. Groups seek to develop autonomy. In the electric power industry, the various groups concentrate on statistics, lobbying, technical information on the industry, public relations, and media campaigns (Wilson 1995, 263).

A famous California politician once said that money is the mother's milk of politics, and that certainly is true for interest group politics. Money is the most convertible of all resources in that it can buy leadership, technology, and even "volunteers." Yet the group with the most money does not always win. Some of the richest and most powerful interest groups (e.g., the AFL-CIO and the NRA) have lost important lobbying battles in recent years against opposition with much less money.

Another characteristic that can greatly assist a group in acquiring financial resources is tax-exempt status. The so-called 501(c)(4) of the Internal Revenue code qualifying a group for income tax exemption is given if it operates exclusively to promote the social welfare of the country and is engaged in substantial lobbying. However, individual contributions to 501(c)(4) groups are not deductible. Groups such as the National Right to Life and the National Taxpayers Union fall under this provision. Another important part of the IRS code to interest groups is Section 501(c)(3), which provides for tax-exempt status and the deductibility of individual donations if substantial lobbying is not performed. The 501(c)(3) groups (charitable) cannot legally lobby Congress but may advocate positions before administrative agencies and may give Congress information on pending legislation. The Heritage Foundation and the Religious Roundtable are Association 501(c)(3) groups. An interest group's 501 status can change if the group gets too involved in politics and the government decides to force it to follow the restrictions of its tax status. The Sierra Club got much more involved in lobbying and established the Sierra Club Foundation to allow it to generate additional income (Berry 1984, 46).

The United Farm Workers (UFW) has received millions of dollars in federal grants in recent decades, which it used to fund UFW programs in the areas of English-language instruction, education and retraining programs, and work surveys. Major veterans' groups are given free government office space in fifty-eight regional Veteran's Administration centers around the nation. Many interest groups receive large portions of their budgets in subsidies or grants from more established groups. Labor unions have been the financial "godfathers" of many of the new left groups, as have various conservative foundations and research think tanks such as the Heritage Foundation for the right.

The National Association for the Advancement of Colored People (NAACP) has suffered through one leadership crisis after another since the 1960s. In 1994 the very survival of the oldest civil rights group in the nation came into question. Headquarters staff was cut by a third and several regional offices were closed. The budget was cut nearly in half, and the Ford Foundation refused to release a $250,000 grant to the NAACP while the leadership was in flux. In 1996 the NAACP named Kweisi Mfume, a former Maryland congressman and chair of the Congressional Black Caucus, to be the new president. Gradually the organization began to recover and became more attractive to foundations while improving its financial situation and its tattered reputation.

Internal Organizational Strength and Lobbying Power

Lobbying power is largely based an interest group's characteristics and resources such as membership, formal organization, leadership, and the staff. Membership is the foundation of any organization. Every organization is both empowered and restricted by its membership. Middle-class organizations such as Common Cause gain lobbying power from the willingness of its membership to give it money for lobbying and to volunteer as lobbyists themselves on occasion. Such a middle-class membership base has high levels of personal efficacy and ego strength, plus a good knowledge of the political process and a sense of obligation that encourages them to participate in politics. Groups with large numbers of lower-class members, such as welfare rights groups, tend to have many members who lack the aforementioned psychological characteristics and thus do not tend to participate to the same extent as their middle-class counterparts.

People join interest groups for a variety of reasons. Mancur Olson suggested in his *The Logic of Collective Action* that it was irrational (in an economic sense) for people to join an interest group unless one of several specific conditions existed: (1) coercion, or being forced to join; (2) the small size of the group means that the addition of even one more member may significantly affect its chances of success; (3) possessing extraordinary resources that strongly enhance the group's likelihood of achieving its goal; and (4) the benefits offered by the group exceed the cost of joining it (Olson 1965). Salisbury (1969) and Wilson (1995) have used *exchange theory* to study people's reasons for joining interest groups. Exchange theory substitutes the idea of a businessperson and a customer for the leader-follower relationship. The leadership provides the "capital" or benefits that are offered to potential members. These benefits are usually grouped as material, solidary, and purposive benefits and can be either selective or collective in nature. *Selective benefits* may be obtained only by those who are members of the organization. The members of an exclusive country club are the only ones who can use the amenities of the club and golf course, in exchange for large amounts of money they have paid for the right. *Collective benefits* are available to all persons regardless of group membership. Usually so-called public interest groups seeking goals such as clean politics or clean air cannot restrict the benefits they achieve to their own members.

The three types of benefits are material, purposive, and solidary. *Material benefits* are items or services that have monetary value. These may include product discounts and political advantages that eventually convert into economic advantages. Some of the most common material benefits offered by many organizations are access to low-priced group insurance or charter air travel. Members of the American Association of Retired Persons have access to low-cost home delivery of prescription drugs.

Purposive benefits usually tend to be collective in nature. They are the result of cause-related activities and include such things as clean air or politics or a prohibition of the death penalty. A general requirement for purposive benefits is that they not benefit the individual members of a group directly. Consequently, these benefits are almost always collective, since it is nearly impossible to restrict them to the formal membership. If politics is cleaned up by banning soft money from the election process, all inhabitants of a political unit might benefit, not just the group membership.

Solidary benefits are defined as psychological rewards that come from associating with certain individuals. Collective solidary incentives are derived from the congeniality and the social attractiveness of the group. Many social groups, such as country clubs, ethnic groups, or fraternal groups, have restrictive memberships that focus primarily on social activities. Selective solidary benefits are given to specific individuals in the form of special honors or offices. Organizations that rely primarily on solidary incentives to attract and maintain membership frequently use selective benefits to encourage additional contributions from members. Some groups have established a fantastic hierarchy of exalted titles. Some groups create titles to artificially enhance the status of their members (e.g., the Ku Klux Klan with Grand Wizards).

The ideal interest group would combine all three benefit types to reinforce the recruitment and retention of members. Many groups are forced to rely more on one type of benefit than another, which may limit the group's political activities. Organizations that rely on material incentives have the greatest freedom of political action as long as the membership is happy with the benefits received. The great freedom of labor unions to support the Democratic party in elections despite the fact that many union members vote Republican is largely a function of the benefits (e.g., job security) that many of their members enjoy. Data from elections beginning in the 1980s indicate that over 40 percent of union household members voted for Republican presidential candidates in each of the three elections of the 1980s. However, in the 1992 and 1996 elections, the Republican vote dropped to 24 percent and 30 percent respectively. Material benefits are seldom effective in encouraging sacrifice by members. Solidary incentives must be selective to be effective. Prestige country clubs can accomplish this by stringent screening processes and high dues. Solidary benefits may also be distributed selectively within an organization to motivate extraordinary membership contributions. But groups relying on solidary benefits must avoid politics, which can be very disruptive to the social environment of the group.

Purposive organizations by their nature and benefit package can be very unstable because they rely on the attractiveness of "the cause" or "the goal" to attract or maintain their membership. When the group fails to achieve the goal or cause, the group is in danger unless it can alter members' perspectives and have them focus on a new cause. Even successful purposive groups are in danger, since once the cause is won, why would the members continue to belong to the group? Groups that survive such successes are able to switch to a new cause and build on their past success. Although the ideal situation for an organization is to have a mixture of the three types of benefits, interest groups that last long enough to become part of the establishment generally discover that material benefits are the most important.

John Hansen (1985) argues that a group must be subsidized to be organized. Economic groups or trade associations are relatively easy to organize and tend to be subsidized by their industries or by the government. Some groups, such as consumer and environmentalist groups, have proven to be difficult to subsidize and must rely on support from charities, foundations, and governments (Hansen 1985). In recent years, conservative foundations or sources of money have supported many of the new conservative groups that have emerged to change the style of American politics. Richard Mellon

Scaife has been a major financial contributor to as many as twenty-five of these new conservative political groups, including the Heritage Foundation and Americans for Effective Law Enforcement (Rothmeyer 1981). On the liberal side, labor unions have been major sources of support for liberal public interest groups. The 1996 campaign finance scandals brought to light this pattern of funding when it was discovered that for years Ralph Nader's reform group, Citizen Action, had been taking money from labor unions for its normal annual budgets. In 1995 various labor unions, including the Teamsters and the United Auto Workers, gave Citizen Action more than $250,000 (Wayne 1997c).

Let us look at a major interest group and see how all these pieces fit together. The American Association of Retired Persons, with more than 35 million members, is the largest interest group in America. Dues are only $8 a year, and in exchange for that small sum, members receive *Modern Maturity* magazine six times a year; a monthly newspaper, the *AARP News Bulletin;* low-cost pharmacy service; discounts at hotels, motels, and car rental agencies; special insurance programs; and access to a special no-load mutual fund. Beginning in the 1986 elections, AARP entered into national political campaigns. But its lobbying operation on issues important to senior citizens has been effective for a much longer time. It has computerized age files on nearly everyone in the nation and mails an invitation to join the organization to each person shortly before his or her fiftieth birthday. AARP calls the membership application "a certificate of admission" and lists numerous membership benefits including; a magazine, pharmacy discounts, group health insurance, and representation in Washington, D.C. However, new benefits have been added in terms of solidary appeals such as AARP Online, where members can chat with other members on-line; volunteer opportunities through the AARP Volunteer Talent Bank; and 4,000 local chapters where "members can meet new people."

The Nature of Interest Group Membership in the United States

Not all Americans play the interest group game in the same proportions. According to Schattschnieder (1975), our interest group system has an "upper-class bias," but in reality, it is heavily dominated by the middle class. The middle class has sufficient income and education to facilitate their interest group activities. The vast majority of the lowest economic class do not belong to any organization (except maybe religious groups). Only 14 percent of the lowest income group belonged to two or more groups, whereas 35 percent of the highest income group had multiple memberships (Hyman and Wright 1971).

The reasons behind this pattern are quite simple. The richest people can afford to belong to more organizations because they have more resources such as money, time, personal political efficacy, social status, and desire. The lower socioeconomic classes do not seem to have these characteristics in the same proportions as the upper classes. Even the aspect of money would seem to confirm this pattern. Many lower-income people belong to a church that accepts voluntary contributions as opposed to an interest group that mandates dues. The problem for potential entrepreneurs of groups aimed at the lower social economic classes is constructing an attractive set of benefits. Immediate monetary benefits might get such a person into the organization, but how does the leadership keep the member in the group over time? Consequently, many such groups start and then fail (Wilson 1995). Many groups that represent the interests of the lower classes tend to be started by middle- and upper-class leaders and are often dominated by these groups in terms of membership as well (Piven and Cloward 1977, 295–313).

Perhaps the classic example of a lower-class group that has been relatively successful is the United Farm Workers, organized by the late Cesar Chavez and composed of California's Mexican American farm workers. The charismatic Chavez was very effective in leading the movement but proved to be much less effective as an interest group administrator. It is still not clear that the UFW will survive as an interest group. The UFW illustrates well the problems associated with interest groups of the lower socioeconomic classes.

The American Interest Group System

Churches and religious organizations are the most frequently joined voluntary associations in the United States. American religious organizations have been involved in politics in one manner or another throughout our history. Usually, such involvement took the form of periodic crusades against some vice such as alcohol, slavery, gambling, war, drugs, or sexuality issues. However, since the mid-1960s, some churches have become more active in the lobbying process and consequently more significant to political scientists as political organizations.

Many religious organizations had become involved in the civil rights revolution of the 1960s and 1970s, but a significant change in the pattern occurred in the 1980s as evangelical Christians joined the political process first under Rev. Jerry Falwell's Moral Majority and then the Christian Coalition sponsored by another fundamentalist minister, Pat Robertson. The Christian Coalition and other organizations such as Focus on the Family, Tradition Values Coalition, and the American Family Association have become powerful political groups in the 1990s.

The second and third most frequently joined association types are sports groups and school service groups such as the PTA, groups that get involved in the political process only on rare occasions. Parent-teacher associations have in recent years broadened their interests beyond the quality of education produced by local school systems to include a nationwide campaign against sex and violence on commercial television. Other types of groups, such as hobby, literary, fraternal, youth, and service groups, seldom become involved in political activities. The major organizations involved in politics that people join are labor unions and professional, veterans, political, farm, and ethnic groups.

Lobbying Resources Derived from Membership Characteristics

Is big powerful? The groups with the largest memberships may not be the most powerful actors in issue campaigns. The two largest political organizations in the United States, the 35-million-member American Association of Retired Persons and the 13-million-member AFL-CIO, have posted very mixed records in recent years as lobbying organizations. It has been a long time since the AFL-CIO has won a major labor lobbying battle in Congress. Such a dismal record was understandable during the antilabor Reagan and Bush administrations during the 1980s and early 1990s, but it was almost as bad with a Democratic Congress and president in 1993–1994. A nearly complete collapse occurred after the Republicans took control of Congress in 1995. Big labor has been declining in political power because its total membership has been declining, as well as its percentage of the workforce. In pure numbers, organized labor peaked in 1975 with 22.2 million members. By 1993, 16.3 million people were union members. In 1973, 25.3 percent of the labor force was unionized; by 1993, this had dropped to only 12.8 percent.

AARP is so huge (35 million members) that it has real problems gaining a sense of direction from its membership. It cannot lobby on many issues because its membership is split between Democrats and Republicans. Its membership may not be interested in a given issue or may be split; thus, it is a giant without real power.

Middle-sized organizations such as the American Bar Association, American Medical Association, and Common Cause, with memberships of several hundred thousand, have been able to convert membership characteristics into successful lobbying efforts. Legal skills, medical knowledge, and middle-class commitment to reforms have driven these often quite different lobbying efforts, but it is important to remember that large numbers alone do not guarantee lobbying success.

Sometimes it is important for a group to have its members in the proper geographic distribution. One reason for labor's weakness in recent decades is that its membership strength is concentrated in the Northeast and Midwest and is weak in the South and West. The South has long been the most anti-union part of the nation and has gained the most political power in the revival of the Republican party in national politics. Almost all the new Republican leaders in the 1995 Congress were southerners. Another group with a maldistribution of membership is the American Civil Liberties Union, the liberal defender of the Bill of Rights. Unfortunately, in exactly those states that pose many of the most serious threats to the defense of the First Amendment (the South and Mountain West), the ACLU has its smallest memberships and fewest resources. Other groups with a more even distribution of membership, such as real estate agents, school teachers, and small businesses, are able to function well anywhere in the nation.

Even small groups may have memberships with characteristics that can be converted into successful lobbying campaigns when necessary. High respect, prestige, and status of either individual members or the general membership can be utilized in lobbying. The National Rifle Association has millions of members. But how many of them are more useful than actor Charlton Heston and his willingness to become the organization's front man in its defense of its interpretation of the Second Amendment? On the left, Jane Fonda and Robert Redford have greatly aided the anti–Vietnam War and environmentalist movements, respectively. The Business Roundtable, consisting of the CEOs of America's largest corporations, is literally the nine-hundred-pound gorilla of lobbying groups. American Medical Association doctors carry significant weight in any discussions of the medical industry. The fact that they represent a well-paid profession that is willing to donate millions of dollars for lobbying campaigns gives the AMA many political options. Some organizations have developed strong positive reputations (American Cancer Society, League of Women Voters, and Planned Parenthood) among the general public. Others such as the Tobacco Institute have real problems with their reputations.

Many people join a collection of organizations that can be described as overlapping. They usually tend to reinforce one another and produce a more effective member. Take, for example, a Utahn who happens to be a devout Mormon, a conservative Republican who works for an anti-union, high-tech firm in his home state. When a political issue emerges with a conservative-liberal dimension, the overlapping memberships all move such a person to action in support of the conservative cause. A relatively small number of people join groups with differing political agendas, such as the ACLU and the Christian Coalition. People who receive conflicting messages from their different groups are "cross-pressured." Such members have to decide which groups are more important and which groups can be ignored. If this determination cannot be made, the person often tries to ignore the issue that is causing the different messages.

Another important membership characteristic that may impact lobbying effectiveness is the degree of commitment held by the membership or activists concerning the organization's policy objectives. Groups with intensely committed members may have a great advantage in asking these members to participate in various types of grassroots actions and receiving a very enthusiastic response. The National Rifle Association, for example, has perhaps 30,000 to 100,000 of its 3.5 million members who are very committed to defending their "gun rights." The AFL-CIO, on the other hand, has millions of members who have joined for economic benefits and do not care at all about the group's political agenda. Many union members, in fact, may strongly oppose some parts of their union's political agenda.

Very committed or intense members may be too much of a good thing for some organizations. They are so committed to a goal or cause that they make it very difficult for the leadership of a group to engage in discussions, compromises, or "politics." Other intensively committed members may get frustrated easily with normal politics and lobbying and may engage in violence or other forms of extreme acts to further their cause. The ecoterrorists who burned an Aspen, Colorado, ski resort in April 1998 represented that type of challenge to more conservative environmentalist movements. The killing of a New York medical doctor who performed abortions and the hundreds of other acts of violence against abortion clinics or their workers also pose serious problems for those who are pro-life but also nonviolent.

Conclusion: Interest Groups, Political Parties, and Modern Campaigns

We have discussed groups and organizations as they have participated in campaign situations occurring in American politics. In terms of functions and roles, both political parties and interest groups provide communications between the American public and their governments. The communications, which may be from the top down or the bottom up, are the essential glue that makes democracy work. The third institution that facilitates citizen-government communications is the mass media itself. We have repeatedly touched on the role played by the media in party and interest group politics. Finally, parties and interest groups have frequently operated in the environment of political campaigns. We have defined campaigns very broadly in this book to include the traditional campaigns of parties, candidates, issues, lobbying, and initiative and referendum elections.

The decade of the 1990s has become the era of the perpetual campaign. Parties and candidates are engaged in the constant fund-raising, organizational staffing, and message testing that characterize modern campaigns. What has changed in the 1990s is the adoption of these strategies, tactics, and techniques from the world of political parties to the world of issue advocacy and issue campaigns. The event that brought the world of issue advocacy to our collective attention was the Clinton health care reform defeat of 1994 and the election campaigns of 1994 and 1996. For the first time in American politics, we can reasonably discuss parties, candidates, and interest groups within the same context of modern political campaigns. What was once a fragmented series of events has become a much more synthesized phenomenon of political campaigning in its various guises.

Campbell and Davidson recently commented on the location of political parties "at the center of extensive and distinctive networks of interest groups"(1998, 135). They note that the ties between parties and interest groups are complex and symbiotic, based on policy decisions in exchange for money and campaign support. They concluded that when voters vote for a political party, they are also selecting a group of interest groups and their policy preferences as well. When one or another of these party–interest group coalitions triumphs, the policy decisionmaking process can be radically altered. New policies and new laws are written, often by the interest groups for their newly empowered party representatives, and the campaign cycle opens up a new phase as the defeated party and its interest group allies reorganize to recapture power in upcoming issue and election campaigns. It is an unending cycle of parties, interest groups, and campaigns. We have touched on just some of the interest features of these cycles. We invite the reader to follow in the media upcoming episodes in this exciting political process.

11

Parties, Interest Groups, and Campaigns

The New Style of American Politics

Campaigns of a variety of types have come to dominate American politics as never before. Each year, thousands of interest groups and both major political parties are deeply involved in a never ending series of issue campaigns in Washington, D.C., and in state capitals across the nation. Every two years, and in off years as well, additional thousands of campaigns are waged in primaries and general elections in each of the fifty states. Increasingly, the major parties are being joined in these campaigns by a growing number of powerful, well-financed interest groups seeking to influence the outcomes of these candidate campaigns. Finally, in the West and Midwest, as well as in a few states in other regions, interest groups conduct powerful campaigns in initiative and referendum elections. Hundreds of millions of dollars are expended in these "popular democracy" campaigns. Such issue-ratification campaigns have sometimes eclipsed the office-filling campaigns being contested in the same elections.

In this book we have explored the overlapping worlds of political parties and interest groups in modern political campaigns. Indeed, both political parties and interest groups have always been part of our electoral campaigns and our legislatures, attempting to influence the outcomes of public policy debates. Throughout our history, Congress and state legislatures have passed outlines of laws and bureaucracies have filled in the "details." Which details are filled in is often the result of campaigns by parties and interest groups.

In the last decade or two there has been an increase in the frequency and the intensity of the overlap between party and interest group activities. Interest groups are more involved in candidate elections, with millions of dollars going to issue advocacy efforts and independent expenditures. Money from interest groups pours into party coffers, and the day of the $100 million single-initiative campaign is nearly here.

The era of permanent campaigns has come. Political consultants, who used to work on campaigns only part of the year or just a couple of months every other year, now move from one election campaign to another and fill the rest of the year with lobbying, coalition building, and grassroots campaigns.

A politics of permanent campaigns is horribly expensive. Lobbying in Washington, D.C., alone is a billion-dollar-a-year activity. Grassroots lobbying costs are unknown because they are unreported on the federal level, but for every dollar spent in traditional lobbying in the nation's capital, another dollar is probably spent on indirect lobbying. In 1998 campaign spending on one ballot initiative on casino gambling in California, Proposition 5, totaled nearly $100 million. Las Vegas gambling interests invested over $30 million in their efforts to limit the type and scope of gambling allowed in Native American–owned casinos in California. Why would they spend that much money? The gambling industry estimated that if the proposition passed (and it did pass), it could cost Nevada casinos a great deal in lost revenues. In 1998 there were over 260 propositions on state ballots. Spending millions of dollars to support or defeat a proposition is often a cost-efficient investment for an interest group.

The cost-benefit analysis of lobbying expenditures is a relatively easy one for many interest groups. Consider the numbers in the never ending savings and loan scandal that emerged on the political agenda in the 1980s and continued to impact the nation in the late 1990s. The cost of cleaning up the financial wreckage of the collapsed savings and loan industry was an estimated $260 billion. But that is not the complete bill. Clever lawyers discovered a way to make the federal government pay additional tax dollars to the purchasers of the failed savings and loans by successfully claiming that the federal government had changed its accounting rules and thus contributed to the collapse of the industry. It is one thing to win such a claim in court; it is quite another to get the Congress to appropriate money to pay the claims. The industry lobbied and got the Clinton administration to support its efforts to have Congress promise to finance billions of dollars of compensation to pay for these claims. The authorization was hidden in the huge budget appropriations bill passed in the closing moments of the pre-1998 election session. The expenditure of perhaps several millions of dollars will probably net the industry billions of tax dollars. That is the comparative benefit of contemporary interest group political campaigns.

The New Nature of American Political Parties

In this book we have suggested that it is useful to analyze the parties by examining party organization and the changes the parties have made over the years. Consequently, we identified four eras of American political party organization and function: (1) parties as elite caucuses (1796–1828), (2) parties as mass organizations (1840–1900), (3) parties as products of state law (1900–1960), and (4) parties as candidate service organizations (1960–present). The era of candidate service functions is the most important one for understanding the role and function of parties in contemporary American politics and government.

Today's parties have weathered serious challenges from campaign consultants and for-profit campaign service providers to emerge as a resource for candidates seeking public office. We are not saying that parties have defeated their private sector rivals in the field of campaign services. Far from it; parties have learned to coexist with their private sector rivals, provide some of the same services, and be competitive in certain types of political environments. Parties have even managed to excel in the area of fund-raising, as evidenced by the enormous amounts of soft money that they managed to raise in the 1996 and 1998 elections.

Change is inevitable, and in politics the pace and significance of change seems to be accelerated. Today's political campaigns, in all the different arenas we have discussed in this book, are a mixture of old styles and new technologies. Door-to-door campaigning and the single piece of printed literature, or "door knocker," left at houses is often as important in lower-level races as the thirty-second television ad. What has happened with much greater frequency and magnitude in recent campaigns has been the entry of interest groups and their many resources into the battles.

Whereas it was once enough for parties to simply turn out their loyal supporters, now a new style of campaign has appeared. The party organization as a vote-gathering machine has largely disappeared and has been replaced by a collection of interest groups that ally themselves to certain parties or candidates and turn out their members to vote in order to achieve certain policy objectives. The parties have fewer loyalists left as the 1990s come to an end, and even they tend to be less intense in their loyalties than their predecessors in earlier generations.

Today's parties and their organizations can offer a prospective candidate for public office several tangible benefits or advantages. First, a party has a nomination to offer, and that places the candidate on the general election ballot in a limited, two-person competition. As we noted earlier, the parties have largely lost their monopoly to nominate the candidates the party leadership may prefer. The rise of primary elections in the twentieth century has taken away the selection function of the parties and has given it to the voters and the individual candidates. However, the parties retain the nomination labels and their access to the ballot. Second, parties have developed a range of campaign services, including media production skills and polling as well as many other high-tech services that they can offer their candidates at prices below those charged by the private sector. Third, the most important benefit parties can offer is money. Campaign fund-raising is a very tough job. Most candidates hate this part of modern politics, but as campaigns get more and more expensive effort has to be put into fund-raising. Even lower-level campaigns in rural states are getting expensive. State senate races in some states can incur general election campaign costs of nearly $100,000. The parties' ability to raise soft money has changed the face of campaign fund-raising. These new sources of money have put the parties back into modern campaigns in a significant way. Now the parties can pour hundreds of thousands of dollars into close races as election day nears and play a decisive role in the outcome. The source of these soft money dollars is, of course, interest groups, and that is another part of the story of the new style of American campaigns.

Party organizations in the United States appear to be hierarchical, powerful structures. They are not. What appears to be a solid pyramid is really a loose collection of relatively independent and often quite weak organizations that periodically come together at conventions but often fail to coordinate their various activities effectively. But this is not necessarily bad. This loose structure offers the advantage of maximum flexibility and adaptability, which has allowed parties to change and adapt to different political environments over time. Their most recent adaptation has been the conversion of party organizations into "service organizations," which currently is the most significant function that parties play in political campaigns.

The New Nature of
American Interest Group Politics

Interest groups are significant actors in a wide variety of American political campaigns. They have come to exert a greater influence in campaigns because they are better organized and have greater resources than before. They use these resources to access the skills and techniques of modern political campaigns to achieve their policy objectives. Interest group campaigns used to be characterized by traditional lobbyists and their appeals for support in legislative chambers in the states and in Washington, D.C. But in today's politics, interest campaigns are often indistinguishable from those run by political parties or candidates for public office. Powerful grassroots media efforts cost millions of dollars and seek to influence public opinion on policy issues that if enacted (or blocked) could mean billions of dollars to the interest sector.

Interest group politics and campaigns have changed in important ways in the past several decades. Cigler and Loomis (1998, 389–390) note the increase in the number of interest groups and the centralization of their headquarters in our nation's capital. New, previously underrepresented interests now have organizations that speak for them. So-called public interest groups (PIGs) have become regular participants in elections and lobbying campaigns. They have acquired the technology of modern political communications (computers, fax, and direct mail, as well as television and radio), which means that their lobbying campaigns can be pinpointed to reach small segments of the nation's population. Interest groups have formed thousands of political action committees, with the largest and most active of these committees pouring tens of millions of dollars into both candidate and issue campaigns. Loopholes in the political finance laws have given interest groups the legal ability to become "major players" in any campaign they wish to influence. Finally, the range of interest group campaigns is much broader than it was just a few years ago. Groups are active at the state and federal levels, in traditional face-to-face lobbying campaigns by professional lobbyists, in grassroots efforts, in media campaigns, in direct democracy efforts in those states that permit initiatives and referenda, and, increasingly, in America's candidate-centered campaigns.

References

Abramowitz, Alan, John McGlennon, and Ronald Rapoport. 1981. "A Note on Strategic Voting in a Primary Election." *Journal of Politics* 43 (3): 899–904.

Abramson, Jill. 1998. "Audit Faults Clinton and Dole for Ads." *New York Times,* December 2.

Abramson, Jill, and Leslie Wayne. 1997. "Democrats Used the State Parties to Bypass Limits." *New York Times,* October 2.

Abramson, Paul R., John Aldrich, and David W. Rohde. 1995. *Change and Continuity in the 1992 Elections.* Rev. ed. Washington, D.C.: CQ Press.

ACIR. 1986. *The Transformation of American Politics.* Washington, D.C.: Advisory Commission on Intergovernmental Relations.

Adamy, David. 1984. "Political Parties in the 1980s." In Michael J. Malbin, ed. *Money and Politics in the United States.* Washington, D.C.: American Enterprise Institute/Chatham House.

Aldrich, John H. 1995. *Why Parties? The Origin and Transformation of Political Parties in America.* Chicago: University of Chicago Press.

Alexander, Herbert E. 1992. *Financing Politics.* Washington D.C.: CQ Press.

Alexander, Herbert E., and Anthony Corrado. 1995. *Financing the 1992 Election.* Armonk, N.Y.: Sharpe.

Allen, Oliver E. 1993. *The Tiger.* Reading, Mass.: Addison-Wesley.

Almond, Gabriel, and Sidney Verba. 1963. *The Civic Culture.* Boston: Little, Brown.

Alvarez, R. Michael, and Matthew Schousen. 1993. "Policy Moderation or Conflicting Expectations? Testing the Intentional Models of Split-Ticket Voting." *American Politics Quarterly* 20 (4): 411–426.

Anderson, Kristi. 1979. *The Creation of a Democratic Majority, 1928–1936.* Chicago: University of Chicago Press.

Andres, Gary J. 1998. "Lobbying for the President." In Paul S. Herrnson, Ronald G. Shaiko, and Clyde Wilcox, eds. *The Interest Group Connection.* Chatham, N.J.: Chatham House.

"Angle of G.O.P. Attack." 1998. *New York Times,* October 29.

Ansolabehere, Stephen, and Shanto Iyengar. 1995. *Going Negative.* New York: Free Press.

Ansolabehere, Stephen, Shanto Iyengar, Adam Simon, and Nicholas Valentino. 1994. "Does Attack Advertising Demobilize the Electorate?" *American Political Science Review* 88 (4): 829–838.

Baer, Denise. 1995. "Contemporary Strategy and Agenda Setting." In James A. Thurber and Candice J. Nelson, eds. *Campaigns and Elections American Style.* Boulder: Westview.

Balz, Dan. 1992. "In Media Res: If You Can't Beat 'Em, Bypass 'Em." *Washington Post National Weekly Edition,* May 25.

Barber, James David. 1965. *The Lawmakers.* New Haven: Yale University Press.

Barnes, James A. 1992. "Voter Turnoff." *National Journal,* August 15, 1895–1898.

———. 1995. "Privatizing Politics," *National Journal,* June 3, 1330–1334.

———. 1996a. "In the Shadows." *National Journal,* July 20, 1568–1572.

———. 1996b. "Party Favors." *National Journal,* May 11, 1038–1041.

Bartels, Larry M. 1985. "Resource Allocation in Presidential Campaigns." *Journal of Politics* 47 (3): 928–936.

Barton, Paul. 1996. "Is Fund Raising 'Job 1' for Politicians?" *Salt Lake Tribune,* July 14.

"Battle over Ballot Initiatives." 1998. *Christian Science Monitor,* October 14.

Beck, Nathaniel. 1991. "The Economy and Presidential Approval." In Helmut Norpoth, Michael S. Lewis-Beck, and Jean-Dominique Lefay, eds. *Economics and Politics.* Ann Arbor: University of Michigan Press.

Beck, Paul Allen, Lawrence Baum, Aage R. Clausen, and Charles E. Smith. 1992. "Patterns and Sources of Ticket Splitting in Subpresidential Elections." *American Political Science Review* 86 (4): 916–928.

Beck, Paul Allen, and M. Kent Jennings. 1982. "Pathways to Participation." *American Political Science Review* 76 (1): 94–108.

Becker, Lee B., and Sharon Dunwoody. 1982. "Media Use, Public Affairs Knowledge and Voting in a Local Election." *Journalism Quarterly* 59 (2): 212–218.

Becker, Lee B., and D. Charles Whitney. 1980. "Effects of Media Dependencies: Audience Assessment of Government." *Communication Research* 7 (1): 95–121.

Beeman, Richard. 1994. "Republicanism and the First Party System." In L. Sandy Maisel and William G. Shade, eds. *Parties and Politics in American History.* New York: Garland.

Bentley, Arthur. 1949. *The Process of Government.* Bloomington, Ind.: Principia.

Berelson, Bernard, Paul F. Lazarsfeld, and William N. McPhee. 1954. *Voting.* Chicago: University of Chicago Press.

Berke, Richard L. 1992a. "Bush Ads Disappoint Many in G.O.P." *New York Times,* July 8.

———. 1992b. "Clinton Addresses Unemployment." *New York Times,* September 17.

———. 1993. "Perot's Support Is Here to Stay, Pollster Reports." *New York Times,* July 8.

———. 1997. "To See Ralph Reed, Take a Number." *New York Times,* September 14.

———. 1998. "Democrats' Gains Dispel Notion That the G.O.P. Benefits from Low Turnout." *New York Times,* November 6.

Berns, Walter, ed. 1992. *After the People Vote.* Washington, D.C.: AEI Press.

Berry, Jeffrey M. 1977. *Lobbying for the People.* Princeton: Princeton University Press.

———. 1984. *The Interest Group Society.* Boston: Little, Brown.

Bibby, John F. 1990. "Party Organization at the State Level." In L. Sandy Maisel, ed. *The Parties Respond.* Boulder: Westview.

———. 1994. "State Party Organizations: Coping and Adapting." In L. Sandy Maisel, ed. *The Parties Respond.* 2d ed. Boulder: Westview.

Birdsell, David S., et al. 1996. "New Forms of Political Participation: A New Political Marketplace." *Public Perspective,* June-July, 33–36.

Black, Gordon S. 1972. "A Theory of Political Ambition: Career Choices and the
Role of Structural Incentives." *American Political Science Review* 66 (1): 144–159.

Bledsoe, Timothy, and Mary Herring. 1990. "Victims of Circumstances: Women in
Pursuit of Political Office." *American Political Science Review* 64 (1): 213–223.

Blum, John Morton. 1991. *Years of Discord: American Politics and Society,
1961–1974.* New York: Norton.

Blumer, Herbert. 1951. "Social Movements." In A. M. Lee, ed. *Principles of Soci-
ology.* New York: Barnes and Noble.

Bohanan, Mark. 1993. "The Clinton Coalition Is No Myth." *Campaigns and Elections,* January, 31–33.

Born, Richard. 1994. "Split-Ticket Voters, Divided Government, and Fiorina's Pol-
icy-Balancing Model." *Legislative Studies Quarterly* 19 (1): 95–115.

Brady, Henry E., Sidney Verba, and Kay Lehman Schlozman. 1995. "Beyond SES:
A Resource Model of Political Participation." *American Political Science Review*
89 (2): 271–286.

Broder, David. 1972. *The Party's Over.* New York: Harper and Row.

———. 1989. "Politicians, Advisors Agonize Over Campaign Character." *Washington Post,* January 19.

———. 1990. "Massive Survey Finds 'Political Gridlock' of Growing Cynicism."
Washington Post, September 19.

Brody, Richard A. 1978. "The Puzzle of Political Participation in America." In Anthony King, ed. *The New American Political System.* Washington, D.C.: AEI Press.

———. 1991. "Stability and Change in Party Identification: Presidential to Off-
Years." In Paul M. Sniderman, Richard A. Brody, and Phillip E. Tetlock, eds.
Reasoning and Choice. New York: Cambridge University Press.

Brown, Robert D., and Gerald C. Wright. 1992. "Elections and State Party Polar-
ization." *American Politics Quarterly* 20 (4): 411–426.

Browne, William P. 1995. *Cultivating Congress.* Manhattan: University Press of
Kansas.

Browning, Graeme. 1994. "Zapping the Capital." *National Journal,* October 22,
2446–2450.

Buckley v. Valeo. 1976. 424 US 1.

Burnham, Walter Dean. 1970. *Critical Elections and the Mainsprings of American
Politics.* New York: Norton.

Burt-Way, Barbara J., and Rita Mae Kelly. 1992. "Gender and Sustaining Political
Ambition." *Western Political Quarterly* 45 (1): 11–25.

"Bush Job Performance Trend." 1992. *Gallup Poll Monthly,* February, 15.

Butler, David, and Austin Ranney. 1994. *Referendums Around the World.* Washington, D.C.: AEI Press.

"Campaign Finance Legal Fight Buries Democratic Party in Debt." 1997. *Salt Lake
Tribune,* November 25.

"Campaign Finance Reform Helped Former Wrestler Post a Headlock on Minnesota Politics." 1998. *Washington Post,* November 4.

Campbell, Angus, Phillip E. Converse, Warren E. Miller, and Donald E. Stokes.
1960. *The American Voter.* New York: Wiley.

Campbell, Colton C., and Roger H. Davidson. 1998. "Coalition Building in Congress." In Paul S. Herrnson, Ronald G. Shaiko, and Clyde Wilcox, eds. *The Interest Group Connection.* Chatham, N.J.: Chatham House.

Carmines, Edward G., and James A. Stimson. 1980. "The Two Faces of Issue Voting." *American Political Science Review* 74 (1): 78–91.

———. 1989. *Issue Evolution*. Princeton: Princeton University Press.

Carney, Eliza. 1996a. "Backdoor PACs." *National Journal*, March 2, 468–473.

———. 1996b. "Defending PACs." *National Journal*, July 13, 1518–1523.

———. 1997. "Taking On the Fat Cats." *National Journal*, January 18, 110–114.

Chambers, William N. 1967. "Party Development and the American Mainstream." In William Nisbet Chambers and Walter Dean Burnham, eds. *The American Party Systems*. New York: Oxford University Press.

Chaney, Carole, and Jonathan Nagler. 1993. "Women, Issues, and Voter-Turnout." Paper presented at the Western Political Science Association Meeting, Pasadena, Calif.

Charles, Joseph. 1956. *The Origins of the American Party System*. Williamsburg, Va.: Institute of Early American History and Culture.

Cigler, Allan J., and Burdette A. Loomis, eds. 1986. *Interest Group Politics*. 2d ed. Washington, D.C.: CQ Press.

———. 1998. *Interest Group Politics*. 5th ed. Washington, D.C.: CQ Press.

Citizens' Research Foundation. 1997. *New Realities, New Thinking: Report of the Task Force on Campaign Finance Reform*.

Clark, Janet, Charles D. Hadley, and R. Darcy. 1989. "Political Ambition Among Men and Women State Party Leaders: Testing the Countersocialization Perspective." *American Politics Quarterly* 17 (1): 194–207.

Clark, John A., John M. Bruce, John H. Kessel, and William Jacoby. 1991. "I'd Rather Switch Than Fight: Lifelong Democrats and Converts to Republicanism Among Campaign Activists." *American Journal of Political Science* 35 (3): 577–597.

Clark, Peter B., and James Q. Wilson. 1961. "Incentive Systems: A Theory of Organizations." *Administrative Science Quarterly* 6 (3): 129–166.

Clines, Francis X. 1997. "Turning to State Campaign Overhauls as Models to Stir Up Congress." *New York Times*, April 6.

Clymer, Adam. 1997. "Few in Congress Support Overhaul of Campaign Laws." *New York Times*, April 6.

Colorado Republican Federal Campaign Committee v. Federal Election Commission. 1996. 116 S. Ct. 2309.

Constantini, Edmond. 1990. "Political Women and Political Ambition: Closing the Gender Gap." *American Journal of Political Science* 34 (3): 741–770.

Converse, Phillip E., and Roy Pierce. 1985. "Measuring Partisanship." *Political Methodology* 11: 143–166.

Corrado, Anthony. 1992. *Creative Campaigning*. Boulder: Westview.

———. 1997. "Financing the 1996 Elections." In Gerald M. Pomper et al. *The Election of 1996*. Chatham, N.J.: Chatham House.

"A Correction: Voter Turnout in 20 Primaries So Far." 1992. *New York Times*, May 15.

Cotter, Cornelius P., James L. Gibson, John F. Bibby, and Robert J. Huckshorn. 1984. *Party Organizations in American Politics*. New York: Praeger.

Council of State Governments. 1996. *The Book of the States*. Vol. 31. Lexington, Ky.: Council of State Governments.

Craig, Steven C., and Michael A. Maggiotto. 1992. "Measuring Political Efficacy." *Political Methodology* 8: 85–109.

Crotty, William. 1994. "Urban Political Machines." In L. Sandy Maisel and William G. Shade, eds. *Parties and Politics in American History.* New York: Garland.

Crotty, William, ed. 1986. *Political Parties in Local Areas.* Knoxville: University of Tennessee Press.

Cundy, Donald T. 1986. "Political Commercials and Candidate Image: The Effect Can Be Substantial." In Lynda Lee Kaid, Dan Nimmo, and Keith Sanders, eds. *New Perspectives on Political Advertising.* Carbondale: Southern Illinois University Press.

Dahl, Robert. 1961. *Who Governs?* New Haven: Yale University Press.

"Democratic Party Returns More Suspect Donations." 1997. *New York Times,* June 28.

"Democratic Primaries Show Drop in Turnout." 1992. *New York Times,* July 2.

Deseret News. 1994. November 1.

———. 1997. August 28.

———. 1998a. April 20.

———. 1998b. May 25.

———. 1998c. July 3.

———. 1998d. October 20.

———. 1998e. October 25.

———. 1998f. November 7.

de Tocqueville, Alexis. [1835–1839] 1956. *Democracy in America.* New York: Mentor.

DeVries, Walter, and V. Lance Tarrance Jr. 1972. *The Ticket-Splitter.* Grand Rapids, Mich.: Eerdmans.

Dexter, Lewis. 1969. *How Organizations Are Represented in Washington.* Indianapolis, Ind.: Bobbs-Merrill.

Diamond, Edwin, and Steven Bates. 1992. *The Spot.* 3d ed. Cambridge: MIT Press.

Dodson, Debra L. 1990. "Socialization of Party Activists: National Convention Delegates, 1972–1981." *American Journal of Political Science* 34 (4): 1119–1141.

"Dole Was Kidding; He Isn't Now." 1990. *New York Times,* October 30.

Donnay, Patrick D., and Graham P. Ramsden. 1995. "Public Financing of Legislative Elections: Lessons from Minnesota." *Legislative Studies Quarterly* 20 (3): 351–364.

Donovan, Beth. 1993. "Much Maligned 'Soft Money' Is Precious to Both Parties." *Congressional Quarterly Weekly Report,* May 15, 1195–1198.

Dunham, Pat. 1991. *Electoral Behavior in the United States.* Englewood Cliffs, N.J.: Prentice-Hall.

Duverger, Maurice. 1963. *Political Parties.* New York: Wiley.

Dwyre, Diana. 1994a. "Party Strategy and Political Reality: The Distribution of Congressional Campaign Committee Resources." In Daniel M. Shea and John C. Green, eds. *The State of the Parties.* Lanham, Md.: Rowman and Littlefield.

———. 1994b. "Should the Parties Play a Larger Role in the Financing of Congressional Candidates?" Paper presented at the American Political Science Association Meeting, New York.

———. 1996. "Spinning Straw into Gold: Soft Money and U.S. House Elections." *Legislative Studies Quarterly* 20 (3): 409–424.

Elving, Ronald D. 1996. "Accentuate the Negative: Contemporary Congressional Campaigns." *PS: Political Science and Politics* 29 (3): 440–445.

Encyclopedia of Associations. 1996. Detroit: Gale Research.

Epstein, Lee. 1985. *Conservatives in Court.* Knoxville: University of Tennessee Press.

Epstein, Leon D. 1986. *Political Parties in the American Mold.* Madison: University of Wisconsin Press.

Erikson, Robert S., and Kent L. Tedin. 1981. "The 1928–1936 Partisan Realignment: The Case for the Conversion Hypothesis." *American Political Science Review* 75 (4): 951–963.

"Ethnocultural Patterns." 1993. *The American Enterprise,* January-February, 92.

Eu v. San Francisco County Democratic Central Committee. 1989. 489 US 214.

"Exit Poll: A Pitched Battle for the House." 1998. *USA Today,* November 4.

Facts on File. 1962. "National Affairs: Elections." New York: Facts on File.

Federal Election Commission. 1996. "1996 Congressional Financial Activity Continues Climb." Washington, D.C.: Federal Election Commission.

———. 1997a. "PAC Totals." Washington, D.C.: Federal Election Commission.

———. 1997b. "Report to the Congress on the Impact of the National Voter Registration Act of 1993 on the Administration of Federal Elections." Washington, D.C.: Federal Election Commission.

Feingold, Russell. 1997. "S.25: Bipartisan Campaign Reform Act." Available at <http://senate.gov/~feingold/cfrsumm.html>.

"53% Oppose Impeachment Hearings." 1998. *USA Today,* October 4.

Finkel, Steven E., and John G. Greer. 1998. "Spot Check: Casting Doubt on the Demobilizing Effect of Attack Advertising." *American Journal of Political Science* 42 (3): 573–595.

Fiorina, Morris P. 1977. "An Outline for a Model of Party Choice." *American Journal of Political Science* 21 (3): 601–625.

———. 1981. *Retrospective Voting in American National Elections.* New Haven: Yale University Press.

———. 1992. *Divided Government.* New York: Macmillan.

Fishel, Jeff. 1971. "Ambition and Political Vocation: Congressional Challengers in American Politics." *Journal of Politics* 33 (1): 25–56.

Fishkin, James. 1995. *The Voice of the People.* New Haven: Yale University Press.

Flitner, David. 1986. *The Politics of Presidential Commissions.* Ardsley, N.Y.: Transnational.

Foster v. Love. 1997. 118 S. Ct. 464.

Fowler, Linda L., and Robert D. McClure. 1989. *Political Ambition: Who Decides to Run for Congress?* New Haven: Yale University Press.

Fowlkes, Diane. 1984. "Ambitious Political Women: Counter Socialization and Political Party Context." *Women and Politics* 4 (1): 5–32.

Fowlkes, Diane, Jerry Perkins, and Sue Tolleson Rinehart. 1979. "Gender Roles and Party Roles." *American Political Science Review* 73 (3): 772–780.

Freedman, Allan. 1997. "Lawyers Take a Back Seat in the 105th Congress." *Congressional Quarterly Weekly Report,* January 6, 27–30.

Freeman, Jo. 1983. *Social Movements of the Sixties and Seventies.* New York: Longman.

Frendreis, John P., James L. Gibson, and Laura L. Vertz. 1990. "The Electoral Relevance of Local Party Organizations." *American Political Science Review* 84 (1): 225–235.

Fritsch, Jane. 1996. "In Dole's Race, Party Money Now a Lifeline." *New York Times,* May 22.

Frymer, Paul, Thomas P. Kim, and Terri L. Bimes. 1997. "Party Elites, Ideological Voters, and Divided Government." *Legislative Studies Quarterly* 22 (2): 195–216.

Gais, Thomas, Mark A. Peterson, and Jack Walker, 1984. "Interest Groups, Iron Triangles and Representative Institutions in American National Government." *British Journal of Political Science* 14 (1): 161–186.

"Gallup Short Subjects." 1996a. *Gallup Poll Monthly,* October, 42.

———. 1996b. *Gallup Poll Monthly,* November, 37.

Gamarekian, Barbara. 1983. "The No. 2 Game: Tennis Everyone?" *New York Times,* May 14.

Gamson, William A. 1974. "Violence and Political Power: The Meek Don't Make It." *Psychology Today,* July, 35–41.

———. 1990. *The Strategy of Social Protest.* Belmont, Calif.: Wadsworth.

Gant, Michael M., and Norman R. Luttbeg. 1991. *American Electoral Behavior.* Itasca, Ill.: Peacock.

Georgia. 1998. *Official Code of Georgia Annotated.* Section 21–2–111.

Germond, Jack, and Jules Whitcover. 1997. "Disclosures from Campaign '96." *Salt Lake Tribune,* October 7.

Gibson, James L., John P. Frendreis, and Laura L. Vertz. 1989. "Party Dynamics in the 1980s: Change in County Party Organizational Strength, 1980–1984." *American Journal of Political Science* 33 (1): 67–90.

Gibson, James L., Cornelius P. Cotter, John F. Bibby, and Robert J. Huckshorn. 1986. "Whither the Local Parties? A Cross-Sectional and Longitudinal Analysis of the Strength of Party Organizations." *American Journal of Political Science* 29 (1): 139–160.

Gienapp, William E. 1987. *The Origins of the Republican Party, 1852–1856.* New York: Oxford University Press.

———. 1994. "Formation of the Republican Party." In L. Sandy Maisel and William G. Shade, eds. *Parties and Politics in American History.* New York: Garland.

Gierzynski, Anthony. 1992. *Legislative Party Campaign Committees in the American States.* Lexington: University Press of Kentucky.

Gimpel, James G. 1998. "Grassroots Organizations and Equilibrium Cycles in Group Mobilization and Access." In Paul S. Herrnson, Ronald G. Shaiko, and Clyde Wilcox, eds. *The Interest Group Connection.* Chatham, N.J.: Chatham House.

Glennon, Michael J. 1992. *When No Majority Rules: The Electoral College and Presidential Succession.* Washington, D.C.: CQ Press.

Goidel, Robert K., and Donald A. Gross. 1996. "Reconsidering the 'Myths and Realities' of Campaign Finance Reform." *Legislative Studies Quarterly* 21 (1): 129–149.

Goldman, Ralph M. 1990. *The National Party Chairmen and Committees.* Armonk, N.Y.: Sharpe.

Graber, Doris A. 1989. *The Mass Media and American Politics.* 3d ed. Washington, D.C.: CQ Press.

Grady, Sandy. 1992. "Carville's Cajun Magic Whisked Clinton into Office." *Salt Lake Tribune,* November 10.

———. 1997. "Chinese Money Buys the Superstars." *Salt Lake Tribune,* March 20.

Gronbeck, Bruce E. 1987. "Functions of Presidential Campaigns." In L. Patrick Devlin, ed. *Political Persuasion in Presidential Campaigns.* New Brunswick, N.J.: Transaction.

Guskind, Robert, and Jerry Hagstrom. 1988. "In the Gutter." *National Journal,* November 5, 2782–2789.

Hagstrom, Jerry, and Robert Guskind. 1986. "Selling the Candidates." *National Journal,* November 1, 2619–2629.

Hall, Donald. 1969. *Cooperative Lobbying.* Tucson: University of Arizona Press.

Hamm, Keith. 1981. "The Role of 'Subgovernments' in U.S. State Policy Making: An Exploratory Analysis." *Legislative Studies Quarterly* 11 (3): 321–351.

Hansen, John Mark. 1985. "The Political Economy of Group Membership." *American Political Science Review* 79 (1): 79–96.

Heclo, Hugh. 1978. "Issue Networks and the Executive Establishment." In Anthony King, ed. *The New American Political System.* Washington, D.C.: AEI Press.

Hedlun, Ronald D., and Meredith W. Watts. 1986. "The Wisconsin Open Primary, 1968 to 1984." *American Politics Quarterly* 14 (2): 55–73.

Herrera, Richard. 1995. "The Crosswinds of Change: Sources of Change in the Democratic and Republican Parties." *Political Research Quarterly* 48 (2): 291–312.

Herrnson, Paul S. 1988. *Party Campaigning in the 1980s.* Cambridge: Harvard University Press.

———. 1990. "Reemergent National Party Organizations." In L. Sandy Maisel, ed. *The Parties Respond.* Boulder: Westview.

———. 1995. *Congressional Elections.* Washington, D.C.: CQ Press.

———. 1998. "Interest Groups, PACs and Campaigns." In Paul S. Herrnson, Ronald G. Shaiko, and Clyde Wilcox, eds. *The Interest Group Connection.* Chatham, N.J.: Chatham House.

Herrnson, Paul S., Ronald G. Shaiko, and Clyde Wilcox. 1998a. "Interest Groups at the Dawn of the New Millennium." In Paul S. Herrnson, Ronald G. Shaiko, and Clyde Wilcox, eds. *The Interest Group Connection.* Chatham, N.J.: Chatham House.

Herrnson, Paul S., Ronald G. Shaiko, and Clyde Wilcox, eds. 1998b. *The Interest Group Connection.* Chatham, N.J.: Chatham House.

Hershey, Marjorie Randon. 1997. "The Congressional Elections." In Gerald M. Pomper et al. *The Election of 1996.* Chatham, N.J.: Chatham House.

Hertzgaard, Mark. 1988. *On Bended Knee*. New York: Farrar, Strauss, and Giroux.

Hertzke, Allen D. 1993. *Echoes of Discontent*. Washington, D.C.: CQ Press.

Hill, Kevin A., and John E. Hughes. 1998. *Cyberpolitics*. Lanham, Md.: Rowman and Littlefield.

Hoadley, John F. 1986. *Origins of American Political Parties, 1789–1803*. Lexington: University Press of Kentucky.

Hofstadter, Richard. 1969. *The Idea of a Party System*. Berkeley: University of California Press.

Hrebenar, Ronald J. 1997. *Interest Group Politics in America*. Armonk, N.Y.: Sharpe.

Hrebenar, Ronald J., and Clive S. Thomas, eds. 1987. *Interest Group Politics in the American West*. Salt Lake City: University of Utah Press.

———. 1992a. *Interest Group Politics in the Northeastern States*. College Park: Pennsylvania State University Press.

———. 1992b. *Interest Group Politics in the South*. Tuscaloosa: University of Alabama Press.

———. 1993. *Interest Group Politics in the Midwest*. Ames: Iowa State University Press.

Huckshorn, Robert J. 1976. *Party Leadership in the States*. Amherst: University of Massachusetts Press.

———. 1991. "State Party Leaders." In L. Sandy Maisel, ed. *Political Parties and Elections in the United States*. New York: Garland.

Hugick, Larry, and Leslie McAneny. 1992. "A Gloomy America Sees a Nation in Decline; No Easy Solutions Ahead." *Gallup Poll Monthly*, September.

Hyman, Herbert, and Charles Wright. 1971. "Trends of Volunteer Association Membership of American Adults." *American Sociological Review* 36 (1): 191–206.

Ivins, Molly. 1998. "Best Election News." *Salt Lake Tribune*, November 8.

Jackson, Brooks. 1997. "Financing the 1996 Campaign: The Law of the Jungle." In Larry J. Sabato, ed. *Toward the Millennium*. Boston: Allyn and Bacon.

Jackson, John E. 1975. "Issues, Party Choices, and Presidential Votes." *American Journal of Political Science* 19 (1): 161–186.

Jacobson, Gary C. 1978. "The Effects of Campaign Spending in Congressional Elections." *American Political Science Review* 72 (2): 469–491.

———. 1980. *Money and Congressional Elections*. New Haven: Yale University Press.

———. 1985. "Money and Votes Reconsidered: Congressional Elections, 1972–1982." *Public Choice* 48 (1): 7–62.

———. 1985–1986. "Party Organization and Distribution of Campaign Resources: Republicans and Democrats in 1982." *Political Science Quarterly* 100 (4): 603–625.

———. 1990a. "The Effects of Campaign Spending in House Elections: New Evidence for Old Arguments." *American Journal of Political Science* 34 (2): 334–362.

———. 1990b. *The Electoral Origins of Divided Government*. Boulder: Westview.

———. 1992. *The Politics of Congressional Elections*. 3d ed. New York: HarperCollins.

————. 1997. "The 105th Congress: Unprecedented and Unsurprising." In Michael Nelson, ed. *The Elections of 1996.* Washington, D.C.: CQ Press.

Jacobson, Gary C., and Samuel Kernell. 1983. *Strategy and Choice in Congressional Elections.* 2d ed. New Haven: Yale University Press.

Jacobson, Gary C., and Thomas P. Kim. 1996. "After 1994: The New Politics of Congressional Elections." Paper presented at the Midwestern Political Science Association Meeting, Chicago.

Janofsky, Michael. 1996. "Report Opposes Low Spending Caps." *New York Times,* June 21.

Jennings, M. Kent, and Richard G. Niemi. 1981. *Generations and Politics.* Princeton: Princeton University Press.

Johnson, Haynes, and David Broder. 1996. *The System.* Boston: Little, Brown.

Johnson-Cartee, Karen S., and Gary A. Copeland. 1991. *Negative Political Advertising.* Hillsdale, N.J.: Erlbaum.

Jost, Kenneth. 1996. "Campaign Finance Reform." *CQ Researcher,* February 9, 123–143.

Just, Marion R. 1997. "Candidate Strategies and the Media Campaign." In Gerald M. Pomper et al. *The Election of 1996.* Chatham, N.J.: Chatham House.

Keith, Bruce, David B. Magleby, Candice J. Nelson, Elizabeth Orr, Mark C. Westlye, and Raymond E. Wolfinger. 1992. *The Myth of the Independent Voter.* Berkeley: University of California Press.

Keleher, Alison G. 1996. "Political Parties, Interest Groups, and Soft Money: Does the Money Flow Both Ways?" Paper presented at the Western Political Science Association Meeting, San Francisco.

Kenworthy, Tom. 1989. "House Democratic Campaign Unit Running into Turbulence." *Washington Post,* August 2.

————. 1991. "NRSC Field Staff Let Go." *Washington Post,* February 9.

Kern, Montague. 1989. *Thirty-Second Politics.* New York: Praeger.

Kernell, Samuel. 1986. *Going Public.* Washington, D.C.: CQ Press.

Key, V. O. 1955. "A Theory of Critical Elections." *Journal of Politics* 17 (1): 3–18.

————. 1959. "Secular Realignment and the Party System." *Journal of Politics* 21 (2): 198–210.

Kiewiet, D. Roderick. 1983. *Macro-Economics and Micro-Politics.* Chicago: University of Chicago Press.

King, John. 1993. "Christian Activists Trying to Make GOP God's Own Party." *Salt Lake Tribune,* September 11.

Kleppner, Paul. 1987. *Continuity and Change in Electoral Politics, 1893–1928.* Westport, Conn.: Greenwood.

Klotz, Robert. 1997. "Positive Spin: Senate Campaigning on the Web." *PS: Political Science and Politics* 30 (3): 482–486.

Kolbert, Elizabeth. 1992a. "Fueled by Words Alone, Radio Ads Are Nastier." *New York Times,* October 5.

————. 1992b. "Low Tolerance for Political Commercials? Just Count to 10." *New York Times,* May 30.

Kollman, Ken. 1998. *Outside Lobbying.* Princeton: Princeton University Press.

Kolodny, Robin. 1998. *Pursuing Majorities: Congressional Campaign Committees in American Politics.* Norman: University of Oklahoma Press.

Ladd, Everett Carll. 1970. *American Political Parties*. New York: Norton.

———. 1991. "Like Waiting for Godot: The Uselessness of 'Realignment' for Understanding Change in Contemporary American Politics." In Byron E. Shafer, ed. *The End of Realignment? Interpreting American Electoral Eras*. Madison: University of Wisconsin Press.

Latham, Earl. 1952. *The Group Basis of Politics*. Ithaca: Cornell University Press.

Lau, Richard R. 1985. "Two Explanations for Negativity Effects in Political Behavior." *American Journal of Political Science* 29 (2): 353–377.

Laurence, Robert P. 1996. "TV Viewers, Koppel Bored with GOP's Infomercial." *San Diego Union-Tribune*, August 14, Republican Convention Supplement.

Lazarsfeld, Paul F., Bernard Berelson, and Hazel Gaudet. 1948. *The People's Choice*. New York: Columbia University Press.

Leege, David C., and Lyman A. Kellstedt. 1993. *Rediscovering the Religious Factor in American Politics*. Armonk, N.Y.: Sharpe.

Lewis-Beck, Michael. 1985. "Pocketbook Voting in United States National Election Studies: Fact or Artifact?" *American Journal of Political Science* 29 (2): 348–356.

———. 1988. "Economics and Elections: An Inventory." In Michael Lewis-Beck, ed. *Economics and Elections: The Major Western Democracies*. Ann Arbor: University of Michigan Press.

Lijphart, Arend. 1990. "The Political Consequences of Electoral Laws, 1945–85." *American Political Science Review* 84 (2): 481–496.

———. 1994. *Electoral Systems and Party Systems*. New York: Oxford University Press.

Lockard, Duane, and Walter F. Murphy. 1980. *Basic Cases in Constitutional Law*. New York: Macmillan.

Lockerbie, Brad. 1991a. "Prospective Economic Voting in U.S. House Elections, 1956–1988." *Legislative Studies Quarterly* 16 (2): 239–261.

———. 1991b. "The Temporal Pattern of Economic Evaluations and Vote Choice in Senate Elections." *Public Choice* 69 (1): 279–294.

"A Look at Voting Patterns of 115 Demographic Groups in House Races." 1998. *New York Times*, November 9.

Los Angeles Times. 1990. March 16.

Lowi, Theodore. 1993. "The Dog That Did Not Bark: Ross Perot and the Prospects for a Permanent Third Party." *Extensions*, Spring, 8–11.

Luntz, Frank. 1988. *Candidates, Consultants and Campaigns*. Oxford: Blackwell.

Madison, James. 1948. In Charles A. Beard, ed. *The Enduring Federalist*. Garden City, NY: Doubleday.

Magleby, David B. 1984. *Direct Legislation*. Baltimore: Johns Hopkins University Press.

———. 1998. "Ballot Initiatives and Intergovernmental Relations." Paper presented at the Western Political Science Association Meeting, Los Angeles.

Martinez, Michael D., and Tad Delegal. 1990. "The Irrelevance of Negative Campaigns to Political Trust: Experimental and Survey Results." *Political Communication and Persuasion* 7 (1): 25–40.

Matthews, Donald R. 1960. *U.S. Senators and Their World*. Chapel Hill: University of North Carolina Press.

May, Clifford. 1988. "Political Mud Can Yield Gold, Analysts Agree." *New York Times,* November 4.

Mayer, Kenneth R., and John Wood. 1995. "The Impact of Public Financing on Electoral Competitiveness: Evidence from Wisconsin, 1964–1990." *Legislative Studies Quarterly* 20 (1): 69–88.

Mayhew, David R. 1986. *Placing Parties in American Politics.* Princeton: Princeton University Press.

McCool, Daniel. 1989. "Subgovernments and the Impact of Policy Fragmentation and Accommodation." *Policy Studies Review* 8 (2): 264–287.

———. 1990. "Subgovernments as Determinants of Political Viability." *Political Science Quarterly* 105 (2): 269–293.

———. 1995. *Public Policy Theory, Concepts and Models.* Englewood Cliffs, N.J.: Prentice-Hall.

McKitrick, Eric L. 1967. "Party Politics and the Union and Confederate War Efforts." In William Nisbet Chambers and Walter Dean Burnham, eds. *The American Party Systems.* New York: Oxford University Press.

Mead, Walter B. 1987. *The United States Constitution.* Columbia: University of South Carolina Press.

Meyer, Chris, and Phil Porado. 1990. "Hit or Miss, Your Guide to Effective Media Buying." *Campaigns and Elections,* August, 37–42.

Michel, Robert. 1962. *Political Parties.* New York: Free Press.

Milbrath, Lester. 1963. *The Washington Lobbyists.* Chicago: Rand McNally.

Miller, Ellen S., and Donald L. Goff. 1998. "Comments on the Electoral Connection." In Paul S. Herrnson, Ronald G. Shaiko, and Clyde Wilcox, eds. *The Interest Group Connection.* Chatham, N.J.: Chatham House.

Miller, Warren E. 1990. "The Electorate's View of Parties." In L. Sandy Maisel, ed. *The Parties Respond.* Boulder: Westview.

Miller, Warren E., and M. Kent Jennings. 1986. *Parties in Transition.* New York: Russell Sage Foundation.

Miller, Warren E., and J. Merrill Shanks. 1996. *The New American Voter.* Cambridge: Harvard University Press.

Mills, C. Wright. 1956. *The Power Elite.* New York: Oxford University Press.

Mitchell, Alison. 1997. "Clinton Pressed Plan to Reward Donors." *New York Times,* February 26.

Moody, Sid. 1992. "Compared to the Past, Mudslinging Tame Nowadays." *Salt Lake Tribune,* June 21.

Morin, Richard. 1996. "Bouncing Along with the Bounce." *Washington Post National Weekly Edition,* August 26.

Morison, Samuel Eliot. 1965. *The Oxford History of the American People: 1789 Through Reconstruction.* Vol. 2. New York: Mentor.

Mushkat, Jerome. 1971. *Tammany.* Syracuse, N.Y.: Syracuse University Press.

Mutch, Robert E. 1988. *Campaigns, Congress, and the Courts: The Making of Federal Campaign Finance Law.* New York: Praeger.

Nagler, Jonathan. 1991. "The Effect of Registration Laws and Education on U.S. Voter Turnout." *American Political Science Review* 85 (4): 1393–1405.

Napolitan, Joseph. 1971. "Zeroing in on the Voter." In Ray Hiebert, Robert Jones, John Lorenz, and Ernest Lotito, eds. *The Political Image Merchants.* Washington, D.C.: Acropolis.

"A Nation." 1995. *Washington Post National Weekly Edition,* July 7.

Nelson, Lars-Erick. 1984. "Frenzied Demos Face a Polished GOP." *Salt Lake Tribune,* July 21.

Nelson, Michael. 1997. "The Election: Turbulence and Tranquility in Contemporary American Politics." In Michael Nelson, ed. *The Elections of 1996.* Washington, D.C.: CQ Press.

New York Times. 1988. January 8.

———. 1995a. January 18.

———. 1995b. May 18.

———. 1995c. May 28.

———. 1996a. February 2.

———. 1996b. March 25.

———. 1996c. April 21.

———. 1996d. July 30.

———. 1997a. June 19.

———. 1997b. July 20.

———. 1997c. August 13.

———. 1998a. March 30.

———. 1998b. April 5.

———. 1998c. June 4.

———. 1998d. June 11.

———. 1998e. July 12.

———. 1998f. October 7.

———. 1998g. October 13.

———. 1998h. October 15.

———. 1998i. October 23.

———. 1998j. October 24.

———. 1998k. October 31.

———. 1998l. November 6.

———. 1998m. November 21.

New York Times Magazine. 1997. October 12.

Nie, Norman H., Sidney Verba, and John R. Petrocik. 1979. *The Changing American Voter.* Enl. ed. Cambridge: Harvard University Press.

Nie, Norman H., Sidney Verba, Henry C. Brady, Kay Lehman Schlozman, and Jane Junn. 1989. "Participation in America: Continuity and Change." Paper presented at the Midwest Political Science Association Meeting, Chicago.

Nimmo, Dan. 1970. *The Political Persuaders.* Englewood Cliffs, N.J.: Prentice-Hall.

Nimmo, Dan, and Robert L. Savage. 1976. *Candidates and Their Images.* Pacific Palisades, Calif.: Goodyear.

Northwestern University Medill School of Journalism. 1996. "No Show '96: Americans Who Don't Vote." Available at <www.medill.nwu.edu>.

O'Leary, Brad. 1994. "Fire Power." *Campaigns and Elections,* December, 32–35.

Olson, Mancur. 1965. *The Logic of Collective Action.* Cambridge: Harvard University Press.

"Opponents of Health-Care Reform Spent $60 Million on Lobbying." 1998. *Salt Lake Tribune,* November 28.

Ornstein, Norman, Andrew Kohut, and Larry McCarthy. 1988. *The People, the Press, and Politics.* Reading, Mass.: Addison-Wesley.

Owen, Diana. 1997. "The Press' Performance." In Larry J. Sabato, ed. *Toward the Millennium*. Boston: Allyn and Bacon.

Payne, Gregory J., and Robert A. Baukus. 1988. "Trend Analysis of the 1984 GOP Senatorial Spots." *Political Communication and Persuasion* 5 (3): 161–177.

Pelling, Henry, and Alastair J. Reid. 1996. *A Short History of the Labour Party*. 11th ed. London: St. Martin's.

Petrocik, John R., and Joseph Doherty. 1996. "The Road to Divided Government: Paved Without Intention." In Peter F. Galderisi, ed. *Divided Government: Change, Uncertainty, and the Constitutional Order*. Lanham, Md.: Rowman and Littlefield.

Pew Research Center for the People and the Press. 1996. "One in Ten Voters On-line for Campaign '96: News Attracts Most Internet Users." December 16. Washington, D.C.: Pew Research Center for the People and the Press.

Pfau, Michael, and Michael Burgoon. 1988. "Inoculation in Political Campaign Communication." *Human Communication and Research* 15 (2): 91–111.

Pfau, Michael, and Henry C. Kenski. 1990. *Attack Politics*. New York: Praeger.

Pika, Joseph A., and Richard A. Watson. 1996. *The Presidential Contest*. 5th ed. Washington, D.C.: CQ Press.

Piven, Francis Fox, and Richard A. Cloward. 1977. *Political Power in Poor Neighborhoods*. New York: Pantheon.

———. 1996. "Northern Bourbons: A Preliminary Report on the National Voter Registration Act." *PS: Political Science and Politics* 29 (1): 39–42.

"Political Operatives Form Government Relations Group." 1997. *Deseret News,* August 28.

Pomper, Gerald M. 1975. *Voter's Choice*. New York: Harper and Row.

———. 1989. "The Presidential Election." In Gerald M. Pomper et al. *The Election of 1988*. Chatham, N.J.: Chatham House.

Pomper, Gerald M., et al. 1997. *The Election of 1996*. Chatham, N.J.: Chatham House.

Pomper, Gerald M., and Loretta A. Sernekos. 1991. "Bake Sales and Voting." *Society* 28 (July-August): 10–16.

Popkin, Samuel L. 1991. *The Reasoning Voter*. Chicago: University of Chicago Press.

"President's Remarks on Rewards for Donors." 1997. *New York Times,* February 27.

Rae, Douglas W. 1967. *The Political Consequences of Electoral Laws*. New Haven: Yale University Press.

Raskin, Jamin. 1992. "Inside Clinton." *Campaigns and Elections,* September.

Rauch, Jonathan. 1997. "Blow It Up." *National Journal,* March 29, 604–607.

Reichley, A. James. 1992. *The Life of the Parties*. New York: Free Press.

———. 1996. "The Future of the American Two-Party System After 1994." In John C. Green and Daniel M. Shea, eds. *The State of the Parties*. 2d ed. Lanham, Md.: Rowman and Littlefield.

"Reno Says It's Legal to Sell Access." 1997. *Salt Lake Tribune,* October 8.

"Rights vs. Revenues." 1997. *Salt Lake Tribune,* November 1.

Robbin, Jonathan. 1989. "Geodemographics: The New Magic." In Larry J. Sabato, ed. *Campaigns and Elections*. Glennville, Ill.: Scott, Foresman.

Rosenbloom, David Lee. 1973. *The Election Men.* New York: Quadrangle Books.

Rosenstone, Steven J., and John Mark Hansen. 1993. *Mobilization, Participation and Democracy in America.* New York: Macmillan.

Rosenstone, Steven J., Roy L. Behr, and Edward Lazarus. 1996. *Third Parties in America.* 2d ed. Princeton: Princeton University Press.

Rosenthal, Alan. 1996. "The Legislature: Unraveling of Institutional Fabric." In Carl E. Van Horn, ed. *The State of the States.* 3d ed. Washington, D.C.: CQ Press.

Rosenthal, Cindy Simon. 1994. "Where's the Party?" *State Legislatures* 20 (6): 31–37.

Rothenberg, Randall. 1990a. "Newspapers Watch What People Watch in the TV Campaign." *New York Times,* November 4.

———. 1990b. "Voters Complain Negative Campaigns Are Driving Them Away." *New York Times,* November 6.

Rothmeyer, Karen. 1981. "Money in Politics." *Common Cause,* August, 13–15.

Rozell, Mark J., and Clyde Wilcox. 1999. *Interest Groups in American Campaigns.* Washington, D.C.: CQ Press.

Rubin, Barry R. 1997. *A Citizen's Guide to Politics in America.* Armonk, N.Y.: Sharpe.

Ryan, Mike H., C. L. Swanson, and Rogene A. Buchholz. 1987. *Corporate Strategy.* New York: Blackwell.

Saad, Lydia. 1996. "Average Convention 'Bounce' Since 1964 Is Five Points." *Gallup Poll Monthly,* August, 8–9.

Sabato, Larry J. 1981. *The Rise of the Political Consultants.* New York: Basic.

———. 1984. *PAC Power.* New York: Norton.

———. 1988. *The Party's Just Begun.* Glenview, Ill.: Scott, Foresman.

Safire, William. 1997. "Broadcast Lobby Triumphs." *New York Times,* July 23.

Salisbury, Robert. 1969. "An Exchange Theory of Interest Groups." *Midwest Journal of Political Science* 13 (1): 1–32.

———. 1986. "Washington Lobbyists: A Collective Portrait." In Allan J. Cigler and Burdette A. Loomis, eds. *Interest Group Politics.* Washington, D.C.: CQ Press.

Salmore, Steven A., and Barbara G. Salmore. 1989. *Candidates, Parties and Campaigns.* 2d ed. Washington, D.C.: CQ Press.

Salt Lake Tribune. 1984a. February 12.

———. 1984b. May 20.

———. 1998a. October 30.

———. 1998b. November 5.

———. 1998c. November 7.

———. 1998d. November 8.

Sapiro, Virginia. 1983. *The Political Integration of Women.* Urbana: University of Illinois Press.

Sapiro, Virginia, and Barbara Farah. 1980. "New Pride and Old Prejudice: Political Ambitions and Role Orientations Among Female Partisan Elites." *Women and Politics* 1 (1): 13–36.

Schattschneider, E. E. 1975. *The Semi-Sovereign People.* Hinsdale, Ill.: Dryden.

Scher, Richard K. 1997. *The Modern Political Campaign.* Armonk, N.Y.: Sharpe.

Schlesinger, Joseph A. 1966. *Ambition and Politics*. Chicago: Rand McNally.

Schlozman, Kay Lehman, and John T. Tierney. 1986. *Organized Interests and American Democracy*. New York: Harper and Row.

Schmidt, Eric. 1996. "New Lobbying Rules, from Bagels to Caviar." *New York Times*, February 11.

Schneider, William. 1992. "Why 'Family Values' Won't Go Away." *National Journal*, September 5, 2042.

Schwartz, Mildred A. 1990. *The Party Network*. Madison: University of Wisconsin Press.

Schwartz, Tony. 1973. *The Responsive Chord*. Garden City, N.Y.: Anchor.

———. 1985. *The Thirty Second President*. Alexandria, Va.: PBS video.

Shade, William G. 1994. "The Jacksonian Party System." In L. Sandy Maisel and William G. Shade, eds. *Parties and Politics in American History*. New York: Garland.

Shaiko, Ronald G. 1998. "Lobbying in Washington." In Paul S. Herrnson, Ronald G. Shaiko, and Clyde Wilcox, eds. *The Interest Group Connection*. Chatham, N.J.: Chatham House.

Shea, Daniel M. 1995. *Transforming Democracy: Legislative Campaign Committees and Political Parties*. Albany: State University of New York Press.

Shepard, Scott. 1992. "GOP Convention Not Your Father's Oldsmobile." *Salt Lake Tribune*, August 23.

Shulte, Brigid, and Jodi Enda. 1997. "Cash Severs Ties as It Cuts Deals in D.C." *Salt Lake Tribune*, January 13.

Silbey, Joel H. 1991a. *The American Political Nation, 1838–1893*. Stanford: Stanford University Press.

———. 1991b. "Beyond Realignment and Realignment Theory: American Political Eras, 1789–1989." In Byron E. Shafer, ed. *The End of Realignment? Interpreting American Electoral Eras*. Madison: University of Wisconsin Press.

Simpson, Janice C. 1992. "Rock the Vote." *Time*, June 15, 66–67.

Smith, Bradley A. 1995. "Campaign Finance Regulation: Faulty Assumptions and Undemocratic Consequences." Washington, D.C.: Cato Institute.

Smith, Hedrick. 1988. *The Power Game*. New York: Random House.

Soloman, Burt. 1987. "Clout Merchants." *National Journal*, March 14, 662–666.

Sorauf, Frank. 1992. *Inside Campaign Finance*. New Haven: Yale University Press.

Sorauf, Frank J., and Scott A. Wilson. 1990. "Campaigns and Money: A Changing Role for Political Parties?" In L. Sandy Maisel, ed. *The Parties Respond*. Boulder: Westview.

South, Gary. 1992. "The Mind's Eye: It Doesn't Matter What You Look Like on the Radio." *Campaigns and Elections*, June, 24–32.

Squire, Peverill, Raymond E. Wolfinger, and David P. Glass. 1987. "Residential Mobility and Voter Turnout." *American Political Science Review* 81 (1): 45–65.

Stanley, Harold W. 1997. "The Nominations: Republican Doldrums, Democratic Revival." In Michael Nelson, ed. *The Elections of 1996*. Washington, D.C.: CQ Press.

"Statistics of the Week." 1983. *National Journal*, April 2, 720.

Stern, Philip. 1988. *The Best Congress Money Can Buy*. New York: Pantheon.

Stone, Peter H. 1993. "Called to Account." *National Journal*, July 17, 1810–1813.

Stone, Walter J., and Alan I. Abramowitz. 1983. "Winning May Not Be Everything, But It's More Than We Thought: Presidential Activists in 1980." *American Political Science Review* 77 (4): 945–956.

Sundquist, James L. 1983. *Dynamics of the Party System*. Rev. ed. Washington, D.C.: Brookings Institution.

Swinyard, William R., and Kenneth A. Coney. 1978. "Promotional Effects on a High Versus Low-Involvement Electorate." *Journal of Consumer Research* 5 (2): 41–48.

Taagepera, Rein, and Matthew Soberg Shugart. 1989. *Seats and Votes*. New Haven: Yale University Press.

Tashjian v. Republican Party of Connecticut. 1986. 479 US 208.

Tate, Katherine. 1991. "Black Political Participation in the 1984 and 1988 Presidential Elections." *American Political Science Review* 85 (4): 1159–1176.

Teixeira, Ruy A. 1987. *Why Americans Don't Vote*. New York: Greenwood.

———. 1992. *The Disappearing American Voter*. Washington, D.C.: Brookings Institution.

Thayer, George. 1973. *Who Shakes the Money Tree?* New York: Simon and Schuster.

Thurber, James A. 1995. "The Transformation of American Campaigns." In James A. Thurber and Candice Nelson, eds. *Campaigns and Elections*. Boulder: Westview.

Thurber, James A., and Candice Nelson, eds. 1995. *Campaigns and Elections*. Boulder: Westview.

Times Mirror Center for the People and the Press. 1990. "A Times Mirror Political Typology." Los Angeles: Times Mirror Center for the People and the Press.

———. 1992a. "Economic Recovery Has Little Impact on American Mood." Los Angeles: Times Mirror Center for the People and the Press.

———. 1992b. "The People, the Press and Politics Campaign 92: The Generations Divide." Los Angeles: Times Mirror Center for the People and the Press.

Traugott, Michael W., and Paul J. Lavrakas. 1996. *The Voter's Guide to Election Polls*. Chatham, N.J.: Chatham House.

Trento, Susan B. 1992. "Lord of the Lies." *Washington Monthly*, September, 11–21.

Truman, David. 1971. *The Governmental Process*. New York: Knopf.

Tufte, Edward. 1975. "Determinants of the Outcomes of Mid-term Congressional Elections." *American Political Science Review* 69 (4): 812–826.

USA Today. 1984. February 12.

———. 1998. November 5.

Van Atta, Don. 1997. "Democrats Skimmed $2 Million to Aid Candidates, Records Show." *New York Times*, February 26.

Verba, Sidney, and Norman H. Nie. 1972. *Participation in America*. Chicago: University of Chicago Press.

Verba, Sidney, Kay Lehman Schlozman, Henry Brady, and Norman H. Nie. 1993. "Citizen Activity: Who Participates? What Do They Say?" *American Political Science Review* 87 (2): 303–318.

Victor, Kirk. 1995. "Labor's New Look." *National Journal*, October 14, 2522–2527.

Vose, Clement. 1958. "Litigation as a Form of Pressure Group Activity." *Annals of the American Academy of Political and Social Science* 319 (1): 20–31.

Wald, Kenneth D. 1992. *Religion and Politics in the United States*. 2d ed. Washington, D.C.: CQ Press.

Walker, Jack. 1983. "The Origins and Maintenance of Interest Groups in America." *American Political Science Review* 77 (2): 390–406.

Ware, Alan. 1996. *Political Parties and Party Systems*. New York: Oxford University Press.

Washington Post National Weekly Edition. 1997. April 21.

———. 1998a. November 2.

———. 1998b. November 16.

Wattenberg, Martin. 1991. *The Rise of Candidate-Centered Elections*. Cambridge: Harvard University Press.

Wayne, Leslie. 1997a. "Congress Uses Leadership PACs to Wield Power." *New York Times*, March 13.

———. 1997b. "Gingrich in 98: Money Gushing Both In and Out." *New York Times*, August 13.

———. 1997c. "Watchdog Group Is Under Scrutiny for Role in Teamster Race." *New York Times*, September 22.

———. 1997d. "With G.O.P. Chief a Lobbyist, Donors Are Clients." *New York Times*, June 8.

Wekkin, Gary D. 1991. "Why Crossover Voters Are Not 'Mischievous' Voters: The Segmented Partisanship Hypothesis." *American Politics Quarterly* 19 (2): 229–247.

West, Darrell M. 1997. *Air Wars*. 2d ed. Washington, D.C.: CQ Press.

West, Darrell M., and Burdett A. Loomis. 1999. *The Sound of Money*. New York: Norton.

Wilcox, Clyde. 1998. "The Dynamics of Lobbying on the Hill." In Paul S. Herrnson, Ronald G. Shaiko, and Clyde Wilcox, eds. *The Interest Group Connection*. Chatham, N.J.: Chatham House.

Wildavsky, Aaron. 1965. "The Goldwater Phenomenon: Purists, Politicians, and the Two-Party System." *Review of Politics* 27 (3): 386–413.

Wilson, James Q. 1962. *The Amateur Democrat*. Chicago: University of Chicago Press.

———. 1983. *American Government*. 2d ed. Lexington, Mass.: Heath.

———. 1995. *Political Organizations*. Princeton: Princeton University Press.

Wines, Michael. 1992. "Bush's Campaign Tries Madison Avenue." *New York Times*, April 27.

Wolff, Michael. 1989. "Say It Ain't So, Joe! Is Political Radio Dead?" *Campaigns and Elections*, October.

Wolfinger, Raymond E. 1991. "Voter Turnout." *Society*, July-August, 23–26.

Wolfinger, Raymond E., and Steven J. Rosenstone. 1980. *Who Votes?* New Haven: Yale University Press.

Zupan, Mark A. 1991. "An Economic Explanation for the Existence and Nature of Political Ticket Splitting." *Journal of Law and Economics* 34 (2): 343–369.

Index

National Association of Small Business, 250
National Conference of State Legislatures, 161
National Conservative Political Action Committee, 228
National Council of Churches, 276
National Council of Senior Citizens, 216
National Education Association (NEA), 228, 230
National Election Studies (NES), 97, 104, 106, 108
National Federation of Democratic Women, 67
National Federation of Independent Business (NFIB), 229
National party committees, 66–68
National party conventions, 22, 61–66
and television, 65–66
National Republican Congressional Committee (NRCC), 68, 153, 158, 179
National Republican party (1832), 20
National Republican Senatorial Committee (NRSC), 69, 158, 180
National Rifle Association (NRA), 217, 228, 279
National Right to Life, 279
National Taxpayers Union, 279
National Voter Registration Act (NVRA), 106
Nebraska, 89
Neilson, Todd, 82
Nevada, 29, 162, 290
New Deal coalition of voters, 33, 34, 38, 117, 120
New Hampshire, 36, 85,161, 189, 207
New Jersey, 25, 52
New Mexico, 82, 161
New York (state), 17, 22, 33, 58, 59, 79, 82, 90, 161
New York City, 27, 28, 42, 50, 196
New York Times, 198, 208
New Zealand, 74
Nicholson, Jim, 67
Nimmo, Dan, 174

Nixon, Richard, 36, 37, 38, 109, 126, 136, 206
Nominations, 78–86
Nonvoters, 111
North, Oliver, 83
North Carolina, 52
North Dakota, 29, 82, 90
No-Show '96: Americans Who Don't Vote, 97

O'Conner, Sandra Day, 140
Ohio, 26, 52, 53, 59, 79, 90, 151
Olson, Mancur, 275, 280
O'Neill, Thomas P. "Tip," 131, 179
Oregon, 30, 162
Organized labor, 228
Ornstein, Norman, 123, 163
Owens, Wayne, 204

Partipulation, 193
Partisan identification, 109
Party activists, 49–51
Party machines, 27, 28, 35, 42, 175
Party organization, 5, 15, 291
as elite caucuses, 9–10, 16, 291
hierarchical, 45, 292
as mass party organizations, 9–10, 42, 291
as public utilities, 52, 92
as reformed parties, 9–10, 291
as service parties, 9–10, 42, 46, 291, 292
See also Democratic party; Political parties; Republican party
Patronage system, 20, 175
Patton Boggs, 245
Penn, Mark, 201
Pennsylvania, 1, 16, 79, 150, 151, 161
People for the American Way, 217
Pepper, Claude, 202
Perot, H. Ross, 40, 41, 63 (box), 95, 107, 112, 114, 127, 131, 145, 192, 201
Pharmaceutical Research and Manufactures of America, 216
Philadelphia, 28, 42
Philip Morris, 216, 233, 235